The Crimean War and its Afterlife

The mid-nineteenth century's Crimean War is frequently dismissed as an embarrassment, an event marred by blunders and an occasion better forgotten. In *The Crimean War and its Afterlife* Lara Kriegel sets out to rescue the Crimean War from the shadows. Kriegel offers a fresh account of the conflict and its afterlife: revisiting beloved figures like Florence Nightingale and hallowed events like the Charge of the Light Brigade, while also turning attention to newer worthies, including Mary Seacole. In this book a series of six case studies transport us from the mid-Victorian moment to the current day, focusing on the heroes, institutions, and values wrought out of the crucible of the war. Time and again, ordinary Britons looked to the war as a template for social formation and a lodestone for national belonging. With lucid prose and rich illustrations, this book vividly demonstrates the uncanny persistence of a Victorian war in the making of modern Britain.

Lara Kriegel is Associate Professor of History and English at Indiana University, where she has served as Associate Editor of *The American Historical Review* and Editor of *Victorian Studies*. Kriegel is the author of *Grand Designs* (2007), as well as several interdisciplinary articles addressing empire, industry, and military culture in modern Britain.

The Crimean War and its Afterlife

Making Modern Britain

Lara Kriegel

Indiana University

CAMBRIDGE
UNIVERSITY PRESS

CAMBRIDGE
UNIVERSITY PRESS

Shaftesbury Road, Cambridge CB2 8EA, United Kingdom

One Liberty Plaza, 20th Floor, New York, NY 10006, USA

477 Williamstown Road, Port Melbourne, VIC 3207, Australia

314–321, 3rd Floor, Plot 3, Splendor Forum, Jasola District Centre, New Delhi – 110025, India

103 Penang Road, #05–06/07, Visioncrest Commercial, Singapore 238467

Cambridge University Press is part of Cambridge University Press & Assessment, a department of the University of Cambridge.

We share the University's mission to contribute to society through the pursuit of education, learning and research at the highest international levels of excellence.

www.cambridge.org
Information on this title: www.cambridge.org/9781108820394

DOI: 10.1017/9781108906951

First published 2022
First paperback edition 2023

A catalogue record for this publication is available from the British Library

Library of Congress Cataloging-in-Publication data
Names: Kriegel, Lara, 1968– author.
Title: The Crimean War and its afterlife : making modern Britain / Lara Kriegel, Indiana University.
Description: Cambridge ; New York, NY : Cambridge University Press, 2022. | Includes bibliographical references and index.
Identifiers: LCCN 2021035033 (print) | LCCN 2021035034 (ebook) | ISBN 9781108842228 (hardback) | ISBN 9781108906951 (ebook)
Subjects: LCSH: Crimean War, 1853–1856 – Influence. | Crimean War, 1853–1856 – Social aspects – Great Britain. | Crimean War, 1853–1856 – Literature and the war. | Crimean War, 1853–1856 – Historiography. | Great Britain – History – Victoria, 1837–1901. | Woodham Smith, Cecil, 1896–1977. | Nightingale, Florence, 1820–1910. | Seacole, Mary, 1805–1881.
Classification: LCC DK214 .K74 2022 (print) | LCC DK214 (ebook) | DDC 947/.073810941–dc23
LC record available at https://lccn.loc.gov/2021035033
LC ebook record available at https://lccn.loc.gov/2021035034

ISBN   978-1-108-84222-8   Hardback
ISBN   978-1-108-82039-4   Paperback

For Alex

Contents

Figures

Acknowledgments

I have, on occasion, referred to this book as my own Crimean campaign. Like the war as administered by Great Britain, there were some blunders at the outset. And, like the conflict as fought on the ground, the end was long in coming. Clearly, there is some overidentification, pathos, and grandiosity involved in comparing a book written in midlife to a war fought in the middle of the nineteenth century. Archives have been likened to trenches, in the best of senses. However, any parallels collapse in the face of war's insurmountable trauma and immeasurable loss. In this book, I write about trauma and loss. I also write about friendship and care. In the Crimea, acts of individual kindness and enterprise compensated for mishandling on the part of the state. Regiments became families on the Crimean Peninsula; icons emerged from the fray to succor the wounded and ailing. Unlike the Crimea's combatants, states and institutions have not failed me. I am fortunate in this regard. On top of this good fortune, I have additionally enjoyed the mentorship, inspiration, and camaraderie of many friends.

For more than a decade now, Indiana University has provided a rich and rewarding home for me and my work. A sabbatical semester allowed for research forays and writing time. Financial support from the College of Arts and Sciences, the College Arts and Humanities Institute, the Institute for Advanced Study, and the Jack and Julia Wickes Fund of the Department of History facilitated research trips. The chairs of my two departments – Jonathan Elmer, Paul Gutjahr, Patty Ingham, and Michael Adams in English; Peter Guardino, Eric Sandweiss, Wendy Gamber, and Michael McGerr in History – created productive work environments in changing and challenging times. I became a better reader and writer through stints as the associate editor of the *American Historical Review* and as editor of *Victorian Studies*. Indiana University's storied Faculty Writing Groups, led by the inimitable Laura Plummer, provided support and strategy to get the job done. The Center for Eighteenth-Century Studies, the European History Workshop, and, of course, the Victorian Studies Program have served up conversation and intellectual play, and, in bygone days, shared meals. Thanks as well to the dedicated staff and distinctive students of the Collins Living-Learning Center, for providing a happy new home. At IU, I am grateful for comments on work in progress and conversations regarding research with Peter Bailey, Judith Brown, Maria Bucur, Kon Dierks, Ke-Chin Hsia, Sarah Knott, Carl Ipsen, Christoph Irmscher, Michelle Moyd, Kaya Sahin, Roberta Pergher, Mark Roseman, Julia Roos, Rob Schneider, and Rebecca Spang. Many of these excellent readers are also excellent cooks, and I am grateful for meals at their tables, as well as those of Gardner Bovingdon, Sara Friedman, Rita Koryan, Krista Maglen, Sarah Mitchell, Alexandra Morphet, Sarah Pearce, and many more. Judith Allen, Mary Favret, Wendy Gamber, and Patty Ingham have provided feminist mentorship and friendship across a decade, along with valued models of institutional leadership and scholarly life. I have had the benefit of working with numerous graduate students, more than my share; their intellects, humor, and generosity hearten and humble me, again and again. Fortune beyond measure has afforded me the rare camaraderie and companionship of my colleagues in Victorian Studies, who are the best of friends in Ballantine, or FBH, and beyond: Rae Greiner, Ivan Kreilkamp, Monique Morgan, and, still in our imagined community, Andrew Miller. Finally, while we gathered more frequently in the yoga studio than around the seminar table, Claudia Breger and Stephanie DeBoer, two dear friends, have been instrumental for this book and much else.

I took the first steps on my long Crimean adventure while still at Florida International University. Over a decade on, I still miss my colleagues there. I've been glad to keep alive my friendships with the Viertes House gang, Kirsten Wood and Rebecca Friedman, as we have navigated mid-career and midlife. I am always grateful for Ken and Elisabeth Lipartito, with whom I have shared so much. Bill and Rita Oates showed us great kindness, as did Jenna Gibbs and her beloved Reills, both Peter and Dominique. There at the start of this project, Peter Reill, Peter Barber, and Aurora Morcillo are all now missed in Miami and beyond.

The North American Victorian Studies Association and the North American Conference on British Studies have long been sites of collegial conversation. Thanks to so very many members of these organizations for their ongoing dialogue. I am also grateful to the Midwest Victorian Studies Association and to the Dickens Universe for welcoming and challenging me. Much gratitude as well to engaged and thoughtful listeners at the City University of New York Victorian Studies Conference, the Newberry Library, Purdue University, Rice University, the University of Texas at Austin, and Yale University. It was, finally, a great serendipity to stumble upon "Charting the Crimean War: Contexts, Nationhood,

Afterlives," organized in 2013 by Rachel Bates, Holly Furneaux, and Alastair Massie.

The Afterlives conference marked the beginning of a rich and generative friendship with Holly Furneaux, who has been a comrade in excavating the Crimea and in embracing adoption. I am one of many people who has been lucky to sit at Helena Michie's extended table. The unflagging support of Philippa Levine, who believed enough in me to offer many opportunities and to share countless phone calls, buoyed me on my way. Jim Epstein long enriched my experience of British history by bringing enjoyment, commitment, and humor to the mix. Michelle Tusan is among many generous interlocutors of warfare in our field; thanks to her scouting in Hawaii, Bristol and Nottingham's veterans found their way into print. Jordanna Bailkin has been a mainstay through thick and thin, since the dissertating days of LLLL and GGGG. I hope that Judith Walkowitz finds traces of her impact as an imaginative researcher, master of historical narrative, and breaker of boundaries in these pages. My gratitude goes as well to the multigenerational Walkowitz sisterhood, including, but not limited to, Anna Clark, Nadja Durbach, Erika Rappaport, and Jennifer Tucker. I am glad still to be a fellow traveler in Victorianist circles with Rachel Ablow. Across the past decade, it was a pleasure to renew a cherished Baltimore friendship with Antoinette Burton at a neighboring flagship university in the Midwest. I will always be grateful for her critiques and her care when it comes to Florence Nightingale, Mary Seacole, and much else.

These pages are the result of many enjoyable trips to England, where I stayed in many wonderful homes, especially in North and East London. The greatest serendipity was the last, when I landed on Hilary Mandelberg's stoop in DeBeauvoir Square. Hilary, in turn, introduced me to the remarkable Cleo Sylvestre. Having played Mary Seacole in a one-woman show, Cleo Sylvestre confirmed for me that the Crimea's afterlife pulsates still. Isabelle Cadignan was always waiting in London with sarcasm and libations; if only Blake, and Anna and Lauren could have joined us there. London found a worthy resident in Bill MacLehose, who spent several happy years in the infernal wen; I was glad to share it with him, and I am sure to feel his absence when I return. Natalie Zacek, finally, has stewarded memories across cities and states, and books and years, from London to Manchester and from Baltimore to Bloomington.

Good friends near and far read drafts of this book in full. For that extraordinary labor, I recognize Roberta Pergher, a model historian and cherished colleague; Ivan Kreilkamp, an extraordinary critic and a generous friend; and Jordanna Bailkin, always on point and always savvy. Sarah Knott was the ideal reader for the afterword, which looks longingly on a beleaguered England from afar.

Numerous archivists and library staff in the United Kingdom assisted along the way; I have been especially grateful to those who have helped in my image quest across successive lockdowns. Closer to home, Abby Ang, Nate Draluck, and Beth Bevis Gallick brought the highest competencies to technical and editorial support. Elisabeth O'Kane Lipartito lavished care and attention on the manuscript more than once; I've been grateful to have my work in the hands of someone who combines a unique appreciation for research, writing, and detail with a lived experience of twentieth-century Britain. I'm glad, finally, that my book found a home at Cambridge University Press. The two reviewers for the press read with remarkable acuity; their commendations have cheered me on my way, and their challenges have made the book much, much better. At once encouraging, frank, and flexible, Liz Friend-Smith, Atifa Jiwa, and Elliot Beck have been a terrific editorial team. Finally, Natasha Whelan in Britain, as well as Vidya Ashwin and Ekta Niwrutti in India, have brought agility, grace, and professionalism to the later stages of production.

There have been many episodes in Crimea's afterlife since the passing of my beloved father, Abe Kriegel, now more than a decade ago. I wish I could have shared my latest entanglements in British history with him. I remain in awe of the generosity, strength, and humanity of my mother, Reva, and the conviction, moxie, and pizzaz of my sister, Mirm. My Uncle Lenny, who wrote about masculinity before it became a category of academic analysis, asks about this book whenever I see him. I'm glad that he and my Uncle Moishe are here for its publication. I'm sorry that Charles Miller, dear husband of my mother-in-law, Cynthia Lichtenstein, won't be able to see this book between covers: a physicist by training, he always took care to ask me about the Crimean War and even to read my manuscript. I wish I would have seen more of Gene Lichtenstein and Jocelyn Gibbs over the years of writing this book. Gratitude goes as well to my extended family, too numerous to name here, but deeply valued for their inquisitiveness and urbanity, and their kindness and humor. Hannah and Max have grown impressively since I last acknowledged them in print; I'm grateful for their company and impressed by who they have each become. For a critical three-plus years, Bianca Irvine became part of our household, providing relief, company, and kindness when we all needed it. We miss her greatly. Lily played her part as the best muse a lockdown lapdog could be. On arriving in Indiana after the long journey from South Africa in late 2017, Ayanda declared that there were "too many flags" along the road (agree) and "too many books" in our home (disagree). She has taught us lessons about love, strength, and style every day since. As always, Alex is the truest partner through thick and thin. His care for me and this project have manifest themselves in many ways. With his love of travel and his desire to stand in the sites of history, he made sure that I found my way to Scutari, where Florence Nightingale once toiled and where Crimean graves still lie. His eye for the repurposing of the past additionally brought artwork and exhibitions into my sightlines. If I had not tarried, he would gladly have made a trip to the Crimea with me. I hope, one day, that we can travel together again. With my deepest gratitude, this book is for him.

Introduction: The Reason Why

Cecil Woodham-Smith was an unlikely historian. Even after writing two best-selling books, the acclaimed popular author remained surprised by her own success.[1] The daughter of a prominent Anglo-Irish military family, Mrs. Woodham-Smith was a well-dressed housewife and erstwhile romance writer turned purveyor of Victorian history. Inspired by a dinner party conversation, she burst onto the scene in 1950 with a successful biography of Florence Nightingale. No one-hit wonder, she followed up three years later with *The Reason Why*, an account of the Charge of the Light Brigade, the tragic culmination of the Battle of Balaklava.[2] The best-seller solidified Woodham-Smith's standing as a historian of national renown. Widely reviewed and broadly acclaimed, *The Reason Why* became required reading across a broad swath of British society. It was even named the *Daily Mail*'s Book of the Month in November 1953.[3]

The through line linking these two works by Woodham-Smith is the mid-nineteenth century's Crimean War, fought between 1853 and 1856, primarily on a Black Sea peninsula now occupied by the Russian Federation. This conflict of recondite and complex causes is best known in Britain for the mismanagement by the Army's hidebound leadership and for the innovations of the moment's resourceful new luminaries. The Army's blunder is exemplified in the Charge of the Light Brigade, a near-suicidal maneuver involving more than 600 cavalry soldiers. The occasion came to characterize a British affection for disaster and even failure, met resolutely and dutifully.[4] The leading light of the war, on the other hand, was Florence Nightingale. Called "The Lady with the Lamp," Nightingale offered a resourceful response to deaths by wartime illness, her can-do spirit coated in an angelic veneer.[5] As she wrote about the Victorian past, Mrs. Woodham-Smith played her part in lodging a tragic blunder and a beloved heroine at the heart of national myth and national understanding. Together, Florence Nightingale and the Charge of the Light Brigade represent the antinomies of the Crimean

War. They also capture two poles of British, and particularly English, self-conception.

I imagined, when I began researching the Crimean conflict some years ago, that Mrs. Woodham-Smith would appear as a footnote in my study, her texts providing a well-regarded foundation in their archival research and lucid prose. But as I dove into military archives, I found myself pulled between letters sent from survivors in the wake of the Charge and plans for auctions of its regalia one hundred years on. And when I surveyed medical papers, my perusals of nineteenth-century newspapers lionizing Nightingale opened up into discoveries of transcripts for BBC radio shows produced a century later. My experience researching other aspects and other protagonists was very much the same. Database searches and archival meanderings had me shuttling between the Crimean War and its legacies, from the nineteenth century to the twentieth century and even to the twenty-first.[6] Time and again, my research revealed, countless Britons have found themselves absorbed by the mid-nineteenth century's war.[7] As I came to apprehend this dynamic, Mrs. Woodham-Smith moved from note to text and from background to foreground.

It is a commonplace to dismiss the Crimean War as an embarrassment, an event better forgotten, and a conflict that has lingered in "semi-obscurity."[8] However, the Crimean War has repeatedly absorbed public attention since its waging. Woodham-Smith and her contemporaries provide a case in point. Cecil Woodham-Smith had a rare and singular talent for bringing Victorian heroes and blunders to life. But she was not alone in her fascination with them. Her knack for narrative and her passion for the archives allowed her to capture the attention of her public of common readers.[9] Her subject matter proved compelling at a moment of modernizing change, with Nightingale offering an exemplar of British ingenuity and the Charge an indictment of dyed-in-the-wool tradition. More generally, the Crimean moment struck a chord – several, in fact – at the moment of its centenary. This anniversary dovetailed with the rise of the Cold War and with the advent of decolonization; it occurred alongside the coming of postwar modernization and the making of the welfare state. For many, the pomp of Victoriana provided surety as the nineteenth century receded into the deep past.[10] The certainties of the nineteenth century offered consolation as Britain lurched toward the end of empire. As they reckoned with their futures in a New Elizabethan Era, many looked back on the past, some critically and others longingly. In the Crimean War, with its blunders and its heroes, they found their ground for launching critique and for navigating change.

This is not, however, a book about Woodham-Smith and her contemporaries. It is, instead, a study of the Crimean conflict and the role played by its ongoing legacies in the making of modern Britain. Florence Nightingale and the Charge of the Light Brigade have long served as enduring touchstones for the production of national histories and national myths. Some years ago, historian Raphael Samuel noted that Florence Nightingale, in her incarnation as the Lady with the Lamp, was a set piece in what he called Britain's "Island Story."[11] An embodiment of the qualities of ingenuity, sacrifice, and humility, Nightingale informed understandings of exceptionalism that bound countrymen and country-women together. In a similar vein, historian Stephanie Barczewski later identified the Charge of the Light Brigade as an epitome of heroic failure, the particularly British penchant for glorifying loss and turning it into victory.[12] Journalist Fintan O'Toole took up this understanding as he illuminated 2016's Brexit referendum and aftermath as the quintessence of the "English capacity to embrace disaster" with "character" and with "pluck."[13] As these examples suggest, the Crimea's set pieces are no static emblems of Victoriana. They are portals to history and memory across the ages; they are bellwethers of nostalgia;[14] they are flashpoints for discussions about belonging in Britain today. Yet, they are only the best-known legacies of the Crimean War, which bequeathed to later generations a set of ideals, practices, and innovations with enduring effects.

Just as this book transcends Woodham-Smith's moment, it reaches beyond her encapsulation of the Crimean War in its two best-known legends to provide a broader assessment of the conflict and its legacies. The Chargers dashed into Balaklava's Valley of Death; Nightingale became a heroic first responder. But there were other responses to the war's demands and mismanagement. From the Crimean moment through to our own time, gallant soldiers who performed acts of bravery have received the Victoria Cross, an award for valor in battle. Woodham-Smith did not write about the Cross, but it was likely on her horizon. The Order was well known at its centenary in 1956, when living recipients from across Britain and the Commonwealth came to London for a recognition ceremony. She would have heard but fleetingly of Mary Seacole, now herself a national institution, though for a time forgotten. This nineteenth-century Jamaican healer made her way to the Crimea despite institutional racism, becoming a heroine in her own day and once again for a post-Windrush Britain. As these examples suggest, the Crimean War provided an opening for now-heralded institutions to develop and for trailblazing figures to enter the breach. Their legacies are evident on the landscape of twenty-first-century London. A gallery of Victoria Crosses has occupied the top floor of the Imperial War Museum since 2010, and a statue playing tribute to Mary Seacole has stood less than a mile away, on the South Bank of the Thames, since 2016.

Other Crimean touchstones elude characterization through names and accolades; they defy materialization in collections and statues. For instance, the Crimean War gave rise to shared experiences of travel and loss that have had continuing reverberations. Long fundamental to wartime, these prospects took particular shape on the Crimean Peninsula and in the mid-Victorian moment. Encounters on the way to war and on the battlefront provided experiences of alterity at a European periphery; in the process, they nourished senses of adventure and senses of home-feeling among the combatants and their fellow travelers. These poles may seem in conflict; yet both are part of British national understanding and English self-conception, historically and today. Ultimately, war is a tragedy involving the deaths of many and the grief of even more. In the case of the Crimea, the ravages of disease and battle led to loss of life and limbs for over 40,000 of the more than 100,000 British soldiers deployed.[15] The numbers pale in relation to the casualties wrought by the wars of Mrs. Woodham-Smith's own century. Yet their consequences were deep and long. Casualties in the East produced heart-rending loss for friends and families; they also bequeathed long-standing challenges for armies and nations. These are most evident in the recurring concerns for the upkeep of the Crimea's graves, which served, time and again, as a focus for collective feeling around the war. Difficult to reach beyond the Iron Curtain in Woodham-Smith's time, they are once again inaccessible in our own.

Statues and collections. Best-selling books and notions of nationhood. Grief and graveyards. The Crimean War has left many legacies, material and immaterial, near and far. To capture their variety and vitality, I employ the notion of afterlife. Those who have sought to understand the lasting effects of wars on home fronts, and particularly their losses and traumas, have long focused upon memory, commemoration, and memorialization as frameworks for study.[16] These rubrics informed understandings of World War I, or the Great War, on the occasion of its centenary. Yet, memorials and ceremonies are but aspects of the Crimea's afterlife. Afterlife is a notion that apprehends the reverberations of the conflict over the ages – its unfinished business and its unanticipated effects, its literary inheritances and its material residues, its structures of feeling and its unanswered questions. It captures the robust persistence of the Crimea's legacies and the reinterpretation of its meanings across both time and space.

In my use of the notion of afterlife, I take my lead from scholars working across disciplines who have sought to understand the ongoing impacts of diverse historical phenomena: the 1856–1857 Xhosa Cattle Killings in South Africa, the events of May 1968 in France, and decolonization as an everyday experience in Great Britain's welfare state, to name some.[17]

Afterlife allows an apprehension of how the past resonates and accumulates in consensual and conflicting ways.[18] It captures how events and their meanings are used and reworked in their long, indeterminate aftermaths. It encompasses representational practices, collective feeling, and shared morals. It signals how things forgotten are expressed, how matters cherished are critiqued, and how the past persists and recurs – for Cecil Woodham-Smith and her readers, for the Victorians and for ourselves.

The persistence of the Crimean War is evident in the texture of everyday life.[19] Through the ages, a cast of ordinary Britons[20] has engaged with the legacies of the Crimea – as veterans and descendants, as acolytes and critics, as first-rate writers and "second-hand dealers in the past."[21] Their venues have been many: the primary school classroom and the dusty attic; the local museum and the national arena; the city square and the country graveyard. As they have stewarded the war's legacies, they have shaped communal fellowship and produced associational life.[22] Veterans' organizations, history societies, and book clubs; nurses' unions, touring groups, and immigrant associations – all have taken up the legacies of the Crimea.[23] The war has provided a set of stories that produce a shared, yet pliable heritage.[24] Its afterlife has enabled the tightening of claims to belonging, the rending of ties of community, and the upending of national pieties.

By charting the Crimean War's robust afterlife, this book participates in a reframing of the narratives of British modernity. In ages of peace and in epochs of wartime, in moments of hope and on occasions of loss, ordinary Britons have made meanings out of the Crimean War. Like Woodham-Smith and her readers, they looked to the Crimean conflict not only as a gateway to the Victorian past, but also as a vehicle for negotiating their own presents. A useable past and an occasion replete with meanings, the war is an anvil on which historical understandings are created and national ideals are forged.[25] The Crimean War's afterlife thus charts, tracks, and engages the major narratives of the modern British past. It recurs with the ebbs and flows of empire and with the waging of wars and the coming of peace. It accompanies the rise and fall of the welfare state and the making of the liberal self. It emerges alongside the remaking of populations and the redrawing of borders. In sum, it indexes the tides and tensions in British history writ large. At the same time, the war's afterlife illuminates how everyday life was lived and how cultural life was rendered, both intimately and expansively. By telling a new story about the Crimean War, this book offers a new perspective on the making of modern Britain, its invented traditions and its cherished heroes, its cultural values and its social life.[26]

***

In national narratives and in the public mind, the Crimean War sits in the shadows of the larger and longer wars that flank the long nineteenth century: the Napoleonic Wars and the Great War.[27] Fittingly, these two conflicts assume commanding spaces on the memorial landscape of London; Nelson's Column occupies a dominant place in London's Trafalgar Square, while the Cenotaph stands conspicuously in London's Whitehall.[28] Taking its place among these monuments is the Guards' Memorial in St. James's Place (Figure 0.1). It pays tribute to the Crimean War, the one truly major conflict involving European powers between the two better-known conflagrations. The Crimean War shattered the so-called *Pax Britannica*, the hundred years of putative peace within Europe, when Great Britain was the globe's foremost power. This notion was, of course, a fiction during a century when insurgency and battle marred the European continent and when Britain, along with other European nations, was involved in imperial conquest and imperial war.[29] The so-called "little wars" of empire were nearly continuous across a century that witnessed the large-scale traumas of the Indian Rebellion

Figure 0.1 Veterans at the Guards' Crimea Memorial. c. 1899.
Photograph by Argent Archer. Mary Evans Picture Library

(1857-1858) and the South African War (1899-1902), to name two of the most significant conflicts.[30]

On the surface, the Crimean War was a contest with obscure causes. Its immediate spark came from tensions over the holy places in Palestine and over territories within the Ottoman Empire.[31] Territorial ambitions in continental Europe and in an imperializing world also propelled Europe to war. These conflicts pitted Britain against a onetime ally, the Russian Empire. They tied Britain to a former enemy: France. Together, and aided by the island nation of Sardinia, they fought on behalf of an ally often deemed unworthy, the Ottoman Turks. The balance sheets of destruction may have paled in comparison to those for the Napoleonic Wars and World War I.[32] However, like the Napoleonic Wars[33] and the Great War,[34] the Crimean conflict was, itself, global in scale,[35] with fighting taking place in far-flung regions, involving both the Army and the Navy.[36] And, like these larger wars on either side of the long nineteenth century, the Crimean War enmeshed the British, perennially reluctant Europeans, in affairs on the Continent, as it led to the redrawing of geopolitics. Negotiated in 1856, the Treaty of Paris ended the war, hastening a French ascent in Europe, a Russian retreat to insularity, an Ottoman decline in power, and a British reorientation of interests – away from Europe and towards its growing empire and its domestic front.[37]

The global dimensions of the conflict notwithstanding, the central and decisive drama – or, at least, the occasions that figure into the war's afterlife – took place largely on the Crimean Peninsula.[38] There, a saga of heroism, sacrifice, and suffering unfolded between 1854 and 1856. In 1854, British troops made the 2,000-mile journey to the East, with some coming directly from stations in the mother country and others arriving from service in the empire. That autumn witnessed a trio of dramatic battles at the Alma, Balaklava, and Inkerman, all allied victories. Fought in quick succession, these occasions tested the mettle of the Army and elevated the status of the British soldier.[39] They linger today as street names in England's inner suburbs, built in the Victorian era, and on placards at pubs and taverns, located across the country. At the time of their waging, these battles broke any hope of a speedy Russian victory, leading instead to the yearlong Siege of Sebastopol, which included the Battles of the Tchernaya and the Redan.[40] This long assault, which provided a dress rehearsal for the trench warfare used in later conflicts, was a slow attrition in advance of the decisive allied triumph in the autumn of 1855. Through it all, the Russians were not the most formidable enemy. Even greater foes were the cold of the Crimean winter, the pangs of hunger, and the depredations resulting from the cholera epidemic: each and every one a failed test of military management.[41]

The overarching story to come out of the battlefront saga thus involves the glory of soldierly sacrifice and the failures of national leadership.[42] The course of the Crimean War witnessed the rise in stature of the rank-and-file soldier. Construed as the "scum of the earth" in Napoleonic times, this figure took hold of the nation's hearts during the Crimean conflict.[43] The soldier was not only an object of admiration for his bravery; he was also an object of sympathy for his suffering.[44] While faith in the soldier grew, confidence in the Army's officers and in the Government diminished. For its part, the Government had embarked on a dubitable war fought by an outdated army. With an officer class left over from the Napoleonic Wars, and with an administrative apparatus not truly tested since, the armed forces showed themselves to be unprepared for full-scale conflict at mid-century. There were failures of military intelligence, as the Charge of the Light Brigade so well demonstrated. There was fumbling by the Commissary when it came to provisioning the troops with warm clothes and sufficient food. And there was a dismal collapse of the medical services in treating the cholera epidemic, taking far more lives than battlefront injury over the course of the war.[45]

There were several well-known and robust responses to this situation, both during and after the conflict itself. The Crimean War has long been understood as an impetus to state modernization and Army reform.[46] Traditionally, Florence Nightingale has assumed a role as the avatar of reforming efforts, credited – erroneously it turns out – with staving off the cholera in the East before embarking on a career of pioneering nursing education and public health initiatives in Britain, India, and beyond.[47] Responses, too, came in the form of a series of Parliamentary interventions. Most notable here are the Cardwell Reforms (1868–1874), devoted to bringing measures of merit and humanity to the antiquated and aristocratic Army.[48] But the war was not only an occasion for engendering modernizing reform; it was, as well, an opportunity for providing succoring care.[49] Concerned citizens on the home front offered monies and goods to the Patriotic Fund, in amounts large and small. They provided outpourings of support in Thanksgiving prayers and at peace celebrations. The battlefront did not lack, either, for quotidian acts of care, in life and in death. The Caribbean healer Mary Seacole, recently anointed as a heroine of the war, looked after British soldiers, offering succor and sustenance in her British Hotel. Officers exhibited paternalistic concern for their men; battlefield compatriots attended to the burials of deceased friends. If the war gave way to a culture of reform, it gave way as well to a culture of care.[50]

These acts, in all of their variety, were made possible within a media ecology that produced shared knowledge and shared feeling. The nation that went to war in the Crimea was a literate society with many forms of written and visual expression.[51] There were, of course, the daily newspapers, most notably the *Times,* in whose pages William Howard Russell, touted as the first battlefront journalist, kindled outrage at the blunders of the war and stoked sympathy for the sufferings of the soldiers.[52] Provincial newspapers amplified these concerns. So did the illustrated press, with its capacities for visual reproduction. Photography became a means for bringing wartime experience and imagery home, with the innovations of Roger Fenton.[53] The field of expression was varied, extending beyond national organs and well-known trailblazers.[54] Homespun tributes abounded in poetry and in homily. Finally, military men, auxiliary supporters, and traveling ladies wrote letters, diaries, and journals at the front.[55] Taken together, these texts helped to produce shared senses of suffering and sympathy, and of concern and outrage. They inspired a diverse set of representational practices that blossomed in the course of the war. These included forward-looking forms like the realist novel as well as more traditional genres.[56] There was no shortage of sentimental literature published in the war's wake. A conflict with religion at its heart,[57] the Crimean War facilitated an engagement with Christian texts and with medieval chivalry.[58] In the end, the war was a pivotal moment in the production of new forms of expression. It was also a landmark moment in the making of a reading, writing, and viewing public[59] that could think, act, and feel.[60]

These representational practices and the wartime experiences from which they derived worked, together, to forge new men and new women.[61] They consolidated and redefined gender ideals for the Crimean moment and beyond. The rich media landscape of the moment played a decisive role in making Florence Nightingale into the exemplar of mid-Victorian womanhood.[62] Newspapers, images, and poems cloaked Nightingale, a paragon of bureaucratic efficiency and an advocate of scientific inquiry, in sentiment and feeling. A heroine for her own time, Nightingale also became a role model for later years: she offered up an avatar of white, middle-class womanhood associated with an idealized figure of the nurse. As the contours of the Crimean War and its afterlife lay bare, this was an ideal to which only some could aspire, and from which many were summarily barred. Mary Seacole, in contrast, made it to the Crimea despite her own experiences of exclusion, where she greeted the troops with boisterous warmth. Models of the female self thus crystallized in the personae of the War's leading ladies. These ideals developed alongside a variety of masculinities that solidified during wartime. Deeds of battlefield heroics and episodes in soldierly valor consolidated a heroic manhood. This ideal found textual expression in the pages of novels promoting muscular Christianity; it found official recognition in the institution of the Victoria Cross.[63] Wartime writing and wartime experience also allowed for the rise of the military man of feeling, who could offer affection and receive care.[64]

A crucible for the making of gender ideals, the conflict was equally a laboratory for the production of nationhood. The War, of course, made the Charge of the Light Brigade and the Lady with the Lamp into set pieces of Englishness. Mary Seacole provided an opportunity to expand the boundaries of Britishness, at least later on. But it was not just the war's icons that enabled understandings of nation and belonging. The process of going to battle at a periphery of Europe amongst new allies and new foes allowed for experiences of difference. In the popular mind, the Crimean War did not stir the terror and trauma that emerged in response to the Indian Rebellion, which gripped the subcontinent in 1857.[65] Draped in English sentiment, the Crimean conflict stands apart from the so-called "savage wars" of empire waged in Africa and Asia across the later nineteenth century, both imaginatively and geographically.[66] Yet, the British understood themselves as the defenders of civilization against Russian despotism in their Crimean undertaking; they did so even while aligned with an Ottoman Empire that many Victorians considered backward. In the end, the wartime experience, like its best-known legends, worked to shore up senses of British nationhood and English home feeling. The Crimea's warriors were reluctant cosmopolitans, needful of home, as evident in their longing for domestic comforts and Christmas dinners while at the front. Britain's Island Story was made, in manifold ways, on the Crimean Peninsula, with its myths ready for reworking, adapting, and exploiting over the conflict's long afterlife.[67]

The afterlife of the Crimean War is, ultimately, a palimpsest for British history as it unfolded within the nation's borders and beyond.[68] It opened out across the life cycles of the Crimean generation and its descendants (Figure 0.2).[69] The Crimean conflict attained resonance at notable anniversaries, such as the centenary that captivated Woodham-Smith and her contemporaries. More broadly, it came to the fore across Great Britain's long, subsequent line of wars, from the nineteenth century onward. Its veterans fought in the Indian Rebellion, the Anglo-Zulu Wars, and the South African War.[70] Its lessons served, alternatively, as calls to duty and as touchstones for rebuke in the era of the world wars.[71] Updated for a modern age, its tales of heroism and blunder reemerged during the Korean War,[72] the Vietnam War, and the Falklands War.[73] Even the twenty-first century conflicts in Afghanistan and Iraq bear traces of the Crimean War's institutions and ideals. The War's afterlife has enjoyed equal longevity

Figure 0.2 Crimean War veterans from the 42nd Highlanders. 1900.
Photograph. COPY 1/447. The National Archives

on the home front. Given its developments in caretaking, the Crimea became germane alongside innovations for the public good, including the rise of the new liberalism and the establishment of the welfare state. Full of its own disappointments and consolations, it proved resonant at moments of loss and change that took their toll on the national psyche: among them, the end of empire, decolonization,[74] and, most recently, Brexit.[75]

It is revealing to catalogue the historical junctures of the Crimea's afterlife. It is more important, however, to consider the purposes of its recurrence. In some regards, the Crimean War embraced the new, its mismanagement opening the way for a set of modernizing reformers. With Nightingale providing a model for professionalism and Seacole a paragon of entrepreneurialism, the Crimean War held purchase at moments when Britons embraced modernity. Yet, in its afterlife, the Crimean War has not only served as a link to history; it has also provided ground for reinvention. Across the ages, a range of Britons have looked to the Crimean conflict to reinvent a romanticized past for uncertain futures. As the nation hurtled toward the changes wrought by mechanized warfare and decolonization, Britons clung to the Crimean War and its legacies.

Relics and lore offered links to tradition and continuity. There were times when cleaving to the Crimean conflict, with its heroes, its artifacts, and its legends, may have been folly. Time and again, however, the war was a prosthetic to a past that offered succor as later generations of Britons faced individual displacement and collective change. A bellwether of tradition and duty, it provided an incarnation of the mid-Victorian age, its logics, and its states of mind.

Ultimately, the Crimea's robust afterlife invites a reconsideration of the imprint of the Victorian age on the making of modern Britain.[76] Why should Victorian Britain matter in the twenty-first century?[77] The epoch fades evermore into the past. Even in 1953, a review of *The Reason Why* declared that the "ever-receding nineteenth century" seemed "as remote as the Pharaohs."[78] Yet, in the 1950s and well beyond, historians and literary critics often looked to the century as foundational for Anglo-American modernity, whether economic, political, or sociocultural. Now, in the twenty-first century, in late capitalism and the later days of the Anthropocene, the glory of industrial and imperial Britain is not just long faded, but also ethically questionable.[79] The period does remain a locus of uncritical nostalgia for Conservative Brexiteers like Jacob Rees-Mogg.[80] Yet, younger generations are toppling its statues and its pieties. The Victorian era has become a site for generating critical understandings of the contemporary world and its racial logics, as the work of a new generation of BIPOC-led scholars to undiscipline the field has indicated.[81]

The Crimea's continued afterlife demonstrates that the Victorian era reverberates still. The war provided an occasion to express, generate, and legitimate a set of Victorian values.[82] Its afterlife has allowed for occasions to transmit, revisit, and transform them. Such Victorian mainstays as duty, sacrifice, and heroism took their shape in the Crimean War.[83] If wartime played its part in developing and institutionalizing these ideals, the Crimea's afterlife provided occasions to sustain and rework them. The mid-Victorian moment thus bequeathed a set of vocabularies, traditions, and ideals to later epochs.[84] These ideas have distinctly Crimean roots; they were the outgrowths of wartime encounters and wartime mediations. They are at once exclusive and malleable; they are simultaneously adaptable and limiting. They inform public practice and govern private hopes; they shape everyday life and inflect landmark events. They produce social cohesion and encourage care; they underwrite violence and allow exclusion.[85]

The Crimean War and its Afterlife places the mid-Victorians' war at the center of our narratives of the making of modern Britain. To do as much, it relies upon a variety of interpretive and archival practices. While attuned to literary and cultural criticism, this book is insistently archival. It draws upon repositories holding materials from the nineteenth, twentieth, and twenty-first centuries. The source base is equally expansive, encompassing military collections and medical papers, as well as national archives and local records. These run the gamut to include schoolboys' notebooks and soldiers' letters, military memoranda and auction accounts, and travelers' diaries and film publicity. Taken together, this range of sources substantiates received narratives even as it offers up hidden histories; it conveys time-honored voices even as it introduces forgotten figures. The pages that follow reveal traces of the Crimea in grand narratives and in small stories; they find it in national traditions and in local examples.[86] They locate the Crimea's afterlife at the levels of the quotidian and the everyday, the ideal and the abstract, and the concrete and the monumental.[87] In many places and on many scales, the Crimean War shaped British history and informed everyday life.

***

The six chapters of this book address different facets of the wartime experience and its legacies across a long historical arc of the modern era, from the nineteenth century through the twenty-first.[88] Each chapter takes as its focus a figure, institution, or practice that emerged from the Crimean War's torsions. The cases are associated, additionally, with a national ideal, a Victorian value, or a character trait. A central contention of this book is that the Crimea's afterlife is not an afterthought or an epiphenomenon. Instead, the seeds of remembrance and reinterpretation reside in the war itself. Each chapter begins therefore in the wartime moment, to show that the event and its mediation provided the conditions for the Crimea's afterlife. All six chapters trace the fate of wartime ideals and institutions from the Crimean moment to the near present. They employ overlapping narratives and recursive trajectories as they demonstrate how values, sociability, and experience were made and remade at flashpoints across history.

The first two chapters address the theme of "Persistence." They underscore the longevity and capaciousness of the Crimea's afterlife as they trouble notions of peripheries and centers. Chapter 1, "The Adventurers," brings the Crimean Peninsula, distant from Britain, into focus. It demonstrates that wartime travel and encounter shaped subsequent experiences of the peninsula, even to our own century. As they made the journey eastward, the Crimea's combatants sought to understand the peninsula and the many peoples they encountered there, both friends and foes. The end of the war was an occasion for mass retreat, but it did not mark the end of British engagement with the peninsula. Rather, wartime writing and wartime experience generated vocabularies and understandings that shaped later engagements with the Crimea as a place of memory and self-discovery, and of tourism and diplomacy. Here and throughout, I refer to the land mass where the Victorians fought as the Crimea. It is today called Crimea. My choice of the earlier nomenclature invokes the nineteenth-century experience of the land and its continuing association among Britons with a Victorian war. Similarly, I refer to Sebastopol, now Sevastopol, by its Victorian spelling.

Although the Crimean War was fought at a distance, on a peninsula at the edge of Europe, it gave rise to one of the most feted events in British military history. The second chapter, "The Dutiful," thus moves from the peripheral locales of Eurasia to the central myths of British history to consider the Charge of the Light Brigade. The Charge occurred over only fifteen minutes of action-packed drama, but it is unusually long lived in the British imagination. It was a highly mediated event, in soldiers' letters, in newspaper reports, and, not least, in Alfred, Lord Tennyson's eponymous poem. Together, these productions worked to criticize the incident while redeeming its protagonists: the 600 or so Chargers who rode resolutely into battle. In its wake, the Chargers became embodiments of patriotic duty, social responsibility, and heroic failure. They remained so across their life cycles. Even after their passing, the ideal of duty stayed fused to the Charge. It proved useful at moments of military pressure and it proved redemptive at times of imperial loss. It could stir men to service in wartime and it could comfort the nation in the wake of disappointment. Its malleability notwithstanding, the ideal of duty did find its own limits, as twentieth-century wars and big screen films lay bare. Yet, the affinity for heroic failure has lingered, as the Brexit moment suggests.

The second coupling of chapters, "Avatars," addresses two different ideals of masculinity that were produced out of the crucible of military mismanagement.[89] They examine bravery and valor, on the one hand, and vulnerability and care, on the other. Chapter 3, "The Brave," traces the institutionalization of a Victorian value and a military ideal in the form of the Victoria Cross. Established at the end of the Crimean War by Royal Warrant, this award recognized acts of valor in battle. It continues to do so today. The Victoria Cross has created a fellowship of bravery that includes Victorian warriors and twenty-first century servicemen; aristocrats and common soldiers; and Britons and imperial subjects. A coveted award with Crimean origins, the Cross is an object of desire. Servicemen have pursued the award; collectors have chased after Crosses. Museums have showcased these treasures, with the largest single collection residing in the attic of London's Imperial War Museum, where it opened in

2010.[90] Its transcendent promises notwithstanding, the Cross itself has not protected its winners from misfortune or hardship. Yet it has functioned all the same as a compensation for loss and a vehicle for consensus at moments of transition across the ages.

Chapter 4, "The Custodians," takes us back to the grounds of the Crimea and the East to consider the vulnerabilities of military masculinity. It foregrounds the challenges wrought by death in wartime, whether on the field of battle or through sickness in hospital. Combatants responded with acts of care – ministering to the sick, acting as brokers with the living, and managing last rites for comrades. Collectively, I refer to these acts as custodianship. In the case of the Crimea, the problem of death in wartime and after crystallized in the challenge of maintaining burial grounds at a distance. Across the centuries, Crimean graves and their upkeep served as a focus for shared emotion and collective mourning. Distance posed a challenge to their maintenance over time, with the world wars, the Cold War, and the Russian invasion of the Crimea making care all but impossible for those good Samaritans, civil servants, and twenty-first century crusaders who took up the task across the years. Like the war itself, their efforts often proved an exercise in futility. The state of the Crimea's graves has served repeatedly as an emotion-laded referendum on the management of the war and its aftermath. Like many episodes in the war itself, the endeavor has proved, time and again, to be an exercise in futility, at no point more so than at the present, with the Peninsula inaccessible to Britain's twenty-first-century custodians.

Under the rubric of "Angels," the final two chapters focus on the lives, mythologies, and legacies surrounding two women who emerged in Victorian times and after as heroines of the Crimean War: Florence Nightingale and Mary Seacole.[91] Chapter 5, "The Heroine," examines the life and legacies of the war's best-known protagonist. Nightingale proved appealing in her own time for the combination of care and organization that she manifested in the crusade against mismanagement. A trailblazing and unorthodox figure, Nightingale was cast as a paragon of white English womanhood. Beloved as the Lady with the Lamp, she was a nursing pioneer and a beacon of reform. She was, in her lifetime and after, a lodestar, a woman who shaped the contours of the nation through her deeds and touched the hearts of the people through her character. Across the years, many sought to burst the myths surrounding this Victorian worthy: the leadership of the Army medical services, pioneers of literary and cultural modernity, and, ultimately, members of the nursing profession itself. To track the ebbs and flows of Nightingale's public fortunes is to track the making and dismantling of an idealized, if constrained, womanhood associated with a variety of Englishness: one connoted by the term Middle England and embodied in the values of rurality, modesty, and practicality.

The final chapter, "The Foremother," traces the emergence of the newest addition to the pantheon of Crimean worthies: the Caribbean healer and hotelier Mary Seacole. Beloved during the Crimean War, Seacole published her 1857 autobiography, the *Wonderful Adventures of Mrs. Seacole in Many Lands*, to claim her place in the War's annals and to secure her livelihood Largely forgotten for more than a century, Seacole enjoyed a renaissance in the last quarter of the twentieth century with the rediscovery and reprinting of her autobiography. Seacole's life provided evidence of the long-standing impact of Black Britons well before the 1948 arrival of the Empire Windrush, which announced the settling of a generation of Caribbean migrants in the mother country; her story provided inspiration for minority communities, especially Black women and health care providers, often overlapping constituencies.[92] On the occasion of her rediscovery, Seacole was, at first, a community heroine, brought to light through labors of love and grassroots efforts. During the first two decades of the twenty-first century, she became a national icon, claiming a place in the National Curriculum and the National Portrait Gallery. A commanding statute of Mary Seacole now stands on the South Bank of the Thames, at St. Thomas' Hospital, where Florence Nightingale once spearheaded efforts in nursing education. The complicated relationship between the two leading ladies of the Crimea has often been cast as a rivalry, with Seacole a foil to Nightingale: a warm hotelier and not a steely angel; a clever entrepreneur instead of a bureaucratic reformer; a subaltern, Black protagonist in place of a white, English heroine. However, like Nightingale, Seacole was an unconventional woman with a long legacy. She became a standard bearer in her own right: an embodiment of distinctive virtues for our own time and a Crimean role model for a twenty-first-century Britain.

***

Born a Victorian, in 1896, Cecil Woodham-Smith passed away in 1977, just a few years after the Lignum Vitae Club, a fellowship of Jamaican nurses, restored Mary Seacole's grave, located in London's Kensal Green cemetery. Although she wrote against the backdrop of a changing Britain, with immigration from the Caribbean on the rise, with decolonization gaining momentum, and with filiations with Europe gaining new steam, Cecil Woodham-Smith could likely not have imagined a moment when Mary Seacole would join the pantheon of Crimean heroes. To be fair, Woodham-Smith was no little Englander. She may have made her name with her rendering of such icons and emblems as Florence Nightingale and the Charge of the Light Brigade. But her consciousness, and her work, extended beyond the island of Great Britain itself. She was a proud descendant of Lord Edward Fitzgerald, a military leader of the Irish Rebellion of 1798. She was, as well, the author of *The Great Hunger*, a book on the Irish Famine of 1848.[93] Her interest in Ireland notwithstanding, it is difficult to imagine Woodham-Smith finding a Victorian worthy in the person of Mary Seacole. As this book shows, the valences of the Crimean War, and its messages, shift across history.

The following pages bring the Crimean War, its heroes, and its traditions to life. This book traces the changing engagements with this mid-Victorian conflict as it charts the making of British pasts and presents. It hones in on a range of actors across the ages. Among them were Mary Seacole, Cecil Woodham-Smith, and the Lignum Vitae Club. All engaged with the legacies of the Crimean War as a way of producing histories and of imagining futures. Each advanced their own understanding of the event in order to create meaning and forge community. With its generative capacities and its shifting resonances, the Crimean War engaged publics of ordinary Britons again and again, shaping their understandings of self and of nationhood. These pages tell the story of that engagement, from Victorian times to Woodham-Smith's time to our time.

Part I

Persistence

1 The Adventurers

In the early months of 1854, as tensions between Russia and Britain intensified, the Caribbean healer Mary Seacole gazed at a map of a distant peninsula. The Crimea lay thousands of miles away from her native Jamaica, where she sat in contemplation of a war in the making. As troops ventured from the Caribbean to the Crimea, Seacole imagined the path that she might one day forge to the East. "I used to stand for hours in silent thought before an old map of the world, in a little corner of which someone had chalked a red cross to allow me to distinguish where the Crimea was," Seacole explained.[1] She captured well the anticipation, promise, and uncertainty of wartime travel as she awaited her place in history. Not long after British troops left the Caribbean, Seacole made her own way to the Crimea on a journey that was both treacherous and heroic. Her travelogue, the *Wonderful Adventures of Mrs. Seacole in Many Lands*, relayed her journey as it boasted of her exploits along the route and of her sacrifices among the Army. Today, Seacole's *Wonderful Adventures* is the most read account of the voyage to the wartime Crimea. Successful at its publication, long forgotten afterward, and rediscovered over a century later, Seacole's text exemplifies the ebbs and flows of the Crimean Peninsula, and the Victorian war waged there, in the collective mind of Great Britain.

Its contemporary renown notwithstanding, Seacole's was just one of countless travel narratives produced in the wake of a war conducted in a little known, rarely traveled corner of Eurasia, some 2,000 miles to the east of England.[2] The conflagration gave rise to a range of travel accounts, both manuscript and printed, written by troops and traveling partners. For Britons bound for war, this landmass on the northern coast of the Black Sea was an exotic, strange, and confounding place.[3] As they chronicled their encounters with a far-away land and its peoples, war-goers produced a collective account of the voyage to the peninsula and back again. Like Seacole, they portrayed the Crimea as a zone of contact and conquest and a place of loss and ruin. When they wrote, they sought to bridge the distance between Britain and the battlefront, and to kindle thoughts of home.

The Crimean War catapulted a small landmass about the size of Maryland or double the size of Yorkshire to a place of prominence in Britain, lodging it in the national imaginary as a site of individual destination and collective concern. However, the narratives written during wartime were not the first to address the Crimea. Nor were they the last. In the years and decades following the conflagration, military men returned to the peninsula; solo voyagers and group expeditions made their ways there, too, as part of the nascent war tourism of the nineteenth century. These voyages were the subjects of diaries and newspaper articles and of periodical essays and memoirs. Across the twentieth century, the Crimea remained on the minds of Britons as they witnessed the demise of empire, the waging of world wars, and the Cold War and its aftermath. As viewed from Britain, the Crimea was a stage for war, a site of atrocity, a locale for peacemaking, and a destination for tourism. These happenings became the focus of a broad and varied archive of news reports, personal reminiscences, and mass media. As they relayed their engagements with the Crimea, twentieth-century interlocutors returned repeatedly to the experiences, events, and affects of the nineteenth-century's war. At times, they evoked it directly; on other occasions, implicitly. Across a long arc of history, the Victorians' Crimea shaped British understandings of this distant land.

The pages that follow examine a cascade of travel narratives like Seacole's as they demonstrate the precarious, if persistent, place of the Crimea in the British national imagination. Official and unofficial, printed and unpublished, these texts drew upon the images developed in wartime as they portrayed the Crimea as a realm of trial and pleasure, of destiny and loss, and of bloodshed and renewal. Their authors came from a wide swath of society; among them were warriors, pleasure-seekers, and peacemakers. Like Seacole, they regarded themselves as adventurers. I employ this term to encapsulate the taste for alterity and the inheritance of Orientalism among Crimean-bound voyagers at different points in time. There is a touch of irony in my usage. In looking to it, I hope to press at the limits of this taste for adventure among a reluctant nation of travelers. Many undertook their travels with alacrity, embarking on their own wonderful adventures as they variably sought out history, fame, and pleasure. At times, they grew circumspect, as they faced homesickness and confusion, or alienation and despair. Taken together, their words show the deep and long-standing role of the Crimea in the making of individual adventure and of collective life, and in the reconceiving of national understanding and of global order.

***

Mary Seacole and her fighting brethren elevated the Crimea to a place of newfound prominence as they traveled "eastward ho!"[4] They were not the first, however, to direct Britain's attention to the peninsula jutting down from the Black Sea. In fact, "that little peninsula to which the eyes and hearts of all England were so earnestly directed," to borrow Seacole's words, had occupied the attention and the pens of English travelers for some decades.[5] In the seventy-five years leading up to the conflict, the rise and fall of empires and the Napoleonic Wars turned British attention eastward. These developments occurred alongside the flowering of travel literature as a genre, the consolidation of Orientalist modes of viewing, and the development of Romantic sensibilities.[6] These geopolitical and cultural trends shaped accounts of the Crimea published from the later eighteenth century onward. From that time, a set of intrepid travelers and vivid writers, both men and women, gave elite readers a budding sense of the peninsula, its land, and its people. Their accounts combined geographical, aesthetic, and proto-ethnographic observations as they described the land, annexed by the Russian Empire in 1783. Taken together, their accounts helped to consolidate a sense of a little-known region. In their textual productions, they offered up an inheritance for later writers to reuse, reshape, and redeploy.

One of the earliest Anglophone writers to discuss the Crimea in depth was Baroness Elizabeth Berkeley Craven, an actress, playwright, and traveler, who wrote a series of letters to her brother. Craven made her way to the Crimea in 1786, three years after the peninsula's annexation by Russia's Catherine the Great.[7] Whereas the nineteenth century's warriors accessed the peninsula from the west and via the sea, Craven reached the Crimea from the east, navigating the land passage from a then-friendly Russia. Hers was far from an inevitable voyage. Craven had been warned away from the land, with its "unwholesome" air and its "poisonous" waters, which augured danger, and perhaps death.[8] Yet, she persisted in her ambitions to reach what was instead a sybaritic and fertile region. Like many Orientalist travelers to eastern lands, she remarked upon the striking women, admired the lush landscapes, and enjoyed abundant repasts with their sweetmeats, lemonades, and wine. These pleasures did not, however, blind Craven to the geopolitical significance of the peninsula. She was impressed by its history. A cosmopolitan locale and a polyglot place, it was home to many invading hordes. The Crimea had long been the site of successive waves of invasion, war, and plunder. With its strategic location on the Black Sea and its strong harbor in Sebastopol, Craven declared, presciently, that the Crimea was sure to become a "treasure to posterity."[9]

In the early nineteenth century, as Russia consolidated its hold on the peninsula, a new generation of English adventurers filled in Craven's view with ethnographic, commercial, and geographical detail. In the account of Mary Holderness, who spent four years in the Crimea as part of an agricultural colony, readers came to apprehend a catalog of the motley inhabitants of the peninsula – the idle, if chaste Tatars, the "litigious" and "parsimonious" Greeks, the enterprising and artisanal Germans, and the industrious and frugal Bulgarians, along with Armenian Christians, Karaite Jews, and Russian peasants.[10] They may have spoken different languages and professed different faiths, but the community as a whole shared in the common pursuit of commerce, Holderness maintained, as she touted the universalizing power of trade. A near contemporary of Holderness, James Edward Alexander, built on these understandings as he highlighted the beauty of the peninsula. In 1830, after tours of duty in Persia, Russia, and the Balkans, this army officer traversed the so-called paradise. Alexander made his way from the vast steppes through the gentle valleys and from the "picturesque hills" to the verdant coast.[11] In keeping with his age, Alexander brought to his depictions a combination of ethnographic detail and romantic sensibility. The striking geography that he sketched was home to layers of cultures and layers of ruins. For Alexander, the Crimea was a land of traces, where mosques, synagogues, and churches stood side by side, as did the tombs of Muslims, Christians, and Jews, with horses grazing among them all. Together, the built environment and the memorable scenery promoted rapt introspection. In the spirit of the romantic adventurer, Alexander claimed that the Crimea presented perfect vistas meant for solitary study and sublime contemplation.[12]

These publications notwithstanding, the Crimea remained remote on the maps and in the minds of most Britons until the 1850s (Figure 1.1). At mid-century, however, this onetime destination for solo adventurers assumed a place at the heart of European diplomatic tensions and at the center of British public attention. What had been a site of rarefied fascination became a focus for collective concern, as international hostilities and diplomatic suspense intensified across Europe in the early 1850s. Newspapers, lectures, and personal accounts all amplified the renderings of earlier adventurers as they focused the attention of an increasingly literate – and increasingly concerned – public on the peninsula. As they forecast the war and covered the conflict, these sources relied handsomely on the renderings of prior adventurers.

A set of lectures written by Anthony Grant exemplifies the shifting audience for Crimean concerns alongside the enduring influences of

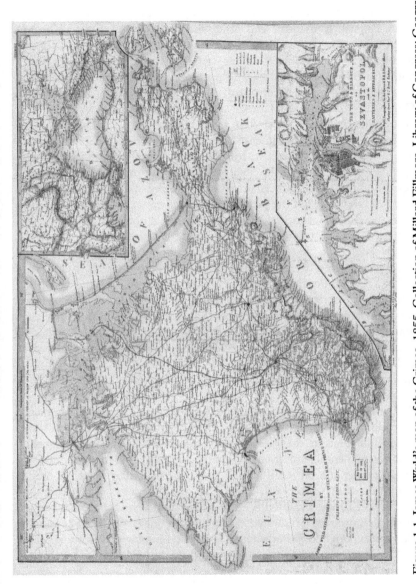

Figure 1.1 James Wyld's map of the Crimea. 1855. Collection of Millard Fillmore. Library of Congress: Geography and Map Division

earlier travelers. Grant intended his lectures for an audience at Hertfordshire's Literary Institute: the concerns of elevated cosmopolitan travelers had become the stuff of provincial rational recreation. In the transcripts, Grant gestured to the deep and preoccupying interest that the English, provincial and otherwise, were taking in the remote land. "Probably no instance can be found of such a sudden transition from obscurity to celebrity as has befallen the Crimea within the period of a few months," wrote Grant, as the conflict catapulted the distant peninsula to the forefront of British attention.[13]

The lecturer charted the Crimea's rise to prominence as a romantic, even sublime, trajectory: the sudden springing of "a terrible manhood."[14] Though he portrayed the Crimea as *terra incognita*, Grant understood that it was no blank slate; it was, instead, a "land literally scarred with the footprints" of history.[15] Like so many others at mid-century, Grant understood the Crimea as a crossroads, temporally, spatially, and culturally. It bore the traces of the past, captured the concerns of the present, and augured the contours of the future. It was a point of contestation between the "gentler refinements of the South" and the "ruthless violence of the North."[16] A "battlefield" and a borderland par excellence, the Crimea confounded categorization. "Is it north, or south? Is it east, or west?" asked Grant of the region that was constantly in contention, most recently as a site of rivalry between the Ottoman and Russian Empires. He expressed a nascent understanding of what would come to be known as human geography in his examination of the region, which he and others viewed as the meeting ground not just of warring peoples but also of "conflicting climates" and physical conditions. In the Crimea, humid summers gave way to frigid winters, and the "desolate steppe" ceded to the "luxuriant coast."[17]

Texts like Grant's lectures began the work of acquainting a Britain that was headed toward war with the historical battleground that was the Crimea. Together, as they reported the rise in hostilities, newspapers, magazines, and letters presented the simmering conflict to their readers.[18] They sustained the representational practices of earlier texts, as they brought the peoples and places of the East into the homes of the reading public. The Crimea saturated domestic consciousness with a speed and intensity that was unprecedented. Thanks to the telegraph, those at home could now experience war at a distance in something approximating real time. While delays of months had characterized the coverage of preceding wars, the lag had shortened to weeks or even days.[19]

These printed renderings were joined by the accounts of a host of Britons who traveled as soldiers and officers, as nursing sisters and camp followers, as medical officers and chaplains, and as historians and journalists. Some wrote for public audiences during wartime, while others addressed loved ones privately. Others still saved their observations for the postwar epoch. As they made their ways, they recorded their encounters in a multitude of venues: in letters, diaries, and ships' logs, to name some. Among the best known in Victorian times and after were William Howard Russell, the *Times*' special correspondent at the front, and Fanny Duberly, an Army paymaster's intrepid and witty wife. Joining in the chorus of adventurers were many young men bound for greatness along with seasoned officers, too. They were accompanied by auxiliary supports, including doctors, chaplains, and nurses. Archived in national repositories and stacked away in county record offices, their texts, together, give a sense of a nation making its way – sometimes gamely, sometimes less so – to an uncertain war on Europe's periphery.

As they traveled, these sundry protagonists turned a place of diplomatic concern and descriptive interest into the terrain of lived experiences and wartime encounters. Their writings attest that they were certainly aware of the tropes of Orientalism sewn into the fabric of travel narratives. They may, too, have been acquainted with the musings of Napoleonic officers and soldiers, who had traversed the continent some forty years before.[20] Influential as well were earlier renderings of the Crimea. Together, these understandings shaped accounts of the journey and of the war itself among the mid-Victorians, who wrote their ways through the conflict in unprecedented numbers. They described, on the ground, a locale that had long been strategically important and historically tumultuous. They rendered a geography filled with cosmopolitan and polyglot populations. And they discussed a terrain overrun with a cast of alarming and dizzying combatants: the formidable Russian enemies along with the mercurial French allies, the vexing Turkish forces, and the exotic Sardinian warriors. Together, they offered up the record of a shared national adventure.

These Crimean adventurers wrote steadily and avidly. They left a formidable archive behind, as they sought to reckon with a perilous voyage, with an onslaught of cultures, and with the dangers of war. They were dogged in their pursuits, writing while perched atop suitcases, leaning on camp stoves, amid heavy musketry, or in the cold winter.[21] They scavenged for paper and for stamps. Their steadiness and determination suggest the importance of writing as a way of confronting danger and difference in the theaters of war. Their correspondences kindled a sense of home feeling while away. They also created ties between the battlefront and the home front. These links were vital ones for the production of Crimean understandings in Britain. As they consumed letters and as they devoured media accounts, a wide readership on the home front participated in a shared adventure and became an imagined community of armchair warriors. Together, they bore witness to a collective, and unfolding, account of war.

**

One of the first acts, for a nation bound for war, is to get its combatants to the front. In the case of the Crimean conflict, troops set off from England's ports in anxious anticipation during the early months of 1854. Accounts of travel to the East began with scenes of embarkation from England and with voyages at sea. In the spring of 1854, there were ample views of the "heart-stirring spectacle" of war's beginning, capturing parades on foot through London and farewells on ships at Portsmouth and Southampton.[22] Found in illustrated newspapers, on prints, and even on sheet music, these views engendered a sense of a shared national adventure (Figure 1.2). Individual chroniclers filled in these stories of send-off as they recorded their departures in letters and diaries.[23] Many echoed the optimism and excitement of the newspapers as they wrote their ways into the nation's shared exploit. They looked forward to luxuriating in a hospitable country while making their names in history.[24] Other travelers, more circumspect, eschewed this early optimism. Mindful that she was saying goodbye to dear friends, perhaps for good, Fanny Duberly was teary-eyed at her departure.[25] In a letter to his father, Major G. G. Clowes was similarly melancholy as he recalled the moment when he "lost sight of England for the first time in [his] life."[26] Read in retrospect, such accounts seem to augur the challenges that were to come: not just the difficulties of a long, mismanaged war, but more immediately, the dangers of the voyage and the perils of the sea. Along the way, the troops faced rough and sickening waves, painful partings at ports of call, and the dreaded cholera that felled soldiers in large numbers, many before they made it to the front.

The voyage, both challenging and fascinating, became a well-rehearsed script, with its stops along the way at Gibraltar, Malta, and Gallipoli. By the time Mary Seacole published her travelogue in 1857, the route had been "worn threadbare by book-making tourists."[27] Its contours went like this. Ships anchored first at Gibraltar, a British possession and a strategic naval base during the Crimean War. It transfixed those passing through with its extraordinary, rocky geography and its industrious, cosmopolitan hordes. Turbaned Algerians, ancient Moors, and Spanish Jews commingled with Scotch Highlanders, British Soldiers, and old women bent with age.[28] Malta, with its bazaars full of kid gloves to take to the front, and its black lace to send back home, sated an appetite for a commercial, oriental East.[29] If Malta offered unanticipated splendor,

Figure 1.2 Unattributed music sheet. *The Parting March*. 1854. Mary Evans Picture Library

with its opera house and its cathedral, then the next port of call, Gallipoli, provided unrivaled squalor. Later immortalized in the Great War, the Gallipoli of the 1850s struck those who disembarked there as a remarkably hybrid and particularly dilapidated mélange, with ingredients of a rickety Irish village, Billingsgate back alleys, and northern Italian towns thrown all together. William Howard Russell called it a "wretched place."[30] The voyagers passed sights of past renown, too, among them, Troy, Sparta, and Athens. When he beheld these cities, Jervoise Smith, who accompanied the Crimean Commissioners on their voyage to the East declared, "for once I did not regret all the work of school."[31]

As they moved beyond the straits of the Dardanelles, Crimean adventurers drew increasingly upon the staples of Oriental encounter.[32] On their ways, they enjoyed abundant fruit, cloudless skies, and bright sun. To journey eastward was to open the pages of a "sealed book."[33] Constantinople, the heart of the Ottoman Empire, lay beyond its covers. It was a vast imperial city, not unlike London in its scope, scale, and bustle, but strikingly different with its colored terraces, striking minarets, and red roofs.[34] As they entered the metropolis, the adventurers reached for Orientalist language to describe what they saw, smelled, and heard. For many, the arrival at Constantinople substantiated stories of a mythical East kindled in childhood. It was, for these adventurers, as if the *Arabian Nights* had come to life. "Everything was strange and picturesque."[35] For some, the tales did not do justice. Such was the case for Lieutenant William Montgomery-Cuninghame, who found Constantinople the "most magnificent sight in the world," with everything he had read in books paling in relation to the reality. Of the Sultan's Palace, he confessed, "it is perfectly impossible to describe or imagine the magnificence of it." While they marveled at the great city for its wonder, the war-bound adventurers praised the surrounding countryside for its languor. It was all "blissful idleness."[36] Typical was the declaration that there was "nothing to do except read, smoke, and eat melons."[37]

If one staple of the nineteenth-century Orientalist travel narrative was delight, another was disappointment. This was certainly the case for many of the voyagers who stopped in Constantinople. Oftentimes, the Ottoman capital did not live up to expectations.[38] Crimean travelers' accounts reveal discrepancies between the panoramic visions of the majestic views and the on-the-ground experiences in the capital. In their negotiations of the streets, the Crimean adventurers evoked assessments not of Oriental majesty but of Eastern decrepitude. They complained of the "dirty, badly paved, narrow" byways.[39] And they displaced their disdain of the Turks onto their "lazy and dirty" dogs.[40] The famous bazaars did not meet their expectations, and they had been "too often and too well described before."[41] It was a hard place to write about. But for those inclined, Constantinople proved a place "soon to get tired of."[42]

Some adventurers moved beyond the antinomies of delight and disappointment, as they understood their day-to-day experiences on the ground through the prism of humor. Their humor was rife with Orientalism, exploiting stereotypes of haggling Turks and pious Muslims.[43] Jervoise Smith relayed the amusement to be had in the bargaining process with one particular merchant, who was forced, continually, to interrupt his business partner in mid-prayer to verify prices; for Smith, to watch the pious man hurriedly pray over the Koran so as not to miss out on the bargain was "not bad fun."[44] Many turned the humor of encounter on themselves, particularly as they navigated the intimacies of the Turkish baths, which provided singular enjoyment for English officers and officials.[45] Smith plainly declared, "I never enjoyed anything more in my life."[46] Frederick Augustus Maxse, Naval Aide-de-Camp to Lord Raglan, took the opportunity to immerse himself in the experience and lay after "with a white turban twisted round" his head and a pipe in his mouth. Thinking of his female relations at home, Maxse surmised that they might laugh if they were to spy him laid out like a "limp wafer."[47]

This was all a mere overture to the September 1854 arrival of the troops at Sebastopol. As the harbor came into sight, focus and mood shifted in public and private accounts alike. Orientalized lolling and melancholy sorrow abated. Instead, a sense of historical gravity and bellicose excitement prevailed on the approach to the city and its grand harbor. Combatants expressed a feeling that they were at the center of history, as the "whole nation" and the "whole civilized world" turned attentions there.[48] "At last we are in sight of Sevastopol," one declared.[49] With its rocky setting, Sebastopol was a distinctly exotic sight, not unlike Gibraltar. But with the bustle of its harbor, it also resembled the cityscapes of England. James Edward Alexander, the early nineteenth-century traveler, had once called it the "Portsmouth of the Euxine."[50] As it came into view on the occasion of his arrival, Colonel Hugh Robert Hibbert reiterated the strategy of familiarizing the foreign city by drawing an English parallel. In this case, he likened Sebastopol to "Birmingham at a distance," its atmosphere filled with smoking chimneys and bustling music.[51]

The wartime campaign began and ended with Sebastopol. It was a lively site at the war's start and an unsettling ruin at the conflict's end. It was not, however, the only town traversed by the troops. There was, of course, Balaklava, whose neighboring valley was associated with the Charge of the Light Brigade. As for the town itself, it appeared squalid and decrepit. Fanny Duberly was no fan of "that stink hole Balaklava." "How it did stink!" she proclaimed.[52] Also on the itineraries of the soldiers were cities like Kerch, brimming with Tatars, Greeks, Jews, and Russians, and, further afield, Yalta, which later became synonymous with a new balance of power in the world at the end of World War II. At the time of the Crimean War, this town on the so-called Russian Riviera was just beginning to make its name as a home of curative waters and seaside leisure. With its scenic views, its abundant wine, and its mild air, it was on its way to becoming "a humble kind of Brighton."[53]

During wartime, at least, much of the attention was on the landscape, the craggy cliffs, the Black Sea vistas, and especially the flowery valleys.[54] "What a country this is for flowers," one officer proclaimed.[55] It was, at times a challenge for the military men to capture the scenery, or so they claimed. For some, the land exhibited wildness and loveliness that exceeded their descriptive powers.[56] Others endeavored to invoke the sensory richness of the undulating land, where wild thyme filled the air with "sweet odors" when crushed by horses' hooves.[57] This appeal not just to the sense of sight but also to that of smell had the effect of bringing readers in Britain, whether recipients of letters or readers of printed matter, closer to the front. Those who desired to bridge the distances looked to material circulation, literally sending bits of the Crimea home in the form of dried plants and preserved flowers.[58] Some of the most heartfelt battlefield missives contained irises and violets. Even beyond offering connection, these floral transactions provided reassurance. Not only did they forge links between home and away; they also made connections between the living and the dead, reminding soldiers and those at home of the cycle of life, even amid war, with winter snow giving way to a steady stream of blooms: crocuses, snowdrops, and violets.[59]

Not only flowers, but other materials too helped to forge sentimental links between home and away. Among the most memorable was human hair, a notably Victorian artifact of remembrance. It was common for mothers and wives, as well as sisters and sweethearts, to preserve locks of hair from their adventurers bound for battle.[60] At times, combatants enclosed locks of hair with their letters in order to close the gap wrought by the miles and to remind loved ones at home of their continued vitality. An extension of the body, hair conjured powerful emotions as it connected the war front in the Crimea and to the home fromt in Britain. As in other matters, humor mitigated the intensity of the encounter upon receiving a lock of hair, not to mention the emotion involved in cutting it. Such was the case for Lieutenant Colonel Hibbert, who noted, in a sharp riposte that bemoaned the sanitary conditions in the East, that he was enclosing, in one of his letters to his mother, "a bit of what may now be called true Crimean hair – thoroughly dirty."[61]

Traffic in handmade objects bridged the gap between Britain and the East as well. Lace from Malta and handkerchiefs from Constantinople found their ways into packages sent home to Britain.[62] There were assurances to return, eventually, with the spoils of war, including

Russian swords, firearms, and charms – often taken from the bodies of the dead. If enclosures provided a sense of reassurance that those at home had not been forgotten, these promises offered a hope for eventual victory on the part of the British and their allies. They incorporated the foreign into British life and domesticated the dangers of the war. Like flowers and like hair, relics and promises bridged the chasms of war.[63]

Much of the ink spilled in the name of navigating the warfront did not, however, involve the natural world or the object world. Instead, it addressed the human world of the Crimea and its combatants. Wartime accounts of the East echoed the writings of earlier travelers as they borrowed from the modes developed by their roving predecessors to portray the local populations of Tatars and others. To this end, they offered up portraits of a colorful population engaged in warm hospitality, of a cosmopolitan multitude absorbed in ambitious trading, and of a simple people living a picturesque life.[64] The adventurers portrayed the Tatar dislike for the Russians with sympathy. That necessarily said, they wrote dismissively of a backward people who had yet to enter the modern world. Taken together, the composite view had the effect of legitimizing the war effort. Even while they humanized the Tatars, wartime interlocutors shored up notions of Russians as savage aggressors and of Britons as improving agents, in an early rendition of the notion of the civilizing mission associated with later nineteenth-century imperialism. As such, their renderings had the effect of drawing attention away from routine atrocities of war that Britons themselves inflicted on local populations and their environs. These depredations included the plunder and drunkenness that they admitted, along with the sexual and physical violence that were only rarely and fleetingly suggested in wartime. Ultimately, the portrayals of the Tatars worked to reassure writers and readers in Britain of their own superiority and of their war's worthiness.[65]

Wartime writers sought also to locate Britons amidst a changing cast of enemies and allies at mid-century, for the Crimean War marked the rearrangement of friends and foes on the European continent and beyond. The Russians and the British had once shared a common cause in the campaign to defeat Napoleon and the French in a struggle that lasted for years and extended across a continent. But the two empires found themselves embattled as mortal enemies in the Crimea. Correspondents from the front did occasionally muster images of the Cossacks as sturdy warriors, with flashing sabers, dependable ponies, and sheepskin hats. They even showed their rivals to be kind, if gullible and ignorant people – at least off of the field of battle. More often, however, English combatants portrayed their Russian foes as filthy brutes: "decidedly a dirty, an excessively dirty people," to borrow from one published author.[66] Subject to the British pen, the Russian soldier was drunken and depraved. To underscore their low habits and their low morals, writers depicted them as animal-like in their tendencies. One compared them to jackals, and another to reptiles, a "secret, stealthy, creeping mass … crawling on the earths' surface … [seeking] to overwhelm its prey."[67] Russian combatants looted with abandon and killed indiscriminately. Flouting the conventions of war, they showed no compunction when it came to murdering wounded British warriors lying on the field of battle. And they left their own to die, too, often groaning like animals and palpitating like wild beasts.[68] When they cast the Russians as depraved, savage, and animalistic, British chroniclers placed them outside of the pale of civilization. In so doing, they bolstered the sense that they fought, in a war motivated by diplomatic and territorial aims, on the side of civilization and humanity.

Capturing the spirit of the allies proved to be a more uncertain endeavor. This was particularly so when it came to the Turks, who evoked ambivalence and acceptance at best and disdain and dismissal at worst.[69] Among the Turks, the Bashi Bazouks, the Army's irregulars, were compelling sources of fascination, described by the English time and again as wild: indeed, the "wildest" of the troops in the campaign.[70] The designation of wild worked strategically, allowing English observers to approach these strange allies simultaneously with judgment and admiration.[71] If the British troops found anything to admire in their Turkish comrades, it was that they were people of faith, "cheered by the pure light" of their holy creed.[72] Even this understanding, however, was difficult to sustain. For many, Islam's ritual observances, including the keeping of Halal law and the practice of prayer, proved not sources for admiration, but objects of ridicule. The Crimean combatants' words anticipated the treatment of subaltern troops on the Indian subcontinent just a handful of years later. While on the Crimean Peninsula, correspondents mocked the so-called "True Believers" – those hungry Turks who shamelessly devoured British supplies of "coffee, sugar, rice, and biscuits," but eschewed the salt beef, lest it be "pork in disguise."[73] At times, the object of derision was not the observance itself, but the departure from it. Mary Seacole, for instance, peppered her account of travels in the East with stories of drunken pashas who stockpiled sherry and became tipsy from champagne.[74] As an outsider herself, Seacole resorted to Orientalist humor and denigration to create filiations with her English readership.

There was little to recommend the Turks in the eyes of the British. To hear the warring adventurers tell it, the Turks, in fact, had much in common with their Russian foes. As they honed rhetorical strategies to portray the Turks, they anticipated Rudyard Kipling's prosodic rendering of the civilizing mission, dark and stark, in the "White Man's Burden."[75] These allies were dirty and depraved – a "crestfallen, depressed, half-fed people."[76] They were primitive and childlike; they showed little respect for the dead. They were prone to thievery. They were blunted in their feelings.[77] They were inefficient and obsequious.[78] They committed atrocities against their fallen enemies. They paraded with the heads of dead Russians on sticks, killed local civilians, and even, at times, flouted their faith, debasing and mutilating women.[79] There was a fundamental difference from the Russians, however. Whereas the Russians appeared reckless in their drunken bravery, the Turks were feckless in their simple cowardice. A "most unhelpful lot of people," they ran away from skirmishes and abandoned positions.[80] When they denigrated the Turks, the English opened a catalog of epithets that left no room to include these unlikely allies in the folds of martial masculinity and European civilization. In the face of these pervasive understandings, Lieutenant Colonel Hugh Robert Hibbert declared that the Turks were "not worth fighting for."[81]

British adventurers in the Crimea looked differently on the other allies in their midst, as they produced a taxonomy of martial masculinities that elevated ornamental grandeur. There were some whose appearances suggested majesty, not debasement. These troops generated admiration rather than disdain. There were, first of all, the troops from Sardinia, the small island off of the coast of Italy that lent its support to the allied cause. These men – draped in green and donning feathered hats – had a theatrical and picturesque look to them. In the eyes of more than one observer, they fulfilled fantasies of the banditry of olden days; they took up far more ink and attention than their mere numbers seemed to merit. There were, too, the Chasseurs d'Afrique, or Zouaves. Magnificent fighters in equally magnificent dress, these members of the French forces via North Africa sported an Oriental costume – a red fez with a white turban and a blue jacket. Their open collars allowed them to boast ample ornaments. Mustachioed and bearded, they cut a fierce-looking sight.[82] They appeared to have taken on the native dress and dark skin of the Arab world – "burnt to a deep copper tint by the rays of an African sun."[83] As such, they were a source of racial and categorical confusion. The Zouaves were, in fact, native Frenchmen and not Arabs, little Napoleons all around, averaging five feet six inches in height. Their appearances proved fascinating to the English adventurers in the Crimea, who devoted a good deal of attention to the exotic fighters, not just in word, but also in image. Mary Seacole was impressed by the "gallant little fellows."[84] So too was Roger Fenton, the photographer at the front. He was taken enough with the Zouaves to have himself photographed, reclined, in their costume. Through his fascination with the Zouaves, Fenton explored an alternate form of manhood while exploring the Crimean front.[85]

The troops from France proved to be more complex figures: the former foes were, simultaneously, comrades and foils.[86] A new alliance provided occasions for fellowship with the newfound allies; there were shipboard visits, meals in camp, theatrical evenings, and sporting competitions (Figure 1.3).[87] This budding friendship did, at times, produce fellow feeling. But it also engendered anxiety and self-doubt. In the first year

Figure 1.3 "Fraternisation at Malta: Highlander and French Infantry Soldier." c. 1854. Watercolor by William Thomas Markham. National Army Museum

of the war, especially, the French Army proved to be far better prepared than the British, particularly when it came to medical readiness, food supply, and warm clothes. Captain Frederick Cockayne Elton, an eventual Victoria Cross winner, was confounded by the apparent contrast between French efficiency and English blunder in the first winter of the war. He declared of the former foes and regarding the Spanish campaign of nearly five decades beforehand, "I sometimes wonder how we ever managed to thrash them on the Peninsula."[88]

It must have reassured those on the warfront and the home front alike when the British righted their supply chains and medical measures in the second winter of the war. This shift improved the well-being of the troops and allowed the English to reassert their preeminence in wartime, at least for themselves. When they did not configure this advantage in administrative terms, they fell back on a sense of moral superiority. Take, for instance, the understandings of William Howard Russell. According to the journalist, while the French tended to bully the natives, the English treated them with respect.[89] And while the French showed disregard for the Turkish dead, the English offered veneration.[90] Although they were military allies, the French did not appear as moral equals. Nor did they present themselves as kindred spirits. In a letter to his sister, Sergeant General Robert Wyatt Meadows encapsulated well the disdain for his fighting fellows, as he dismissed the "little frog eating and snail swallowing soldiers of La Belle France."[91]

The wartime journeys to the Crimea allowed Britain's adventurers to come into contact with foreign lands and foreign troops. As they traveled, they maneuvered between the familiar and the unfamiliar, and between the English and the foreign. Some did so reflectively, others reluctantly, and still others eagerly. The tour to the Crimea proved to be a demanding trajectory, taking the adventurers thousands of miles from home and acquainting them with unfamiliar peoples. While many of the adventurers set off to the Crimea following service elsewhere, some had arrived on the peninsula after saying goodbye to England for the first time. They may have greeted the adventure with optimism and opportunity, but the long war, with its cold winters and material privation, and with its bloody battles and its interminable siege, made the combatants, by and large, yearn for home (Figure 1.4).[92] They were, in the end, the bulk of them, reluctant cosmopolitans, needful of home comforts. Eager to set out for greatness, they happily returned home at war's end.

"What a delightful change it will be to feel the comforts of home & England again," declared John Netten Radcliffe, a surgeon who had rubbed elbows with the Turks during his time spent in the headquarters

Figure 1.4 Men of the 77th Regiment in winter costume by Roger Fenton, 1855. Library of Congress Prints and Photographs Division/ Mary Evans Picture Library

of Omar Pasha.[93] Military officers offered up similar sentiments. The words of Lieutenant George Waller of the 7th Fusiliers, who went seeking greatness in the East, departing a boy and coming home a man, provide a case in point.[94] Waller relished the East, with its scenery, its people, and its produce. He served with pride, becoming a credit to his family. But after the war, he captured his feelings of his return to England with a simple word: "Hurrah!"[95]

***

George Waller took leave of the peninsula and headed home to England in February 1856, just a month before the signing of the Treaty of Paris, which ended the war. At that time, the young Lieutenant declared, "I hope I shall never see the Crimea again."[96] Most of the troops shared Waller's feelings. Their wishes were realized, with no regiments making repeat tours of the peninsula in the years to follow. Some returned to England, while others made their ways to far-flung parts of the British Empire, including Canada and India. The Crimean Peninsula and all that had unfolded there did not, however, recede from British consciousness. The blunders of the Crimea became the topic of official inquiry in the years following the war, with commissions devoted to investigating the failures of food provisioning, sanitary arrangements, and army intelligence. The Crimea remained on the periphery of the Eastern Question, which involved the treatment of religious minorities by the Ottoman Empire in its twilight amidst ongoing anxieties about Russian territorial ambition. There were other forms, as well, through which the Crimea persisted in the public mind, particularly when it came to visual and literary culture. At the war's end, Roger Fenton displayed his famous panorama of Sebastopol, along with hundreds of other photographs, at the Royal Watercolour Society in London. Over the following decades, Alexander Kinglake, an intrepid voyager and a noted Orientalist, sustained the literary world's engagement with the peninsula. His celebrated, multivolume history, *The Invasion of the Crimea* (1861–1887), was itself an outgrowth of the traveling gentleman's onetime ventures on the faraway peninsula and continued correspondence with the war's *dramatis personae*.[97]

During these years, the Crimea was the destination of solo travelers and group tours concerned, by and large, to return to the landmarks of the war. Although they were intermittent and sporadic, these visitors followed the fashion of earlier British pilgrims voyaging to the battlegrounds of the Napoleonic Wars; they joined in the practice of contemporary American brethren sojourning to the killing fields of the American Civil War.[98] Among their ranks were military men and royal tourists as well as New Women and traveling students. When they recorded their journeys, they recast wartime adventure into return narratives. As they ventured, they addressed the tensions wrought in the face of the Eastern Question, the Franco-Prussian War, and the New Imperialism. On their minds was not just the Crimean past, but equally, and if not more, the global future.

One early account of return comes from a medical officer – M.S. – who had served in the war and who sojourned on the peninsula in 1861. His reflections, published as "Ten Days in the Crimea" in *Macmillan's*

Magazine, condense in pithy form the elements of the return narrative
and the workings of memory. This solitary traveler's tour helped to
consolidate some of the staples of the wartime return narratives which
pivoted between portrayals of wartime clamor and quiet aftermath. As he
made his way through deserted harbors, ruined cities, and erstwhile
trenches, the medical man took in scenes of desolation and devastation.
There was detritus in abundance – piles of war materiel and bones
of horses and dogs. In narrating his paces through this landscape,
M.S. relied upon contrasts. The cloudless August 1861 was a stark
departure from the cold winter of 1854–1855. The quiet of the
Sardinian Camp, where there was nary a sound but "the chirping of
grasshoppers," was a world apart from the commotion of wartime, and
the emptied-out harbor at Balaklava was unrecognizable in relation to its
appearance just a handful of years before.[99] These differences aside, the
war's traces remained evident on the landscape: "All the scenes of the war
winter came before one – the noise, the confusion, the accumulations in
that small place," he explained.[100]

This 1861 journey predated by a handful of years a far more public
tour: that made in 1869 by the Prince and Princess of Wales. They were
accompanied by a set of incisive interlocutors, including William Howard
Russell of the *Times* and an artist employed by the *Illustrated London News*,
both making return visits to the land, along with Teresa Grey, a lady-in-
waiting to Princess Beatrice, traveling to the East for the first time. The
journey enjoyed ample publicity in a memoir by Russell, in the pages of
the illustrated newspapers, and in a printed diary kept by Grey.[101] Fifteen
years on, the Crimea may have become a "bore" in the collective mind,
where it had become synonymous with mismanagement and with
blunder.[102] Yet, the chroniclers of 1869 furnished the region with
renewed flair and relevance as they situated it in the context of the raging
Eastern Question and the Suez Canal's opening.

The royal party took a different route to the Crimea than its warring
predecessors had, passing through continental Europe and enjoying
a sojourn in Egypt – a country which Lady Grey, who enjoyed its feasts,
harems, and pyramids, regarded as the "beau ideal" of the East.[103]
Returning to the course of the Crimean army, the 1869 procession
stopped in Constantinople, a familiar port of call. The travelers saw
a city that was, at once, similar and changed, shaped by the great fire of
1864 and the building of an ambassadorial network. After their magical
stay in Egypt, however, the visit to Constantinople seemed a perfunctory
obligation. Reflecting on her experience of the celebrated locale, Lady
Grey echoed the Crimean War's adventurers as she declared, "I never saw
a place I felt so little inclined to fall in love with."[104]

The *Illustrated London News,* for its part, sought, explicitly, to accentu-
ate this historical path from Constantinople to the Crimea in its
announcement of the royal party's arrival at Sebastopol. "Few places,"
it declared, were "more familiar to English newspaper readers" than the
Crimea.[105] The newspaper pointed to the seeming incongruity between
the historical weight of the war in the national memory and the geographical size of the small peninsula that had played the host. It was
a discrepancy with which all of the chroniclers among the royal party
sought to reckon as they meditated on arrival there, some fifteen years
after the Crimean invasion. Sighting Sebastopol left the usually prolix
William Howard Russell grasping for language; it engendered a "feeling
too deep for words."[106] Russell imagined, instead, the feelings of others,
among them the first-time visitors Princess Beatrice and Teresa Grey. He
surmised that the modest proportions of the stage of the war must have
proven disappointing to these ladies, particularly when contrasted with
the larger-than-life legends of the place. In her own diary, Lady Grey
reckoned with her own senses of incongruity and oddness in arriving at
a place "so very different from what one had then imagined to one's
self."[107]

The 1869 tour was an effort at reckoning on many scores – not simply
with the geographical scale of the Crimea against the historical weight of
memory, but also with the transformed landscape of the peninsula compared to its appearance in wartime. In Sebastopol and Balaklava alike, all
was "empty, void, and waste." Like their returning predecessor, the
medical man, members of the royal party produced contrasts between
the Crimea of wartime and the Crimea of their time. What had been
bustle was now quiet; where there had been development was now ruin,
noted the sojourners, as they sharpened staple elements of the return
narrative.[108] Ruins were everywhere, and in heaps, to use a word that
recurred through Russell's writing and that of his fellow travelers. There
were "heaps of broken stone," "shapeless heaps," "harmless heaps," and
"ruined heaps."[109] The Crimea had become pastoral.[110] The noisy ports
of call – Sebastopol, Balaklava, and others, too – were now left to "the
wild duck and the sea gull."[111] The "roar of guns and the rattle of
musketry" had given way to the "lowing of the kine, and the song of the
crested lark."[112] Such nods to the pastoral must have offered moving copy
for readers at home. More significantly, they allowed the authors to
sidestep critiques of the war and its violence, aestheticizing its ravages,
minimizing its pains, and painting a bucolic resting place for the dead.

The Crimean returnees extended the notion of a pastoral Crimea from
their observations on landscape to their portrayals of the local populations. Depopulated, the Crimea had shrunk tenfold in numbers of

residents. While the allied combatants had departed, the Crimea remained a multicultural locale, the home of diverse peoples. Of particular interest were the Russians, no longer formidable foes. They were, in fact, on their ways to becoming allies in the region as they engaged in a Christianization campaign on the peninsula, and as Turkey floundered and committed atrocities. Russians served, for the royal party, as hospitable guides, obliging with their guests and resigned to or even "in love with ruin" themselves.[113] For the most part, the Tatars equaled the Russians in hospitality, offering up loaves of black bread and cups of salt as signs of welcome. There were, among them, some who greeted the entourage with caution, however. In one such incident, the *Illustrated London News* found some humor. It relayed the alarm of a young Tatar shepherd, too young to have remembered the British occupation, who greeted a member of the traveling party with the anxious cries of "*Anliksi*," meaning Englishman. It was as if he had witnessed a devil. The young shepherd may have lacked for worldliness, but he was not alone. Had an "Irish cow boy" in Connemara laid eyes on a Russian, the newspaper averred, he would, certainly, have behaved the same.[114]

Accounts of interactions with Tatar natives, and especially native children, were among the most memorable and affecting features of the return narratives. Time and again, poor children approached the traveling entourage, offering old bullets, shell splinters, and musket locks for sale. In purchasing them, the returnees followed in the footsteps of their battling predecessors, securing souvenirs of their trips and reminders of the war. Lest his readers grow too easeful about a wartime landscape turned into tourist terrain, William Howard Russell, still a critic of the war, refused to coat these exchanges in pastoral sentimentalism. The transactions, however quaint, gave but "little notion" of the scale and the violence of the war and the ravages of the land, where "smoke, fire, and projectiles" had "vomited, volcano-like, over the plain from month to month."[115]

The sojourners concerned themselves primarily with remembering the past as they reassessed the war from the vantage point of fifteen years on. But the returnees gestured, too, to the future of the Crimea as they turned their attention to Yalta and its Livadia Palace. At the southern tip of the peninsula, Yalta was off the beaten track of the Crimean campaign. Yet, its blossoming flowers and picturesque views were objects of admiration on the 1869 tour, which tied sites of war and sites of pleasure into a single itinerary. Yalta's realization as a vacationer's paradise was well underway by 1869, when the royal party made it the final stop on the Crimean tour.[116] Teresa Grey admired the opulence and taste of the Livadia Palace, the summer retreat of the Tsar built in the 1860s and the eventual home of the Yalta Conference at World War II's end.[117] As he extolled the virtues of Yalta, William Howard Russell offered what read like an early travel brochure, touting the "beauties of the south coast of the Crimea," which was particularly well suited for yachting and vacationing.[118] There was much to behold for the military buff on the nearby war-torn landscape and much to enjoy for the bon vivant in the free-flowing wine and beautiful scenery. As 1869's tour revealed, the tiny peninsula held great promise in the intertwining of war's history with tourism's future.

Several travelers followed in the royal party's footsteps across the remainder of the long nineteenth century, an epoch marked by the intensification of diplomatic tensions and the modernization of tourism. The 1890s, in particular, witnessed what the *Times* called "a very remarkable revival of interest in the story of the Crimean campaign" for reasons both demographic and diplomatic.[119] At this time, the veterans of the Crimea were moving into old age. Even more significantly, the hostilities in sub-Saharan Africa, culminating in the South African War, made the Crimea once again a subject of popular attention. Eyes were on Russia, too, at the time, with the death of Tsar Alexander III. Accordingly, travelers approached the Crimea in search of lessons, and of warnings, for a new world and a new century.

It was in this context that Evelyn Wood, a great naval hero, a Crimean veteran, and a Victoria Cross winner, made his return to the peninsula. In periodical installments and later in a book, Wood discussed the Crimean War at a forty-year distance. *The Crimea in 1854 and 1894* used the visit to the peninsula as a meditation on war.[120] Wood waxed about the deep tracks cut by memory forged in youth – tracks reinforced, in his case, by the naval habit of journal-keeping that he cultivated in his Crimean years. Like the visitors who preceded him, Wood focused on the power of the landscape, much-changed but still highly evocative of a painful past. The peninsula, with its picturesque views, dredged up forgotten memories of suffering as they restored the war to Wood's consciousness. When he made it to the field a half-century later, Wood found that it was grown over with flowers and weeds. While it might have been unrecognizable on the surface, its contours were unmistakable. "Nothing can so change the look of a place as to cause any difficulty to a visitor who can read a map," the returned hero declared.[121] This personal recollection of the Crimea served a broader social purpose. As he recalled the war and its blunders, Wood pointed to a set of "grim lessons," or cautionary tales, for present and future.[122]

Writing at a moment of generational transition, Wood was among the last of the Crimean returnees to leave an extended record of his visit.

Across the following years, a new crop of visitors made their ways from Britain in search of edification and history. In 1903, for instance, a young William James Garnett traveled to the Crimea with the London-based company, World Travel. Garnett and his fellow voyagers toured the Black Sea region, stopping in Salonica, Constantinople, and, eventually, the Crimea. The eastward excursion sated the travelers' appetites for things Oriental, as it exposed them to Turkish baths, cemeteries, and coffee. As his warring predecessors had, Garnett toured mosques and cemeteries; he beheld whirling dervishes and veiled women. There were scenic views to be had as well. Writing to his mother aboard the *Argonaut,* Garnett rhapsodized of an evening vista, "As the sun set the snow became pink; I nearly fell into an ecstasy!"[123] World Travel's voyage offered shipboard lectures as mainstays of its travel-study programs. One especially memorable lecture came on the forty-ninth anniversary of the Battle of Balaklava. It served to whet Garnett's anticipation of his experience at the warfront. He was not disappointed. Upon disembarkation, he beheld sites of 1854's heroism at the Alma, Balaklava, and Inkerman and monuments to 1855's tenacity at the Malakoff, the Redan, and the Mamelon. Seasoned returnees had discerned a transformed landscape, yet one that bore unmistakable traces of the past.[124] For the young Garnett, however, the peninsula offered unmediated access to history. "Everything is as it was left fifty years ago," he declared of the fields at Inkerman and the sights at Sebastopol.[125] There was, for the young man, palpable excitement in standing in front of history: "One could fight the siege of Sebastopol over again as well as if one had been present at the actual time."[126]

A nearly concurrent account of another adventurer, Ménie Muriel Dowie, upends Garnett's youthful enthusiasm.[127] This peripatetic New Woman writer and traveler lived a life that took her from Liverpool to the European continent and from Kenya to Tucson, Arizona. She voyaged to the Crimea in 1899, against the backdrop of the Second Anglo-Boer War. Like many of her contemporaries, Dowie delighted in a glorious Yalta. However, she found herself troubled by a haunted Sebastopol. As she described her sojourn, Dowie dispensed with the certainties of Garnett's narrative. Passing through the landscape of war, she imagined not the glories and victories of battle, but its pains and violence instead. The Crimean terrain was saturated with rebuke. It did not invite her to celebrate the British soldier. Rather than view the battlefields as a tribute to duty and sacrifice, Dowie could only imagine them as "turf nourished actually with the blood" of young men.[128] And unlike Evelyn Wood, who found guidance for the future on the ravaged, if overgrown, landscape, Dowie saw a chiding for lessons unlearned.[129] The peninsula's past held no salvific promise and no redeeming potential. Looking back on the Crimean conflict at the height of the South African War, Dowie declared, "we possess, as fine as ever, our deathless courage- but we have learned nothing from the years in strategy, nothing in intelligence to estimate an enemy's capacity." Such was the unfolding of history. "Would it were untrue."[130] In the end, she found the Crimean Peninsula not a monument to heroism, but a symbol of futility: a victory deplorable in its uselessness.[131]

***

The fin-de-siècle's visitors to the Crimea found on the landscape the lessons of history and the forebodings of the future. For her part, Dowie captured well a collective mood of concern at the dawn of a new and anxious century. During the first half of the twentieth century, the peninsula became a stage, once again, for aggression and terror. The twentieth-century history of the Crimea condenses the horrors of world war in the East, the drama of diplomacy at the beginning of the Cold War, and the allure of travel behind the Iron Curtain. During the first half of the century, in particular, the Crimea became a site for struggles of global and moral significance. It remained, at the same time, a land saturated with history. As it covered the events on the peninsula, the popular press thus acquainted readers with the destinations of nineteenth-century warriors and introduced to them the narratives of the mid-Victorian war.

The route that the Crimean adventurers took to the East in the mid-nineteenth century saw great devastation during World War I. Names like Gallipoli became synonymous with destruction and sacrifice. Soon after the fighting, Constantinople became the site of an allied occupation. Sebastopol itself was the target of bombing in 1914, helping to push Russia into the Great War. During the conflict, ultimately, the peninsula became a point of embarkation and disembarkation for Russian troops, both healthy and injured.[132]

The peninsula enjoyed extensive coverage in the British press during the Russian Revolution and its aftermath. Commentators echoed Victorian predecessors as they portrayed the peninsula as a terrain for a battle between civilizations and a stage for the combat of good versus evil – in this case, the White and Red Armies.[133] This was, to hear English newspapers tell it, a battle between democratic rule and "Bolshevist tyranny."[134] When the latter won out, the peninsula, on the way to becoming a happy and salubrious resort, took a downturn. English newspapers featured tales of twentieth-century Soviets who resembled their barbarous Russian predecessors from Crimean War days. The Crimea

was newly filled with "horrors," "stagnation," and "filth."[135] Others
suggested Soviet depravity as they offered headlines announcing
"Bolshevist Atrocities on Moslems" and even "Cannibalism in the
Crimea."[136] During the years after the Great War, British readers bore
witness to a starving, savage Crimea, still a hub of populations in motion
across Europe. Tatar and dissident refugees fled Bolshevist tyranny on
the peninsula; Russian Jews made their ways there to create agricultural
settlements in hopes of better lives.[137]

The struggle between good and evil that played out on the peninsula
continued during the dark years of World War II, when it was home to
a grave, ongoing battle between the Allied and Axis Powers. Invading Nazi
forces took the majority of the peninsula shortly after their entry in 1941
and claimed Sebastopol, the ultimate prize, in 1942. Organs of the press,
such as the *Times*, whose special correspondent, William Howard Russell,
had covered the nineteenth-century campaign so evocatively and forcefully
once again told of a dramatic conquest of the Crimea. The Nazi forces
hammered on until 1944, when the Soviets – this time in their guise as
civilization's agents[138] – managed to push back. The newspaper recalled
the landmarks of the prior century's war, as it rolled out headlines declaring
"Inkerman captured"[139] and "Sevastopol captured."[140] Frequently, it
covered these turning points in staccato lines. However, on the occasion
of the Soviet capture of Sebastopol, the *Times* lingered as the conflict came
to an end. Once a picturesque vista with welcoming houses and blooming
flowers, Sebastopol had turned yet again into a ghostly ruin, with hollowed-
out skies and rubble-filled streets. The tour prompted musings on the war
the century before. The *Times* recalled the hallowed battlefields of the
nineteenth century, including the Alma, Balaklava, and Inkerman. It tied
together the two wars, waged nearly a century apart, as it scripted the
Crimea as an ongoing stage for moral, and mortal, combat. In the process,
it remade the Crimea into a ground for recurring British victory.

This sort of coverage set the tone for the world-historic event that
followed at the end of World War II. After the capture of Sebastopol in
the winter of 1945, the Crimea became the site for another storied
moment in the history of Western warfare and diplomacy: the Yalta
Conference. Synonymous with the forging of the postwar order, this
meeting brought to the peninsula the leaders of the Allied Forces:
Britain's Churchill, the Soviet Union's Stalin, and the USA's Roosevelt.
Together, they negotiated the contours of the postwar world as they
gathered at the Livadia Palace, the onetime home of the Russian
Tsars.[141] A longtime battlefield for civilizations, the Crimea thus became
the negotiating ground for the end of Nazi tyranny and for the West's
remaking.

Among those who accompanied heads of state to the Crimea were civil servants and support staff. Their ranks included a contingent of British men and women who set off for the peninsula in early 1945 to play their part in forging the postwar world. Among them were Lieutenant Colonel T. J. Cowen, the scion of a Cumberland farming family who kept a travel diary, and Ilene Hutchinson, a top-security stenographer who recorded her time in the East in letters to her sister. Their words give an impression of the day-to-day process of peacemaking on the ground. They also demonstrate the lasting imprint of the annals of a Victorian war at the moment of the forging of a twentieth-century peace.

The twentieth-century diplomats embarked on a journey that was, in many ways, strikingly different from that of their nineteenth-century predecessors. Whereas the Victorian adventurers undertook a difficult journey, the postwar peacemakers traveled in style. They voyaged in comfort on a luxury aircraft, which was the "very acme of air comfort," and on a converted cruise liner, the Franconia, which was "as smart and comfortable as a West End Hotel."[142] Among its amenities were facilities for sunbathing and deck tennis; along the route there were signs of a transformed world, including electric lighting and American music.

Even in this changed world, however, the earlier scripts of Victorian adventure had staying power.[143] While their modes of travel differed, Cowen and Hutchinson followed the familiar route of the Crimean warriors. When his plane descended through the clouds as it approached Malta, Cowen glimpsed fishing boats, stone walls, and a "splashing sea."[144] The streetscapes of Malta recalled those of the past century: yellow stone buildings, a gay street life, and "swarthy and dark haired" throngs. Breaking up the splashes of yellow and black were the harbor and the sea. Together, they offered up a "magic interplay of green and blue and white, merging imperceptibly into the pale sky."[145] Malta was, in Cowen's own words, infused with the "gentle flavor of the East."[146] Istanbul similarly recalled its Victorian incarnation, offering up what Cowen saw as a "curious admixture of East and West" and "of old and new."[147] Hutchinson too drew upon a persistent Orientalism to describe the city. For her, it was the first port of call to "have a definite Eastern look about it," as signaled by its mosques and minarets. Like her Victorian predecessors, Hutchinson measured the region against the expectations of the popular and literary culture of her day. "I've always heard of the romantic nights in the Med. (sic)," she wrote to her sister, "but I never really thought that was true. I thought it was all just cheap fiction."[148]

Not only did these ports of call sustain their Victorian imprints; so too did the ultimate destination of the Crimea itself. There, Cowen and Hutchinson both found much that was reminiscent of a century before.

A varied population filled the cityscape, while Tatars dominated the countryside. The region remained a crossroads, where Greek Orthodox churches and a Moorish atmosphere commingled. There was, still, a sense of a decayed pastoral, with tumbledown marble and overgrown gardens. Finally, just as it had been at the end of the Crimean War, the harbor city was a scene of "stark desolation," with ruined roads and barren structures everywhere.[149]

These continuities notwithstanding, the Crimean landscape bore the marks of the world wars. There were signs everywhere of the twentieth-century's tools of destruction, with burnt-out tanks, crashed aircraft, and twisted metal occupying the land. The desolation was reflected, nay, magnified, in the "melting snow and the leaden, darkening skies." Ragged German prisoners toiled on the landscape as if they were "animals" in the "mud."[150] And whereas the Sebastopol of the nineteenth century appeared deserted, hollowed out of its inhabitants, here the streets were populated, and grimly so. Faces everywhere were marked by resignation, devoid of ambition, and denuded of hope. Sebastopol's citizens had borne witness to the death of society, the ruin of their cityscape, and the hollowing of the social structure. Life was only struggle – for food, for sleep, and for shelter. Its demands were etched onto the weary visages. "The people of Sebastopol did not laugh – they seemed hardly ever to talk – they did not bustle," wrote Cowen.[151] Ilene Hutchinson similarly told, "I've never seen a town look so devastated."[152] It was "desolation and misery" all around.[153]

Not far from the ruins, the postwar peacemakers gathered for negotiations to remake the world. It was an atmosphere of heady excitement for Ilene Hutchinson, who "rushed to and from the Palace" to "take down shorthand" in the pursuit of the peace. In the process, Hutchinson encountered "a lot of the bigwigs," including Anthony Eden and Winston Churchill.[154] Filling the streets in the Crimea were American GIs, many of them drunk on vodka.[155] There was, among the victors, a "general state of holiday."[156] There were entertainments worthy of London venues: a male choir, a brass band, and a dancing troupe. "I found it hard to appreciate and firmly grasp the fact that there I was in Russia seeing with my own eyes Russians dancing Russian dances," Cowen, an Englishman abroad, wrote, as he sought to square his experiences on Europe's periphery with his own everyday life.[157]

Aware of history and heritage, Cowen found himself drawn to the Crimean War's monuments and battlefields. He made no fewer than three visits to the Panorama of the Siege of Sebastopol, painted by Russian artist Franz Roubaud at the turn of the twentieth century. Though located in a commodious park, this tribute to Russia's initial successes a century before was worse for the wear by 1945, having been bombed during the German siege of the city in 1942. Moving beyond the city itself, Cowen stopped at the many monuments erected by the British and the French to honor the fallen. He also visited the battlefields. On his meanderings, he made assessments that echoed those of earlier British returnees. Cowen meditated on the layering of history upon the landscape, while also luxuriating in the persistence of the past around him. "It was not easy at times to differentiate between the events of 1850 and the events of 1941–44," he remarked. Yet he took great pleasure and gained "personal benefit" in "seeing at first hand the places where history was made."[158]

One particularly striking site for Cowen was the Tchernaya Valley. Located just a few miles outside of Sebastopol, this quiet spot was the place where the heroes of the Charge of the Light Brigade had "rode to their glory."[159] Cowen was not alone in visiting this storied locale over the course of the Conference. Winston Churchill, himself a purveyor of the British values of duty and sacrifice so wrapped up with the Charge, offered his respects there too.[160] The Yalta Conference was a moment to reckon with the carnage of war, and it was equally an occasion to forge the postwar order. It was, as well, an opportunity to stamp the World War II as an occasion of British sacrifice and triumph, although the future seemed uncertain. Winston Churchill played a decisive part in this effort, as his tour of the Crimea suggests. In Cowen's recounting, Churchill joined the celebrating party aboard the Franconia in advance of his return home after the proceedings had ended. As he prepared to depart the Crimea in February 1945, Churchill made a deliberate and stylish exit. Slowly, he stepped onto his boat whilst puffing on a cigar. As he crossed Sebastopol harbor, he waved his cap and gave his trademark "V for Victory sign."[161] Once again, the Crimea appeared as a landscape of British victory, albeit pyrrhic, fleeting, and uncertain in this new age.

**

A site of diplomacy at the end of World War II, the peninsula developed into a destination for tourism in the Cold War and after. Modern tourism had a longer history on the peninsula, dating to the 1920s. In that decade, intrepid solo voyagers continued to make their ways to the Crimea, just as their predecessors had. For instance, Claire Sheridan followed in the footsteps of lady travelers and New Women from bygone centuries as she rode to the Crimea via sidecar in 1925, taking in everything from Soviet warships to the Czarina's bedroom.[162] During the 1920s, more generally, however, Crimean travel came increasingly under the aegis of the state. In the year 1921, Vladimir Lenin had signed a decree encouraging the cultivation of the Crimea as a site of health and recreation for Soviet workers and peasants, and for foreign visitors, too.[163] The end of that decade witnessed the institution of Soviet-run tours of the peninsula, planned and advertised by Intourist. Founded in 1929, this Soviet travel agency sought to show the face of a new nation, forward looking, pleasure-seeking, and prosperous. The Crimea, known as the "Russian Riviera," was a cornerstone of this campaign. Sleek posters and streamlined brochures offered promises of a modern Sebastopol, a majestic Livadia Palace, and a breathtaking coast (Figure 1.5). The small peninsula promised much: a grand Russian past, a bright Soviet future, and an environment of timeless beauty.[164]

World War II interrupted the forward march of tourism, but as the reminiscences of Cowen and Hutchinson attest, Yalta held out many pleasures in the years that followed. The reopening of the peninsula to tourists in a young Cold War during the 1950s offered up the region as a destination for travel once again in an epoch of recovery and prosperity.[165] In the middle years of the decade, the Soviet government welcomed tourists to behold the beauties of Yalta. At the end, it exposed them to the grandeur of Sebastopol. This was a possibility welcomed in Britain. "Drive your car to the Crimea," encouraged the *Daily Mail* in 1955.[166] What would those adventurers who set sail from Portsmouth, traveling through Malta, Gallipoli, and Varna, have thought of such a journey? One hundred years after the nineteenth-century war, the Crimean Peninsula seemed closer than ever before, though much of it remained out of reach, with the historical sites of Victorian military victory off limits to tourists. In the 1950s, at the Crimean War's centennial, Britons knew well the histories and myths surrounding the conflict. Although they could not behold the sights of battle as Cowen had, they could travel to the peninsula amply armed with stories.

At the height of the Cold War, Intourist continued to boast the riches of the peninsula as it lured visitors from the West on its highly choreographed tours with well-designed brochures. Yalta, the so-called "Gem of the Crimea," was a focus of the advertising campaign. With its warm climate and its healthful water, this "first-class resort zone" rivaled the Mediterranean in its pleasures. It was a place of recreation and a hub of health. There were flowers and trees, beaches and parks, and rest homes and sanatoriums. Intourist borrowed from the Russian writer, Anton Chekhov as it promoted the destination. Of Yalta's environs, he had claimed, "the sea is marvelous – blue and caressing – where you can live for a thousand years and never experience a dull moment." There was much to see beyond the shore itself, too. Those visitors eager to unlock

Figure 1.5 Vintage InTourist travel poster for Soviet Russian Crimea.
1930s. Shawshots/Alamy Stock Photo

the Russian past could stop by Chekhov's home; they could additionally
enjoy the peninsula's folk museums. History lessons of a different order
were on offer at the historic Livadia Palace, which encapsulated the
advance of Russian, and later, Soviet, power. Once associated with
Imperial Russia, and then the Yalta Conference, it was, by the 1960s,
the site of a workers' sanatorium. Day-trips beyond Yalta made the glories

of Soviet society evermore evident. Via special arrangement, British tourists could make their way to the so-called "hero-city Sevastopol," site of the siege of 250 days during the "Great Patriotic War." Rebuilt "in record time" after Nazi destruction, it had returned to its state as "one of the most beautiful cities in the Soviet Union," at least according to Intourist.[167] Intourist brochures not only cultivated a sense of pride in the Soviet sacrifices of the mid-twentieth century. They also performed their own acts of cleansing. The brochures did not display all the realities of the present, nor all of the hardships of the past. Cold War adventurers to the Crimea would not have found traces of Tatar ethnic cleansing on the salubrious peninsula; nor could they have seen the battlegrounds of the nineteenth century.

Visitors were aware of these limitations, but they were not stalled from traveling to the peninsula. In an article discussing Crimean travel, the *Guardian* warned its urbane readers that they would not be able to visit the hallowed battlegrounds were they to make the journey. "There is plenty to see all the same," it reassured. The greatest attraction was the atmosphere.[168] "The clean and gentle sea breezes mingle with the pine fragrances of the mountain forests to make breathing a pleasure and to give tired London lungs a new lease on life."[169] There were other pleasures as well for those budget travelers seeking the good life behind the Iron Curtain. While in Yalta, visitors could feast on plentiful meals of salad, borscht, and ice cream. For nightlife, they could enjoy discos, bars, and cafés. Not only a tourist resort, Yalta was also a monument to Soviet ambition. Tributes to Russian bravery and Soviet victory were everywhere on display. Statues of soldiers and posters of workers abounded. The seaside town and the surrounding region offered a true showcase of Soviet success, with abundant orchards, plentiful housing, and lavish entertainments. In short, the Crimea was a convenient and comfortable destination for a nation of curious, if sometimes reluctant travelers. At least this was the case until the later years of the Cold War, when the Eastern Bloc was foundering. By the 1980s, the long queues and the empty shops associated with the era were all too apparent.[170]

The contours of tourist traffic to the Crimean Peninsula in the late days of the Cold War and in the quarter century after provide a bellwether of the times. They reflect the opening of the region after independence in 1992 and the closing once again with the Russian invasion of 2014. Tourism from Britain had its own perestroika as it sought to capture the changing appetites of potential visitors in the late 1980s. At that time, one tour offered a chance to delve into the woman-centered mythologies of the region. This joint initiative of Intourist and Thomas Cook Travel sought to reach those more interested in "goddesses than in Gorbachev."

With its signature cheeky wit, the *Guardian* declared of the package holiday, "In May, Glastonbury gives way to Glasnost."[171] Opportunities for niche marketing only multiplied after the 1992 opening. "The chaotic world of the Ukraine is opening its doors to travelers prepared for anything," quipped the *Guardian*. From the early 1990s onward, pleasure tourism, medical tourism, and historical tourism proliferated. These ventures were enabled by entrepreneurial initiatives based in Britain and in the Crimea itself; they were propelled by cheap flights from English airports to Simferopol. Taken by budget travelers, pleasure seekers, and elderly tourists, these latter-day journeys were speedier by far than those of the nineteenth-century's adventurers. The landscape that this new generation of tourists saw was, in many ways, unrecognizable, transformed by the passage of time and by the ravages of the twentieth century. But it featured once again the battlefields where British history was made, covered with tulips as before and littered with tractors in this new age.[172]

The old sites of British glory were once again on display after 1992, when British travelers were free to enjoy package holidays in the post-Cold War, post-Soviet Crimea. An article printed in the *Daily Mail* in 2004 at the moment of the Crimean War's sesquicentennial attests to the allure. The "Charge of the Holiday Brigade" recalled the brave history of the nineteenth-century's adventurers, while it forecast a bright future for the twenty-first century's vacationers. In the hands of the *Daily Mail,* the peninsula, long the stage for monumental struggles, had become a destination for budget vacations. There was enrichment to be had in the history of the peninsula, with its lessons in British heroism, Nazi depredation, and Soviet aspiration. There was enjoyment to be sought in the land of the Crimea, with its pleasures of scenic beaches, warm weather, and tasty fare. Adding to these attractions was affordability: a Crimean vacation was far cheaper than a budget holiday to Turkey or to Greece. The Crimea remained an "obscure place" in 2004, though undeservedly so. The *Daily Mail* urged its readers to book their tickets ahead of the traveling hordes to come. It exhorted them to go at once to this historic and alluring land, before the secret was out and before the British invaded again.[173] In its jocular manner, the *Daily Mail* made a land of ongoing historic struggle into a beckoning vacationer's paradise. It turned a distant, war-torn peninsula into a welcoming port of call.

There would, of course, be no such British invasion of the peninsula, whether for purposes of vacation or of war, in the coming decades. Instead, the 2014 Russian incursion on the region, a part of Ukraine since the 1990s, put an end to the romps of latter-day adventurers. Long a *terra incognita*, the Crimea is, once again, all but inaccessible to

Western travelers today. The *Daily Mail*'s article remains useful, however, as evidence of the enduring role of the Crimea in generating fantasies and possibilities for English adventure in peacetime and in wartime alike.

In its 2004 promotion, the *Daily Mail* relied upon the most mythologized event of the Crimean War: The Charge of the Light Brigade. With its choice of headline, the newspaper played off of the widespread recognition of the event, especially among its patriotic readership. At the Crimean War's sesquicentennial, the Charge remained a piece of common cultural currency among ordinary Britons. The following chapter addresses the Charge and the mythologies surrounding it during wartime and well after. If the narratives of travel to the front helped to solidify a sense of adventure and its limits, the legacies of the Charge cemented a notion of duty in military conduct and in social life. The peninsula may have been precarious in the British mind, but the Charge is undoubtedly pervasive. Its myths and its recurrence help us to understand another facet of national character: a penchant for leaping, dutifully, into the abyss in the face of possible, and even certain ruin.

No military action is more immediately associated with the campaign in the Crimea than the Charge of the Light Brigade: the tragic, yet heroic culmination of the Battle of Balaklava waged on October 25, 1854.[1] On that occasion, five regiments of the Army's Light Cavalry rode dutifully and unflinchingly into harm's way, as they descended into a valley to be attacked by Russian artillery. The fatal charge was the result of a mysteriously mangled order, the riddle of which has preoccupied military historians and military buffs across the ages. This confounding event has long functioned as the epitome of the military adventures and misadventures of the Army in the East. A synecdoche for the war and a prosthetic to memory, an occasion associated with the sacrifice of the soldiers and the miscalculations of the officers, it has come to stand for the campaign as a whole. Its fifteen minutes of action-packed drama condense the vicissitudes of the long campaign into a single, sad episode. The mismanagement of the war, the bungling of the Army's officers, and the duty of the British soldier: all were on display in the Charge of the Light Brigade.

The riddle of the Charge offers one reason for its persistence in the popular mind. The Charge's immortality was sealed, however, by the December 1854 publication of a landmark poem by Britain's Poet Laureate. Alfred, Lord Tennyson published "The Charge of the Light Brigade" in *The Examiner* a few months after the great loss. This exemplar of war poetry brought the Charge's glory and sorrow, and its sacrifice and its senselessness, into lyrical unison.[2] With his poem, Tennyson sought to commemorate the tragic event and to unite a divided population. He transformed defeat into victory as he immortalized the Charge. Through his moving and memorable verses, Tennyson nodded to the uncertainties of the Charge while paying tribute to the Chargers, the "Noble Six Hundred" who rode into the "Valley of Death." The poem has enjoyed a robust afterlife, shaping understandings of the Crimean War and molding national character. Portable across the ages, it has been memorized, recited, and parodied. Its longevity has allowed, time and again, for collective and individual engagements with the Charge and, by extension, with the Crimean War.

Like Tennyson's verses, the Chargers themselves have occupied an enduring place in the making of British national life and the shaping of English national character. As they recorded their experiences on the fateful day of the Charge, its protagonists shaped themselves as the embodiments of duty, immovable in their resolve. During wartime and after, those who survived clung to the occasion. They sought to wrest meaning from its carnage, to create reputations out of their sacrifices, and to secure resources for their participation. Celebrated at the time of the war, they remained part of the civic landscape of Britain across their lifecycles, as young avatars of military sacrifice, as middle-aged personifications of associational fellowship, and as elderly recipients of civic largesse. Those who survived into the twentieth century became living relics of Victorian duty in the context of a new epoch's wars.

The afterlife of the Charge extends beyond the lifetimes of its protagonists. Long after the Victorian heroes passed away, their relatives and descendants cleaved to the event. They asserted their relations to bygone heroes and avidly sought out cherished artifacts, including military regalia and musical instruments. Taken together, these links to history mediated the Charge across time and space, knitting past and present, victory and failure, and heroism and loss. The Charge has therefore endured not only as a riddle in military history, but also as a resource in forging a national collective.

Persistent across a long durée, the Charge was also pliable, its connotations changing across venue and time. The Charge was renewable and recyclable, and sometimes emptied of its meaning. A tool for social cohesion, it could, equally, be an instrument for social dissent. A focus for veneration, it was also subject to critique. At moments of social tension and on occasions of military crisis, critics invoked the Charge not deferentially, but reprovingly. They looked to the Charge to remind the public of its failures of collective compassion and to suggest the folly of war. In the process, they lodged the Crimean conflict squarely at the heart of practices of shared remembrance and collective critique, in all of their fractiousness and vitality.

***

Not long after they reached the Crimean Peninsula, in the autumn of 1854, British Army regiments engaged in three dramatic battles. The names of these battles – Alma, Balaklava, and Inkerman – are legendary

Figure 2.1 Toy theater with scenes of Balaklava and Inkerman. Interfoto. Bildarchiv Hansmann. Mary Evans Picture Library

in the annals of military history. They quickly found their ways into the daily life of Great Britain, whether as the names of public houses or as the subjects for children's games (Figure 2.1). Fought on October 25, 1854, the second of these occasions, the Battle of Balaklava, has become the best-known battle of the Crimean War. In the morning hours on that day, the Battle commenced when Russian artillery units overran the Turkish redoubts at Canrobert's Hill, just outside of the town of Balaklava. Two British actions – the movement of the much-mythologized Thin Red Line, composed primarily of the celebrated 93rd Regiment of Highlanders led by Sir Colin Campbell, and the Charge of the Heavy Brigade, a formation of Cavalry regiments commanded by General Scarlett – proved successful in staving off further Russian attack.[3] It seemed to be a day of success for the British forces.

In the end, the British won the battle. But this was not an unmitigated success. In truth, the culminating maneuver, the Charge of the Light Brigade, was a crowning Russian victory and a crushing British loss, though it quickly enjoyed reinterpretation as a triumph. On this occasion, the British Army's Light Cavalry – comprised of the 4th and 13th Dragoons, the 8th and 11th Hussars, and the 17th Lancers – descended into the Tchernaya Valley. The outnumbering Russian artillery, firing from the Causeway Heights, decimated the British troops as they raced into breach. The ill-fated action resulted in casualties for nearly half of the Brigade, leading to the christening of the Tchernaya as the Valley of Death. The victorious Russians held on to their guns and their position. In strategic terms, the Russian triumph was little more than inconsequential, both when it came to the battle and when it came to the war. In symbolic terms, however, the occasion had unprecedented repercussions. As an example of intelligence failure, it was long a subject of interest.[4] As a military mystery, it remains a topic of debate to this day.

How was it that the Light Brigade came to make its fatal charge? This horrific instance of soldier sacrifice was the result of a grave miscommunication among the officers. An order that was vague, bungled, and misinterpreted led to the quick and spectacular destruction of the five regiments of the Light Brigade. The fatal charge was wrought out of the imprecise orders of the legendary Army General, Lord Raglan. His directives were delivered via the tragic Captain Nolan to the unlucky Cavalry commander, Lord Lucan. Raglan's order to "Attack the Guns" was puzzling enough. Nolan's gesture of waving his arm had the effect of confounding, not clarifying. It remained a mystery for the ages, with Nolan the first man killed, his body charging down a hill after his head fell off in a textbook example of *rigor mortis*.[5] With Nolan dead and gone, military men, government officials, and the general public were left to ponder the reason why the debacle had occurred. In Parliament and on the page, they grappled with the questions of culpability and responsibility for months, years, and decades to come.[6]

More immediately, a nation in wartime struggled to come to terms with the disaster. The Crimean Commission scrutinized the records and testimony of officers and generals in the aftermath of the war. But in the days, weeks, and months following the Charge, this process of collective reckoning occurred, by and large, in the press. To pore through the daily and weekly newspapers printed in Britain a week after the infamous Charge is to get a sense of the unfolding of the happenings on the home front.[7] On November 2, 1854, just a little more than a week after the Charge, the *Morning Chronicle* broke the news of what it called a great "misfortune."[8] Unable to transmit accounts of the Battle as quickly as it might have liked, the *Times* bemoaned the problems of tardy news and faulty intelligence that bedeviled the mid-Victorian world at war.[9] The nation's households waited with "painful anxiety" in the meantime until the news of "immense loss and suffering" began to trickle in.[10] Soon enough, a portrait of devastation took hold. "We now know the details of the attack on Balaklava on the 25th," the *Times* leader declared on November 13, 1854. It offered a sobering account and a harsh judgment, maneuvering between the languages of romantic longing and modern disaster as it reflected on the carnage. The Charge was a "melancholy loss," an "annihilation," or even a "grand military holocaust." With these assessments came an indictment. The result of a piteous "mistake," the Charge was an utter "disaster," a "causeless and fruitless" undertaking. If there was any consolation to be had, perhaps it could be found in the conduct of the rank and file, whose sacrifice stood as a "grand heroic deed." As the *Times* noted, "the British soldier will do his duty, even to certain death," although the "the victim of some hideous blunder."[11]

In its spirit and its wording, the *Times* drew heavily on the report of its special correspondent at the front, William Howard Russell, who had witnessed the occasion firsthand.[12] Printed in the *Times* on November 14, Russell's stirring narrative remains, to this date, one of the most famous pieces of war correspondence in the newspaper age. It was embellished liberally and reproduced widely. It became the authoritative account of the event, appearing in venues from *John Bull* to the *Illustrated London News*. Russell's reportage thus seared the Charge into the nation's consciousness, making it a part of its shared conception. Much of its appeal derived from the journalist's own careful staging of the Charge as grand military theater as he blurred the lines between heroism and failure. He managed well his part as an eyewitness to the "fearful spectacle," with the "smoke of the batteries" and the "halo of flashing steel." In Russell's hands, the Charge put "brilliant valor," overflowing "courage," and chivalric "daring" on display. A compelling event, it was a struggle of "courage" beyond "credence" and against "atrocity" without parallel. There were enemies not only without, but also within. "Alas!" Russell exclaimed of the unhesitating Chargers. "Their desperate valor knew no bounds, and far indeed was it removed from its so-called better half – discretion." The result of this immoveable dedication was not a grand victory, but a "melancholy catastrophe."[13]

At the very moment that Russell's narrative appeared in the English press, letters from officers and men who had been present on the battlefield arrived home. Written directly to loved ones, to parents, to siblings, and to spouses, letters were cherished, personal possessions. But, in a war that was waged both in person and on the page, they often had public lives that exceeded their receipts in private households. One need only flip through the pages of the daily and weekly papers, and the leaves of the local and national press, to apprehend the porosity between the private household and the public stage. In the Crimean War, cherished letters were copied and shared. A fair number found their ways into local and national newspapers, handed over by proud relatives, sometimes in spite of the pleadings of the letter writers themselves. Printed prominently and plentifully, they made the dutiful Light Cavalry into leading protagonists of the war.

What did the survivors of the Light Brigade report in their letters from the front? Taken together, the multitude of accounts from the survivors of the Charge coalesces into a collective narrative of trauma, gratitude, and resolve. Those who wrote in the Battle's immediate aftermath sought first and foremost to reassure loved ones of their survival. They endeavored, too, to provide accounts of their exploits. By so doing, they sought to write themselves into the moment's history and to reckon with their own experiences of what we recognize today as battlefield trauma.[14] In vivid detail they rendered the attack by shelling and shooting.[15] One correspondent compared the experience to putting one's "head into a hive of bees."[16] Others likened it to a great and "concentrated storm": a deluge in the "thickest shower," a walk through a relentless rainstorm, or an onslaught of "perfect hail."[17]

As they reached for language to capture the occasion, they grappled with what it meant to have survived in the face of the carnage, which left over one-third of the Brigade as casualties and nearly one-fifth of the force as dead. Correspondents from all classes reached for the divine as they sought to apprehend the event and offer gratitude for survival. Time and again, they regarded the catastrophic ride as a "great lesson to put one's trust in God"; they gave thanks for God's "unbounded mercy" and great "goodness."[18] "Thank God I am spared to write," told one survivor.[19] Others assured their mothers that their prayers had been answered.[20] In the minds of many, it was God, and only God, who had allowed them "to survive and escape" the "most dreadful fire" that Britain's Cavalry had ever known.[21] The odds had been utterly against their coming out unscathed.[22] Letters from all social ranks converged in paying homage to a divine guardian. Ultimately, as one semiliterate cavalryman reported, to come out of "Ballieclaver" with life and limb intact was nothing short of a "mirricle" [sic].[23]

For these survivor correspondents, the Charge offered not only a proof of God, but also a tribute to national character. The event gave ample evidence of the long-standing virtues of "British swords and pluck," those capacities that hearkened back to the mythologized warriors of yore and that forecast idealized versions of Tommy Atkins, a figure of indeterminate origin who became the apotheosis of the dutiful British soldier in the modern age.[24] Journalist Fintan O'Toole recently referred to pluck as the "most English of English words."[25] Accordingly, the Charge gave every reason to believe in the virtues of "English blood," both individually and collectively.[26] "I do not think one man flinched in the whole brigade," one officer declared.[27] In the end, freeborn Englishmen won the battle against lowly Russian serfs.[28]

Praise for the Charge was not unanimous, however, even if it was pervasive. There were critics who dismissed the display of unity as an excess of military punctilio. In the mind of one, the unhesitating action did not represent the best of Englishness. Instead, the brash rashness was worthy of the Spaniard, Don Quixote.[29] Eyewitnesses complicated the image of an orderly advance, as they recalled a scene where the Light Brigade's regiments, "too glad to be let loose," took off at "a thundering gallop – cheering more like mad men than men with common sense."[30] These critiques notwithstanding, there was, generally speaking, an over- whelming sense across the ranks that the Charge had unfolded in a fashion that was true to national ideals. "We only did what was ordered," one survivor reflected, "and we did it like Englishmen."[31] Decades later, even a Russian officer recalled the "simple unassuming heroism in the British character." It was not, the Russian officer sug- gested, "glory" or "vanity" that led Englishmen to follow their orders. It was, instead, "duty for duty's sake."[32] Through declarations such as these, the Charge took its shape, in its immediate aftermath and across time, as a quintessentially English occasion, one where order emerged out of chaos, liberty out of obedience, and heroism out of disaster.[33]

It is evident that participants and eyewitnesses understood the Charge as an occasion of national significance and historic proportions. As such, they clung to the event from a very early date. Almost immediately, it was clear that participation might ensure family distinction and bear personal rewards.[34] In the Crimean War, where many languished in boredom and still others died from disease, there was a strong desire to be a part of the action. Some military men regretted missing out on important battles when their regiments arrived too tardily for the occasions; others worried that their voyages to the Crimea would be for naught, as they reached the peninsula well after things were underway. Lieutenant Earnest Peake Newman candidly expressed such a concern in his diary, where he reflected on his belated arrival: "How I hope the war won't be over too soon, for I should not like to say I was too late for everything."[35] It was an honor to claim a part in a heroic action. There was no occasion more singularly glorious than the Charge of the Light Brigade, which con- densed great sacrifice of historic proportions in mere minutes of military struggle. For men at the beginning of their careers, especially, the Charge was considered to be a "hard apprenticeship." Yet it was also "a good start in life."[36] "Having been present at such a conflict of giants" was sure to be "a great feather in any man's cap."[37]

Survivors of the Charge thus cast themselves as the avatars of duty and the heroes of the nation. Shrewdly and carefully, they parsed the dynamics of the event and assessed the opportunities for glory. But their missives were not solely laudatory. Even while they framed themselves as heroes, they searched as well for villains in their morality tales of dutiful action. Time and again, commentators lambasted the Turkish forces for their abandonment of the redoubts, which had made the British positions all too vulnerable. Their assessments sustain the understandings of those adventurers who had dismissed the Turks as unworthy allies, both craven and superstitious. Letters universally blasted the "cowardly Turks," the "rascally Turks," and the "brutes of Turks."[38] Far more troubling for the correspondents was the internal mishandling of the matter, with the fumbled order to charge. "Everyone is outrageous at the order, whose ever it was," one officer noted.[39] Dismissive of the Army's intelligence, another complained, "A child might have seen the trap that was laid for us." As they reckoned with the senseless command, commentators pointed fingers all around: at the obstinate, even "wicked" General Raglan, at the stupid, and pitiful Lord Lucan, at the overzealous and "hot-headed" Captain Nolan, and most especially, at the ineffective and unfortunate Lord Cardigan, Commander of the Light Brigade.[40] This question of responsibility bedeviled the Army during the war and long after, even into the twentieth century.[41]

In the more immediate aftermath of the Battle, a few months on, Alfred, Lord Tennyson stepped headlong into the fractious media ecology of the Crimean moment. In his verses, he sustained the concerns with duty and courage, and with heroism and blunder, addressed in the print press and in personal letters. Tennyson sought, however, to shift attention away from the finger pointing so prevalent elsewhere. As literary critic Stephanie Markovits has demonstrated, Tennyson transcended questions of individual culpability in his verses. With his gentle assessment that "someone had blundered," he took the collective gaze off of individual actors. With his ingenious notion that "all the world wondered," he portrayed a globe united in uncertainty. And, finally, with his subtle rhyme "Noble Six Hundred," he brought attention to the rank and file.[42] These were the Chargers who were to "do and die" – to follow orders and to ride into harm's way. Their lives were a monument to duty. In his homage, Tennyson lent to these tragic heroes an aura of immortality, "When will their glory fade?" he inquired of the Cavalry. "Honor the Light Brigade," he directed to the readers.[43]

In advance of Tennyson's publication and well after, countless authors of doggerel and rhyme had offered up their words with the hopes of venerating the great sacrifice.[44] Their fleeting verses proved evanescent. This was not the case, of course, for Tennyson, whose "Charge of the Light Brigade" has become the best known and most enduring artifact of the Crimean War: its longest lasting "monument," to use the formulation of literary critic Trudi Tate.[45] As Tate has shown, it was no static or simple tribute: the Charge itself, along with Tennyson's poem, carried the capacities for "admiration and mockery" and for "inspiration and despair."[46] Reproducible and recyclable, Tennyson's poem became an object for repetition and reprinting, for performance and parody, and for remembering and forgetting. Its verses informed political responses both in Britain and abroad, extending even into Haiti, as literary critic Daniel Hack has demonstrated.[47] Tennyson's verses thus transported the so-called glory of the Charge, and of its dutiful heroes, across the ages. It held a remarkable power to recall a hallowed event, prompting private recollection and stirring public feeling in its own time and beyond. All the while, it carried, in its form and in its content, the possibilities for imitation and critique.

The staying power of Tennyson's "Charge," momentous and capacious, was stunning on all scales. It was memorized in schools; it was recited at military reunions; it was made into song.[48] Across the years, Tennyson's verses acted as a prosthetic to memory, stirring up individual recollections. Such was the case for Charles Lamb of the 13th Dragoons, who, looking back on the Charge some sixty years on, in 1907, reached for Tennyson's verses to shore up his narration of the event. "There wasn't much more than six hundred of us in all," Lamb declared. "There was a mistake, you've likely heard," he explained. "And so we got back, all that was left of us. I've heard the verses that calls it that, and good solider verses they are. Good soldier verses, just like galloping and slashing and the sounds of guns."[49] Lamb thus incorporated the poet laureate's words into his own recollections of the event, and, in the process, into his own understanding of himself. While Tennyson's verses created unity in the face of discord, they also shored the Chargers into paragons of duty, in their own minds and in the minds of others. They ensured, moreover, that Balaklava would be a "name" "handed down to posterity" and an occasion "unsurpassed in history."[50]

***

Many had perished in the Crimea due to the failures of intelligence and readiness, but a majority of the Chargers survived the debacle to live into middle and old age. They lived out their years within the contexts of the rise of a mass society focused on entertainment and the growth of an associational culture devoted to charity. They also aged alongside the rise of a popular monarchy at the twilight of Queen Victoria's reign. In their middle years, as they looked back on their youths, the Chargers became embodiments of sentimental masculinity. Later on, as elderly men, they grew into vulnerable figures, needful of care. Finally, as the Great War approached, they functioned as the living avatars of duty, coaxing others on to battle. Across all of these incarnations, Tennyson's verses, and adaptations of them, became recurring refrains. They linked the dutiful Chargers to their glorious past and allowed for multiple reworkings across many presents.

By the 1870s, the Charge was a canonized episode in British military history. Renditions accentuating theatrical trauma circulated widely in illustrated print (Figure 2.2). Its heroes attracted the attention of newly renowned painters, like Elizabeth Thompson, Lady Butler, who showed her works at the Royal Academy to great acclaim.[51] The Charge also encouraged a commemorating impulse in civic culture more broadly, as a twenty-first anniversary celebration that took place in October 1875

Figure 2.2 Charge of Light Cavalry at Balaklava. *The Pictorial World.* 1879. Colindale. The British Library Board

made manifest. This occasion vaulted the Light Brigade to renewed attention. The grand scheme took place at the Alexandra Palace, a newly opened pleasure ground in the outer reaches of suburban London. After struggling to get off the ground, it enjoyed the benevolent support of military widow Countess Cardigan, the Lion Brewing Company, and a handful of army officers. They combined their largesse to provide an event where veterans of the Charge, both comfortable and poor, could enjoy a day in their own honor, along with their loved ones and some 30,000 other guests.[52] For the occasion, the middle-aged Chargers took the train to the suburban pleasure grounds. There, they and the recreating multitudes enjoyed an afternoon's entertainment, which included band performances, dramatic farces, and flying trapeze. There were relic displays and animal showcases, including the appearance of a living, high-caste chestnut Arab horse. An animal veteran of the Crimean War, the horse was touted as the oldest in the entire British service. After relishing these entertainments, the seventeen surviving officers and 128 rank-and-file veterans enjoyed a sumptuous banquet, including courses of soups, fish, sweetbread, jellies, and, of course, Balaklava pudding (Figure 2.3).[53]

Figure 2.3 Mounted illustrated menu for the Balaklava commemoration banquet. 1875. National Army Museum/Mary Evans Picture Library

The plenty of the banquet and the comfort of the day were a far cry from the hunger of the war and the trauma of the Charge. But the organizers recalled the gravitas and significance of the occasion as they rehashed and revisited the pivotal texts that shaped public understandings of the event two decades before. Lavish programs reprinted William Howard Russell's report. Several newspapers recalled the experiences of the survivors. Finally, the evening's proceedings included a recitation of "The Charge of the Light Brigade" offered up by Thomas Pennington, one of the survivors who had made his celebrity in the intervening years as an actor in London's West End.[54] Tennyson's poem, itself, encapsulated the antinomies of the event, with its grandeur and nostalgia, and its bombast and reflection. Pennington's recitation, moreover, transformed the plaintive suffering of the verses into a public performance for his day.

All in all, the occasion allowed not only for a reconsideration of the Charge, but also for a reconfiguration of its heroes. Twenty years on, the survivors, who had staged themselves as dutiful, fearless, and pious, appeared as reverent, reflective, and sentimental. Young warriors no more, the survivors had transmogrified in the public mind and grown in their own bearing into reflective men who mourned at a temporal and geographic distance. This transformation was evident in a poem presented by Lydia Melland to commemorate the twenty-first anniversary of the Charge. Imagining the collective mindset of the Light Brigade's remnants, Melland offered a rhyming couplet: "But now as we recall it; The weight of bygone years; Melts form our hearts in mem'ry; And yields us manly tears."[55] The dutiful Chargers of Balaklava had turned into military men of feeling, as literary critic Holly Furneaux has called them. On this occasion, moreover, tears, those "liquid social bond[s]," to use the words of historian Thomas Dixon, linked past to present and soldier to soldier.[56]

The Chargers themselves had a hand in producing, and in protecting, these bonds as the century unfolded. They cultivated friendship and fellowship as they cleaved to the dignity and exclusivity of their bonds. The Chargers eagerly guarded their fellowship with one another in the years following the Alexandra Palace banquet, as the formation of the Balaklava Commemoration Society indicates. The society held an annual private dinner to mark successive anniversaries of the Charge, either at a London club or at a restaurant. Membership was a distinct privilege, only extensible to those who had been "actually present on the field of action" at Balaklava. In this protected space, a hallowed society came together to mark the passage of time, to rekindle the fellowship of the dutiful, and to honor their brethren who had died. Like the banquet hall at the Alexandra Palace, it was a venue of associational fellowship that stood at a remove from the demands of everyday masculinity and civilian life. In these confines, the survivors could freely exhibit "friendship's warm and sorrowing tear."[57]

Across the century, poetry remained a vehicle for linking the Chargers to their pasts and for bringing them together in the present. It had still more critical effects at the end of the century. Poetry and its power to evoke public sentiment catapulted the Chargers to the forefront of public attention once again in 1890. The occasion was the publication of a poem in the conservative *St. James's Gazette*. Here, Rudyard Kipling bemoaned the plight of the survivors of the Light Brigade and its "wretched remnant." The bard of the British Empire and the British soldier alike, Kipling revealed an inconvenient truth: many survivors of the Charge were living into their dotage in penury and facing their deaths in the workhouse.[58] Kipling's "The Last of the Light Brigade" engaged in his typically wry use of a meter befitting a children's ballad to lure readers into a startling revelation about the fate of the remnants of the Six Hundred:

> There were thirty million English, who talked of England's might,
> There were twenty broken troopers who lacked a bed for the night.
> They had neither food nor money, they had neither service nor trade;
> They were only shiftless soldiers, the last of the Light Brigade.[59]

As it wove its tale of woe, Kipling's poem conjured up the image of an indifferent nation, Britain, and the specter of a "Master-singer," Tennyson, who had, together, turned a deaf ear on those survivors who sought their aid.[60] To hear Kipling tell it, the empire had failed in addressing its duty to its heroic veterans, the onetime avatars of patriotic sacrifice who were becoming objects of paternalistic charity. Ultimately, in Kipling's hands, the Chargers, the very embodiments of splendid military duty in the past, became living rebukes of failed social responsibility in the present.

The poetic indictment galvanized the energetic work of the Light Brigade Relief Fund.[61] For two years, an ad hoc committee worked in the service of those "destitute survivors" memorialized by Kipling, raising funds to be used for pensions.[62] Its members included politicians and painters, and even the poet laureate, Tennyson. Persuasively and actively, the Committee appealed to the nation, tugging at its heartstrings and pulling at its purse strings. It beseeched the nation to do its duty to the veterans. In shillings and in pennies, funds flowed in from around the country. Donors included "a laborer who has two sons in the Army," "a Soldier's son," and "one who remembers the battle." "Poor Jimmy" and "Percy, who is learning Tennyson's poem" contributed as well, cloaking the effort in schoolboy sentiment.[63] The citizens of York and the mayor of Brisbane pitched in, too. Finally, a wealthy Muslim from Bangladesh gave 1,000 Rupees to the cause, and spurred others to do the same. In his own interpretation of the Crimean War, he was convinced that the Light Brigade had "fought in the cause of Islam," presumably since the British Army had allied itself with the Ottoman Empire.[64]

When it came to aiding the veterans, this new sense of public duty took the form not only of fundraising for soldiers in need, but also of providing comforts to men in their twilight years. Buffalo Bill shows and kettledrum bazaars, roller skating races and cricket matches – all were on offer in London and elsewhere to provide pleasure to the survivors and to raise funds for their care. Such enterprises were part and parcel of a broader effort to aid the mid-century veteran at the fin de siècle, as military conflicts across Africa and the Middle East hardened and escalated.[65] Although the tenor of the events changed, the accoutrements remained the same. Recitations of Tennyson's Charge were commonplace, with the veteran Pennington reappearing in his old age to rehearse the verses. Relic displays featuring regalia and remains also attracted attention. As a sign of the times, however, there were new curiosities, most notably the recorded words of Alfred, Lord Tennyson, preserved on the phonograph and reciting "The Charge of the Light Brigade."[66] At the century's end, these modern technologies pressed the poet laureate's voice into the service of duty.

Thanks to these and other efforts, the Fund raised nearly £7,000 to be devoted to the aid of the poor veterans, who numbered upwards of 100 still.[67] "Whatever else may be said against our treatment of our soldiers," noted the *Morning Post*, "it can no longer be alleged that the country has quite forgotten the heroes of the Crimea."[68] The fund certainly helped many "genuine survivors," including a handful living in the "extreme poverty" of the workhouse. But the efforts also opened up questions. Who, precisely, deserved the succor of the Light Brigade Relief Fund? The Fund did not provide indiscriminate aid; like many other Victorian efforts, it drew a line between the deserving and the undeserving as it meted out support. There were a few hopeless cases.[69] The most notable among these was poor James Brennan of the 17th Lancers, who met his death in 1891 in the Marylebone Union Workhouse. Lacking in funds but proud in principle, he had refused to wear the Queen's medals on his workhouse uniform.[70] He remained beyond the pale of charity, however, having "drifted" to the workhouse after forfeiting employment opportunities. "We were warned that it would be useless, and, indeed mischievous, to make any direct grant of money to him," the members of the Light Brigade Relief Committee claimed, as they defended their decision in the face of this "hopeless case." Brennan may have been a "very fine soldier," but he had "fallen into very bad habits" late in life.[71] There were others, too, who lost out, not so much because of failings of their own but due to the limits of bureaucracy. A man whose leg was "shattered to bits" in the Charge missed the application deadline, only to find himself headed for the workhouse.[72] Others, like George Gibson of the 13th Dragoons, failed to show sufficient "privation and want." Gibson, although poor, did not fall below the Committee's poverty line.[73]

Cases like these constituted the unluckiest among the lucky. As the example of the Light Brigade Relief Fund attests, the remnants of the Six Hundred – those who had survived the horrific Charge nearly half a century before – enjoyed a peculiar form of "good luck" that allowed them to "shine in the front of history." Participation in the Charge and survival against considerable odds had bought its veterans a set of unanticipated privileges. It is not to say that they were free of privation: more than a few died in the workhouse, as the case of Brennan suggests. Still others displayed their share of traumatic scars, though the ceremonial spectacle and sentimental rhetoric surrounding them sought to deflect attention away from war's horrors against the backdrop of rising military tensions. These truths notwithstanding, the survivors of the Charge, those paragons of duty, did enjoy the access to lavish banquets, exclusive clubs, and special aid that came with national adoration. Certainly, they played their part in protecting this privilege, stipulating, as they had at the inauguration of the Balaklava Commemoration Society, that all members must have been present on the field of battle at the time of the Charge. Segments of the press were quick to note the inequities produced by and on behalf of the Chargers. This matter was a persistent preoccupation for the *Saturday Review* across decades. In 1875, on the heels of the fetes and feasts at the Alexandra Palace, it had foretold, "there will be Alma Banquets, and Inkerman Banquets, and possibly Abyssinian and Ashantee [sic] Banquets, till every day of the year is filled up."[74] Its signature hyperbole, rife with racism, was not realized. However, its real object of concern – the adulation of the Chargers at the expense of other heroes – did persist. Some fifteen years later, when it witnessed the inception of the Light Brigade Relief Fund, the *Saturday Review* harped once again on the inequity. The Chargers had conducted themselves with great gallantry, yet their hallowed status was an effect of history's happenstance rather than a singular quality. A different set of soldiers would certainly "have borne themselves no less well if called on."[75] The *Saturday Review* was not alone in this assessment. *The Graphic*, too, was of the opinion that the special succor granted to "one little band of British heroes" had what it termed "a somewhat invidious look."[76]

Crimean veterans themselves joined in the critique of the celebrated Light Brigade's strange privilege. We can only imagine how galling the special recognition was for the Battle of Balaklava's other participants, including the Highlanders who comprised the Thin Red Line and the Heavy Cavalry Brigade. Their maneuvers on October 25, 1854, had been far more successful than those of their charging brethren. Cavendish L. Fitzroy, Major of the 68th Light Infantry who fought in the Crimea, expressed these sentiments well. "Why are the survivors of this portion of one battle signaled out for a special public appeal?" he demanded. "The idea is almost ludicrous were it not unjust," he declared. The injustice extended far beyond the Crimean campaign to all others who had "bled for their country."[77] More critics followed, as they appealed for all "Old Campaigners" in need, including those who had served in China, India, and Afghanistan.[78]

Resentment of the Chargers on the part of their battling brothers hearkened back to the war itself. Aristocratic in bearing and splendid in dress, the Cavalry had long been the pride of the Army. The instantaneous celebrity of the Light Brigade was thus a ready cause for resentment, even among usually judicious men. Bitterness accrued, especially, around the practice of awarding military honors in the war. To accompany the Crimea Medal, combatants might win one of four clasps, given for the battles at Alma, Balaklava, or Inkerman, or for the long siege at Sebastopol. There were no temporal equivalencies among the medals, however. The siege at Sebastopol had required weeks and months of forbearance, while the Battle of Balaklava was the work of a day, and the Charge an occasion that took fifteen minutes. The fact that a quarter of an hour of bravado received equal recognition to months of perseverance troubled Edward M. Wrench, a surgeon in the Crimea, to no end. He confessed that he was "intensely disgusted" by the injustice.[79]

All cavils aside, the celebrity accorded to the Light Brigade endured, and even grew, at the fin de siècle as it enjoyed stages evermore public.[80] The Light Brigade functioned to redefine and to reignite the ideals of duty in an epoch of pomp and circumstance and in an era of escalating war. Time and again, the aging band of brothers was trotted out to mark Queen Victoria's Jubilees and Britain's Anglo-Boer Wars. This increased visibility ignited new efforts to aid the aging Chargers. In 1897, Lord T.H. Roberts, a publisher and a philanthropist, initiated a fund that ultimately sent all seventy-four of the living survivors to London for Victoria's Diamond Jubilee. Roberts's ambitious scheme involved tracking down the veterans, transporting them to the metropolis, and providing dormitory lodging. These grand designs had the effect of pulling the monarchy and the military into even closer alignment. They had more enduring effects, too, for T.H. Roberts's energies revealed the unpleasant truth that many Light Brigade survivors remained destitute, despite the efforts to aid the veterans in the preceding years. In the face of this discovery, Roberts made it his life's work to rescue these "old and worn" soldiers. Supported by women worthies ranging from Queen Victoria to Florence Nightingale, Roberts tended faithfully to this "labor of love" over the following two decades, from 1897 until his own death in 1915.[81] Annually, he wrote to the papers to drum up support for the shrinking ensemble of heroes, especially at Christmastime and in the winters. On these occasions, he took recourse to Tennyson's verses, relying upon them to tug at his readers' heartstrings and to replenish his dwindling fund. Plaintively, he asked of the twenty-nine veterans still living, "When shall their glory fade?" Roberts pressed a "great, rich country" to save its "old soldiers" from the workhouse.[82] In so doing, he tapped into broader efforts at the time of the South African War, when campaigns across the country sought to save old veterans from privation.[83]

Perhaps the most remarkable aspect of Roberts's scheme was the provision of an annual anniversary dinner for the Chargers. Like those in years past, Roberts's banquets provided welcome opportunities for the "war-scarred heroes" to gather for fellowship and comfort. Time and fortune had affected the "old fellows" differently, with some arriving to the dinners "hale and hearty" and others exhibiting "want and privation." For the public at the doorstep of a new century, accounts of the banquets provided "delightful and touching scenes."[84] For historians working today, the annals of the dinners provide a balance sheet of mortality, showing the number of participants dwindling from year to year. On the occasion of the 1910 dinner, a mere thirteen out of the twenty-eight living veterans attended the dinner, the remainder being "too feeble." With their full beards and their staggering gaits, the death riders cut a strange sight in a modern and mechanized world as they took taxicabs to the destination. By the time of the last of the dinners, in 1913, only six of the thirteen survivors managed to attend. Until this final gathering, they remained bound by their moments of glory and by Tennyson's poem too, as a souvenir commemorating "all that was left of them" suggests so well (Figure 2.4).[85]

The cumulative effect of these rituals was to portray the veterans as quaint relics and as happy fighters, not as injured veterans or as traumatized souls. It is difficult to find evidence of trauma on the surface of these records. However, the 1907 interview of Charles Lamb preserves a sense of the scars of battle in a manner approximating what we recognize today as post-traumatic stress disorder. Late in his life, Lamb reported that he was, still, haunted by the Charge of the Light Brigade. The memories

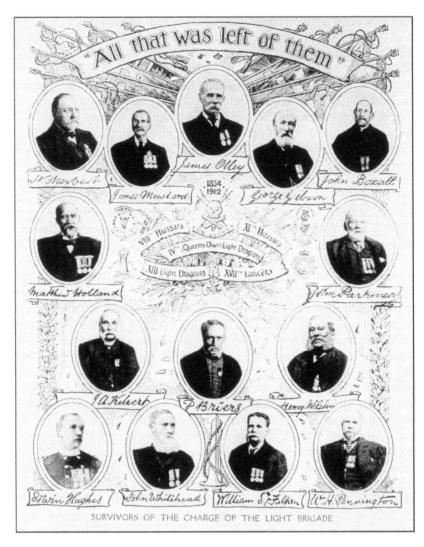

Figure 2.4 Charge of the Light Brigade survivors. c. 1912. KGPA/
Alamy Stock Photo

rushed upon him in everyday moments. When he crossed the Strand in
London, for instance, the elderly veteran felt himself engulfed by "cabs
and 'buses and big roaring motors." "The noise and the clutter and clatter
and rush and hurry and tangle of people and horses all made me think of
that retreat up the valley," he declared. At least there was in London

a secure waiting ground between the lanes of traffic and in the midst of the hubbub. The same had not been true in the Tchernaya Valley: "There warn't no isle o'safety there!" The Charge haunted Lamb not only in his waking hours, but also in his sleep. "I often wake in the night fighting it all over again," he confessed. In a comic banter characteristic of the Cockney, his wife replied, "He shouts and roars like a 'nelephant [sic]." These rich anecdotes verge on the ludic as they illuminate the antiquated Victorian elder out of place in the modern Edwardian moment and as they render the warm, if humorous repartee of the elderly couple's marriage. Ultimately, even as they brought trauma to the surface, narrative and performative strategies such as these had dampening effects: they contained the horrors of wars past as Britain was hurtling toward new conflicts in the twentieth-century world.[86]

***

The era of the world wars unsettled the British hegemony and the Victorian certainties of the nineteenth century. In this context, the role of the vaunted Light Brigade and of the dwindling band of Chargers came once again into question. On the one hand, the Chargers retained their last bit of patriotic punch, with Crimean veterans stepping out to do the work of recruiting in World War I before the coming of conscription. But the Chargers were, more and more, the outdated emblems of the nineteenth century.[87] The diplomatic landscape had changed. In the Great War, the British and the French once again found themselves together in an extended conflict, but other alignments had shifted. Russia was, on this occasion, an ally, and the Ottoman Empire, an adversary. The ideological landscape was changing as well. Among the lofty ideals that the Great War called into question was the notion of duty, at least as it had existed in the Victorian age. And, among the martial technologies that total war put to a near end was the cavalry charge, symbolizing the military practices of the past.[88] More and more, the Charge and the Chargers seemed antiquated, relics of a lost world.

The Chargers and their Crimean brethren were well beyond their fighting years when the Great War broke out. Yet they remained in the public mind as avatars of duty to country; annual banquets were regular news items, as were stories of the passing of Crimean veterans. There was, as well, a spate of human-interest stories in local and provincial papers that told of the efforts of the veterans of the mid-nineteenth century's conflicts trying to enlist. One of these men, eighty-three-year-old Christopher W. Horne of Ashton-Under-Lyme, tried, in fact, to rejoin the Army four times. "Too old I may be in years, but not in spirit," he declared. Horne may not have been a veteran of the Charge, but, as a Crimean fighter, he had absorbed its spirit exceedingly well. Driven by duty, he was eager to do his "bit" for the nation's cause.[89] Though thwarted in his drive to reenlist, Horne might have taken comfort from the fact that he, and others like him, served as enduring symbols of the virtues of military duty for a new era. Young men read about the sacrifices of elders like Horne in the pages of the press. In some circumstances, they would, additionally, have seen veterans of the mid-nineteenth-century's conflicts – both the Crimean War and the Indian Rebellion – recruiting for the twentieth century's first grand conflagration. Such was the case in Bristol – a city that, along with Nottingham, boasted an active organization for veteran support (Figure 2.5).[90] There, members of the Crimea and Indian Mutiny Veterans' Association stood together in 1914, calling a younger generation to enlist in the fighting: "We have done our duty," their placards read. "Now come and do yours."[91]

In the years and months leading up to the institution of the draft in 1916, some might have dismissed the exhortations of the mid-nineteenth-century's veterans as the misplaced patriotism of an older generation. The wide eyed among them may have found the invitation hard to press against, particularly when accompanied by the military regalia of parading veterans and their sentimental staging in the nation's papers. It proved impossible, however, to sustain these understandings in the twentieth century, with the extended, mass slaughter of the Great War and with the rise of newer languages to express the conflict's physical and psychological tolls. Not least among these was the medical diagnosis of shell shock. One effect was to discard any Victorian certainties about the duty of military service that lingered during World War I. The iconic battles of the Great War – Gallipoli, fought on the very tracks of the nineteenth-century's Crimean warriors, and the Somme, waged in the trenches of Western Europe – were just two to recall the costs of service in the face of survival's indomitable odds. They were, of course, far larger in scale and longer in duration than the Battle of Balaklava, with its culminating Charge. In the end, battles such as these produced significant breaks with the confidences of the Victorian world as they engendered disillusionment and despair.[92]

In particular, World War I's soldiers and officers railed against the notion of serving dutifully against the odds. Like their predecessors, they expressed these understandings in their war poetry. The trenchant criticism of Wilfred Owen, who was killed a week before the armistice in 1918, is well known. "Dulce et decorum est, Pro patria mori," he concluded one of his best-known texts, as he reversed the Latin poet Horace's pro-war maxim about the beauty of sacrifice for country in wartime.[93]

Figure 2.5 Program for the Bristol Crimean and Indian Mutiny Veterans' Association. 1907. Bristol Archives

The wry conclusion discards any sense that patriotic duty leading to wartime death is at all worthwhile. It is a firm rebuke of efforts like those of Bristol's Crimean veterans, who beckoned young men seeking glory into war. It is a far cry, too, from the sense that soldierly sacrifice – "to do and die" – could be ennobling, even while tragic.

More generally speaking, at a moment when patriotism and critique stood in stark opposition, there was little room for the sensibilities of a Tennyson, who had sought, in "The Charge of the Light Brigade," to uphold the soldier's duty, even while lamenting the leadership's blunder. At the moment of the Great War, Tennyson, himself, was a subject of satire and dismissal once again by Rudyard Kipling. Kipling's was a war of heartbreak, with his own son passing away at the Battle of Mons (1914), early on in a conflict that the father had initially championed. In the midst of the loss, Kipling looked, poignantly, to poetry to confront his grief. In verse, he addressed not just the questions surrounding the death of his son, whose body was not found in Kipling's lifetime. He attacked too the certainties propping up the waging of war, as they were received from prior generations. His trenchant couplet "Common Form" upends the hope of Tennyson's world view: "If any question why we died, Tell them, because our fathers lied."[94]

Hope in a shared purpose and a shared understanding as expressed by Tennyson were on the wane in World War I. So too were the very military unit, and the very military undertaking, that the Victorian poet laureate had sought to sanctify: the Cavalry and the cavalry charge. The last significant cavalry charge had occurred in the Sudan, during 1898's Battle of Omdurman, where Winston Churchill, himself a champion of Victorian duty, was present for the fighting.[95] On the heels of the battle in the Sudan, the South African War showed the Cavalry to be anachronistic, if also flexible and capable of change, with mounted riders using guns rather than swords.[96] The Cavalry's fitness for mechanized warfare was very much in question over the following years. Long renowned for its luster and tradition, it was a vestige in the modern age. Even so, cavalry brigades made early appearances on the Western Front in World War I, where they remained the stuff of legend. At the Battle of Mons, an English cavalry rider notably shot the first German soldier to die in World War I's hand-to-hand combat.[97] But the critical role of the Cavalry was elsewhere, in the Middle East, where it saw its final victory in 1918 at Megiddo. This was a bright moment for the Cavalry in what was otherwise a frustrating, futile outing that saw an antiquated unit galloping "Balaklava style," as it hearkened back to the nineteenth century, in glory and futility alike.[98]

Artifacts of an antiquated, if enduring, part of the British Armed Forces, the last of the Crimea's acclaimed Chargers passed away against this backdrop.[99] The last surviving officer, Colonel James Mustard, died in 1916, and the longest-lived veteran, Edwin Hughes, passed away in 1927, when he reached the ripe old age of ninety-six.[100] Known as "Balaklava Ned," Hughes was a Victorian relic by the time of his death in the interwar era. A scrappy figure who rose through the ranks, he had enlisted in the Army as a private in 1851 and retired as a Sergeant-Major in 1871. A faithful attendee at the Balaklava dinners, he was "a spare man with upright carriage" whose visage bore the marks of battle, his cheek boasting the "deep scar of a sword cut received in the mad onward rush." The Charge had left his left leg wounded, but he stayed out of hospital. "I was lucky to get nothing worse," he later declared of his plight. Because of his role in the Charge, Hughes benefitted from the largesse of the T.H. Roberts Fund and, later, the Royal Patriotic Fund. Outlasting them both, he received a pension from the War Office for the last two years of his life. With his passing, the last of the "Noble Six Hundred" were no more.[101]

By the interwar era, the Chargers were but traces of an age that had passed. The values that they represented had worn thin. The Great War unsettled any certainty in the ideals of sacrifice and duty. The cavalry charge on horseback was, moreover, on its way to obsolescence, with the last instance coming in World War II.[102] Even at this late date, however, Tennyson's tribute to the Chargers and their Charge retained its traction. The poem was an artifact of Victoriana in a changed world. But it was also a piece of common currency, widely known. This dual quality of being antiquated and everywhere is evident in the work of Virginia Woolf. Woolf published *To the Lighthouse* in 1927, the very year that Balaklava Ned passed away. Her characters repeat and misquote its lines, with Mr. Ramsay declaring, time and again, that "someone had blundered." As Trudi Tate has noted, Woolf's contemporary readers would not have needed a reference as they, themselves, grappled with the legacies of the past century.[103] Their descent into the Tchernaya Valley may have taken mere minutes, but the Chargers and the verses commemorating them remained persistent and pervasive, vestiges of the Victorian age.[104]

***

Ever relevant and recyclable, the Charge of the Light Brigade enjoyed a renewed significance in the decades of the 1950s and the 1960s against the backdrop of the dwindling of the British Empire and the remaking of a postwar world. At that time, there were efforts to reinvigorate Victorian notions of duty in public and in private alike. The focus of study, veneration, and nostalgia, the Charge represented a heralded link to the past at the end of the age of empire. Ordinary Britons and English royals sought out connection to this past, clinging to its artifacts and legacies. They read about its history, coveted its material culture, and traced their lineages. Connections to the event kindled comfort and consolation in the postwar world, as Victorian values became, for many, a thing of the past. There were others, however, who found in the Charge a target for reproach. This was particularly the case in the 1960s, with antiwar sentiment and countercultural currents at high tide. For critics and skeptics, the Charge was no monument to Victorian duty and resolute sacrifice. Instead, it became a rebuke against tired pieties and senseless war.

The Charge enjoyed renewed popularity at the moment of its centenary. One example came, of course, with the literary success of Cecil Woodham-Smith's *The Reason Why*. In 1953, almost a century after the Crimean War, Mrs. Woodham-Smith, a master storyteller, published her reappraisal of the Charge of the Light Brigade. Her best seller engaged with the long-standing questions about culpability and with the venerable lines of Tennyson as it sought to memorialize the occasion and to adjudicate responsibility. Woodham-Smith did not, ultimately, succeed in resolving the question of responsibility for the grave mistakes of the military. "Perhaps 'Everybody blundered' would have been a sounder verdict," the *Illustrated London News* reflected.[105] She did, however, whet untapped appetites for the mystery, as she familiarized a new generation with the names of Raglan, Cardigan, Lucan, and Nolan.[106] Heralded as "lucid," "clear," and "panoramic," Woodham-Smith's masterpiece became the *Daily Mail's* Book of the Month selection in November 1953.[107] The stewards of the Charge's memory at the moment of its centenary ranged from Mrs. Woodham-Smith to the Queen herself. A young Queen Elizabeth II, herself an embodiment of duty, made an appearance at the Balaklava Ball, held in November 1954. There, she danced with one of the Army's Major Generals, J. F. B. Combe, who donned the regalia of the Earl of Cardigan, 100 years on. Arrayed in the costume of an earlier epoch, the pair fused past and present. They became a living tribute to military service and monarchical tradition in a postwar world.[108]

Not only a concern of historians writing for national audiences or for monarchs occupying a grand stage, the Charge held allure across a wide swath of society, both high and middlebrow. In the 1950s and 1960s, it continued to serve the prosthetic purpose of providing connection to a glorious past associated with tradition and duty. It inspired acts of remembrance, both public and private; it occasioned campaigns for possession, whether sentimental or spectacular. In the 1960s, preservationists, genealogists, and collectors, all custodians of the past, sought to safeguard their stories of the Light Brigade. In Manchester, for instance, local interests endeavored to provide a suitable grave for Sergeant Richard Brown, whose plight moved many well over 100 years after the Battle of Balaklava. A veteran of the 11th Hussars, Brown survived the Charge but died a pauper, buried in a common grave.[109] Like those subscribers to the relief funds who sought to do their duty to the living at the fin de siècle, those residents of Manchester who looked after Sergeant Brown subsequently aspired to meet their responsibility to the dead. Along with these civic acts of public duty, there were personal acts of family pride. Take, for instance, the case of septuagenarian Arthur Allwood, who published the biography of his mother's great uncle, Sergeant Major James Nunnerley, a rider with the 17th Lancers in the fateful charge. In offering this monument in print, Allwood sought to boost local legend and to gild family history. He aimed, too, to mend a wound that hearkened to his own youth. As a schoolboy, Allwood's claims of relation to a Charger had met the "derision and disbelief" of his classmates. Allwood's pride was great, and his scar was deep, so much so that he waited, as he explained, some seventy years to "justify" his "childish boast." It was a chance, many years on, to vindicate his own reputation and to safeguard his family's name.[110]

Perhaps Allwood was being uncharitable to his younger self when he labeled his tenacity in the face of his taunting classmates as mere boyish pride. There was, after all, a good deal at stake in the claim of a link to the Chargers. It was not a matter merely of individual vindication or even of family pride. It was, even more so, a bid for belonging in a sanctified national past at a moment of imperial decline and in an epoch of generational upheaval. There was social capital to be had and individual comfort to be gained in forging a connection to the hallowed Victorian event. So many years on, the Charge recalled a moment of righteous strength and moral certitude. With this in mind, it should be no surprise that men like Arthur Allwood cleaved tenaciously to the Battle of Balaklava, and, by extension, to duty's lineage. Allwood sought to safeguard his role as a stakeholder in the occasion by taking possession of his family's story. Others, on far more public stages, aimed to claim a relationship to the event through acts of literal possession. Such is the case, for instance, with the Balaklava Bugle. This episode brought a famed British auction house and two transatlantic celebrities into the fray over the ownership of a relic of the Charge, redolent with fame and duty.

It was in 1964 that the tense and tender ties wrought by relatives and relics came together most publicly in the case of the Balaklava Bugle. This was the instrument that had sounded the Charge of the Light Brigade, its mythologized notes condensing the virtues of duty and loyalty, even in the likely event of death. In 1964, Sotheby's hosted a much-publicized auction. Here, a coiled bugle pierced by a Cossack lance fetched a price of £1,600. It had once been blown by Trumpet Major William Brittain, who died at Florence Nightingale's Scutari Hospital. Across the century, his bugle passed through various hands. It ultimately became the property of two unlikely custodians, British actor Laurence Harvey and American television personality Ed Sullivan.[111] The daily press and the tabloid newspapers made the most of the occasion, billing it as an "unprecedented scene" and an occasion of "high drama," not unlike the Charge of the Light Brigade itself. The media coverage of the occasion gave the Charge a new prominence in popular culture; in so doing, it made the instrument into a crucial tool of the special relationship. Enacting his largesse on the small screen, Sullivan planned to present the object on live television to the 17th Lancers' Museum in Nottingham, where it still holds pride of place today.[112]

The auction accorded great publicity to Sullivan and Harvey; it provided the Lancers' Museum with an invaluable cultural treasure. But it did not offer unadulterated affirmation all around. Sixty-three-year-old Bertha Kearns of Middlesex was, along with her extended family, particularly distraught over the sale. She claimed that the auctioneers had the Bugle's provenance all wrong – that it was not William Brittain who had blown the Bugle, but instead her grandfather, Trumpet Major Henry Joy.[113] Long-standing family lore attested as much, and there was a newly refurbished headstone at the cemetery in Chiswick Churchyard that appeared, additionally, to bear out this claim. Joy's bugle had its own robust history. At the fin de siècle, an earlier, celebrated auction had delivered the family treasure into the hands of a philanthropist, J.G. Middlebrook, who put it to good use, lending it out for charity functions and military fundraisers against the backdrop of the South African War. By the year 1904, the bugle once blown by Sergeant Major Henry Joy had generated £5,000 to be directed to the aid of soldiers' widows and orphans. It then came into the possession of John Jacob Astor, who preceded Sullivan as an American of note to gain publicity through philanthropy. He generously donated it to the collections that eventually comprised Britain's National Army Museum. There, Joy's bugle remains today.[114] Its storied history notwithstanding, questions about the provenance of this bugle bedeviled its career, from the turn of the century to the 1960s, when Sotheby's settled it once and for all: the verdict favored William Brittain. As for Joy, it turned out that he had sounded the Charge of the Heavy Brigade, which had preceded the Light Brigade's actions at Balaklava. In bearing the brunt of this decision, Bertha Kearns and her family must have shared the frustrations of the very participants in the Charge of the Heavy Brigade some 100 years before. Although more successful at Balaklava than the Light Brigade in their military maneuver, the Heavy Brigade never attained lasting celebrity.

With this issue solved, Sotheby's orchestrated the spectacle of commerce impeccably. The highly profitable sale was a well-staged occasion exploiting nostalgia and longing for a bygone era, while relying upon the engines and actors of modern media. It married auction-room trading and military spectacle. It tempered the vicissitudes of the market with the duty of custodianship. The day was to culminate with a symbolic event: the sounding of the Charge by a latter-day trumpeter donning traditional regalia. So eager was Harvey and Sullivan's agent to gain possession of the prize, however, that the bidding concluded in fifty-five seconds. Efforts at impeccable choreography notwithstanding, the trumpeter, Philip Costen, had not yet reached the auction house. Learning of the sale, he rushed to Sotheby's in a taxicab, where he received accolades for his great "initiative." Upon his arrival, Costen sounded the Charge to stirring effect. The juxtaposition of past and present was, however, lost on the young man. When asked about his connections to a venerable lineage of trumpeters, Costen replied, "I don't worry about history. This is 1964" (Figure 2.6).[115]

The episode of the Bugle's sale captures nicely the double registers carried by the Charge in the 1960s. A part of the Victorian past, it was redolent with history for some and devoid of meaning for others. It

Figure 2.6 "Into the Valley of Death." Sale of Balaklava Bugle. 1964. Keystone Press/Alamy Stock Photo

recalled a traditional order, while engaging celebrity culture. It stirred the sounds of duty, while offering opportunities for entertainment. These dualities, and the challenges posed by them, are even more evident in a large-screen venture that hitched itself to the Light Brigade's history. This was English filmmaker Tony Richardson's 1968 feature, *The Charge of the Light Brigade*. Leading the way in this screen drama were John Gielgud, who played the doddering, if well-meaning Lord Raglan, and Trevor Howard, who acted the part of the haughty and magisterial Lord Cardigan. *The Charge* also featured David Hemmings as "the upstart officer" Captain Nolan, who was vaulted to an especially central role in Richardson's film, which was based on the screenplay of Charles Wood, himself a onetime rider in the 11th Hussars. Hemmings played across Vanessa Redgrave, who starred as the entirely fictional Clarissa Morris, a Pre-Raphaelite beauty who served the dual purposes of providing an occasion for an imagined sexual liaison and an opportunity for added star power. The *Guardian*, in fact, dubbed the star-studded cast the "heavy-weight brigade."[116]

Neither opportunity nor expense were spared in the production of the film, the grandest production to date for the Bradford-born and Oxford-educated Richardson, who had won a 1964 Oscar for his *Tom Jones*. While the thirty-nine-year-old Richardson billed himself as a "luxurious communist" who was critical of "dollar imperialism," he relied upon Hollywood funds to finance *The Charge*.[117] The lavish costumes and the location costs were considerable for a film that was shot in both England and Turkey, on a carefully scouted site in the province of Anatolia, just 350 miles away from the Tchernaya Valley. The result of more than three years of planning and production, it augmented its star power with heavy auxiliary and heavy fireworks – there were "5000 extras, 1100 horses, 6000 pounds of TNT and 3000 cannonballs."[118]

The promotional materials for United Artists, which distributed the film, boasted not only the epic ambitions of the color, widescreen film, but also its "complete, large-scale realism." With his hyperrealism, Richardson offered a response to the lyrical rendition in Tennyson's poem, which had mythologized the Charge, and the loose interpretation of a filmic predecessor, 1936's *The Charge of the Light Brigade*, starring Olivia de Havilland and Errol Flynn.[119] In distinction to its predecessor, Richardson's work relied upon what its promoters called an "ultra-realistic style," one facilitated by deep historical research into the archives produced during the war – the diaries, newspapers and letters, and especially the rich "pictorial record."[120] Recourse to portraits, paintings, and sketches ensured that "every detail down to the curl of a man's mustache was

authentic," or so the promoters claimed. The film showcased
Victorian shoehorns, clay pipes, and umbrellas. In so doing, it satis-
fied a contemporary appetite for Victoriana that was manifest on
Carnaby Street, the center of sartorial fashion and of Swinging
London.[121] Not only did Richardson's *Charge* seek to satiate fashion-
istas. It aimed to please military buffs as well. The film made use of
Russian cannons, British warships, and Victorian tents. A cast of
hundreds marched and charged in the exact formation of the Light
Brigade. In the making of Richardson's *Charge*, fidelity to detail was,
clearly, a high duty.

This was, however, no bland antiquarianism.[122] Along with its
embrace of the verisimilitude of costume drama, Richardson's film
aspired to a social realism that sought to critique the antinomies and
hypocrisies of Victorian society. Specifically, Richardson sought to unsettle mid-nineteenth-century ideas of military duty. He cast a critical eye on
the privileged and hidebound officer class, whose members had looked
myopically back to Waterloo, the last occasion when several had served
on the field of battle. Many had won their commissions through purchase,
not service. Their lavish weddings, frivolous banquets, and haughty sociability were far removed from the lives of the rank and file, as the film's
stark contrast between the officers' balls and the privates' mess halls
showed. To press this point, Richardson's film provided a view onto an
army whose members were recruited from the lowest ranks of society: the
untutored, the unmoored, and the unwashed. Military families lived
cheek by jowl, with men and women commingling in bawdy sociability.
Those privates who violated the whims of officers found themselves, as
The Charge showed quite graphically, subject to the lash; corporal punishment remained permissible in the Army until 1868, when the Cardwell
Reforms began to take hold. If barrack life in Britain was hard, even more
difficult were the rigors of the voyage to the front and the extremities of
the weather. To demonstrate the folly of military duty, Richardson
showed the men dropping off of horses to their deaths in quick succession
in the Crimea, where they fell victim to the heat, the cold, and the cholera.
The lessons about the futility of war culminated, of course, in the Charge
itself. As the promotional materials explained, "Richardson shows the
disaster for what it was – a series of flag-waving blunders, led by myopic
militarists." There was, in his rendition, nothing to be gained by the
obedience of the rank and file.[123]

In Richardson's hands, the Charge was a battle between innovation and
tradition, between professionalism and amateurism, and, finally, between
bravery and obsequiousness. Against the backdrop of Vietnam, he drama-
tized the event to illustrate the "comic futility of war."[124] The film nodded

in the direction of antiwar sentiment as it showcased a gathering of pacifist campaigners, likely Quakers or other nonconformists, who carried placards that declared, "Blessed are the peacemakers for they shall be called the children of God." The most important figure for this aspiration, in Richardson's rendition, was Captain Nolan, Raglan's Aide-de-Camp who delivered the orders to charge. As they charted Nolan's oppositional identity, the promotional materials cast the character as a youth who struggled for "intelligent individuality amid official apathy" in a "classic clash of old and new generations."[125] Nineteen sixty-eight's film audiences might well have understood Nolan in the tradition of Jimmy Stewart from the film *Look Back in Anger*. He was, in the parlance of the day, an Angry Young Man. In playing this part, Richardson's Nolan upended the duty long associated with the Charge as outdated and pointless, even destructive. Well over 100 years on, the Charge's unresolved stories of blame and blunder held great purchase, once again, in a violent and volatile world.

Taken together, these gestures to the folly of war and the righteousness of its critics should have resonated well with the intended audience in 1968, as the conflict in Vietnam trudged on and as opposition grew on both sides of the Atlantic. However, the film met skepticism from the critics, who found that it had a straining and compromising effect. The mixture of costume drama, epic film, and social realism did not go down well. The *Times*, for instance, judged Richardson as a "heavy-handed political moralist" and an "eclectic movie stylist."[126] Adding to the drollery for the critics was the experience of watching with the crowds. *Illustrated London News* critic Michael Billington had to contend with "a broad-backed, needlessly tall gentleman" in front of him, a man with "a bottomless supply of sweets" who "munched and munched and munched" on his left, and "a lady who exclaimed with audible pleasure every time an animal appeared on the screen" on his right. There was, too, sitting behind him, "a man who gave his wife a running commentary on the history of the Crimean campaign." If the Charge itself had been tragedy, the viewing experience was farce. By 1968, the Charge itself was "neither myth nor very well remembered history."[127] Its past pervasiveness notwithstanding, the occasion and its meanings had become opaque. Rebuke of duty through appeal to realism had gone wrong. Despite the filmmaker's ambitions, the cinematic experience was prosaic.

The Light Brigade's legacies long cycled between myth and history, between remembering and forgetting, and between epic and mundane. One extreme example of the decline from dignity to bathos occurred on the tails of the film's release, with the nearly simultaneous opening of an unlikely theme restaurant in London's West End. This institution was typical of what the *Guardian* dismissively called an "expanding gastronomic anomaly": that is, the "mass specialty restaurant." Called The Charge of the Light Brigade, it joined the likes of the New Chicken Inn and the Kentucky Palace Pancake Kitchen. A seafood restaurant, it offered up a series of incongruities in its descent into kitsch. Restaurant-goers could enjoy meals served on marbled tables in an ambient setting with military décor and martial music. Waiters in the uniforms of the 11th Hussars served dishes like Lobster Balaklava and Raglan's Fish Pie. These items appeared on a menu that was bordered, of course, by Tennyson's poem. It was, the critic determined, "an experience historians will dislike and gastronomes rather despise." An anomaly and a disappointment, it demonstrated not the lofty acclaim that the Chargers had once enjoyed, but the kitschy bottoms of mass culture that the legend had reached.[128]

***

Fintan O' Toole has recently remarked that the tendency to blur the ordinary and the epic, along with the habit of confounding success and failure, it is at the heart of Englishness. It also governs the afterlife of the Charge of the Light Brigade.[129] This tendency was made possible through the capaciousness of Tennyson's verses. It was evident too in the jokes of the Victorians, for whom the poem was so familiar that it became the punchline of a one-line riddle. In 1882, the comic serial *Judy* printed the following one-liner, which combined the novelty of illumination with the tradition of the cavalry charge: "The Charge of the Light Brigade: The Gas Bill."[130] Similarly, Mr. Ramsay's repetitions in *To the Lighthouse* relied on common knowledge, devoid of referent. The developments of the 1960s took these developments to new heights, or depths, at a moment when consumer culture was on the rise and the ideal of duty on the decline.

Across its long afterlife, the Charge summoned Englishness of a dutiful and praiseworthy, or perhaps of a fruitless and ill fated, variety. Even so, the Charge itself and those objects connected to it did not lose their luster wholesale. *Antiques Roadshow*, that arbiter of Englishness and authenticity, provided a stage for a reconsideration of the Charge in the autumn of 2013. At that time, nearly 160 years after the outbreak of the Crimean War, the BBC television series featured a latter-day trumpeter, Captain Holtby, sounding the Charge on William Brittain's bugle, its tones muted by age. The Bugle was a thing of no small value: it was worth between £30,000 and £40,000.[131] Its broader worth lay in the connections of past and present that it crystallized. "It is a fantastic piece of British military history," declared *Antiques Roadshow* firearms expert Bill Harriman. "You can reach out and actually touch history," he proclaimed.[132] When Captain Holtby blew the Charge, he connected past, present, and future with the dutiful reveille.[133]

The BBC staple of *Antiques Roadshow* is a fitting place to end a story of the Light Brigade and its legacies. This is not the only artifact connected with the Crimean War to appear on the show, however. There, experts have assessed the worth of Crimean sketchbooks and warfront letters as they have offered lessons in history and patrimony to loyal viewers. On several occasions, *Antiques Roadshow* has also featured the Victoria Cross, the military award for uncommon valor dating to the Crimean conflict. If the Charge of the Light Brigade became a conduit for considering duty in British cultural and social life, the Victoria Cross became a touchstone for honoring bravery at home and abroad. Its career as a commemorator of courage provides yet another thread for apprehending the impact of the Crimean War and its long legacies.

Part II

Avatars

3   The Brave

Established in 1856, the Victoria Cross is the highest honor granted by the British Armed Forces. Its namesake, Queen Victoria, instituted the award via a Royal Warrant as the Crimean War came to a close.[1] The award recognized a selected few, the bravest of the brave, who had distinguished themselves through their extraordinary acts in battle.[2] In the granting of the award, rank was of no consequence; courage in the face of an adversary was all that mattered. With the Warrant, the Queen created knights for a new day. The Crimean War was only the beginning of this order, which has celebrated bravery in battle ever since. At the centennial celebration of the Cross, Victoria's great-great granddaughter, Elizabeth II, addressed the awardees who had congregated from across the globe. The young Queen declared that the Cross bound them and their predecessors in a "golden thread of extraordinary courage."[3]

Like the Charge of the Light Brigade, the Victoria Cross is a product of the Crimean War. Those who venerated the Charge honored a select few, the noble 600 who dashed into the valley at the culmination of the Battle of Balaklava. In celebrating the Chargers, they upheld a broader value: that of duty. Like the Charge, the Victoria Cross created an exclusive fellowship around a guiding ideal. Intended as a rare award, it was granted a mere 111 times in the Crimea. To date, there have been fewer than 1,400 recipients of this royally sanctioned honor. Like the Charge of the Light Brigade, the Victoria Cross also embodies a Victorian value and a military ideal: that of bravery, or valor. Its *sine qua non* is the military man of action, who responds unerringly to war's demands, no matter the cost.

Like the Light Brigade, the Victoria Cross has a venerable legacy and a telling afterlife. While the Charge was a hallowed event marking a national trauma, the Cross is a treasured institution signaling British might. It is a mainstay in national life, with its lore the stuff of Victorian schoolboy stories and of twenty-first-century celebrity culture. The coveted medal itself provides a palpable connection to military heroism and to battle glory, making the Cross into a fetish. The Cross has been an object of desire across the ages. Warriors have sought out the distinction; families have safeguarded ancestral awards; regiments have showcased the accolades; and national museums have accumulated the medals.

Those Britons who commemorated the Charge of the Light Brigade, cleaved to its artifacts, and recited its verses all engaged with a noted legacy of the Crimean War. In contrast, those who venerated the Victoria Cross did not explicitly hearken back to the Crimean conflict. Yet, the Order was born out of the antinomies of the war. While the Charge was an example of the leadership's failures, the Cross was an effort to address mismanagement in wartime and beyond. It responded to the blunders of the hierarchical armed forces in egalitarian terms. It sought to substitute the bureaucratic and democratic in place of the privileged and outdated, all while offering a royal sanction coated in chivalry. It was, in short, an effort to compensate and console. It made war assimilable, even admirable, sanitizing its violence and turning it into a character lesson.

Born out of the exigencies of the Crimean moment, the Cross has had staying power well beyond. It has been offered up as a salve at junctures of violence, like the Indian Rebellion, and a hope in epochs of trauma, like the Great War. It has been a response to discontentment and unrest, extended, over the years, to subaltern troops across the empire. It has taken on particular importance at moments of imperial contraction and geopolitical change, looming large as a bond across the Commonwealth in the epoch of decolonization. And it has been an answer to modernization, as it has reached back, nostalgically, to an invented era of tradition. Although forged in the crucible of the Crimean War, the award's capacity to console has endured well beyond. Across its long career, the Victoria Cross has held the power to comfort and to compensate: soothing war-weary populations at times of loss, placating insurgent nations at times of disgruntlement, and providing fellowship at times of change.

This chapter traces the warps and wefts of the Cross's thread of courage. It considers the resilience, and the flexibility, of this award from the Crimean moment onward. The Cross was notably pliable. Imagined as an award for bravery in hand-to-hand combat of a romantic kind, it extended its reach to recognize the airplane fighters and the submarine warriors of the twentieth century. Offered first as an award to Britons, it included imperial subjects within its ranks. Intended explicitly for men at the outset, it may now be granted to women, though women remain eligible still in name only for membership in what remains an all-male brotherhood. In fact, the lived history of the honor – including the administration of the award, the careers of the recipients, and the traffic in the crosses – complicates any stories of transcendence. The Cross does not reside above the fray of pettiness and politics or outside of the logic of markets and media. Nor is it a talisman. It has not protected its wearers from errors of judgment or from reversals of fortune; nor has it shielded them from the indignities of poverty and the currents of racism. The thread of courage shows its knots along the way.

***

In the early days of 1856, the British had, at long last, achieved their elusive goal in the Crimean War: the capture of Sebastopol. The Treaty of Paris, whose passage marked the end of war's hostilities, was near. At that time, on January 29, 1856, Queen Victoria issued a Royal Warrant intended to create a "New Order of Valor." This highest military decoration was to be bestowed upon the bravest of the brave: those in the Army and Navy who had performed a "signal act of valor" and done so "in the presence of the enemy."[4] Successful recipients were to be nominated by Commanding Officers, approved by the War Office, and awarded by the Queen. This was an honor different from any preceding it in the history of the British armed forces. It married bravery and bureaucracy; it conjoined democracy and derring-do. The award was to be given solely according to merit, and not with regard to rank. As it reported the inauguration of this honor, the ever-critical *Saturday Review* declared, "The era of chivalry has not departed."[5] It had, in fact, begun again: by the Crimean War's end, there were over one hundred knights in this new Order of Valor.[6]

The emblem of this new order, at once the most egalitarian and the most exclusive in the British military, is the Victoria Cross: a simple Maltese Cross, struck, legendarily, from Russian cannons seized at Sebastopol. Held by a ribbon in crimson red for the Army or dark blue for the Navy, the Cross carries the words "For Valor" on the back. To convey the close relationship between monarchy and army, the Cross bears a lion atop a crown. From the 1850s, the medal has been produced solely by Hancock's Jewelers of London, struck only on order of the War Office. From the outset, critics decried the physical medal as a "plain and homely" object, "poor looking and mean in the extreme."[7] Yet it remains the sign of an exclusive fellowship of bravery. Its wearers enjoy, to this day, the privilege of appending the initials V.C. after their names and the security of receiving a lifetime annuity.[8]

The Cross, an invented tradition, was a response to the exigencies of the Crimean War.[9] Britain had entered the War with an Army untested in Europe since the days of Napoleon. The military leaders of that epoch – Nelson and Wellington – were no more, with Admiral Nelson having met his death in 1814 and Wellington, more recently, in 1852. And while hyperbolic, the allegation that the mid-century Army had been, in fact, "frozen in time at the moment of its victory at Waterloo" carried some truth.[10] Although some regiments had been involved in "little wars" across the empire, Britain entered the Crimean conflict with an Army that had not seen combat on the European continent since the days of Napoleon. In the subsequent years, as it sought to maintain its image and to boost morale, the peacetime Army had devoted much of its attention to the spectacular practices of drills and parades.[11] It was a living anachronism: beautifully dressed, but ill trained and ill equipped, as the Charge of the Light Brigade so well demonstrated.[12] Although the Army might have looked impressive, its organization was poor, its equipment inadequate, and its organization atrocious.[13]

The stock in the military's leadership was on the wane during the war. However, the star of the rank-and-file soldier was on the rise. His rising status represented a shift from the early nineteenth century, when an army of outcasts had fought for Great Britain. Castigated as "drunken, thieving, whoring" men, the Army's ranks had come from the meanest corners of society.[14] Wellington had characterized the men of his own forces as the "scum of the earth."[15] The Crimean War was a turning point, however, marking a decisive shift in the public regard for the common soldier.[16] During the conflict, the long-suffering soldier, who had endured privation, cold, and hunger, became an object of sympathy, affection, and pride. The *Morning Chronicle* noted that, "for the first time the soldier" had managed to excite "the interest of those at home beyond the narrow circle of his relatives and friends."[17] The Victorian public, skeptical of the Army's high command, came to believe that the Crimea's battles were won on the backs of the rank and file, "long-suffering, shrewd, and stolid."[18] No longer did British soldiers appear as scofflaws and oppressors. Instead, they were the brave defenders of British liberty against Russian despotism.[19]

In the face of the war's trials, and in the face of the leadership vacuum that it laid bare, there was a definite hunger for heroes. The Light Brigade's heroes were one such cast of characters. But the home front public was primed for more. An appetite for chivalry, valor, and bravery was ripe at the time of the war's fighting, kindled at least in part by the publication of Thomas Carlyle's *On Heroes, Hero-Worship and the Heroic in History*.[20] As literary critic Stefanie Markovits has noted, writers engaged in the wake of the Crimean War with this newfound appetite for chivalry as they produced tales of muscular Christianity, which looked back to the Elizabethan age as a stage for manly action fused with morality. Building upon these desires, the Victoria Cross promised, as an institution, to provide new knights for a new era.[21]

The project of enshrining new heroes – of legitimating chivalry through bureaucracy – had already taken root elsewhere. Across the European continent and across the Atlantic, states developed "national standards of heroism" as they sought to recognize rank-and-file soldiers, and not simply officers.[22] The French created the Legion of Honor in 1802, and orders sprang up as well in Prussia, the Netherlands, and Belgium. The American South showed a great interest in the regulated aggression of chivalry, with codes of honor hearkening back to a knightly past. Given these trends, the absence of a national award to recognize the rank-and-file soldier in Britain was especially notable at mid-century.[23]

It was in this climate – in the face of disenchantment with a hereditary aristocracy, in the wake of a hunger for heroes, and in the context of international reforms – that Queen Victoria called for a new Order of Valor.[24] Given by the War Office and bestowed by the Queen, the Cross was a prize that worked within the established military and political hierarchies. Even so, there were many who applauded the award for its transformative capacities. A "step in the right direction,"[25] it promised a "democracy of merit."[26] It recognized men regardless of rank.[27] "Valor in Private Jones is to be alike distinguished with valor in Major Mayfair," proclaimed *Lloyd's*.[28] General John Codrington, a real Crimean officer, and the humble "Sandy M'Ivor," an imagined Irish soldier, could both join its ranks, the *Saturday Review* noted approvingly. Even the "poorest house" could become the "abode of honor."[29] Captain, boatswain's mate, and seaman all stood on level ground.[30] The warrant promised to transform each and every one of these men into gallant knights in a new "order of chivalry."[31] "Private soldiers may now look forward to wearing a real distinction which kings may be proud to have earned the right to bear," the *Times* declared.[32] The *Morning Chronicle* anticipated welcoming "knights" of a "new class," all chosen, it imagined, "without distinction to professional rank."[33] The award did not derive from "error or favor," but rather from the "gallant prompting" of the recipient's "own stout heart."[34]

Accounts of the great gallantry of the Victoria Cross's recipients appeared in the *London Gazette*. Aficionados of the award believed that these citations provided insight into the character of the honorees.[35] They were, therefore, reproduced widely, sating the appetites of a public hungry for accounts of newfound chivalry. The first Victoria Cross winner, Naval Rear Admiral Charles Lucas, threw a live shell from his ship, the *Hecla*, saving the entire crew.[36] On a subsequent occasion, Captain William Peel did the same (Figure 3.1). Army Brevet Major Charles Lumley shot two Russians at the Redan and maintained his position though wounded.[37] Private John Alexander brought wounded soldiers

Figure 3.1 Captain William Peel depicted in his Act of Bravery. 1854.
Supplement to the *Illustrated London News*, June 20, 1857, *Illustrated London News Archive*, Mary Evans Picture Library

and an officer away from enemy fire.[38] Others held the colors amidst danger, repaired embrasures under fire, rescued wounded comrades, or fought hand-to-hand with enemies. These accomplishments appeared "like sets of extracts from the old chivalrous romances, or from old heraldic chronicles, telling the deeds of early chiefs."[39] Taken together, the citations of Victoria Cross winners provided excellent raw materials for those tales of pluck and bravery that the reading public so enjoyed. Time and again, they offered examples of "supreme courage" and "disregard for danger." The citations exemplified a "resolute boldness and a readiness for self-sacrifice that g[a]ve the lie to the cautious, the hesitant, and the defeatist."[40]

The Victoria Cross warrant privileged a "signal event" as the hallmark of valor when it came to offering up its rewards.[41] This event had particular contours. It was, more often than not, an "improvised" or "isolated act."[42] Under the warrant, a heroic individual engaged in hand-to-hand combat emerged as valor's apotheosis. Granted, in a war that combined such diverse elements as cavalry charges and trench fighting, the Victoria Cross was already anachronistic in its specifications, even at its very foundation. The expectations for the award required updating in the twentieth century, in the face of submarine and airplane warfare. Even as the award's stipulations shifted, however, the ideal of the "signal event" remained constant. There was a sense that the act, often performed in a split second, suggested qualities beyond itself. It was a mark of "steady, sturdy British valor" and an index of character.[43] Alongside the detailed descriptions of acts of "conspicuous bravery" performed on the battlefield or at sea, Victoria Cross citations abound with mentions of the "great enterprise," "determined resolution," and "great coolness" of the recipients.[44]

From the outset, there was a common understanding that the Victoria Cross might not only offer military distinction, but also augur future success. For this reason, young men from the officer classes and their families sought out the award, often flouting established protocol and usually in vain. Such was the case for George Waller, who served in the Crimea with the 7th Fusiliers. For young Waller, born in 1837, the Crimea represented his launching into an army career that lasted until 1891 and occasioned his rise to the rank of Lieutenant Colonel. It signified, equally, his entrance into manhood. During wartime, Waller endeared himself to many, cultivating a reputation that would please his family at home. His shining moment came at the Redan, where he, as a Lieutenant, volunteered to join a group of soldiers in storming a rifle pit under fire. "He will do a good thing or two someday," reflected an impressed Colonel Yea to a fellow officer.[45] Convinced of the same, the family later appealed to the War Office as part of a post-Crimean campaign for the Cross.[46]

In a similar, if more dogged fashion, Sir John Page Wood, the father of Henry Evelyn Wood, launched an appeal on behalf of his son, then a Lieutenant in the 13th Light Dragoon Guards. The senior Wood held that his son had been passed over for his gallantry, also at the Redan, where he rose from his sick bed and planted a ladder at a strategic location while under fire. His companion on the field of battle received the Victoria Cross for the feat, but Wood did not. Seeking to vindicate his son, Sir John Page Wood compiled an extensive dossier of letters attesting to the young man's "beautiful courage," "extreme intrepidity," and "exemplary" conduct. "Rely on it that none of his class can be recommended for the Victoria Cross without your brave boy being one," one advocate declared. Of the son's actions, another proclaimed, if this "be not valor, I know not what can deserve the name." However, the War Office did not concur.[47] But the young Wood was undeterred. He enjoyed an illustrious career in the armed forces, securing a Victoria Cross for his heroics in India only a few years later.

The cases of Waller and Wood suggest that, despite its democratizing aspirations, the Cross remained the prerogative of privilege. Yet, applications for the Cross came from humbler quarters, too, with noncommissioned officers and family members making equally vigorous and impassioned appeals. Lieutenant Corporal William Courtney put up a valiant fight, but to no avail.[48] In the longest lasting appeal, Thomas Morley continued his quest across the century.[49] He too fell short, as did Mrs. Jary, a widow. In 1856, she wrote proudly to the War Office of the successes enjoyed by her husband, who had fought illustriously in the Xhosa (Kaffir) War, where he had made, a daring "escape from a horde of savages." With their racist overtones and their hyperbole, her encomiums read as if lifted from the adventure literature of the day. To her disappointment, she learned that the Cross was not to be awarded retrospectively.[50] Also denied was paternal supplicant John Godfrey, whose late son, Lieutenant Godfrey of the 1st Battalion Rifle Brigade, had silenced two Russian artillery guns while under fire in the Crimea. The disconsolate father discovered that the Cross was not to be given posthumously.[51] Similarly aggrieved parents would have to wait for years for reprieve; by 1920, an updated warrant allowed for posthumous recognition.

Taken together, the efforts on the part of the privileged to grease the bureaucratic machinery of the Cross and the challenges faced by the less fortunate in navigating the cogs show the limitations of the award. These were not lost on public critics who pointed to the capricious and stinting nature of the honor. According to the *Daily News,* the troops believed that the authorities had been "too niggardly" in doling out the honor: there were only 111 awards in the entire war, with over half going to officers. Despite the democratic pretensions, the award still emanated from the "cold shade of the aristocracy."[52] This was perhaps unavoidable in a scenario where officers were to make the decisions. In fact, this stipulation gave way to a host of inconsistencies and irregularities. While many officers had long exhibited concern of a paternal nature for their men, there existed in other regiments a "wide, unbridgeable gap of social standing and human sympathy."[53] This was a chasm that the award could not bridge. Adding to the randomness of the honor was the fact that, while some officers had an "excessively low threshold for heroism," others held the bar impossibly high.[54] Despite the aspirations to the predictable and the democratic, the Victoria Cross was fundamentally hierarchical and idiosyncratic. As the *Saturday Review* so inimitably put it, "all deserved the Cross who got it, but some did not get it who deserved it quite as well."[55]

Even more than idiosyncratic, the most stringent criticism was that the Cross was malign in its purpose: in the dazzle of its ornament, it deflected from the inequities of the day. This was the critique launched in the radical *Reynolds's Newspaper*. From the outset, it dismissed the Cross as a moral fig leaf, meant to distract soldiers from injustices in the Army. Most notable was the perpetuation of corporal punishment via the lash, deployed for punishment until 1881. Soldiers shared the burden of flogging at this time with felons alone. Along with a handful of other news outlets, *Reynolds's Newspaper* mourned the persistence of, and even the uptick in, the use of the cat o' nine tails as the war lagged on to its end. In the late months of the conflict, soldiers were flogged for offences that ranged from desertion to sleeping to drunkenness.[56] It was an "ignominious punishment" for an English soldier to be "whipped like a hound" or, for that matter, a slave, to use an especially charged analogy in the 1850s.[57] Its persistence was an abomination among a people who extolled British liberty and decried Russian tyranny.[58]

These criticisms were minority opinions, however, at a time when the broader public hungered for heroes and for pageantry. Such an appetite was evident on the morning of the first investiture ceremony, held on June 26, 1857. At that time, Queen Victoria bestowed the Cross on sixty-two of the honor's original winners in London's Hyde Park. It was a sunny and breezy day, perfect for the grand pageant that had been planned. A crowd of thousands, coming from all social ranks, had gathered for the occasion, while still more crowded on the Park's outskirts.[59] At the sound of a gunshot, the Queen entered the Park dressed in a dark blue suit complete with military tunic to preside over the occasion and to award the Cross to the exemplars of bravery who paraded before her.[60] Some recipients were dressed in military regalia; others were bedecked in the uniforms of their current vocations, as policemen or as park keepers. A galling reminder of the tragedies of the war, several were injured. Parades of the injured became a common sight at Victoria Cross investiture ceremonies in subsequent years, as many recipients carried bodily markings of bravery's costs. As she passed by the awardees on her Roan Charger, the Queen inspected the men, pinning the Cross, a treasured talisman, directly on the officers' breasts.[61]

One witness to the occasion was liberal journalist and antislavery advocate Frederick Chesson who wrote for the *Morning Star*, a radical, anti-war publication founded by the likes of Richard Cobden and John Bright. In his diary he himself had decried the "evil barbarism" of war.[62] But, on the morning of June 26, 1857, he found himself affected by the goings on in Hyde Park. It was, he reported, "the grandest military spectacle" he "ever beheld" in his life. He sketched the "splendid sight" in great detail, with its grand royal procession, its parade of heroes, and its "military evaluations of the most dazzling and exciting character."[63] Though a critic of the war, Chesson was a fan of the ceremony. Such was the allure of bravery and its trappings. The *Saturday Review* was correct: the "age of chivalry" had "not departed"; it had only just begun.[64]

***

Across the remainder of the nineteenth century, this new era of chivalry unfolded under the sign of the Victoria Cross. Bookended by the Indian Rebellion and the South African War, those years were no *Pax Britannica*. They were, instead, marked by successive imperial wars in Asia and in Africa, the Anglo-Afghan, Ashanti, and Anglo-Zulu Wars among them. In the wake of these conflicts, the fellowship of the Cross expanded to include hundreds more Britons and colonial troops.[65] These awards worked to sanitize violence, making conquest palpable and agreeable whilst building empire abroad and cohesion at home. In Britain, public culture and print culture celebrated the Cross, promulgating stories of bravery for a nation of armchair warriors.[66] With its ability to condense personal fortune and national history into morality tales, the Cross provided lessons about courage and character. One of the virtues embodied by the Cross was that of loyalty to both Crown and country. Reinforcing this understanding, Queen Victoria and her descendants added legitimacy and luster to the honor, as they steered the shape of the royal warrant and as they committed the medal in ceremonies large and small.

The need for the Cross was especially great in the immediate aftermath of the Crimean War. Frederick Chesson and all of those who enjoyed the Victoria Cross investiture in Hyde Park would have been painfully aware of events going on across the globe, in India, at the same time. May 1857 witnessed the outbreak of the Indian Rebellion, when Sepoys stationed in Meerut turned on the British Army. The violence meted out over the following months by both sides was horrific. Civilians, women, and children were not immune. From the vantage point of the British at home, the situation seemed to invite feats of heroism worthy of the Victoria Cross. As they assessed the aftermath of the Indian Rebellion, Britons could learn about the heroics of Evelyn Wood, who was denied the Cross in the Crimea.[67] In a later, successful campaign for the Cross, he singlehandedly attacked a band of robbers and rescued an imperiled merchant. They could discover, too, the deeds of Field Marshal Earl Roberts, then a lieutenant, who killed two sepoys to save a standard.[68] And they could revere the acts of common soldiers, like Valentine Bambrick, who slayed a rival without fear or compunction.[69] Taken together, the grisly citations had the effect of legitimating – and even celebrating – the armed, imperial violence wrought by the British on the subcontinent. They raised the Victoria Cross heroes above the fray of the melee, while they lowered the rebels as unworthy antagonists. In the end, they played a small part in soothing a traumatized home front with tales of British overcoming.[70]

An important chapter in the mainstreaming of the Victoria Cross and, with it, in the domestication of military violence, transpired just after the Indian Rebellion, when a Victoria Cross Gallery opened in London in 1859.[71] This was a project masterminded by Victoria Cross recipient Robert Lindsay, who won a Cross at the Battle of the Alma, and by artist Louis Desanges, a celebrated portrait painter for the *beau monde*.[72] Together, they aspired to produce a gallery of bravery containing portraits of Victoria Cross winners. The enterprising Desanges endeavored to capture those who had won the honor in the Crimean War and in the Indian Rebellion, all engaged in the acts that had brought them glory. His method involved working from live sittings and gathering eyewitness accounts; his style melded history painting and parlor aesthetics. Energetic in his habits and swift with his brush, Desanges debuted his collection of fifty Victoria Cross portraits at Leicester Square's Egyptian Gallery. Critics praised Desanges for the intent of his works, which provided a monument to Victoria Cross heroes.[73] Many believed that the painted portraits did far more to portray the bravery of the VC recipients than had the written notices. But others were not convinced by the renderings of the brave. The *Athenaeum* found that Desanges' subjects had a "drawing room aspect" and a "rose water delicacy."[74] They lacked a sense of heroism or gravitas appropriate to war. These criticisms notwithstanding, the collection enjoyed longevity, moving to Sydenham's Crystal Palace and later to Oxford's Wantage Gallery, where it remained for some forty years, until dispersal and neglect prompted the gallery's end at the turn of the twentieth century.[75]

Although limited in their execution, Desanges' portraits enjoyed a vigorous afterlife on the page. The *Illustrated London News* conveyed the painter's work to an audience far beyond the gallery. And even more significantly, printing entrepreneur Samuel Beeton brought the painted renderings of Victoria Cross heroes to ever-larger readerships. They appeared first in serial form in the *Boys' Own Magazine* and subsequently in the dedicated volume, *Our Soldiers and the Victoria Cross*.[76] Alongside these renderings of the portraits, Beeton showcased biographical sketches of Victoria Cross winners, whose daring exploits offered up lessons about pluck, endurance, and bravery. His was a "capital boy's book," pitching itself to the nation's youth.[77] In the annals of the heroes of the Crimean War and the Indian Rebellion, young readers could gain valuable lessons about conduct. As Beeton noted, "boys – worthy to be called boys – are naturally brave."[78] He therefore offered the exploits of these military exemplars to his audience. His strategy was akin to that employed by contemporaries like Samuel Smiles, author of *Self-Help*, who preached the virtues of perseverance, method, and self-sufficiency as he spun the biographies of men like the inventor James Watt and the potter Josiah Wedgwood into success stories.[79] In similar fashion, Beeton provided his young readers with lasting lessons in "chivalrous courage and excellent conduct" as he introduced an array of Victoria Cross heroes.[80]

It did not take long, in such a context, for enterprising Victoria Cross winners to capitalize on their own stories, as they sought to transform military heroism into popular celebrity. The most avid self-promoter was Thomas Henry "Lucknow" Kavanagh, the first civilian to win the Victoria Cross and one of only five to do so. An Irish civil servant, Kavanagh earned his Cross at the Relief of Lucknow, where he successfully disguised himself as a native.[81] So great was his renown that friends suggested he write a book on the matter. In 1860 he delivered *How I Won the Victoria Cross*, which added wealth to his fame.[82] Yet, in rushing into print, he may have tarnished his Cross.[83] His deed, one reviewer noted, appeared in the autobiography as "a plain and unvarnished picture of a brave man performing a perilous duty." However, his account more generally evinced the "worst evils of the autobiographical class," which led to puffery and braggadocio.[84] This was a critique that fell in line with a broader contemporary concern that the Victoria Cross engendered brash action and self-seeking fame.[85] In Kavanagh's case, unhinged ambition extended from the printed page into his daily conduct. It led, in the end, to his downfall. Kavanagh's star rose with the award of the Victoria Cross, but it fell with his removal from the Civil Service in Oudh in the 1870s in the face of his excessive debt.

In the nineteenth century, good credit and good character worked in alignment with one another. Implied in the granting of the Victoria Cross was the recognition of character. Its warrant sought to recognize "signal acts of valor" performed in the heat of battle. Its progenitors, moreover, understood these "signal acts" as exactly that: acts that pointed to larger expressions of exemplarity. To deviate was to sully the Cross. Lucknow Kavanagh may have engaged in behaviors questionable for a VC winner, but he did not relinquish his medal. There were, however, other Victoria Cross recipients who were less fortunate in the consequences of their subsequent actions. In Queen Victoria's day, a VC winner charged with "treason, cowardice, felony" or another "infamous crime" forfeited his prize.[86] James McGuire lost his Cross for stealing a cow; James Collis relinquished his for bigamy; and Valentine Bambrick gave up his award when he faced assault charges.[87] These were three of the eight VC winners to lose the coveted medal. This Victorian stranglehold went out with George V, who determined, in 1920, that the Cross was inalienable: "Even were a VC to be sentenced to be hanged for murder," the King declared, "he should be allowed to wear his VC on the scaffold."[88]

George V's declaration signals the monarchy's centrality in shaping the Victoria Cross, whether in terms of policy or ceremony. This role hearkened back, of course, to George V's grandmother, Queen Victoria. The Queen had inaugurated the Cross and presided over the initial investiture ceremony at the dawn of the era of royal spectacle.[89] Across her lifetime, she appeared at ceremonies large and small. While her stewardship of the Cross began with the mid-nineteenth century's Crimean conflict, it ended with the South African War, occurring at the century's close. Like the Crimean War, this latter contest pitted European combatants against one another. Like the Crimean War, it revealed an Army unprepared in military vigor and military intelligence. Here, once again, the Cross proved to be a signifier of bravery and a source of consolation. The moment, in fact, prompted an important innovation in the granting of posthumous awards. This practice was discouraged, or at best irregular, in the years leading up to the South African War; it did not receive official sanction until the institution of the 1920 Warrant. But the striking case of a young Lieutenant Frederick Hugh Sherston Roberts, the son of Field Marshall Earl Roberts, who won a Cross himself after the Indian Rebellion, vaulted the possibilities of a posthumous honor to the forefront: the award had the capacity to comfort a family and to console a nation. At the Battle of Colenso, Roberts, only twenty-seven, had lost his life when he tried, valiantly, to save the guns.[90] Even more publicized than the act of bravery was the manner of giving the posthumous award. "Here is something that I have tied with my own hands and that I beg you not to open until you get home," Queen Victoria told Lady Roberts.[91] Woman to woman, the elderly Queen thus extended comfort to the military mother, in a gesture that reveals at once the intimate qualities, and the personal privilege, of the celebrated medal.

Taken together, the royal recognition and the celebrity that came with the Cross at the turn of the twentieth century were difficult to resist. The award remained particularly compelling, and frustratingly elusive, for one long-suffering veteran of the Crimea, Sergeant Thomas Morley. Morley had repeatedly sought the Cross at the war's end and long after. He renewed his pursuit one last time, in the year 1902, when he was seventy-two years of age. The wake of the South African War had brought the

Victoria Cross ever more polish and luster; it had, additionally, offered to the aged veterans of the Crimea a newfound concern and respect. A member of the celebrated 17th Lancers, Morley had charged with the Light Brigade. The action for which he sought recognition occurred, however, at the Battle of Inkerman, where he had pulled Coronet Archibald Clevland, young, beloved, and injured, off of the field of battle. The action may have been for naught: Morley did not win the Cross and Clevland did not survive the war.[92] But it opened up a decades-long quest, wherein Morley appealed severally to the War Office, to the grieving family of Archibald Clevland, to his regimental brethren, and, eventually, to King Edward VIII. Despite the King's interest, the appeal again fell short. Perhaps the old soldier took some consolation in the fact that he came away from the encounter with an increased pension of fifteen pence a day.[93] And, though spurned by the War Office, the thwarted Morley was embraced in his hometown. In Nottingham, he became something of a local personality, known for his "long pointed beard" and his remarkably "erect carriage." The Cross may have eluded Morley, but not so good will. With the support of Nottingham's Crimea and Indian Mutiny Veterans Association, he enjoyed a ceremonial burial, accompanied by men from the First Battalion, the Leicester Regiment, and his own beloved 17th Lancers. Morley may have lacked the Cross. However, he became a warmly regarded character, an exemplar of patriotism and a beacon of courage, by the time of his 1906 death. He was, despite it all, a military man to the death. As the *Nottingham Daily Guardian* told it, "There was none prouder than he of the medals pinned on his breast."[94]

***

Morley's passage reminds us that the ranks of the Crimea's veterans were passing away as Great Britain moved toward World War I. While it dealt the death knell to Victorian ideals of duty, World War I witnessed the largest number of Victoria Crosses given in any single conflict. There were, in the end, a staggering 620 awards, besting the 500 granted in the decades leading up to the Great War by far. The intensity and velocity of total war meant more awards to more men. Technologies of modern warfare challenged the premise for the awarding of the Cross, which had been predicated upon hand-to-hand combat, already an anachronism in the mid-nineteenth century. Submarine warfare in the Navy and remote attacks in the Army upended the traditional understanding of the award's parameters. So too did the matter of airplane bombing. A belated response, the 1920 Warrant, signed by then War Secretary Winston

Churchill, sought to meet the new circumstance in extending consideration to the Royal Air Force. Additionally, this warrant allowed officially for the granting of posthumous awards, thereby sanctioning the practice that had begun some years before. In fact, in World War I nearly a quarter of the awards went to the deceased. Finally, the 1920 Warrant allowed the provision of the Cross to women. However, its fellowship remains a masculine preserve in practice and in spirit to this very day.[95]

The proliferation of the Cross during the Great War is not a story of benign institutional inevitability. It was deeply political as well. There were attempts, at the time, to use the Cross as a tool of unity in a fracturing empire. This is evident in the extension of the award to Indian troops – a provision developed, notably, before the war, but highly serviceable during its course, when the Cross signified that loyal fighters had not given their lives in vain.[96] It was evident, too in the celebration of Irish recipients – most notably, Michael O'Leary, a nationalist who came to fight for the British cause, performing the superhuman feat of single-handedly storming two German barricades, killing many German soldiers, and injuring others in February 1915. This display of an Irishman's raw bravery and remarkable loyalty had its uses in London and in Ireland. O'Leary was feted as a hero on the occasion of his award and at his investiture later that summer; he became the face of a recruitment poster used in Ireland (Figure 3.2).[97] But he attracted the ire of the Ulster Volunteers. The occasion became the subject of a satirical, and critical, one-act play written by George Bernard Shaw in 1915, but not performed until 1920. The play told of the predicament of a Victoria Cross hero, Dennis O'Flaherty, who returns to Ireland to recruit soldiers for the British Army after his great personal victories. At home, he is caught between his mother, a nationalist who believes he is fighting for the German cause, and his fiancé, who hopes to depend on a Victoria Cross pension. And he is left, too, to explain imperial double standards to a naïve, if well meaning, English squire. In the end, Shaw's trenchant critique ranges widely, with no group coming out unscathed. It exposes the opportunism of the British in their recruitment of the Irish; it also foregrounds the limited minds of the local peasantry. It points, finally, to the arbitrary limits of the awarding of the Victoria Cross which come down to luck, as O'Flaherty demonstrates so well.[98]

Critiques like Shaw's notwithstanding, the Cross retained an allure in World War I and its aftermath, even in the face of disillusionment. It remained an instrument of consolation and consensus, supplying a steady stream of heroes for a new age and inspiring a host of admirers. One interwar tribute came from Rudyard Kipling. In *Land and Sea Tales for*

Figure 3.2 Recruitment poster from World War I: VC Michael O'Leary. c. 1915. Mary Evans Picture Library. Onslow Auctions Limited

Scouts and Guides, Kipling rehashed the history of the Cross for an interwar audience of young readers. With admiration, he looked nostalgically on the hand-to-hand combat of the Crimea, as he longed for the days of yore. Yet, in keeping with the intentions of the progenitors,

Kipling cast the Cross as a flexible and living institution, designed to award chivalric impulses in changing times. He especially admired its egalitarian spirit, if within limits. As Kipling explained the requirements for the Cross, he reminded his readership of interwar youth that "conspicuous bravery" was the sole requirement. "Nothing else makes any difference."[99] Yet, while he hewed to notions of meritocracy, Kipling held on to hierarchies of rank and race. In jarring and painful language that bears the racist mark of its moment, he proclaimed that anyone was worthy of the Cross, from a "Duke" to a "Negro." By the time of Kipling's writing, the Cross had been extended to Sikh, Gurkha, and West Indian soldiers, not to mention to the Irish. Echoing a refrain from earlier days, he reiterated that the Cross was an index of character; the act of an instant indicated the mettle of a man. To earn the Cross, one had to lose his head, while holding on to it all the same. "The order is a personal decoration and the honor and glory of it belongs to the wearer," explained Kipling, "but he can only win it by forgetting himself, his own honor and glory, by working for something beyond and outside and apart from his own self. And there seems to be no other way in which you get anything in this world worth the keeping."[100]

***

Kipling's character type found its expressions in the men who won the Victoria Cross. One of the 620 men to receive the VC for his heroics in World War I was Sir John "Jackie" Smyth, who performed valiantly on the Western Front, where he led a conveyance of bomb supplies near enemy territory in 1915.[101] Smyth epitomized the Victoria Cross hero as typified by Kipling and, before him, by Beeton. In a foreword to his 1959 autobiography, Smyth's wife cast her husband as an orderly, purposeful man of action – never wasting time, yet "never in a rush." Like so many Victoria Cross winners, her husband was as gentle and modest off the field of battle as he was forceful and prepossessing on it, with a "rocklike courage which shows itself in ordinary life just as much as in war." It was, Mrs. Smyth explained, "a moral quality far more than a manifestation of physical bravery."[102] Once again, the Cross came down to character.

Smyth exemplified the fellowship of the Cross, with its strengths and limitations. Despite its democratic aspirations, the Cross continued to recognize a particular, and anachronistic, elite military masculinity. Smyth was every bit the upper-class Victorian, born in the year 1893 to a prominent family. His education culminating at Sandhurst, Smyth went on to become an officer in the Indian Army and then to serve in the world wars. He fought as well in the interwar struggles on the Indian frontier. In the years following the wars, he devoted himself to broader aims – to the service of country as a Member of Parliament for the Conservative Party, to the service of sport in writing the rules of lawn tennis, and to the service of the Victoria Cross as the long-standing chair of the Victoria and George Cross Society. These roles suited well the passions of the indefatigable Smyth. He was a defender of the British Empire and an apologist for it, too. He was an enthusiast for the monarchy, who delighted in royal recognition. Finally, he was a no-nonsense conservative, dedicated to fighting communism during the Cold War. With his character, career, and values, Smyth provides a view onto the twentieth-century career of the Victoria Cross. The annals of Jackie Smyth allow for an understanding of how the Cross sustained a particular variant of Victorian values as it brought imperial nostalgia, Conservative values, and monarchical majesty into union.

Smyth frequented public ceremonies around the Victoria Cross in the twentieth century and planned his share of them, too. He made an appearance at a Garden Party hosted by George V and held at Buckingham Palace on June 23, 1920 (Figure 3.3). In his autobiography, Jackie Smyth described the event as an especially moving occasion. Held in the aftermath of the war, it offered up a living museum of VC winners.[103] Though there were no Crimean VCs in attendance, 1857's bravery was represented by the presence of Sir Dighton Probyn, a veteran nearing ninety years of age who had won his Cross on the subcontinent in the mid-Victorian era. Mustering all the vigor that was left to him, he insisted on getting out of his wheelchair for royal inspection at the Palace. Probyn was one of 324 winners in attendance, representing the Army, the Navy, and the Royal Air Force, which sent three of the newest recipients of the Cross. Ambitiously designed and impeccably choreographed, the Garden Party was the culmination of a day of celebration and remembrance that included a luncheon at Wellington Barracks and a public procession from there to the Palace. Newspapers lauded the occasion as "'the most wonderful sight in the history of the war'" and "'the most remarkable procession the world has ever seen.'"[104] The parade may have provided a consolation in the face of the war's losses, but it was also a distraction from the war's costs. To adulate individual heroes was to obfuscate the war's carnage and casualties. As Smyth himself noted, on the occasion of the 1920's Garden Party, many of the Great War's recipients were too disabled to attend.

A subsequent reunion, in 1929, also gathered holders of the Victoria Cross. Held in November of that year to coincide with the anniversary of the Armistice, it brought together 321 Victoria Cross winners, some crippled, from the over 400 then living. The list of honorees, from England, Canada, Australia, and India, serves as a reminder of the global reach of the British armed forces, and, with it, of the mother country's great dependence

Figure 3.3 Souvenir Handkerchief. Garden Party of Victoria Cross Heroes. 1920. Mary Evans Picture Library

on its colonies. Coming nearly a decade after the 1920 reunion, 1929's gathering provides a stark marker of the passage of time. Three veterans of the Indian Rebellion had attended in 1920; nine years later there were no more. Instead, the event focused on the losses of the Great War with an occasion that combined a celebration of bravery with a ritual of remembrance. In his recollections, Smyth relayed that the site of the sumptuous dinner, the House of Lords, was decorated with an ornament of poppies taking the shape of the Victoria Cross.[105] The Great War and its aftermath were front and center throughout, in all sorts of ways, with a special production of the World War I play, *Journey's End,* for the honorees in a London theatre, and with a procession to the Cenotaph, the World War I memorial at Whitehall.[106] There, a moving choreography linked the Victoria Cross to a history of family sacrifice and family pride. Wearing the Cross won by her deceased father, a young girl laid a wreath at the monument, while her maternal grandfather, also a VC winner, looked on.[107]

As they contained war's atrocities in ritual, ceremonies such as these sought to endorse the Cross. But they could, as well, reveal cracks in the order, limitations to the award, and shortcomings in the brotherhood of bravery. In 1929, for instance, the chilly November day proved a trial for some of the Cross winners, despite their feats of bravery in past wars. One poor recipient, wearing only a thin suit and lacking a coat, shivered with malaria as he stood in the cold and wet. As if to materialize the brotherhood across class and across time, a man of rank, Lord Jellicoe, draped a mackintosh around the "little cockney."[108] Smyth may have relayed this incident as part of an effort to portray the bonds of brotherhood. But it showed, as well, the failure of the state to care sufficiently for veterans, even the most decorated, in the midst of economic upheaval and in their old age.

Strewn across the country and appearing in print, the archives of the Cross reveal similar situations of privation. They demonstrate, too, the lasting trauma of war. Such was the case for James Hewitson, a VC winner in World War I.[109] It was not uncommon for VC winners to suffer the worst of the ailments wrought by war trauma.[110] A longtime sufferer of neurasthenia, Hewitson had been in and out of hospitals for the better part of twenty years. In fact, 1951's Armistice Day was the first observance that found him at "home sweet home," in his own words. For the occasion, the old veteran was invited by the British Legion to lay a wreath on the war memorial in his Lancashire village. It was, he believed, a "great honor." The only problem was that the crimson ribbon on his Victoria Cross had grown worn, threadbare, and shabby. Could the War Office, he wondered, "kindly forward a few inches of VC ribbon?" The War Office received the request from Hewitson too late to address the need by Armistice Day, but it passed on new ribbon all the same. We are left to wonder whether Hewitson laid the wreath, nonetheless, worn ribbon, broken soul, and all.[111]

The case of Hewitson and Armistice Day points forward to an uptick of interest in the Cross, and in military ceremony, in the 1950s. This growing interest occurred in the aftermath of World War II, which gave the Cross new luster. Winston Churchill, that great orator of bravery, was fascinated by the Cross.[112] Against the backdrop of his premiership, World War II vaulted the honor back into the public mind. Its 180 winners personified the modernity of the moment while recalling the chivalry of yore. James Brindley Nicolson, a pilot who stood a striking 6 feet 4 inches, was the sole winner of the Cross in the Battle of Britain. James "Frogman" Magennis, an Irish daredevil diver, rose to great celebrity after his heroics in the Pacific.[113] As these two examples demonstrate, Englishmen and Irishmen continued to win the Cross during World War II. So too did troops from the settler colonies of Australia, New Zealand, and Canada. Finally, the award went to combatants from across the imperial globe, often with great fanfare. During the War, *Times* readers could find in abundance notices such as the following: "Another VC for the Gurkhas," "Posthumous VC for Punjabi," "Another Burma VC," and "VC for Maori Subaltern."[114] Human interest stories focused on Sefanaia Sukanaivalu, who grew up in undeveloped Fiji, for the sacrifice of his own life in the Solomon Islands. Such stories played well in the papers in Britain.[115] Grantors and publicists alike may have seen in these small gestures the possibilities for building a loyal flank in Asia. If so, the era of decolonization would have left them disappointed.

In the tumultuous years after the World War II, the Cross became a powerful symbol of the British monarchy, the Conservative party, and especially the British Commonwealth. It was an object of desire in public and in private life.[116] Its potency was especially evident during the 1950s as Britain embraced a new Queen and faced a new world order. Ceremonial events across the decade provided occasions to knit together the Monarchy and the Cross, in the hopes of honoring a brave past and envisioning a bright future. Yet, these occasions were also moments where longing and loss came to the fore. The 1953 Coronation of Queen Elizabeth II is one such example. For the occasion, Victoria Cross winners and their spouses enjoyed special seating. Maud Sylvester, the elderly daughter of a Crimean War veteran, found herself shut out of these provisions. Eager to attend the Coronation in select company, Sylvester wrote directly to Prime Minister Winston Churchill. "Can you help in any way to enable me to see Her Majesty's Coronation Procession?" she entreated. Her father had won the Victoria Cross nearly one hundred years beforehand, at the Siege of the Redan. Although she was a direct descendant of the original fellowship of the brave, Sylvester was ineligible for a ticket, as a daughter and not a spouse. "I feel very hurt," she confided in the Prime Minister of her exclusion, "and you are the only person who can assist me." There is no evidence of Churchill's leaping to Miss Sylvester's aid.[117] But perhaps she was among the audience that heard an address by the Prime Minister two years later, in 1955, at a Centenary luncheon for daughters and sons of those who had fought in the Crimean War, held at London's Connaught Rooms, where fifty-six septuagenarians, octogenarians, and nonagenarians gathered. "People will not look forward to posterity who never look backward to their ancestors," Churchill told them, as he borrowed a line from Edmund Burke, and glossed across a violent century, to sketch a long lineage of bravery in Britain.[118]

By far, the most high-profile event involving the Victoria Cross in the 1950s was a set of centennial celebrations taking place in June 1956, 100 years from the time of the issue of the initial warrant and 99 years to the day that Queen Victoria had feted the original recipients. This celebration of the brave fused together the Monarchy, the Commonwealth, and the Cross. Organized by a Joint Services Working Committee, this week-long series of events at the onetime heart of empire was a year in the planning. Its occasions included a relic display at Marlborough House, a remembrance service at Westminster Abbey, a special visit to Hampton Court, and even an evening of entertainment at the BBC's studios.[119] A celebration of Commonwealth courage for a postwar world, the impeccably planned occasion brought to London 100 Victoria Cross winners from abroad and 200 from across Britain, along with some 900 relatives. Its centerpiece was a grand military parade of the brave through London's Hyde Park culminating in the Queen's speech.[120] It was a fitting ceremony for a nation that, having lost an empire, was searching for a role.[121]

Eager to capitalize on the occasion of the centenary, the Commonwealth Relations Office sought to bring as many Victoria Cross winners from across the globe to London for the festivities as possible. Enabling these pilgrimages required lengthy negotiations for the Office, which found itself in the role of diplomatic arbiter and travel agent, as it brokered arrangements with India and Pakistan, with Canada and South Africa, and with Australia and New Zealand. Its work paid off in enabling the journeys of far-flung VC winners to London. Veterans from Australia and New Zealand made the long trek to the mother country. Sikh and Gurkha winners came in their traditional dress. Relatives of Fijian and Maori posthumous awardees made their ways, too, representing their slain kin.[122] These very travels kindled excitement for the occasion. The press, in turn, translated these adventures into human-interest stories, as it documented the many approaches to London. In the process, it repackaged the loss of an empire as a story of Commonwealth courage.

Taken together, the several elements of the week in London sought to produce this understanding. To do as much, they gestured, simultaneously, to the past and to the future, as they situated the Victoria Cross within a long tradition of bravery, one that dated back to the nineteenth century. The ambitious exhibit at Marlborough House highlighted the historical origins of the Victoria Cross in its showcase of the Russian guns used in the Crimea, its display of the original Victoria Cross Warrant, and its hanging of the first award ever given, that granted to Charles Lucas of the Royal Navy.[123] It included, as well, the dress that Queen Victoria had worn in Hyde Park and the disguise that Thomas Kavanagh had donned in Lucknow. There were, additionally, showpieces from more modern moments in the Cross's history – a World War I tank and an Air Force uniform. Those who visited the exhibit thus attained an appreciation for the Victoria Cross across its hallowed career.

In the week's culminating occasion, Queen Elizabeth II offered homages to the past and gestures to the future in her Hyde Park address to the 300 Victoria Cross winners, men of many ages, races, and classes, who had fought in conflicts from the South African War to the Korean War (Figure 3.4). The young Queen evoked the spirit of 1856 in her Centenary remarks. She recalled the day when her great-great grandmother had pinned the award on the chests of sixty-two winners. Ninety-nine years on, the men assembled before her in Hyde Park stood in a distinguished line of history. They were, in Queen Elizabeth's words, "successors of that first gallant band." When she paid heed to the Cross and its winners, Queen Elizabeth celebrated the ties forged by acts of bravery across the ages and across the globe. She linked past, present, and future; she bound nation, empire, and Commonwealth. In this spirit, she welcomed those who gathered before her, whose lives and stories were "linked by a golden thread of extraordinary courage."[124]

The celebration was wrapped in the trappings of the past. However, the broader intent of the event was to look forward in an effort to fashion the Victoria Cross as a fellowship for a new day. Along with the *Times* and with the Archbishop of Canterbury, Queen Elizabeth II declared courage to be "the commonplace inheritance of all citizens of the Commonwealth." To hear them both tell it, courage was the glue that bound the Commonwealth together, even after its soldiers, once subjects of the British Empire, had come to inhabit their own republics. As the vessel for courage, the Commonwealth could enable belonging in all sorts of ways. According to the young Elizabeth II, the VC winners were "men of all ranks and they came from all walks of life. They were of different colors and creeds. They fought in many lands and with many different weapons." But they had bravery in common. If, at its inception, the Victoria Cross had sought to contain wartime critique through the trappings of chivalry, it might, a century on, contain imperial fissures in a rhetoric of Commonwealth diversity. Although separated by race, religion, and region, the winners of the Cross were bound by bravery. As the Queen told it, "Each man of them all gave the best that a man can give."[125] With its empire dwindling, Britain was poised to become the custodian of the courage of the Commonwealth and its diverse populations.[126]

Figure 3.4 Victoria Cross Parade in Hyde Park. Queen Elizabeth II talks to veterans during inspection. 1956. Trinity Mirror. Mirrorpix. Alamy Stock Photo.

On the heels of the 1956 Reunion, the rhetoric of Commonwealth brotherhood attained institutional realization. Those who had assembled might "disperse to the ends of the earth," but they remained bonded within a fellowship of the brave.[127] At the close of the occasion, Jackie Smyth rose to lead a new organization – the Victoria and George Cross Society. The venerable society included among its members not only winners of the Victoria Cross, but also recipients of the George Cross, a civilian order established during World War II by King George VI. The fledgling organization sought, in Smyth's own words, "to cement the brotherhood of the orders of the Victoria Cross throughout the Commonwealth," and, in so doing, to kindle world peace.[128] Over the years, the Society sponsored reunions, which brought recipients of the Cross, free of charge, to London for ceremonial dinners. These occasions were nostalgic displays of bygone valor, royal pomp, and orientalist flair (on one occasion, a recipient's widow came out of Purdah to meet the Queen), not to mention conservative politics. Attendees included the likes of Harold Macmillan, Lord Mountbatten, and Michael Profumo. These exercises in nostalgia continued through the 1970s and even beyond, with the "bravest of the brave" gathering in London even then for fellowship and ceremony.[129]

In the postwar era, respect for tradition, nostalgia for a bygone era, and longing for empire all added to the luster of the Cross.[130] These dynamics were on display in the reunions of the Victoria and George Cross Society. They were additionally evident in a set of global dynamics that made Crosses themselves into objects of desire. Crosses had been lost, forged, or stolen for decades. A growing interest in the honor during World War II, combined with a slowdown in awards after the conflict, kindled a passion for the Cross itself. Military regiments seeking to preserve their grandeur aimed to secure the medals of servicemen who had won the award.[131] Fundraising exhibitions across the English-speaking world endeavored to display the Cross, thereby collecting monies for the troops. In the face of these developments, stories of stolen, copied, and counterfeited medals abounded. With this spike in interest, the War Office found itself in the unexpected position of gatekeeper, patrolling the movement of objects through auction houses, deciding when to issue replacements, and considering how to regulate the production of fakes. Crosses went missing in Johannesburg, Montreal, and Nepal. To the surprise of many would-be owners of Victoria Crosses, it had not been uncommon for winners to obtain duplicate copies over the years, whether for the purpose of selling the originals, offering doppelgangers to sweethearts, or guarding against thievery.[132] Concerned to regulate the traffic in Crosses, Jackie Smyth – whose very own Cross had been stolen – stepped in to govern the sales. He railed against fakes. In the unlikely event that a Cross needed selling, he urged families to give right of first refusal to regimental museums across Britain.[133] An object of desire and a symbol of bravery across the ages, the Cross offered a tangible connection to tradition and to history at a time of loss and at a moment of change.

Finally, for those who could not possess a Cross, there were other ways to gain proximity to a lineage of bravery at the end of empire. Archives from the 1950s onward reveal a trail of Victoria Cross enthusiasts, especially schoolboys, who gathered signatures of award holders. Signatures were things of value. It was not uncommon for those in attendance at a commemorative event – a dinner or a theater performance – to sign a program as a trace of their presence and participation. In the 1950s, in the aftermath of the centenary, schoolboy Alan Cumberland wrote assiduously to regimental associations to obtain the signatures of Victoria Cross recipients. He dutifully pasted these, along with hand-copied citations of Victoria Cross notices, in a cherished scrapbook.[134] Such pursuits continued over the coming decades. Although the Victoria Cross had fallen out of view by the 1970s, with the slowing of the awards to a mere trickle, it attracted schoolboy attention still. Twenty years after Alan Cumberland had collected his own signatures, another student, Peter Sharpe of Coventry, spent months copying the citations of all of World War II's VC winners into a scrapbook. To hear him tell it, a letter from "that splendid old soldier" Jackie Smyth provided a real "bright patch" as the young Sharpe prepared to take his school exams.[135]

Other ordinary Britons continued to cultivate an interest in the award during the 1970s, as the case of Linda Clarke, of Stoke-on-Trent, attests. Clarke gathered autographs from Victoria Cross recipients who fought in the world wars. Judging from their responses, the old warriors appreciated this attention in their later years. Major David Jamieson, who earned his Cross in World War II, was "delighted" by the request. He took some reassurance in the fact that Linda Clarke knew "what VC stands for." "The other day someone asked me if it meant Vice Chairman!" he confided. The reply of Captain Richard "Dick" Annand, a World War II veteran, suggests, at least, that Ms. Clarke was not alone in her pursuit of signatures. Annand noted his appreciation for the self-addressed and stamped envelope that Ms. Clarke had included with hr request. "Many don't bother!" he exclaimed. And, in his correspondence with Ms. Clarke, an elderly Jackie Smyth took the opportunity to recommend his latest book on the Victoria Cross. Exchanges like these must have confirmed to Ms. Clarke that her collection of autographs was a thing of value. Years later, in 1992, concerned about burglaries near her home, she sent her treasured book to the Imperial War Museum, so that it might not be stolen. There, she hoped, it might become part of a monument to national bravery in modern war.[136]

***

Brigadier General Smyth, himself a relic of the Victorian age, passed away in 1983 at the age of ninety, as Britain under Margaret Thatcher was embracing neo-Victorian values. He took with him, as the last of the Crimean veterans had done some sixty years before, the trappings of an earlier epoch. Even after his death, the Cross remained a link to a long lineage of bravery dating back to the Crimean War. It was notably malleable, rooted in the Victorian moment, yet strikingly usable in the current day. Margaret Thatcher's Britain provided a fertile ground for reassessing the meanings of the Victoria Cross and its nineteenth-century underpinnings. The contexts of the Falklands War and neoliberal economics, together, brought the Cross and its Crimean origins once again to the fore.[137] In the fraught, early years of Thatcher's regime, the Cross played its role in refashioning Britain as a military power in the later twentieth century, while linking it to the gallant past of the Victorian age. Simultaneously, the award exposed the parsimony of the Thatcher years.

In 1982, the Falklands War vaulted the Victoria Cross, along with its mid-Victorian grammar, into the public consciousness.[138] War with Argentina provided the occasion for the awarding of two Victoria Crosses, both given posthumously.[139] These winners – Sergeant Ian McKay and Herbert "H" Jones, both members of the Parachute Regiment – occupied separate ends of the class spectrum.[140] Dubbed "the last hero of the twentieth century," Sergeant Ian McKay was instrumental in the assault on Port Stanley.[141] Born to a modest South Yorkshire family, he had once dreamed of becoming a footballer. Crowned as the hero of the Falklands War, H Jones had sacrificed himself in a direct rush into an Argentine machine gun nest at Goose Green. Born to privilege in Putney, he was educated at Eton and Sandringham. The dashing and well-heeled H Jones was, in particular, a fitting hero for Thatcher's Britain. He combined the trappings of the past with panache of the present. Born in the midst of World War II, he was duty bound and eager to serve. It was said, in fact, that he hurried back from a skiing holiday so that he could set off for the Falklands. Every bit as much a celebrity as H was his glamorous and photogenic spouse, Sara Jones. In the months following the War, she captured the hearts of Britain – or certainly of Tory England – with her visit to the Falkland Islands and her appearance at the Conservative Party Convention of 1983.[142] These occasions knitted the affiliations between the Conservative Party and the Victoria Cross ever closer together. Mrs. Jones brought the glamor of Jacqueline Kennedy Onassis and the stiff upper lip of the Blitz together to be a wifely profile in courage for Thatcherite Britain.[143] In later years, as she became an active philanthropist and supported her two sons' military careers, she was dubbed a "role model" for army widows.[144] She was, in fact, the perfect mouthpiece for the war, the ideal self-sacrificing subject and the perfect embodiment of neo-Victorian values.

The story of Sara Jones shows, once again, how the Victoria Cross functioned as a tool of consolation and consensus. It had the capacity to shift attention away from a controversial war in the difficult early years of the Thatcher regime. But the Victoria Cross did not always work in this fashion. Indeed, the early 1980s offer a countervailing example of how the Victoria Cross could expose fissures in the efforts to use war widows and dead heroes in the interests of militarism. Specifically, in the year 1983, the plight of Mrs. Muriel Nicolson and her son Jack occupied national attention when the family decided to put a Victoria Cross up for sale. The Cross had been won by Mrs. Nicolson's husband, Wing Commander James Brindley Nicolson of the Royal Air Force. He had been the lone recipient of the Cross in the Battle of Britain, another historic touchstone for duty and bravery alike. Nicolson was injured, and his Hawker Hurricane, the iconic airplane of the RAF, on fire, when he shot down a German Messerschmitt and parachuted to safety, landing in a school's playing field. The feat earned the Cross for Nicolson, unusually tall at 6'4" in height and notably modest in his eschewal of personal recognition. The Battle of Britain's VC hero did not, however, survive the war: he met his death in 1945 in the Bay of Bengal when his plane failed due to engine trouble. Tragically, his then young wife learned of his death on the last day of the war. With her heroic husband downed in the conflict, Muriel Nicolson was left with an infant son, a newlywed cottage, and a meager pension – and, of course, the Victoria Cross.

What did the Cross mean to the widowed Mrs. Nicolson? Once a year, on Battle of Britain Day, she took it out of a bank safe, unwrapping its brown paper and wearing it for ceremony.[145] But the Cross offered little comfort beyond that for Muriel Nicolson, who received a paltry pension of £60 per week. She and her son, Jack, a Tadcaster wine merchant, decided, thus, to auction the Cross. Their purpose was twofold – to bring Mrs. Nicolson material comfort in her old age and to raise awareness of the plight of World War II widows. Long forgotten, they had yet to reap benefits from the "ballyhoo" that surrounded the Falklands War.[146] At the highly publicized auction, the Cross fetched more than any of its predecessors had by threefold: £110,000, some of which was donated to the Rainbow Trust for British War Widows.[147] It was purchased by a coalition of buyers, large and small, who deposited it in the Royal Air Force Museum in Hendon, North London. The outcome of the sale was not only the transfer of the Cross from the private safe in a bank to the public collections at Hendon. The transaction also generated, as the

Nicolsons hoped it might, a platform to critique the lack of support for war widows.[148] The VC hero's son led the charge here, writing a letter to Members of Parliament attacking the parsimony of the pensions, which he called "disgracefully meager."[149] The assault led to a bitter exchange with Margaret Thatcher, who rushed to defend the Government's generosity in a manner that the younger Nicolson deemed hypocritical.[150] Quickly, and predictably, the furor became partisan, with Jack Ashley, Labour MP for Stoke-on-Trent South, calling the transactions one of the "saddest sights" he knew.[151]

The sale of the Nicolson medal did manage, if for a news cycle, to bring attention to the limits of the Victoria Cross. That said, the Nicolson episode was fleeting, with the celebrity of the Cross, and the glamor, proving longer lasting in the public mind, or at least in the daily press. Of the two Victoria Cross episodes in the early Thatcher years, it was the story of H Jones that endured in the public eye. The Jones family long remained a subject of interest, both as military royalty and as tabloid fodder. Along with Sara Jones, sons Rupert and David have drawn sustained attention. Both followed their father into the military, with Rupert, becoming a Major General in the British Army, and the youngest ever to attain the ranking. He even held his wedding, fifteen years after his father's death on the anniversary of the ending of the Falklands War.[152] The spotlight has continued not just to shine on the legacy of H Jones, but to glare as well, with questions arising, years after, about the true nature of Jones's actions. An embodiment of valor, he was initially billed as the "architect" of the victory, his "leadership and courage" paving the way to the war's end.[153] But years on, the questions about whether H Jones was a "hero or hothead" resurfaced.[154] The myths of Goose Green eventually came crashing down, with revisionists charging that "H" was "hotheaded" and that his "fatal charge" was ill conceived.[155] Perhaps he had more in common with Captain Nolan, who headed impulsively into the Valley of Death in the Crimea than he did with Charles Lucas, the first winner of the Cross, to whom he had once been compared.

These critiques notwithstanding, H Jones retains his eminence in the annals of Victoria Cross heroes. His medal is displayed on the top floor of London's Imperial War Museum, in the Lord Ashcroft Gallery. There, it takes its place among the largest collection of Victoria Cross and George Cross Medals to be assembled at one site.[156] The gallery, which opened to fanfare in 2010 against the backdrop of the wars in Afghanistan and Iraq, is the fusion of a collection of Crosses previously owned by the Museum – nearly fifty of them – along with 164 artifacts collected by Michael Ashcroft, a businessman, an erstwhile Conservative Party Deputy Chair, a former member of the House of Lords, and, finally, a philanthropist. With the donation of his medals and a £5 million gift, Ashcroft made the permanent exhibit, "Extraordinary Heroes," a possibility. At the Imperial War Museum, visitors can now admire Victoria Crosses won across the ages, by Lucknow Kavanagh, Frogman Magennis, H Jones, and more. And thanks to the inclusion of the George Cross, they can appreciate the boldness of Doreen Ashburnham, who fought a cougar, hand to claw, on Vancouver Island and the sacrifice of Odette Sansom, a World War II agent who spent time in a concentration camp.[157]

Opened in 2010, the Ashcroft Gallery was the fruit of a decades-long pursuit that grew from childhood. Born in 1946, Ashcroft came to consciousness in the aftermath of World War II. The war was a family affair, with Ashcroft's father, a veteran of the D-Day operations, regaling his son about the landing throughout his youth. For the young Ashcroft, the result was a schoolboy's fascination with bravery – a fascination that led him, in his young adulthood, to pledge, if he were ever to make money, to buy a Victoria Cross. This childhood dream became a reality in the year 1986, not too long after the Falklands War. By then a successful businessman, Ashcroft purchased a Victoria Cross at auction. Having grown up with heroic stories of World War II, it was only fitting that he would seek out the treasured Cross of James "Frogman" Magennis, the navy diver from Belfast who was famed for his exploits in the Pacific theater. The sale was to be a one-time pursuit, or so Ashcroft had assumed. But the frisson of the experience overwhelmed him. He was certainly not the first Victoria Cross buyer to experience the thrill of the auction room. Other collectors before him had found the process exciting and enthralling. "I wish you had been at the sale," one VC buyer wrote to a collaborator in the 1950s, as he recalled the intrigue of the auction. "You would have loved it."[158] For these men, the heady action of the auction room was, perhaps, a fitting substitute for the military muscle of the battlefield. In both instances, split-second decision-making was a must. Ostensibly, though Ashcroft did not claim a place in history for his exploits as a warrior, he made a name in Britain for his ambitions as a collector. The thrill of possession unleashed a relentless pursuit for Ashcroft, who came to own 164 Crosses, nearly one-eighth of all of those earned. As he bought up Crosses, the relentless collector bought into the understandings that underpinned the award. Namely, he came to regard the Cross as an instrument for the greater good. In this way, he was not unlike his Victorian predecessors, the painter Louis Desanges and the publisher Samuel Beeton. Nor did he stand at too great a distance from the organizers of the centenary exhibition at Marlborough House. In putting his Crosses on display, along with those owned by the Imperial

War Museum, he aimed to bring the Cross, and its lessons, to a new generation of museumgoers.[159]

What shape did "Extraordinary Heroes," the Imperial War Museum's Victoria Cross Gallery, take? When he described the aims of the exhibit, perched in the attic rooms of the airy museum, historian Nigel Steel declared, "We are trying to create a space where people can think about courage."[160] "Extraordinary Heroes" captures the heroism of the holders of the Victoria and George Cross in a series of wooden cases. Each holds a recipient's medal – oftentimes, a full medal set – and a photograph, wherever available. These cases bring the heroes to life. They are accompanied by other personal belongings – in some cases, handwritten diaries, and, in other rare instances, weapons, which might gesture to the acts of violence that garnered the Cross. The tribute case devoted to Sergeant William Gardner, an Indian Rebellion Victoria Cross, includes the kukri, or the curved knife, from the so-called "fanatic" he killed; that honoring Major Gonville Bromhead, who earned one of the twenty-one Victoria Crosses awarded at the Battle of Rourke's Drift during the Anglo-Zulu War, features a spear blade, an Assegai, that he turned into a paper knife. Once again, the violence of empire becomes an aesthetic practice through the public life of the Cross. There are, additionally, riding crops, binoculars, revolvers, dolls, barbed wire, and comic books, as well as larger-scale artifacts, among them, battle knapsacks and diving costumes. Where objects alone do not communicate the magnitude of heroism, multimedia experiences, with film, interviews, and animation, complete the task. As visitors travel through the gallery, and later, when they purchase souvenirs, they face the open-ended and soul-searching question: "How Brave Are You?" There is, finally, something in the exhibit for all ages. Just as adults are encouraged to engage with the individual stories of the remarkable heroes, children are invited to earn badges as they pace through the display.

Those who visit the gallery, with its Crosses and photographs, and its artifacts and films, move through seven thematic sections. Character-driven, this organizational scaffolding revolves around seven traits, all aspects, expressions, or "types of bravery," to use the words of the Museum's official press release. Among these we can count aggression, boldness, endurance, initiative, leadership, sacrifice, and skill. It was, to use the curators' own words, a "close reading of the formal language" of the Victoria Cross citations that allowed the Museum to discern the common thread of bravery and its linguistic expressions. In the hands of the gallery's curators, these seven virtues appear as universal ideals. Borrowing once more from the Museum's formulation, "bravery itself transcends time."[161] Accordingly, the exhibit's publicity material eschews historical distinction as it knits the stories of VC winners together, from the Crimean War to the twenty-first century. "What one person did in the 1850s was really not so different from what another did in the 1940s, or the 2000s," it avers.[162]

As it uproots the Victoria Cross from history, the exhibit unhinges it from dated notions of race and nation. Even Kipling had, in a disparaging and disconcerting way, suggested that the Cross had a capacity to extend across classes and races. Yet, the Cross was a tribute to distinctly British values, conceived in the nineteenth century as Anglo-Saxon virtues and purveyed by the legends of muscular Christianity. The awards to colonial and Indian troops later on sought to expand these ranks, if in measured ways. Finally, the rhetoric of Commonwealth at the time of the centenary endeavored, once again, to extend and to bind the fellowship of the Cross. Admittedly, the Museum's publicity underwrites the bravery and courage surrounding the Cross as aspects of so-called "Western Civilization." This is a telling appraisal, with the most recent VCs coming from the conflicts in Afghanistan and Iraq, which trace long-ago roots to the British Empire.[163] But the exhibit, like the Cross, cleaves to a latter-day rhetoric holding that the reward is open to anyone, regardless of class, color, or creed. Included are many Sikh and Gurkha VCs, and Caribbean winners too. As it invokes racial categories and national identities in a postcolonial context, the exhibit cuts both ways – at once acknowledging and eviscerating them. Imperial and post-imperial subjects are not, in the understanding of the exhibit, representatives of their places of origin. Instead, they are simply "remarkable people" who have exhibited "extraordinary courage."[164]

In the exhibit and beyond, Lance Corporal Johnson Beharry, a Grenadian-born soldier, emerges as an important hero.[165] At the time of the gallery's opening, Beharry was the most recent winner to wear the Cross. There, visitors can find Beharry's medal, a portrait of the hero sporting a tattoo in the form of a Victoria Cross, and a helmet featuring the signatures of the men he saved in Helmand Province. Beharry's life story fuses elements of a Dickensian childhood with the narrative of a postcolonial everyman. The son of an alcoholic father and a struggling mother, Beharry grew up in a large, extended family on the island of Grenada. A lover of fast cars and of heady adventure, Beharry left the confines of the tiny island to seek broader horizons in London. To avoid a life of drugs, drink, and dissipation, he eventually joined the Army in 2001, becoming the driver of a Warrior Armored Fighting Vehicle in Iraq. In May 2005, he performed two feats of "extraordinary courage," driving through enemy ambush to bring his platoon commander and disoriented troops to safety, although he was, himself, severely wounded in the head.

After Iraq, Beharry experienced both the pleasures and the perils of the Cross. The fact that he was the first recipient since the Falklands War – and the fact that he was a living recipient too – certainly helped to vault him to celebrity.[166] Beharry appeared at the Cenotaph with World War I veterans; he carried the Olympic Torch in 2012. His portrait now resides in the National Portrait Gallery (Figure 3.5). But the traumatic legacies of war have left their mark as well; they led, distressingly, to a suicide attempt in 2010. Incidents like this are, all too often, the unhappy afterlife of valor.[167] For Johnson Beharry there were further twists as well. Despite his heroics, and despite his celebrity, Beharry has not been immune from the injuries and inequities of race and nation in the current day. At the beginning of 2017, Beharry was on his way to a charity event in New York when authorities detained him at John F. Kennedy Airport in the aftermath of Donald Trump's travel ban. Beharry made the newspapers, but missed the occasion. In the end, Beharry's story crystallizes the great promise and the limited power of the Cross.[168]

***

As long as there are wars to fight, and as long as there are Victoria Crosses to sell, the award will linger in the public consciousness, resurfacing at times of conflict and controversy, large and small. Since Johnson Beharry earned his Victoria Cross, three more heroes have been added to the rolls of bravery that extend back to Charles Lucas and the Crimean War. Only

Figure 3.5 VC Soldier's portrait unveiled: Johnson Beharry, National Portrait Gallery. 2007. Photograph by Cathal McNaughton. PA Images/Alamy Stock Photo

one is living. This is Corporal Joshua Leakey, who fought in Afghanistan. There, while under direct fire, Leakey rescued a wounded officer and activated a machine gun. To hear his mother tell it, Leakey is the proto-typical man of action who exemplifies the bravery of the Victoria Cross. A onetime history student, Leakey told her before enlisting, "Mum, I'm fed up of reading about wars. I'm going to go and be in them."[169]

There have been two posthumous Crosses given to Corporal Bryan Budd and Lance Corporal James Ashworth as well for their heroics in Afghanistan. The awards to living recipients remind us of the vigor of manly action, but those to the deceased soldiers recall the vulnerability of soldierly sacrifice. Across the years, wartime losses have opened up ques-tions that are medical and military, and emotional and logistical. All of these matters came to the fore during the Crimean War and after. Because the mid-Victorian era was a transitional moment in managing the war dead, the challenges were particularly acute. Affection for the troops kindled a sense that a proper burial was important, but the wholesale organization of this project was in its infancy. Burial is, however, just one aspect of military caretaking that includes the upkeep of monuments and the welfare of veterans. To consider these matters and the challenges they have posed, the following chapter focuses on loss, rather than heroism. It considers the dead, as well as the veterans and memorials produced in the war's wake, to understand the custodial practices that developed out of the conflict. The Crimea's legacies, as we have seen, are many. It bequeathed to modern Britain not only the bureaucratic recognition of bravery, but also many Victorian practices of care.[170]

4   The Custodians

Perhaps because of their inevitable connection, the associations between war and death are curiously underexplored.[1] This relationship was hardly unique to the Crimea, where death occurred everywhere in the conflict – on the battlefield, in the hospitals, and even at home.[2] Many died in battle and from their wounds. More, however, lost their lives as results of hunger, cold, and disease. Cumulative totals vary wildly, with the toll for the British forces coming in at just above 22,000.[3] This figure may be far smaller than the body count for the Napoleonic Wars; it pales, additionally, in relation to the death toll in the Great War. Yet, death and dying preoccupied the warring nation during the Crimean War and well after. In the course of the war, combatants, helpmeets, and regiments all ministered to the dying. They engaged too in the mournful tasks of burying the dead, notifying their families, and disposing of their effects. Meanwhile, a nation at home looked on with concern as it mourned. Care for the dead did not end with the departure of the last troops from the Crimea in 1856. Instead, in the decades and centuries after, good Samaritans, and, eventually, the state, endeavored to maintain far-flung British graves.

I refer, in this chapter, to those who cared for the dying, the dead, and their resting places as custodians. Like adventurers, this is a cross-temporal category that encompasses a broad range of people and practices. During the war and after, the Crimea's custodians came from the ranks of combatants and non-combatants, of Britons and foreigners, and of civilians and government officials. Like the Crimea's adventurers, the custodians left a vast and varied archive. It includes the many personal letters from the front, articles in the printed press, and spates of government reports. The archive of custodianship is, thus, a varied one, filled with individual emotion and bureaucratic red tape, and with public sentiment and political brinksmanship. It provides a view onto the ferment of Victorian feeling as well as the management of foreign affairs. It demonstrates the ways in which labors of love drifted into the spadework of maintenance, and the ways in which outpourings of grief turned into endeavors in diplomacy.[4] Ultimately, the acts of custodianship were varied and wide ranging, but loss and mourning remained at their core.

Taken together, these efforts anticipated the development of what historian Drew Faust has called, in the case of the United States, a "republic of suffering." In the wake of the American Civil War, the collective throes of mourning and grief served to bind and ultimately to heal the citizenry.[5] Similarly, in the Crimea, regiments became families as they grieved their lost warriors.[6] Additionally, readers at home lamented loved ones and countrymen. Yet, while the Civil War took place on home ground, the Crimean War was waged at a distance. As a result, tending the graves of the fallen presented particular challenges during the Crimean conflict and after. The dead left the world in a place far from home. They were buried thousands of miles away, in cemeteries that were vulnerable and often neglected. With upkeep a challenge, the condition of the cemeteries became yet another site for mismanagement in a war marred by blunder. Across decades and centuries, their state became a moral referendum. Campaigns for their upkeep joined the better-known crusades for army reform and sanitation management that flowered in the struggle's aftermath. Through it all, the resting places of the Crimean War dead became a focus for shared emotion, as well as moral outrage.

In wartime and after, the focal point of collective emotion, shared hope, and national frustration was a complex of cemeteries on the Crimean Peninsula and beyond. Most significant was the Officers' Cemetery at Cathcart's Hill, which overlooked the Black Sea on a commanding perch not far from Sebastopol. It was here that many leaders of the war effort were buried. This cemetery became the primary focus for endeavors in custodianship and care during and after the war. It was not, however, the only burial ground to become an object of concern in the war's aftermath. In a conflict whose battles were far flung, graveyards extended well beyond the Crimean Peninsula itself. They were located in liminal spaces connected to Britain and its empire, yet sovereign or colonized by others. They became, moreover, a focus for complex relationships with a growing empire in the East and with a changing Europe across the decades. No mere monuments to the past, they were stages for the unfolding of history in a century of hot and cold war alike.

The previous chapter considered the innovation of the Victoria Cross as an effort to deflect from mismanagement by celebrating war's valor. This chapter looks to the pursuit of custodianship as a response to military blunder and lives lost. Like Chapter 3, this one fosters a view onto the mixed modernity of the Crimean War. Just as the War marked a formative moment in the recognition of heroism, it was a transition point in the

maintenance of death. The Crimean War fell midway between the
Napoleonic Wars, which witnessed early attempts to inter soldiers in
mass graves near the sites of battle, and the Great War, which saw the
inception of the Imperial War Graves Commission, later the
Commonwealth War Graves Commission. Like the prior chapter, this
chapter, too, uncovers the war's role in the making of masculinity. While
the preceding chapter addressed the celebration of valor and action, this
chapter makes visible the roles of suffering and care.[7] Namely, it reveals
the vulnerability of Victorian generals and soldiers; it displays the pastoral
labor of nineteenth-century regiments; it chronicles the heartfelt concern
of postwar travelers; it uncovers the painstaking work of twentieth-
century bureaucrats. There has, of late, been some discussion of the
true nature of manliness in the Crimea. Was the military man the prototype of a bellicose masculinity, or was he an expression of a sentimental
manhood? The story of the Crimea's custodians, during battle and after,
demonstrates that this figure could be both.

***

The Crimean War coincided with the development of a distinctive Anglo-
American culture of bereavement that was evident on many fronts. Death
was a preoccupation of the literary productions of the age. The public that
consumed William Howard Russell's dispatches from the Crimea also
read contemporary works such as Tennyson's *In Memoriam* along with
Dickens's *Bleak House* and *Little Dorrit,* the latter of which responded
directly to the excessive deaths in the Crimea. These texts, moreover,
provide evidence of an intensification of social practices concerning
death, including epitaph writing, paupers' funerals, and undertaking, in
everyday life.[8] Not only did a concern with death shape the conventions of
social life. It also determined the physical shape of towns and cities, with
large, urban cemeteries becoming part of the modern landscape.[9] If
a preoccupation with death was ubiquitous in this era, so too was an
ideal of dying. Victorians held fast to the ideal of the good death. This
notion, an inheritance of philosophical liberalism and evangelical
Christianity, enshrined an ideal way to leave the physical world that
involved a painless, peaceful passing.[10] In the regime of the good death,
those who were deserving passed away not alone but surrounded by loved
ones; they spent their last moments not far away but ensconced at home;
they expired not in pain, but at peace; and perhaps they even took their
last breaths not in dread but in anticipation of the world to come.[11]

Like the record of the culture at large, the archival record of the
Crimean War provides abundant traces of efforts to reckon with death.

These are especially evident in the letters written by men in uniform from all ranks and sent to friends and family in Britain.[12] Men on the front wrote to their loved ones of their trials and tribulations, and of their longings and losses. They sought, in their letters, to reassure those at home of their own health and well-being.[13] Try as they might, however, they could not keep death at bay. As letters home indicate, death came in many ways in the Crimea. Men lost their lives in battle and on sick beds, of course. Additionally, during the conflict in the East, thousands died prosaically, having succumbed to hunger, cold, and disease. It was not, in fact, until World War I that the majority of those dying in military conflicts lost their lives in battle.[14]

All told, wartime did not produce favorable conditions for the good death.[15] Letters sent home from the front bear this out in stark detail. Many writers shied away from depicting the horrors of battle, but there were those who described it vividly. This was the case from the very beginning of the war, as a missive from Sergeant Yeasbley of the 67th Regiment sent to his parents in the aftermath of the Battle of the Alma indicates all too well. The Alma was the site of chilling combat and non-stop action with "no time for reflection," in Yeasbley's words. But if the battle itself was overwhelming, the aftermath was far worse. It was then that the "dreadful sights" of the struggle – its "grotesque" results – were arrestingly clear. There were men and horses with "heads blown to pieces," and others cut in half by cannon balls, "some with one leg and many with both blown off and left to bleed to death."[16] As another correspondent wrote, "men made in God's own image" were "torn to pieces by a shell, or smashed into a pulp by a round shot."[17]

Burials after battle were attempts to restore the humanity of those who survived and the sanctity of those who died.[18] To be sure, these strayed far from the ideal of the good death. More often than not, wartime burial involved the interment of several bodies together – from a handful to dozens. Those who had fought each other in life lay cheek by jowl in death.[19] There was a rank order to this practice. In January 1855, in the thick of the Siege of Sebastopol, one chronicler lamented the mass grave of five dozen privates. It was a "melancholy sight," to be sure, with no heed paid to sacramental differences yet with plenty of evidence of the depredations of a long war: "*One* grave in which 41 Protestants and 20 Catholic soldiers were laid, merely sewn up in blankets, poor fellows, they looked not bigger than children, so wasted away they appeared."[20] This was a far cry from the notion of a proper grave. Another interlocutor, a Lieutenant Howell, defined the last rites, such as they were, by what they lacked: "A funeral here is a very solemn, but a very common thing, no coffin, no mourners, a blanket is all you are conveyed in on a litter and the body rolls from one side to another as it is conveyed to the last resting place and no more thought of it."[21]

Observations such as Howell's bemoaned that war's hardships had whittled away proper burial practices. Yet, British commentators retained a sense of their own superiority all the same. As many noted, the British Army in the East did not distinguish between brothers, friends, and foes when it came to battlefield burials. Its men took care to bury all the dead. This was a stark contrast to the Russians, who left their dead on the field, or to the Turks, who paraded with enemy bodies on stakes.[22] In a regime where the treatment of the dead was an index of civilization, these differences were of no small consequence. Instead, they helped to justify the reasons for fighting a questionable war.

Taken together, the foregoing examples demonstrate that the good death was difficult, if not impossible, to achieve in the Crimea. Yet many in the East strove mightily to approximate it. They labored to ensure that their brothers in arms, the men in their command, and the soldiers they served all passed away in conditions that bore at least some resemblance, however faint, to the good death. They tended to the dying at their last breaths; they buried the dead in their graves; they kept up the plots in the aftermath. They played additional roles, too, in passing on news, and sometimes effects, to the bereaved at home. Some of the most poignant letters to reach England from the Crimea came from third parties who bore the news of a loved one's death. Whether the demise was the result of battle or illness, the letter sought to reassure the recipient – oftentimes a mother or a father – that the soldier had passed in a manner resembling the good death. Particular circumstances may have varied, but there were constant themes throughout. In his last days, or perhaps in his last hours, the dying man had wanted for nothing. On his deathbed, the deceased had remembered his parents and said his prayers. He made his peace with his imminent departure from this world as he prepared to move to a better place. He had, ideally, taken his last breaths in the company of others – fellow soldiers, chaplains, or nurses. There was, additionally, news of a burial and of effects to make their way home soon. Finally, as if to narrow the distance between the dead in the Crimea and those mourning at home, these letters might contain material traces from the East: sketches of graves, pressings of flowers, and cuttings of grass.[23]

Take, for instance, the missive sent by John Reid to the family of his dear friend Joseph. Before his death, Joseph had savored his time in the East, like many of the war's adventurers. As he prepared to fight, he had joked about Aladdin's lamp, searched for snuff, and longed for action. These things he had shared with his parents in letters sent from the

Crimea. In his early days there, Joseph had made a pact with John Reid. The two men, bound by a shared surname, forged a more meaningful allegiance as well. Should one of the friends lose his life, the other would be sure to communicate the loss to the fallen warrior's family. When his comrade Joseph passed away in January 1855, John Reid did just that. In his letter, he relayed the news. Joseph died of illness, but he had received wounds in battle beforehand. This was no small incident: The wounds made what may have seemed a futile and senseless death, the result of the failure of the Army's bumbling medical services, all the more heroic and worthy. If Reid sought to comfort Joseph's family members by reminding them of the battle wounds, he aimed to mitigate their sadness, too, providing an image of a man surrounded, in his last days, by all he desired. "I can assure you that he got every attendance that a man could be got," John Reid wrote. In his last days, Joseph partook of wine, poultry, mutton, oranges, and, generally "everything that he wanted." This is, in truth, a rather stunning inventory, given the privations in the Crimea during the winter of 1854 to 1855. Perhaps John Reid allowed himself some hyperbole in the service of mercy. Finally, Reid promised that the family would soon receive his friend's medal and three clasps, all richly deserved, along with his back pay.[24]

In wartime, letters announcing the death of loved ones came from all ranks. There were those written by newly literate privates and noncommissioned officers, such as George Ratcliff of the Land Army Corps, who sent sobering news that was doubly heartbreaking, since it came in the winter of 1856, on the occasion of the peace, just as the war ended. "I am very sorry to enform [sic] you that poor Joe Saddler is Dead he died on the 4th of feby with feaver," [sic] wrote Ratcliff. He sought, at least, to provide reassurance with the news of a proper burial. "I folered [sic] him to his last home on the 6th of the same month," he declared.[25]

Missives like Ratcliff's exist oftentimes as single specimens, artifacts handed down through generations and secured in archives thanks to luck, accident, or happenstance.[26] There are, as well, more developed collections that archive the death of Britain's beloved sons in the Crimea. One such archive is that of the family of Archibald Clevland, a young officer in the 17th Lancers, who was adored by his regiment, his mother, and his community. Clevland's death, like Saddler's, was especially poignant because of its timing. He had survived the Battle of Balaklava, where he charged heroically with the Light Brigade, only to fall a few weeks later at the Battle of Inkerman.[27] It pained the commanding officer of the 17th Lancers, Geoffrey Morgan, to notify Clevland's devoted mother, recently widowed, of the tragic news: a shell splinter had taken the young officer's life. "You have lost I am sure an affectionate and amiable son," wrote

Morgan, "and I need not tell you how deeply I sympathize with you on this melancholy occasion, as we have also lost a brave and good brother officer." Morgan did recognize that no praise, however fulsome, could comfort. But he promised, at least, to send home some of Archibald Clevland's belongings, among them, his sword belt and his gold ring.[28] Such possessions would surely have been welcomed home to Barnstaple, in Devon, where Archie's life was celebrated in locks of hair, newspaper tributes, and sentimental poems.

During the Crimean War, a diverse range of actors served as guardians to the dead and as comforters of the living. George Ratcliff and Geoffrey Morgan occupied different stations at home and in war, but they participated in common custodial roles. Those who tended the beds of the sick – nurses and chaplains – also acted as helpmeets to the dying.[29] A formidable and prolific letter writer, Florence Nightingale sent her share of condolences from Scutari Hospital. Although she wrote hastily, Nightingale assured families, time and again, that their young sons had died the good death.[30] Such was the case in her communication to the family of Edward Nixon Spofforth, who had run away from home to join the Army. She promised the family that Spofforth benefitted from access to religious books and to arrowroot until the very end. "I am sure, my dear Madam, that you need be under no anxiety about him," Nightingale assured Spofforth's mother. "He was resigned, deeply thankful, good and well principled. He did his duty fully and was not neglected. He never complained. He liked the service and I hope you may believe that he enjoyed this life and will be happy in another."[31] Chaplain J.E. Sabin also attended deathbeds at Scutari. Using a similar formula to Nightingale's, he relayed to poor Harry Teesdale's parents – Colonel and Mrs. Teesdale – news of their son's decline and death. As he lay dying, a Testament given to him by his mother was a "constant companion."[32] In his final hours, the dying man professed his love for his parents and his joy at the thought of meeting God.[33] Perhaps knowledge of these intimate and solemn scenes might comfort the devoted and grief-stricken parents. So too might the fact that the young man was buried with military honors. Sabin closed with yet more offers of consolation, offered in the form of two promises: one, to adorn the grave far from England with a monument, should the family desire it, and two, to send Harry's cherished belongings – books, papers, and a telescope – home.[34]

A common concern of those who stood watch at death beds or recovered bodies from battle was to ensure that prized objects returned to England. Sword belts, gold rings, and prayer books were among the precious items that were saturated with meaning. They connected the battlefront to the home front, and they linked the living and the dead.

They also imbricated erstwhile strangers in unforeseen relationships – some of them sticky. As they performed the tasks of sending goods and funds back to Britain, those who had assumed duties as guardians and helpmeets found themselves inserted into often intimate, and sometimes problematic relationships with the families of their fallen comrades. In their capacities as brokers between the living and the dead, between the military and the family, and even between brother and sister, they could, at times, enter unknowingly into family disputes. Such was the case for Edward Steffe. He and George Burdis had become fast friends in the East. Life brought them together and death bound them as well. They had vowed to communicate the news of loss and to convey cherished belongings home. It had been Burdis's hope that his possessions – his prize money, his personal effects, and his war medals – would make their way to his sister after his death. The laws of England dictated, however, that these objects of desire were to become the possessions of Burdis's brother. Steffe had the mettle to survive at the front, but not to quarrel with his departed comrade's family. Edward Steffe may have managed to fulfil the first part of his mission, in communicating the difficult news of his comrade's death; he was unable, however, to complete the second, in assuring the intended deposit of the treasures.[35]

Stories like these make visible in the most material of ways the ties that bound Britons in a shared culture of suffering.[36] This traffic in goods connected onetime strangers during wartime, producing intimacies out of loss and kinships out of suffering. This network of relationships nourished the understanding that there was not a household untouched by its tragedies. In the most literal, or limited, of terms, this may have been hyperbole. To be sure, the British death toll was great at just over 22,000.[37] Yet, it came nowhere near the balance sheet of the American Civil War, which occurred just a decade later and counted nearly three quarters of a million dead.[38] It paled too in comparison to that of World War I, when the death toll across Britain, its dominions, and its empire surpassed one million. But while the death toll was comparatively modest, the sense of loss was everywhere apparent. It was manifest not only in the traffic in letters and in goods; it was also evident in the printed culture of the epoch.[39] Letters sent home from the front found their way into local and national newspapers. In this way, these private communications about a loved one's death became collective meditations for a nation at war.

One widely reprinted missive was a "manly and feeling letter" from Major Freese, of the Royal Artillery, to Captain Childers. Childers's son, also a Captain, died in the trenches before Sebastopol in October 1854. The letter told of the young man's great bravery and notable promise: had young Childers survived, he would have become an "ornament to the profession." It assured the father of an instantaneous death. Major Freese reported a worthy burial: a custom-made coffin was lodged in a secluded valley lying near to the camp, if far from home. As it made its way into print, this instance of a family's sorrow became a manifestation of a nation's tragedy.[40]

Printed letters offered an affecting way to communicate and to collectivize this experience of loss: to render death in black and white. More generally, across the conflict, the annals of print sought to address mortality and loss. Reports of the funerals of generals, fulsomely covered in the press, similarly gave expressions to a nation's pain. There was some risk in publicizing such ceremonial events that paid tribute to fallen commanding officers, for they contrasted starkly with the unceremonious interments of privates. Yet, a good part of the mid-Victorian reading public had a taste for such coverage, which bound Britons in collective remembrance and shared emotion. Just a few years before the outbreak of the war, in 1852, the printed page had brought Britons together in mourning the loss of the Duke of Wellington, the military hero who had vanquished Napoleon and later become Prime Minister.[41] With great verve, and in infinitesimal detail, newspapers across the land had recorded the rituals of the occasion, pictured the funeral car of the Duke in its elegant splendor, and outlined the order of procession. It was a farewell to a hero and a farewell to an age.

In similar fashion, accounts of the funerals of military leaders brought the Crimea's tragedy to the hearths of the nation. The ceremonies devoted to generals in the Crimea may have been lacking in the majesty and stateliness accorded to Wellington, but they were not wanting when it came to solemnity and sorrow. They allowed for a connective and coordinated outpouring of grief alongside the regal and regimented performance of pageantry. Such was the case when it came to the funeral of Lord Raglan, the original leader of the Army in the East, whose disastrous performance led to his own destruction. Raglan died near Sebastopol in June 1855; his body was returned home to be buried shortly after. Raglan's passing garnered reverent attention from writers and artists at the front. The passage of his corpse, similarly, received generous coverage in the newspaper press, where it was extensively narrated and lavishly illustrated. Attention to the funeral produced consensus at a time of discord as it redeemed the shortsighted General.[42] Attention to ceremony papered over the failures, as it highlighted Raglan's good intentions. In so doing, the press contributed to the English habit of venerating heroic failure, in the tradition of the Charge of the Light Brigade.

In contrast to the ill-fated Raglan, many subordinate officers found their last resting places in the East. Their rites also filled the pages of newspapers. One of the first of these to fall was George Cathcart, a general who boasted a model career across the first half of the nineteenth century. He had served, as a young man, as an aide-de-camp to the recently deceased Wellington at Waterloo and had gone on to become the Governor of the Cape of Good Hope. After his death at the Battle of Inkerman, Cathcart enjoyed a somber burial attended by the troops.[43] Cathcart found his final resting place on a piece of land perched above Sebastopol harbor. This majestic spot assumed the name of Cathcart's Hill and became the burial ground for several officers.[44] With its collection of memorials, this "spot of melancholy interest" was, in the words of the *Illustrated London News*, at once "picturesque" and "affecting" in its "pure simplicity."[45] It was a fitting place for the burial of officers and an effective focus for the emotions of the nation. This dual function was evident in the *Daily News*'s coverage of the burial of Lieutenant General Thomas Fox Strangways. Beloved by his men and cherished by his nation, Strangways fell in action in 1855. In Cathcart's Hill, the newspaper found a fitting, albeit distant, resting place. "While the ashes of these warriors rest here," the *Daily News* wrote of the magisterial vista, "their glory will live in many a heart far away."[46]

The *Daily News* sought to assuage, on a collective level, the very concern addressed in letters sent to England – that those who died in the Crimea would rest in peace in a land far away. It was joined by the *Times*, where the correspondent at the front, William Howard Russell, offered narrative closure to the British effort in the war with a farewell missive entitled "Our Graves in the Crimea." It was not the first time for Russell to address the Crimean resting places. During wartime, Russell had portrayed the burial grounds of the Crimea with a gothic naturalism. When the war was over, Russell revisited the gravesites, and the burial efforts, this time with a more reassuring, if melancholic tone. Writing in July 1856, he portrayed the rump of an army working methodically, assiduously, and diligently at its last rites, after the last marches had ended and after the last cannons had roared. In anticipation of the time when the "last Englishman" would quit Sebastopol, the "soldier fragments" labored long. "For many long weeks," wrote Russell, the living toiled in an effort to build monuments for their deceased brethren who would not make it home. He rendered the peninsula as a massive graveyard filled with "stark white stones." Erected by brothers in blood or placed by brothers in arms, these small markers offered "monumental stories" in the form of simple tributes, biblical verses, and sentimental rhyme. With the fighting over, "numberless wild flowers" had begun to grow around them. The focal point of this landscape was, of course, the Officers' Cemetery, built atop Cathcart's Hill. Here, as elsewhere, "the care and love of friends" sought to bracket the violence and bloodshed of war. The men remembered there had passed away far from home, and their deaths had ranged far from the Victorian ideal. But these small acts might allow repose for the dead and peace for the living. If this was not a good death, perhaps it was good enough.[47]

***

Tributes such as these transformed Cathcart's Hill into what Pierre Nora once called a *lieu de memoire,* a place where memory and emotion "crystalize."[48] In this capacity, the graveyard was a repository for the feelings of love, longing, and loss that accrued around the war dead. The site answered the mournful hope that those who were felled in the war would rest in peace, albeit in a land far removed from their home. Because Cathcart's Hill was replete with such meaning, it is not surprising that those in Britain, and especially those who had suffered losses in the war, sought to bring the site closer, incorporating it into their domestic lives. One especially poignant instance involved a Mr. C.B. Curtis of Acton. Curtis painstakingly rendered a model of the cemetery at Cathcart's Hill in the summer of 1856; he subsequently donated it to the United Services Institution. Working from drawings made on the spot, Curtis offered up a likeness in stunning detail. "Every tombstone with its exact inscription – every nameless mound," the *Morning Post* noted, "all [were] presented in exact facsimile." There was, clearly, some cathartic purpose involved in the endeavor for Curtis, whose son, a Lieutenant of the 46th Regiment, was buried there. If he could not reach his son's gravesite, he could, perhaps, bring it home.[49]

The model rendered by Mr. Curtis of Acton provides just one example of the continuing presence of Cathcart's Hill in home front hearts and in metropolitan minds.[50] Visual culture, too, played its part in producing *memento mori.* The Crimean War, of course, coincided with the great age of image reproduction. Lithographs rendered the solitary site in gentle color.[51] Lavish, collectable books offered keepsakes memorializing the bravery of the officer class.[52] Cathcart's Hill appeared time and again in the illustrated press. And the photography of Roger Fenton preserved the site, sparse and stone-laden, in sepia tones (Figure 4.1).[53]

Such representations were the closest most came to the Crimea and its burial grounds in the years following the war. The peninsula was, of course, difficult to reach and treacherous to visit, as the wartime adventurers and those who followed learned well. At the war's end, despite the

Figure 4.1 The Tombs of the Generals on Cathcart's Hill. Roger
Fenton. Library of Congress Prints and Photographs Division/Mary
Evans Picture Library

finality of the departure from the Crimea, there were hopes in some
quarters that the graveyards might, over the years, receive sojourners
bound for the East. In words that were widely reproduced, William
Howard Russell expressed a wish that the Crimea might become
a "chosen terminus of Saxon pilgrimage." Though far afield, the "little
spot" beckoned to those with "British blood" coursing through their
"veins."[54] The Crimea never drew the crowds that the American Civil
War battlefields, located on home soil, subsequently enjoyed. Nor did it
assume the shape of the memorial complex on the Western Front.[55] Yet
the peninsula did attract its share of adventurers in the years after the war.
Cathcart's Hill and nearby cemeteries became featured stops for those
military officers, family relations, and touring groups who ventured to the
East.[56] They also became destinations for representatives of the War
Office and the Foreign Office. But what they found when they arrived
was of little comfort.

When they reached the peninsula, travelers discovered that the cemeteries had all too quickly descended into states of disrepair. The graves
were located in a faraway land where they were vulnerable to the elements

and to the local populations. The poor quality of custodianship on the part of Great Britain did not help matters. The hopes for venerating the dead and comforting the living were dashed. There was consternation all around, on the part of the visitors, the families, and the government. If the treatment of the dead provided an index of civilization in wartime, so too did the maintenance of a nation's graves long after. Britons may have met the first bar with distinction during the war, but the government abysmally failed the second in the aftermath.

In the years immediately following the war, it was not the British themselves, but foreigners who kept an eye on the cemeteries in the Crimea. One visitor to report on this phenomenon was James Fergusson of the Royal Engineers, who made his way to the Crimea in 1858. At that time, he reported favorably on the status of British graves at the Alma. Credit was due here not to the British state, but to a Russian woman resident in the Crimea, a Madame Belovodsky. Fergusson imagined that the Russian woman's labors in the East would be a comfort to Englishwomen at home, notably to those wives and mothers who had lost companions and sons.[57] Mourners such as Archibald Clevland's mother were sure to feel their burdens eased by Madame Belovodsky's "kindness of heart," which knew no national borders. It may seem surprising to find a Russian woman as a caretaker of British graves. However, those who returned to the Crimea after the war discovered that, while the Russians were formidable in battle during the conflict, they were noble in defeat in the years following. Conversely, the British were ignominious in their victory. This was evident at the Redan, whose memorials were defaced with graffiti. As Fergusson explained, this was not the work of the enemies. Instead, it was wrought by the very "hands of Englishmen." In his dismay, Fergusson turned the hierarchies of civilization that had operated in wartime upside down. "Can any barbarism equal this?" he cried.[58]

It was not only the Russians who came to the aid of the British, helpless and hapless after the Crimean War. Ultimately, an American military officer resident in the Crimea became the most prominent, and the most celebrated, custodian of the graveyards. This was Colonel Gowen, who labored regularly and assiduously at Cathcart's Hill. He saw that rose bushes and cypress trees were planted at the graves, so that they would not be left barren. He extended his kindness to the grieving families of slain officers, including Archibald Clevland, as he insisted to poor Archie's mother that he would tend the burial plot at his own expense. Gowen sought, ardently, to protect the resting places of the fallen from the "ravages of time."[59] For these efforts, Gowen became a postwar hero, lauded by the British Army and feted by the British public. He toured

London, where he enjoyed a hearty welcome, regaled in newspaper notices and swamped by calling cards.[60] The Colonel remained a friend to fallen Britons in the Crimea and an advocate as well. In the year 1869, he appealed to Parliament to provide financial support for the monuments to the fallen. To bolster his case, he offered up the example of the US Congress, which had allotted two million dollars to support memorializing the dead after the American Civil War. It was a shame that the mother country had to look to the riven American nation as an example.[61]

Gowen's 1869 plea came against the backdrop of the most publicized journey to the Crimea of the postwar years: the tour of the Prince and Princess of Wales. The visit of the royals and their entourage restored the peninsula to the forefront of British attention.[62] The traveling party reflected, of course, on the ports of entry and the sites of battle. Another highlight for the adventurers and their readers at home was a pilgrimage to Cathcart's Hill. There, the visitors surveyed the site, viewed monuments, and picked flowers. It was a "pensive hour." While among the graves, they reckoned with the legacies of the conflict, collectively and individually. "There were few of the party who had not a friend or relative lying there," noted William Howard Russell. For many, it had been a very personal war.[63]

The 1869 visit was not simply a moment for personal reflection. It was also an occasion for national stock-taking. As they reflected on the losses of those near and dear to them, the voyagers also reckoned with the ravages of fifteen years. The graves were "as much in ruins as Sebastopol itself," to borrow Russell's words.[64] The tour amplified concern about the dilapidation of the burial sites.[65] Winter's "wind, rain, and snow," combined with summer's "intense heat," had wrought their destruction. Monuments were "smashed to fragments"; stones were "chipped and split."[66] The location of the burial sites exposed the stones to the infelicities of the weather, which had bedeviled the British in the Crimea. It also made the sites vulnerable to the ravages of the Tatar population, who, at best, ploughed over the graves as they cultivated the land, and, at worst, plundered them in search of fortune.[67]

Reports of these discoveries during the 1869 visit helped to publicize the state of the graves. In the process, they worked to consolidate a framework for assessing the sites and critiquing their upkeep. One central ingredient here was that of national comparison. If the British cemeteries appeared forlorn in their own right, they were disgraceful in relation to those of the French. Lady Grey noted as much in her own travelogue.[68] Others too rendered the contrast graphically, juxtaposing the upkeep of the French cemetery to the decay of the English one.[69] Commentators freighted this contrast with a moral equation – the second feature of the discourse on the cemeteries to come into focus in 1869. This was especially evident in the words of William Howard Russell, who had, during the course of the Crimean War, brought home the effects of aristocratic misrule and bureaucratic bungling to the readers of the *Times*. If the Army had blundered during the Crimean War, the Government similarly fumbled in the aftermath. Mismanagement bedeviled the British in the Crimea in wartime and frugality wrecked the graves beyond it. The state of the cemeteries was, in Russell's words, a "national disgrace," the result of "sordid parsimony."[70]

Others, too, picked up on this understanding across the following months and years.[71] The radical *Reynolds's Newspaper*, for instance, responded to the reports with a nearly identical language to the one that it had used to critique the limitations of the Victoria Cross. The state of the cemeteries was, in *Reynolds's* estimation, just another injustice wrought by an "aristocratic system of Government." Never mind the fact that the graves, themselves, marked the resting places of the leaders of the Army and not the men, whose corpses lay, unmarked, in the Crimean soil. For *Reynolds's Newspaper*, the royal tour brought home, yet one more time, a national indifference to the common military men: those "gallant fellows who fought, bled, and perished in the Crimea."[72]

The uproar set into motion an official inspection of the tombs and graves, administered in 1872 by Brigadier General Sir John Adye and Colonel Charles Gordon of the Royal Corps of Engineers, who set off on the *HMS Antelope* to see the dilapidated burial grounds for themselves (Figure 4.2). Their *Report on the British Cemeteries in the Crimea* confirmed what the visiting parties and the national press had already exposed: that the Crimean graveyards were in a state of ruin, with tumbling headstones, wretched fences, and overgrown grounds. In particular, the inspectors and their correspondents noted the pillaging of the Tatars, whose greed and infidelity had prompted them to disinter bodies, ruin Crosses, and smash stones.[73] Lamentably, the fact that the Tatars held the Christian burial ground in such little regard separated them from other Muslims, who tended to hold graves as sacrosanct.[74] In the face of these ravages wrought by people and environment, the *Report* urged the employment of a guardian to superintend the Crimea's burial grounds. It also suggested an enclosure movement of sorts. This effort would involve the consolidation of memorials, stones, and Crosses strewn across the Crimea in over 100 sites within eleven cemeteries. In particular, the *Report* advised that cemeteries lacking worthy monuments should be covered over and the graves themselves abandoned. Exhumation was, officials concluded, offensive to the notion of the good death in Britain and to the dignity of the immortal soul. Elsewhere, tombs, tablets, and Crosses should be

Figure 4.2 Ruins of the British soldiers' graveyard. Wood engraving by
RCH[?]. Wellcome Collection

repaired and removed. This, too, was a delicate matter, for it involved
negotiations with local property owners, on the one hand, and with the
families of the deceased, on the other. The first group was eager to defend
their territorial interests, and, at times, to extract rent, while the second
was anxious to preserve the memories of their dead. The *Report* recommended, finally, the erection of protective fences, plain and unadorned in
their design.[75] Perhaps they might make good neighbors.

The recommendations offered in the *Report* may seem to be modest
proposals for practical custodianship and successful guardianship.
However, they proved difficult to implement across the vast distance
that separated England from the Crimea and within the eighty square
miles that comprised the burial sites. Taken together, communication
within Foreign Office files and letters printed in the newspapers reveal
frustrations and disappointments. Everywhere, there remained "headstones overturned," "monuments defaced," and "walls thrown
down."[76] The consolidation of the graves of those slain on the peninsula
and the reconstruction of monuments to battles at the Redan, the Alma,
and Inkerman proved slow, ongoing work.[77] Even the hiring and maintenance of a guardian, a seemingly simple task, was beset with difficulties.

It proceeded at a snail's pace. The successful employment of a "respectable and sober man" only brought more fiscal demands – a proper roof for the guardian's cottage and a pony to ride across the miles.[78] The far-flung geography of the graveyards meant that the guardian had to trudge over a great expanse of steppe, carrying his spade and other tools with him. He lived, additionally, three miles away from the nearest provisions. The blundering work did take a turn for the better in 1875, when Captain Anstey of the Royal Engineers began to oversee the task of repairing and consolidating the gravesites. In a cosmopolitan effort, he pressed into service an Italian stonemason, a German gardener, and a Russian builder. By 1877, they had managed to consolidate the monuments from 139 locations at eleven sites, where they repaired and restored the stones.[79]

Not all travelers to the Crimea were willing, however, to see the project as successful, as the 1880s visit of Colonel George Villiers laid bare. He upended any sense of complacency with his comments, widely publicized, about the continued deterioration of the gravesites. The British Consul at Odessa, G.E. Stanley, sought to counter the critique, as he compared the burial grounds of the Crimea to the cemeteries of England. They might not have resembled the cemeteries of English towns, with their "neatness and trimness." But, with their pleasing walks, blooming flowers, and leafy trees, they surely approached the appearance of the "ordinary English Churchyard before the grass is cut for hay." And Cathcart's Hill, for its part, exceeded this yardstick in its tidiness.[80] In other words, it offered every bit of home comfort that the Crimea might provide. It was surprising, Stanley said, that Villiers could have transformed what was, in truth, a "pretty oasis" into "so bleak and exposed a situation." Those who came to such a conclusion were, simply, "misinformed."[81] In his retort, Villiers sustained this use of the domestic burial ground as the measure. Yet, while he retained this rhetorical strategy, he rejected Stanley's conclusions. To his mind, there was no place "so unlike an English cemetery" as Cathcart's Hill.[82] It was a dispute that was troubling and impossible for a home front public to adjudicate at a distance.[83]

Concern with the graveyards took a turn to the sensational and the gothic just a few years on. In 1883, new disturbances to the gravesites came to the notice of the Foreign Office and the British public. "Shocking accounts" not simply of the decay springing from general neglect, but also of the desecrations wrought by Tatar herdsmen, continued to predominate.[84] There was troubling news of the defacement of a monument in the cemetery of the 4th Division, as well as the harrowing account of the opening of a coffin. Even more unsettling was the news that a bag tied around the neck of the corpse had been ripped asunder. Attempts at this sort of plunder extended beyond this burial ground. One highly publicized instance of vandalism occurred in the cemetery at the British Headquarters. Among the officers interred and memorialized there was General George Estcourt. His grave and the surrounding sites had long been the focus of cultivation and care, with Gowen and Anstey both working, across the decades, to build walls, repair stones, and plant trees. Although she resided at a great distance, Lady Estcourt had paid close attention to the state of her late husband's remote grave across the years, like so many wives and mothers of deceased officers. No amount of safeguarding or vigilance was enough, however, to protect the grave from the ravages of the local population. It was said that Tatar herdsmen out for plunder had opened the tomb. They did not manage to disinter the body, which was secured under concrete, but they did manage to stir great "grief and anxiety" for the widow, who pondered whether she might have her husband's bones moved nearby to Cathcart's Hill or even brought all the way home to England. Assured at long last that her husband's remains could be disturbed no more, Lady Estcourt let them rest where he had been buried.[85]

Taken together, these events, along with the visits to the Crimea of many widows and daughters of the military heroes buried there, prompted a new set of efforts to safeguard the graves.[86] The work of a custodian, however well meaning, was not enough.[87] In an 1883 meeting held at London's United Services Institution, and subsequently, in the pages of the *Times*, General Codrington appealed to the nation as he recommended the decisive gathering of the monuments at the central site of Cathcart's Hill. The plan garnered support from the Board of Works, from the Royal family, and from the armed services, not to mention from the Russian government. An act of consolidation brought to the elevated locale nearly all of the memorial stones from other cemeteries. Walls were razed and monuments moved. Left elsewhere were only stone crosses at Balaklava that marked the graves of the Sisters of Mercy, a Nightingale Cross, and assorted monumental obelisks. At Cathcart's Hill, a strong wall secured the newly gathered stones, which were flanked by corner monuments that commemorated the principal battles at Alma, Balaklava, Inkerman, and Sebastopol. At long last, these tributes in stone were united on a commanding site – a central memorial to the cherished deceased.[88] The 139 burial places had become, finally, one memorial ground. It was a home fit for heroes, if, still, too sparsely landscaped. To recognize the occasion, the Bishop of Gibraltar consecrated the consolidated graveyard in 1884 at a gathering that brought together the friends and foes of the Crimean conflict in solemn unison. At the ceremony's conclusion, an honor guard composed of Russian seamen fired three volleys in salute.[89]

Implied within the consecration ceremony was the hope that the graves, and, by extension, the Foreign Office, would be left in peace. This was, however, not to be the case. In the early 1890s, the Foreign Office found itself bedeviled by the case of the ill-fated tomb of Captain Horace Cust of the Coldstream Guards. Cust had fallen in the early days of the war, at the Battle of the Alma, his body buried in a nearby orchard, with a stone laid there in 1857. In the immediate aftermath of the war, Madame Belovodsky, the good-hearted Russian, had cared for the grave, which was situated on her property.[90] But the land had changed owners in the intervening years, coming into the hands of a family of Karaite Jews. In the early 1890s, the proprietress, a widow named Zaharievna Shokai, contacted the British Vice Consul at Sebastopol about the grave, which had remained in place, despite the efforts at consolidation.[91] As she explained, the fact that the grave lay on her property cost her money, as it stopped her from growing and harvesting within the valuable and fertile orchard. In need of the funds, she gave the Foreign Office three options: to purchase the site for a considerable sum; to provide rent, both going forward and retrospectively; or to pay a removal fee to have the grave relocated elsewhere. Lest the government should become intransigent, the lady promised to destroy the grave, or to show otherwise that she was "not joking."[92] These were threats that the Foreign Office lamented as "preposterous and outrageous," tantamount to blackmail.[93] Yet, the Foreign Office proved powerless when it came to standing up to the widow, who lived beyond the pale of nation and convention. The Russians could not either offer a promise of protection. After much handwringing and consternation, the British government moved the remains, and with them, the monument, to Cathcart's Hill. The British may have left the Crimea long before, but they could not shed the ongoing responsibility of serving as custodians to the dead in a distant, and confounding, land.[94]

***

The Crimean War claimed thousands of lives well beyond the peninsula itself. The adventurers *en route* to the war front lamented those who died at sea. There was fighting, of course, in naval theaters that ranged far from the East. And the death toll in the hospitals at Scutari and elsewhere was staggering. Accordingly, monuments reflecting the wide geographical reach of the war and its casualties extend far beyond the Crimea. There were, notably, a range of burial grounds extending from Greece and into

Turkey, at Therapia, Smyrna, Abydos, and New Phaleron, to name some locales.[95] Of all of these, the focal point was Hadarpasha cemetery at Scutari, now Üsküdar, just down the hill from the hospital where Florence Nightingale ministered to the ailing troops. This burial ground with its handsome vista was situated on the Asian side of Constantinople, across the Bosporus from the European part of the city. Whereas Cathcart's Hill was unfamiliar ground for the British at the time of the Crimean War, the cemetery at Scutari developed on a well-known landscape, adjacent to English populations and in a storied locale. Consequently, its career provides both a complementary and a contrasting story to Cathcart's Hill. While the maintenance of the Crimea's graves developed piecemeal, that at Scutari devolved from the outset, from the state. Whereas the cultural navigations at Cathcart's Hill remained quotidian and uncertain, those at Scutari were academic and deliberate. And while the Crimean graves' upkeep was bedeviled by remoteness across its history, the cemetery at Haydarpasha was shaped, over the years, by its proximity to a British expatriate population.[96]

The eastern bluffs of the Bosporus, where a British cemetery began in 1854, were well known to English observers in the years before the Crimean War. The Asian side of Constantinople boasted vast and storied cemeteries for the Eastern metropolis's Islamic population, who preferred to be buried on the same continent as the holy places of Mecca, Medina, Jerusalem, and Damascus. Graced with cypress trees, adorned with fezzes, and filled with visitors, these cemeteries were long a source of fascination for English writers and travelers.[97] The British press turned anew to the Bosporus's eastern bluffs in May 1855, when the graveyard was consecrated. In that month, the Bishop of Gibralter presided over a small, intimate, and somber affair. For the occasion, British clergymen, some thirty nurses, military officers, and 100 soldiers in arms joined in a procession. Assembled around them were a mere dozen convalescent soldiers. It was a humble affair, yet it was a fitting tribute to the deceased heroes in the East and a welcome nod to English modesty in a realm associated by the British with Oriental pomp.[98]

There was an immediate sense that this burial ground for English heroes needed protecting in a foreign land. In a contrast to Cathcart's Hill, the War Office made sure, from the outset, to press for the employment of a guardian. To borrow directly from the language of the War Office's files, the need was for a *custos* – from Latin, literally, a guard. The ideal candidate would be a respectable married man and a pensioner, perhaps from the Royal Sappers and Miners. Such a figure would be able to live on site and to perform the necessary repairs, not only at Scutari, but also at nearby burial grounds.[99] For travel, the guardian would require a pony. For shelter, he could use a small house already located in the cemetery, which might be purchased from the Turkish government. To augment his small stipend, he might, too, receive a garden for cultivation, to be walled off from the rest of the land. And finally, to make his role official, he would wear a uniform while employed. In the end, Sergeant W.H. Lyne of the Royal Engineers took up the task, making it his life's work to cultivate and beautify the cemetery where the English heroes were buried.[100]

In another contrast to Cathcart's Hill, there was a sense of urgency when it came to safeguarding the burial grounds at Scutari. This was due in no small part to the much-anticipated arrival, in 1857, of a 100-foot obelisk (Figure 4.3). Begun in London in 1855, this monument was the work of the Italian-born sculptor, Baron Carlo Marochetti. Made of granite, Marochetti's imposing tribute was flanked by four weeping victories, each colossal in size. Once installed, it would occupy a commanding place on the sea cliff, becoming easily visible to friends and strangers as they approached Constantinople. As it anticipated the monument's installation, the War Office looked for a guardian, so as to protect the obelisk from intrusion or injury. This was not the only concern to occupy Whitehall at the time, however. During the course of the monument's construction, Marochetti and the War Office found themselves engaged in lengthy negotiations having to do with both religious and linguistic expression. In the 1850s, these concerns proved a challenge to diplomats and scholars. In retrospect, their discussions provide important reminders of the difficulties involved in remembering *in situ* those who perish in wars fought at a distance from home.[101]

As he constructed his monument, Marochetti imagined, initially, that it would feature, at its pinnacle, a Cross. The crucifix would function as a tribute to those soldiers who had fought and died as Christians in aid of their Muslim allies. The Cross may have been well suited to the monument in terms of both design and meaning. It was not, however, especially well suited to the location. As designed, the obelisk would loom on the skyline above the Islamic metropolis of Constantinople, with the Cross drawing attention from all sides. There was a risk, Marochetti and others noted, as they relied upon disparaging stereotypes, of drawing the "umbrage of the fanatics" and of inspiring "unfriendly feelings." Perhaps it was unwise to showcase the Cross in what one critic derogatorily called "such close juxtaposition to a fanatical and dominant Mahomedan population."[102] The jury was out on how the locals might behave. There was, on the one hand, the sobering story of a monument to a doctor, put up at Smyrna, where a crucifix was defaced, thrown down just a night after the monument's erection. But there was, as well, on the other hand, evidence of more reassuring behavior. Nearby, at the Scutari

Figure 4.3 Crimean War Memorial. English cemetery. Haydarpasha Cemetery. 1923 Postcard. Mary Evans Picture Library/Grenville Collins Collection

Barracks, the Turks had treated the display of Crosses with respect, or at least with indifference: there had been no reports of vandalism. Perhaps, in the case of Marochetti's monument, there might be a middle ground.

In lieu of a shining gold cross sitting atop the monument, the sculptor considered a less conspicuous bronze one to be embossed on the obelisk. But in the end, the desire to protect the obelisk in a foreign land exceeded any verve to honor Christian heroes. Marochetti determined that the monument could answer its purpose without a Cross. For this reason, the secular course won out.[103]

Debates about the monument continued well after its arrival at Scutari, in 1858. If one set of questions involved the religious iconography of the obelisk, another concerned the words engraved upon it. As planned, the monument was to feature a carved inscription paying tribute to the fallen of the British Army and Navy, who had perished in the war against Russia. This tribute was, additionally, to appear on all four sides of the monument, and in each of the languages of the four allies: the British, the French, the Sardinians, and the Ottomans. The linguistic politics of translation proved complex on literally all sides. There were questions asked about the translation to the French, and particularly about whether *Anglaises* or *Britanniques* would be the better term for the monument's sponsoring nation.[104] There was deliberation, as well, about the Italian, with the Foreign Office even consulting with the Florentine *Accademia della Crusca*. One particularly ponderous question involved whether to use the word *Soldati* or *Gregary* for the armed forces. *Soldati* was preferred, but there was a risk that this choice might favor the Army's fighters over the Navy's heroes, who were all too often forgotten.[105] Ultimately, it was the fourth side, devoted to the monument's host nation, which proved the most perplexing. Was it Arabic or Turkish that was the proper language for this side of the obelisk? And how much accommodation to local religious custom and linguistic practice should there be? This discussion extended into the reaches of Orientalist scholarship, with the linguistic scholar James Redhouse submitting three Turkish translations for consideration – one literal, another more robust, and the third positively ornate. As Redhouse explained, the direct translation would verge on unintelligible for the local population; it was important, after all, that they understand something of the gravity of the monument. The ornate version could seem excessively flowery to British sensibilities, on the other hand; yet it was more accessible in the local context. On top of this, there was, as well, the matter that Islamic sacred monuments included the phrase, "God is the enduring one." It was true that such an addition might create an inconsistency, yet it was, in the end, far more respectful of local custom than an omission would have been. Ultimately, a moderate path seemed sensible to the War Office. It explained its decision, however, with an ill-advised and perhaps deliberately Islamophobic phrasing, proclaiming that it would not go "whole hog" with its translation.[106]

All of this careful deliberation about the Turkish proved wasted, however. An opposing, and influential, view favored Arabic, not Turkish, for the monument. In the mind of one advocate, it was more suitable to "pious commemoration."[107] To this suggestion Redhouse retorted that Arabic inscriptions were uncommon, indeed "almost unknown" in Constantinople. As he explained, "Turkish is universal, from the tombs of the Sovereigns to those of the peasant." Arabic, moreover, would prove impenetrable to the local population. To supply the statue with Arabic text would be to engage in an archaism not unlike employing Latin or Greek on a monument in England. Yet, Redhouse offered an Arabic translation, albeit grudgingly.[108] He cautioned that a native linguist should scrutinize the translation, to avoid offense and impropriety. In the end, Redhouse's labor was wasted and his expertise was for naught: the Embassy worked locally to devise an Arabic translation on its own.

This monument, much debated at its inception, remained the focal point for the Scutari Cemetery. It was subject to reinterpretation and refashioning one hundred years on, at the moment of the Crimean War's centenary, when a plaque was installed there to honor Florence Nightingale and her band of nurses. The intervening 100 years were varied ones for the cemetery, which had a vibrant career well after the thousands of Crimean War dead were buried there. In the years following the war, the cemetery became home, increasingly, to the graves of civilians, members of the elite of Britain's community in Turkey. The use of the cemetery for civilian purposes did, in fact, prompt the War Office to wonder, eventually, whether it was the Foreign Office instead that should cover the costs of upkeep. The cemetery was not the only memorial to the Crimea in Constantinople and environs to occupy the attention of the British in the years following the war and beyond. There was, as well, the Crimea Memorial Church, designed by George Edmund Street and built in the 1850s and 1860s in the city's English quarter. In the later nineteenth century, it provided a hub for Anglican worship. In the later twentieth, it provided a focus for a different kind of custodianship in its rehabilitation and rescue.[109] Remote in its location, Cathcart's Hill may have had an attenuated relationship to Britain in the later nineteenth century, though it was never fully absent from the English imagination. Scutari was, however, different, as it continued its career as an operational graveyard throughout the nineteenth century and as part of a broader memorial complex.

The Great War had the effect of returning British attention to the cemetery at Scutari, its uses, and its origins.[110] In 1923, a *Times* correspondent, an heir to William Howard Russell, paid a visit to the cemetery.

The reporter described its singular beauty to his interwar readership in a manner recalling that of the eastward travelers of the nineteenth century, bound for adventure and bound for war. "There is, perhaps, no burial ground in the world so beautifully situated," the journalist declared of the land, which was "perched on a rugged hill on the Asiatic shore." Sojourners could look out onto Constantinople and the Bosporus; they could turn in to admire Marochetti's obelisk and later tributes, including a monument to prisoners of war and a pillar commemorating the British Foreign Legion. The cemetery told a history of Britain's cosmopolitan engagement with the world. Yet it was also, as those who buried their dead abroad in the mid-nineteenth century hoped it might be, a preserve of Englishness. In capturing the qualities of the graveyard – its "trim and homely orderliness" and its "rambling fashion" – the correspondent drew upon a refrain used in the nineteenth century as he compared it to an English country churchyard. It appeared all the more English in its Asiatic environs, a preserve of home on a distant continent: it had a striking capacity to conjure Britain in Asia. "As one walks in the feeling is always present that this is England, not Turkey," wrote the journalist. "Of all the spots throughout the world 'that is forever England', there is probably none more unique or sacred to the British born than the Crimean Cemetery at Scutari" (Figure 4.4).[111] As we shall see, there was, in the twentieth century, plenty of tumult in the cemetery and its environs. But, at least for the *Times* correspondent, the Victorian labors of those who had planned, decorated, and cared for the burial ground had succeeded in creating a haven that would be an eternal England.

***

By the moment when the *Times* correspondent visited Constantinople, the Crimean War was a thing of the distant past. The last ranks of its heroes were dying away at home, many in straitened circumstances. National and local newspapers provided heart-rending accounts of warriors who died in despair inside the workhouse and in poverty beyond. One particularly moving story involved a seller of bootlaces. This onetime hero had performed the service of burying his comrades in the Crimea, but by the time of his death, fifty years on, there was nobody to bury him.[112] Such accounts, along with the direct appeals of veterans themselves, inspired efforts to provide for the old warriors in their twilight years and in their deaths. In cities across the country, and notably in Nottingham and in Bristol, local worthies stepped up to augment the efforts of the Light Brigade Relief Fund and the Lord Roberts Fund. They sought to ensure that Crimean veterans were spared the pains of

Figure 4.4 British Cemetery at Scutari. Photograph by an American Red Cross Relief Worker, 1920, Library of Congress, Prints & Photographs Division, American National Red Cross Collection, LC-DIG-anrc-11821

destitution in their later years and the indignities of pauper burials at their deaths. In Nottingham, for instance, H. Seely Whitby worked tirelessly over the course of more than thirty years to guarantee that the old heroes of the Crimea and of the Indian Rebellion received fitting burials, complete with a journey on a gun carriage and the sounding of the last reveille. Elsewhere, aid societies and Army regiments ensured proper ceremonies (Figure 4.5). These efforts at latter day custodianship persisted into the 1930s, when the last of the centenarian veterans finally passed away.[113]

These longest-lived Crimean veterans spent their final years in the shadow of World War I (Figure 4.6). The very last of them even witnessed the rise of Nazi aggression on the way to World War II. The previous chapters demonstrated just some of the ways in which the era of world wars transformed the geopolitical map, not to mention received notions of bravery and of heroism. The Great War additionally brought changes to the ways of addressing death and dying. Throughout the cataclysmic global event, encounters with death were pervasive and the balance sheet of destruction was incomprehensible. One effort to manage these grim

Figure 4.5 Burial of a Crimean War veteran, Holt, Norfolk. 25th Battalion Forms Honor Guard before departure for India, 1916. Photograph. National Army Museum

and nightmarish realities came in the founding of the Imperial War Graves Commission, later renamed the Commonwealth War Graves Commission. The Commission was the brainchild of Fabian Ware, a British businessman. Too old to fight in World War I, the story goes, Ware was determined, still, to play his part. He found his way into the British Red Cross, in whose ranks he encountered death and dying on a daily and an unprecedented scale. To render some order amidst the chaos, he began keeping records of the war dead, along with their places of burial, in 1915. His efforts attained formal recognition by Royal Charter in 1917 and enjoyed global reach in the Commission's subsequent work following the Armistice.[114] At that point, the Commission enlisted the labors of eminent architects to design thousands of cemeteries that would pay tribute to the sacrifices of the war, both individual and collective. The Commission employed the talents, too, of Rudyard Kipling, who became its spokesperson, publishing *Graves of the Fallen* in 1919.[115] The efforts of the Commission, still extant, have been far-reaching. It now administers

Figure 4.6 Crimean veteran and Chelsea pensioner, 1914. Postcard.
Chronicle. Alamy Stock Photo

1.7 million graves of Commonwealth war dead, known and unknown, in
154 nations across the globe.[116]
    The foundation of the Imperial War Graves Commission marked
a shift from the practices of the nineteenth century. During the
Crimean War, regiments, friends, and families worked together to
comfort the dying and to bury the dead. There was, of course,
a hierarchy built in to burial practices, with commissioned officers
receiving more extensive funerary rites and more exclusive resting
places than noncommissioned officers or privates. The War Graves
Commission did away with these hierarchies. Under its stewardship,
everyone who fought in the armed forces –whether soldier or officer,
British citizen or imperial subject, Christian or otherwise – would

receive similar recognition. This was evident in the uniform headstone style.[117] Along with the philosophical and aesthetic departures, there were bureaucratic differences, too. In the Crimean War's aftermath, custodians cultivated funeral grounds and tended to monuments, with the hope of making these resting places fitting homes for British heroes. Though well-intentioned, these efforts were scattershot and piecemeal. With central coordination and with attention from the start, the Imperial War Graves Commission succeeded in many places where the earlier efforts failed. Even so, this did not mean that their cemeteries were free from the violence wrought by natural disaster or by local vandalism.

Although the Imperial War Graves Commission was a departure from earlier practice, it literally built on earlier custodial efforts. Nowhere was this more evident than at Scutari graveyard, renamed Haydarpasha Cemetery, where the land abutting the Crimean burial ground became home to the graves and memorials of the Commission. In fact, the cemetery was not just a burial ground for World War I, but a staging ground too. It had a lively history during the Great War, which saw Britain and the Ottoman Empire, onetime allies, become foes. With its proximity to the heart of Constantinople, the cemetery was, itself, an extension of the conflict zone. Crimean graves were ransacked during the war, possibly, though not certainly, by Turkish soldiers, who were quartered in barracks and in camps nearby. In the course of the conflict, the cemetery became a holding place for ammunition.[118] During the war's later stages, Turkish soldiers used it to bury Commonwealth prisoners of war. Finally, after the war's end, and under the guidance of the Imperial War Graves Commission, the cemetery on the bank of the Bosporus became the home to over 400 graves of individual heroes from the world wars. It came, as well, to accommodate memorial tributes once located elsewhere, in Russia, Georgia, and Transcaucasia. One memorial, moved to the site in 1961, was a monument to Hindu soldiers whose remains had been cremated in line with religious custom. Another was a tribute to Commonwealth soldiers whose graves are either unmaintainable or unknown. To fantasize that the Scutari Cemetery was the most English spot on the earth, as the *Times*'s interwar correspondent did, was to erase the cosmopolitan and violent histories of the site.[119] Rather than an English country churchyard, Haydarpasha was a monument to global war and the management of its legacies.

The Scutari burial grounds may have been singular in their role as a focal point of Crimean memorialization beyond Cathcart's Hill. Yet, the story of the site was reflective of a larger history of the management of graves in postwar Europe. There was another locale where nineteenth-century histories of memorialization, twentieth-century efforts at management, and postwar engagements coalesced, in the suburbs of Athens, Greece. Established in the nineteenth century, the Anglo-French Cemetery at New Phaleron served as the final resting place for Crimean combatants. By the mid-twentieth century, the ground lay surrounded by the working-class suburbs of Athens. Nearly one hundred years after its foundation, the cemetery had become a decrepit locale found at the end of a mud-covered road and maintained by a guardian who lived in a waterlogged house. These conditions had not allowed for an easy upkeep. Indeed, the cemetery proved something of a headache for the British Foreign Office. A visit to the site in December 1949 revealed a cemetery in a "very shabby state," one that was "over-run with weeds and badly in need of tidying up."[120] The land remained vulnerable in the 1950s, if not to Crimean Tatars, then to other local threats. At New Phaleron, neighborhood boys scaled the walls to recuperate their lost footballs and nearby lovers trespassed in search of an isolated spot.[121]

While the cemetery was an object of concern for the British Foreign Office, the site was an object of desire among Athenian reformers. In the 1950s, with the hundred-year lease set to expire, local officials and municipal reformers set their sights on the land.[122] It seemed to offer new opportunities for a new epoch. There was talk of building a church for the working-class neighborhood that was needful of one. There was consideration of a football ground or perhaps a children's playground. By far the most ambitious reimagining came from the Committee for the Olympic Games. Established in advance of the 1896 Olympics, its members had maintained an interest in the site since 1907.[123] They envisioned that the hallowed ground might allow for a stadium expansion. In this way, it would aid in the Olympic endeavor of addressing national and international ideals, including the "maintenance of an athletic spirit" and the promotion of sport.[124] Perhaps the land that had been used to commemorate the services of those who fell in wartime could be employed for the pursuits of those who played in peacetime. It was a fitting goal for the postwar era, sure to benefit a new generation of youth and to enable the regeneration of Europe.[125]

Weary from the requests for repairs and for gardening tools, the Foreign Office was eager to unload the site. It saw in the opportunity to offload the cemetery an occasion to exercise a magnanimous form of graveyard diplomacy. A gift would allow for a generous gesture to the Greeks and a smooth departure from New Phaleron. Less eager to part with the land without turning a profit was Her Majesty's Treasury, pennywise and pound-foolish. Ultimately, the wisdom of the Foreign Office won out over the parsimoniousness of the Treasury, with the remains removed and the land returned to the Greeks in an act of largesse.[126] Since 1966, the graves of the fallen Crimean soldiers buried outside of Athens reside at the Phaleron War Cemetery, a site run by the Commonwealth War Graves Commission. There, they joined the company of the graves and monuments to soldiers from the Commonwealth who had fought in the Greek Civil War and in World War II. Once again, the Commonwealth War Graves Commission provided a venue for embedding the Crimean War within the topography of Commonwealth sacrifice, in a land far away from the heroes' homes.[127]

***

Along with the memorials to their twentieth-century successors, the resting places of these Crimean heroes located in Scutari and at Phaleron are accessible to visitors seeking to pay tribute in the cemeteries run by the Commonwealth War Graves Commission. The same cannot be said of the cemetery at Cathcart's Hill, the focal point for the grief of Great Britain at the end of the Crimean War and the gathering point for the monuments erected across the peninsula in the decades after. If the nineteenth-century narrative of the cemetery was characterized by frustrations and fixes, the twentieth-century history was marred by destruction and decay. The Russians may have been willing custodians of the site after the Crimean War, but they proved unable to safeguard it from the desires and designs of the local population, not to mention from the ravages and infelicities of nature. In the twentieth century, the peninsula became a staging ground for conflict once again, as a site for the struggles of the Russian Revolution and the battles of World War II. The epic contest on the peninsula with the Germans, covered amply in the British press, made Cathcart's Hill into one of its casualties. The graveyard of the Crimean heroes was ravaged by the war, with bomb attacks and shell explosions destroying the stones. The earlier attempts to protect the monuments were for naught. The home to Britain's Crimean heroes became yet another loss on World War II's balance sheet of destruction.

A tribute to the fallen in a conflict from a century past, the cemetery at Cathcart's Hill represented just one small and local casualty of World War II. Its fate was tied, ostensibly, to a larger consequence of the war and its aftermath: an end to the Anglo-Russian alliance and the rise of the Iron Curtain. With the relationship between Britain and the Crimea attenuated by the Cold War, the cemetery at Cathcart's Hill languished for the next half-century or so. In the 1950s, Nikita Khrushchev saw that the

Crimean graveyards were bulldozed, almost to rubble.[128] Even in the face of this destruction, the Foreign Office and the Commonwealth War Graves Commission paid little attention to the gravesites behind the Iron Curtain, which were frustratingly out of reach. With information sparse and access impossible, it was difficult to monitor the cemetery during the Cold War, much less to imagine caring for it.[129] By the end of the 1980s, it was a dilapidated preserve, filled with cooperative gardens used by those living nearby.[130]

This downward course reversed at the end of the Cold War. As the region emerged from behind the Iron Curtain, the Crimea became newly accessible. For a time, the site, off the beaten track of Cold War travelers, attained renewed vitality and visibility. There were new monuments erected at Cathcart's Hill and nearby. But the project was beset by challenges strikingly reminiscent of those that had hampered custodial efforts in the Victorian age.[131] In the Crimea, there arose questions about ownership of the land and episodes of jockeying for influence. In Britain itself, there was a vacuum of responsibility: the Crimean War fell outside of the direct remit of the Commonwealth War Graves Commission and outside of the immediate concern of the public, particularly against the backdrop of World War I's centenary. The project of protecting the graves of those buried in a remote land once again proved challenging, just as it had in Victorian times.

On the upside, the graves at Cathcart's Hill found their advocates, as they had in the past. The most prominent of these was Louise Berridge, who became a sort of latter-day William Howard Russell as she took up the mantle of champion of Cathcart's Hill. A onetime executive producer of the British soap opera *EastEnders,* Berridge found a new calling as the author of historical novels. Published in 2012, Berridge's *Into the Valley of Death* featured the fictional soldier Harry Ryder. It was a research trip the year earlier, in 2011, that allowed Berridge to come face to face with the graves. At that time, she happened upon what she herself called, on a now defunct website, the "wreck on Cathcart's Hill." Berridge's descriptions of the site, and her lamentations about its state, recall the words of her Victorian predecessors. Specifically, Berridge assessed the dense memorial landscape through the prism of comparison. She inventoried the monuments to the dead of all nations. The Russian monuments were well maintained. There was a marble obelisk recalling the dead of Sardinia. The resting grounds of the other allies provided yet more chastening contrasts. Turkey boasted a memorial garden that was diligently cultivated by a family of Crimean Tatars. Even more striking was the French site, nicely landscaped, well maintained, and gracefully adorned with flowers sent by France's government. But the British memorial stood in ruins. At Cathcart's Hill, Berridge found a crumbling obelisk, rampant weeds, and rusty railings. Echoing Russell and his successors, she reported that overgrown grasses covered the site where headstones had disintegrated to dust.[132]

Berridge's description of Cathcart's Hill recalled Russell's not only in its deployment of a language of comparison. It resembled the Victorian journalist and crusader's words, too, in its resort to a language of moral judgment. As in the nineteenth century, Britain had turned its back on its heroes and on its history. The cemetery and its monuments were not fitting tributes to the dead. Instead, they were sobering bellwethers of a nation's complacency – in Berridge's words a "shame and disgrace on who we are now." "It's all out there," Berridge wrote, "everything that defines us. Our pride, our glory – and our shame."[133] These parallels to Russell's rhetorical project are striking. But even while drawing them, Berridge did not simply echo her predecessor. There may have been a persistent structure of feeling, but the language of emotion and affect had changed. In the place of Russell's sorrow came melodrama. And in the place of collective mourning was individual grief: "I cried my eyes out when I saw it."[134] "I felt I'd been kicked in the gut," Berridge claimed of the cemetery.[135] These differences reflect changes in media ecology and in emotional regimes. These shifts notwithstanding, a constant remains. To use the words of historians Luc Capdevila and Daniele Voldman, the war dead hold the striking capacity, across the ages, to "haunt the collective memory of the living and disturb their peace."[136]

On her return from the Crimea, a haunted Berridge launched a call to action and made a plea for support. Frustrated at first, she found allies in the Historical Writers Association, the Crimean War Research Society, and the British Embassy in Kiev. The partnership, announced at a wreath laying at the Guards Crimean War Memorial in 2013, launched the Crimean War Memorial Appeal. On a rainy Friday, September 13, the date marking the arrival of the British troops in the Crimea 159 years before, representatives of these groups gathered to play tribute to the heroes of the mid-Victorian war. The somber ceremony occurred in central London with hardly a notice. Yet the appeal struck a contemporary chord all the same, moving regiments, buffs, and descendants to action. Organizing through websites and message boards, they pitched in to support the upkeep of the site and the construction of worthy monuments.[137] By 2014, the fundraising campaign enjoyed a vigorous momentum. It was short lived, however, in the face of the Russian invasion of the Crimea and the return to volatility on the peninsula. In the winter of 2014, the peninsula became increasingly treacherous and inaccessible.[138] Berridge and the Crimean War Memorial Appeal found themselves thwarted, bedeviled by the remoteness and tumult of the peninsula again. In 2016, they made a sad retreat from their campaign after a valiant fight. A comrade in the struggle, posting on a message board, reached to the words of the Duke of Wellington, who had passed away just before the Crimean War, in order to offer solace and understanding. "To know when to retreat and to dare to do it": this was the great wisdom of a military leader.[139] Like many before her, Berridge had tried patiently and valiantly to honor the Crimean War dead. Once again, this labor and its fulfilment would have to wait for another day.

***

The campaign to restore and renew the resting places of the dead may have stalled in the East, but efforts to safeguard the history and legacy of the Crimean War have endured on the home front. Contemporaneous with Berridge's appeal, for instance, was the push, in Sheffield, to restore a monument to the city's Crimean War dead that languished in storage. Constructed in 1858, the monument graced the city center. It had been moved to Sheffield's Botanic Gardens in 1960, and then removed in 2004, when the gardens returned to their Victorian design.[140] This localized effort demonstrates a civic interest in the Crimean War, even against the backdrop of the Great War's centenary. The Crimean War and the Victorian peninsula are far removed, but efforts to remember the dead, and to nurture their legacy, persist all the same.

The languishing monument was not the only site in provincial England to attract the attention of the Crimea's custodians in 2014. In that year, the grave of Florence Nightingale became a focus for concern, too. Along with her band of nurses, Nightingale had cared for soldiers in the wards at Scutari Hospital, just up the hill from Haydarpasha. She and her nurses had tended to men on their deathbeds. Nightingale had, herself, written countless letters to relatives from the bedsides of the dying men. The legend of her work in the Crimea grew in her lifetime and well after. It was fueled at her own death, in 1910, when her passing attracted international attention. At the time, commentators and hagiographers noted the differences between the global concern Nightingale's death attracted, certainly not desired by a notably private woman, and the intimate place of her burial, in a country churchyard in Hampshire. It was there that Nightingale was buried in a family plot, at St. Margaret's Church in East Wellow, and it was to this gravesite that attention turned, once again in 2014. Long the site of pilgrimage, the grave, and the surrounding churchyard, were damaged by a Valentine's Day storm. The ancient church had often struggled, and it had been the subject of a theft in

2010, when a window featuring a Cross made out of Crimean bullets and gifted to Nightingale was stolen. In 2014, concern focused upon the churchyard once again so that the grave might be restored. Swiftly and effectively, it was put back in order in a matter of a few months, in time for Nightingale's May 10 birthday, which had become the date for observing International Nurses Day.[141]

The prompt and notably decisive action offers a strong contrast to the slow and often inconclusive work at Cathcart's Hill. We can attribute this disparity, in part, to proximity. No matter how remote they were in the public mind, the corners of Hampshire were, after all, far more accessible than the reaches of the Crimea, thousands of miles away. We can attribute it, as well, to the fact that Nightingale became, during the War and long after, the foremost heroine of the Crimean War. It is thus to the production of Nightingale as the leading light of the campaign that the next chapter turns.

Part III

Angels

5   The Heroine

Conventional wisdom has long told that Florence Nightingale was the most outstanding figure of the Crimean War.[1] Known today as a progenitor of modern nursing, Nightingale became a guiding figure during the conflict. During wartime, she led a band of amateur nurses to the East, spending twenty-one months at Scutari Hospital, across the Bosporus from Constantinople. There, she and her so-called Angel Band waged a storied battle, not against the Russians who prolonged the war, but against the cholera, which felled the troops. In so doing, she and her nurses offered a rebuke to medical and military mismanagement. From her acclaimed arrival at Scutari in November 1854 to her quiet return to England in August 1856, Nightingale captured the hearts and minds of a nation at war. A nurturing presence, she became known as the Lady with the Lamp as she offered up an avatar of greatness that took the form of mercy. Those who followed Nightingale from the halls of Scutari Hospital, through her visit to the Crimea, and back to England again found in her story a tale of national redemption in the face of a national trial. If the Crimean War was a pivotal occasion in the making of masculine bravery and manly compassion, it was, even more, the stage for the production of womanly sacrifice and feminine heroism.

Nightingale was not only the leading figure during wartime. She was also a guiding light long after. Her fame endured well beyond the Crimean War, through the Victorian era, and after her 1910 death. Among the heroes of the Crimea, Nightingale is singular in her persistence. Having fulfilled the need for spiritual connection during a war with distinct religious overtones, Nightingale became something of a secular saint in its long aftermath.[2] She was a moral exemplar and a national lodestone. Nightingale appeared on figurines and sculpture and on stamps and bank notes. Across the centuries, a host of ordinary Britons clung to reminiscences and relics associated with her, all the while seeking connection to Nightingale's glory, the Crimean past, and the Victorian age. Bridging secular and sacred, and past and present, Nightingale became a focus for mass culture in the twentieth century, the subject of popular books, radio shows, and pageantry.[3]

Florence Nightingale's longevity as a Crimean heroine did not simply hinge on her pervasiveness, but also on her pliability. This was particularly so when it came to gender. Across her life cycle and afterward, Nightingale became an avatar of womanhood in many forms. The production of Florence Nightingale was an extensive project of fantasy, containment, and self-fashioning. As feminist critics have shown, the notion of a ministering angel was, in many regards, a myth developed atop the actualities of a stern and bureaucratic persona. Nightingale was, in truth, an iconoclastic daughter who defied her parents' desires as she pursued nursing, declined to marry, and challenged the medical profession. If the notion of a ministering angel enabled the acceptance of a difficult daughter during the Crimean War, the image of an invalid returnee papered over the challenges of a formidable presence in the aftermath. Although she lived in seclusion on her return from the East, Nightingale remained an energetic reformer who transformed nursing education and public health. Atop this legacy, Nightingale became a professional model in the twentieth century, when nurses and humanitarians looked to her for inspiration, guidance, and messaging.

Race, region, and religion have been equally important, if less considered, in the making of Nightingale as an English heroine. In her lifetime and after, Nightingale epitomized a set of virtues connoted by the idea of middle England: rural, Protestant, and Anglo-Saxon. She displayed "firm English character," to use the words of one admirer.[4] Her tastes and proclivities were exemplary of a sort of upper-middle-class Englishness that became associated, at once, with Christendom and civilization, and with piety and progress. Legendarily fond of animals, she was a model of pastoral care in her girlhood.[5] Buried in a country churchyard, she was attached to rural England at her death. She was chaste, modest, and respectable, in her deeds and in her words. There was a measure of fantasy in this rendering of Nightingale as a rural, English idyll, just as there had been in the fashioning of the Lady with the Lamp. Nightingale was, literally, made abroad, born in Italy, educated in Europe, and triumphant in the East. She later lived and toiled in London. Yet, encomiums associated her with the villages of Hampshire and the countryside of England across her life and afterlife.

Across a long arc of history, Nightingale, the Crimean heroine, has served as an organizing figure for national life, an avatar of Englishness and a vision of womanhood. Yet, the contemporary era has laid bare her limitations. Nightingale, a pioneer of nursing, long had her skeptics, but her most decisive critics came from within the profession she had a hand in developing. As the new millennium approached, the nurses of the National Health Service turned on Nightingale. Deemed excessively privileged, sanctimonious, and deferential, she was no longer a worthy figurehead. A white Briton born into wealth, she was an unsuited inspiration for a diversified profession, a mismatch for modernity and multiculturalism alike. Florence Nightingale may have been remarkably resilient as the great exemplar of the Crimean War in British public memory. But even her legend has found its limits, like the very island story it has constructed and underwritten.

***

A nation at war met Florence Nightingale in 1854, not long after the fighting in the Crimea began (Figure 5.1). The young woman who stole the hearts of England in the first difficult winter of the Crimean War was born thirty-four years earlier, in 1820, in the Italian city from which her parents derived her name. The daughter of learned and liberal parents, Nightingale had already, by the time of the Crimean War, traveled far in diverging from familial expectations and pursuing nursing education. By 1854, Nightingale served as the superintendent at the Institute for the Care of Sick Gentlewomen in Harley Street, London; she had assumed this post in the summer of 1853. Years of training on the European continent preceded Nightingale's ascent to this station. A path of study had taken her to France and Germany, where she learned her vocation, the art of nursing, from Catholic and Protestant orders.[6] In Germany, especially, she gained an understanding of hospital discipline as efficient and orderly and of nursing demeanor as circumspect and serious.[7] European travel and European exchange thus shaped an English heroine and an English profession, as Nightingale's early life lays bare.

When it came to the unfolding of the Crimean War, Florence Nightingale's travel in Europe was decisive in more ways than one. It was on the continent – in Italy, to be exact – where Nightingale met Sidney Herbert, the eventual Secretary of War, in the early 1850s. It was Herbert who ultimately sent Nightingale to Scutari, where she ministered to the British troops suffering from cholera. The cholera, and the medical mismanagement that had allowed it to spread, were causes for great concern at the time, with "dire distress and bitterest agony piercing England nearly to the heart," in the words of one early hagiographer.[8] In a legendary missive, Herbert called upon Nightingale to bring her energies to the East.[9] The plan was to gather a band of lady nurses to be deployed at the British Hospital at Scutari, situated on the eastern side of

Figure 5.1 Florence Nightingale by William Edward Kilburn. 1856. Albumen Carte de Visite. National Portrait Gallery, London

the Bosporus.[10] There, members of the Royal Army Medical Corps and members of Catholic nursing sisterhoods were already at work against the cholera's ravages. Even so, Nightingale's new mission provided hope for the doubtful public and the beleaguered troops. Perhaps it could answer the "cold unfeeling iron heel of routine, and the heavy murderous hand of mismanagement."[11] There were, it turned out, more than enough women willing to rise to the occasion. Working-class matrons, middle-class ladies, and even minor aristocrats answered the call. The ranks quickly filled with thirty-eight nurses, handpicked by Nightingale.[12] These volunteer nurses became, in popular parlance, members of her "Angel Band."[13]

While Nightingale and her nurses prepared for the journey to the East, the public learned about the woman at the helm of the "Angel Band." Accounts of Nightingale's rare experience and testimonials to her exceptional character abounded. Taken together, they produced an image of Nightingale as the archetype of English womanhood: nurturing, devoted, and Christian. Sarah Anne Terrot, a Sellonite sister from Edinburgh who served among the thirty-eight nurses, confessed "an impulse to love, trust, and respect" Florence Nightingale.[14] Goodness and wisdom, intelligence and devotion – all were evident in her very bearing. In the dailies and in the weeklies, and in the provincial papers and in the national organs, letters and leaders pointed to Nightingale's focus, character, and "singleness of purpose."[15] Accounts reached back to Nightingale's younger years, consolidating for popular consumption, and for perpetuity, the aura of destiny.[16] Annals of her youth focused on Nightingale's efforts at healing animals and visiting villagers. Legendarily, the young lady was called to her vocation as an adolescent. "God spoke to me and called me to his service," Nightingale had declared.[17] Such an understanding had broad uses, lending an air of inevitability to Nightingale's mission and rendering acceptable her eschewal of marriage. Being a nurse, after all, was a mean profession in the early nineteenth century, when the dominant figure resembled Charles Dickens's Sairey Gamp, the intemperate and immoral nurse of *Martin Chuzzlewit*.[18] But Nightingale, conversely, was like the "martyrs of old."[19] In her "abnegation and self-denial," she resembled Joan of Arc.[20] Hers was, similarly, the "humility of true greatness."[21] Nightingale's sacrifices stood out, in the end, as a most "Christian episode in a Christian war."[22]

Fulsome coverage of the journey of Nightingale and her nurses to the East followed upon these encomiums. Personal and public accounts alike suggest the fanfare and celebrity that the party enjoyed. They traveled by ship and by rail, making their way across the English Channel from Folkstone to Boulogne, and sailing once again from Marseilles to Constantinople. Like the soldiers who had preceded them, the nurses enjoyed good cheer upon departure. They were feted at banquets and hailed by crowds, who regaled them with wishes of "God Speed." They met a hearty welcome at Boulogne, where they enjoyed the sisterly assistance of fisherwomen, who carried their luggage from the port into the town. It was a warming gesture of transnational solidarity among women in wartime.[23] The much-heralded nurses made it to their journey's end point, the Barrack Hospital at Scutari, just across the Bosporus from Constantinople, in perfect time.[24] They arrived to meet the troops that had been wounded at the Battle of Inkerman, where, on November 5, Britain's soldiers had distinguished themselves for their great bravery. As the injured men came in, the ladies washed their wounds and cleaned their bodies. It was, as popular accounts spun it, the perfect meeting of English womanly duty and soldierly sacrifice.[25]

From the point of the nurses' arrival at Scutari to the very end of the war, accounts of the succoring presence of the women abounded. William Howard Russell christened Nightingale as the "Lady with the Lamp." A chorus of correspondents joined in praise of the "incomparable woman" – that "ministering angel" who had the power to soothe the soldiers with her very presence. "When her slender form glides quietly along each corridor, every poor fellow's face softens with gratitude at the sight of her," the *Illustrated London News* noted.[26] This was a capacity that extended to the nursing band, whose members meted out the miracles of feminine care with tenderness and abundance.[27] It was almost as if their very presence could cure the suffering masses at Scutari. As Sarah Anne Terrot reported, the arrival of the nurses made the men feel that they had returned home to their mothers. "The sight of a woman does a world of good," one declared.[28] It was enough to press these military men to manly feeling. In the years and decades to come, stories of "poor fellows" bursting into tears at the sight of the nurses were both characteristic and legion. "'I can't help crying when I see them,'" one legendarily exclaimed.[29] The womanly presence of the nurses elicited tears and gratitude among the soldiers. In this way, male frailty revealed itself in the face of female strength.

These sentimental narratives were moving in moral and material terms alike. They captivated a public at home, kindling affection for Nightingale's mission and generating support for the suffering troops. This was important work in symbolic terms. It made what might have been seen as an inappropriate mission – with English womanhood under threat at Scutari Hospital, or, conversely, with female presence extending itself into unwanted quarters – into a domestic idyll appropriate for home consumption. One additional byproduct was to generate support in the form of funds and goods. The coverage of the early work of Nightingale's band in Scutari inspired a cascade of contributions to the Sick and Wounded Fund, also known as the Patriotic Fund. In towns across the nation, men, women, and children came forward to give their pennies and shillings to the Patriotic Fund. They answered the call, too, for those "comforts and luxuries" that would succor the soldiers, whether these be shirts, stockings, or even drink, which at least one nurse requested in order to soothe those who suffered. Arrowroot and tapioca arrived in plenty, as did chess sets and magic lantern slides.[30] In the face of these donations, Miss Nightingale herself made special appeals for the most simple items: lint and linens, necessary for the treatment of wounds.[31]

The disjuncture between Nightingale's needs and the actual donations is telling, for it points to a misunderstanding – at the time of the Crimean War and well after – of the real work of nursing in the Crimea. Though the rhetoric might have suggested otherwise, it was not all sentimental succor. It ranged far beyond the emotional care of the soldiers, which was secondary, and, at times, irrelevant. Nursing was a "fluid" endeavor at the time when Nightingale and her band arrived in Scutari.[32] It involved the menial and mundane tasks of laundry, needlework, and cooking. It could be stern and arduous work.[33] Immediately upon arrival, Nightingale and her nurses set themselves to washing, scrubbing, and even rat catching. Miss Nightingale herself was known to be an "expert rat-catcher."[34] She was efficient and fearless, as her demanding journey to Balaklava during wartime soon suggested. In short, nursing required ability, industry, and decisiveness; it demanded grit, courage, and valor. In these ways, it was not unlike soldiering. Additionally, if nursing was physical in nature, it was also managerial in focus, as Nightingale subsequently explained in her *Notes on Nursing*.[35] Nightingale had more interest in organizing the hospital than in ministering to the men. She had little patience, in fact, for the middle-class women who pottered about, tending to the soldiers and making beef teas. She may have performed bedside rounds, but Nightingale was far more concerned to transform systems than to aid individuals – a preference that proved a great disappointment to novelist Elizabeth Gaskell, one contemporary admirer who contributed to the Nightingale myth.[36]

To be sure, there were still more cracks in the legend of a Nightingale who was angelic and nurturing. Relentlessly and mercilessly, Nightingale antagonized the leadership of the Royal Army Medical Corps and of the Catholic nursing sisterhoods. Some Army officers found her "over bearing and presumptuous."[37] Others saw her as "bullying" and "sanctimonious." and as interfering and misinformed. She could be unpopular with staff, doctors, and troops.[38] There were those among Nightingale's band who had their run-ins with her as well. Those who found much to admire in Nightingale could object, at times, to her stern bearing. Among Nightingale's nurses, even her partisans admitted that she was controlling. She had as well tendencies toward self-aggrandizing behavior. She was, to hear one member of her Angel Band tell it, all too keen for the limelight.[39]

Yet for all the cracks in the legend, there were still more stories that countered these flaws. Take, for instance, the account of Nightingale's return from the Crimea, which helped to consolidate a notion of the beloved nurse as the avatar of English modesty. To the consternation of the nation, Nightingale herself was felled by cholera late in the war. It was, ultimately, well after the conflict's end that Nightingale, elevated in stature by her labors in the Crimea yet weakened in strength by the travails of illness, found her way back home. A sign of her promise, Nightingale had arrived in the East in November 1854 to great fanfare. A testament to her modesty, she returned home to England in August 1856 under secret cover. Traveling under the name of Miss Smith, her hair cut short after her illness, she made her way, *incognito*, back to her parents' home in Derbyshire. It was, in many ways, an anticlimactic homecoming occurring after the departure of the troops from the Crimea and after the celebrations of the peace in England. But in its modesty and in its simplicity, it echoed Nightingale's conduct at Scutari and in the Crimea.[40]

So pervasive were these understandings that they inflected assessments of Nightingale's possessions. Among these was a simple Russian-built wood carriage that Nightingale had used for transport in the East. A "homely vehicle," it was a perfect complement to her "womanly simplicity."[41] This simplicity was evident on Nightingale's unobtrusive return to her motherland. She was an example of grace and discretion. As such, General Grey noted, she might serve as a lesson, and a rebuke, to many boastful generals.[42]

The truth is that Nightingale's return did not go unnoticed or unrecognized, whether at the highest station or among the lowest ranks. Queen Victoria awarded Nightingale a St. George's Cross, inscribed with the words "Blessed are the Merciful." The award reflected Victoria's military enthusiasm, as did an invitation to a ball at Balmoral, where Nightingale appeared in October 1856, displaying her newly cropped hair.[43] In the months after Nightingale's return, there were, as well, many people from elevated stations who wrote to Miss Nightingale's parents to offer gratitude and congratulations. Several had, themselves, welcomed their own sons back from war. But none, they imagined, would be "crowned with honor and glory and immortality" quite as the heroic daughter promised to be.[44] There were, finally, Britons across the land, including no fewer than 1,800 laborers from Newcastle-upon-Tyne, who offered up testimonials in Florence Nightingale's honor.[45]

As these examples suggest, Nightingale was, at the war's end, beloved across ranks. She was "'the heroine of the cottage, the workshop, and the alleys.'"[46] Tributes to the Lady with the Lamp assumed multiple forms at this moment, which biographer Mark Bostridge has called the height of "Nightingale mania."[47] Steamships and racehorses bore her name; porcelain figurines and simple dolls resembled her likeness. And, in the months and years that followed, parents across the nation gave their infant daughters the name of Florence.[48] Nightingale was on her way to assuming the role of secular saint.[49] In this vein, mid-Victorian pilgrims paid visits to Nightingale's childhood home, located in the quiet hamlet of Lea, with its lush scenery, picturesque views, and beautiful environs. To know Lea Hurst was to know Nightingale, noted James Croston, an admirer who suggested that the home itself was generative not just of Nightingale's "tender solicitude" and "humanizing influence," but also of her "holy ministerings" and her "self-denying zeal."[50] Lea Hurst also conjured up Nightingale's "Christian devotion" and "saint-like endurances."[51] Its location, both "quiet" and "secluded," seemed to foretell the shape that Nightingale's character would take in the years following the war.[52] Like Nightingale, Lea Hurst was sure to enjoy a renown that was not only "imperishable," but also "immortal."[53]

By the time the Crimean War came to a close, there was no question but that Britain had found a new heroine. However, this casting of Florence Nightingale as the heroine of the war generated a set of questions about the nature of the heroic, and about the gender of heroism. There was the opportunity, for some, to recast the very notion of care. Perhaps heroism had changed its contours, for men and women alike. There were those who welcomed this shift, noting that heroism in war did not simply translate into manly action. It did not correlate merely to "dashing up the heights of the Alma" or "seeking glory at the canon's mouth."[54] These were, to be sure, the sorts of feats that could gain a man the Victoria Cross. Yet heroism in the war's aftermath extended to performing the quotidian work of care, as done, allegedly by Nightingale's female nurses and as performed, too, by the Army's male orderlies.[55] But there was not always the sense that heroism could be an expansive, or a fluid category. For most commentators, it presented itself as a zero-sum game. This understanding emerged quite clearly at the war's end in the encomiums offered up to Nightingale. At that time, there was a pervasive sense, to use the words of the *Illustrated London News*, that "the chivalry of England ha[d] changed sexes."[56] Time and again, those who heaped praise on Nightingale determined that "England's greatest glory in the bloody fields of the Crimea" was achieved not by a man, but by a woman.[57]

Such formulations anticipate a broader shift in the gendered order of things, associated most notably with World War I, when women rose to the occasion on the home front and when men returned forever changed from the battlefront.[58] Across the experiences of the combatant nations, these developments produced great anxieties in the wake of the Great War. The emergence of a woman as the avatar of national heroism at the time of the Crimean War elicited a related uncertainty, producing a host of accommodations and responses. There were those who tried, in the face of Nightingale's rising star, to frame her as male. Even before the War, Nightingale's very family had played with notions of gender pliability as it sought to accommodate a daughter of unusual ambition. In a family without sons, Nightingale had been known as "the young squire."[59] And, as she defied that family's wishes in traveling in pursuit of her vocation, Nightingale referred to herself, in a letter to her mother, as "your vagabond son."[60] Later on, admirers compared her talents and her accomplishments to those of statesmen and generals. It was said that her work in the Crimea demanded "the courage of a Cardigan, the tact and diplomacy of a Palmerston, [and] the endurance of a Howard."[61] Such a gesture might compare Nightingale to the leading men of the day, or, tellingly, to those who fell short of expectations. There were others still, who went further, making Nightingale into a member of the stronger sex, at least rhetorically. "I have only met two men in the Crimea," an admirer had once claimed, "and one was Florence Nightingale."[62] This remark evinces an effort to stabilize heroism as a male quality, while cordoning women off from war. It also appears as a backhanded compliment, acknowledging Nightingale's efforts in the Crimea, while castigating the established leadership. Deceptively decisive in its rhetoric, it was a form of praise that opened, rather than answered, questions about the gender of military heroism at the Crimean War's end.

Responses to such ambivalences took their shape in the form of cultural products that sought to reassert the feminine aspects of Nightingale's personae – among them, her altruism, her charity, and her saintliness. To this end, the most enduring tributes to Nightingale portray her not as a formidable warrior, a fearless reformer, or a trenchant critic. Instead, she emerges as a ministering angel, a domestic archetype, and even a national saint.[63] Sentimental and lyrical verses cast Nightingale in a decisively feminine light. As in the case of the Light Brigade, poetry proved an effective vehicle for focusing attention and producing consensus. Such was the case with Henry Wadsworth Longfellow's "Santa Filomena" (1857), which was just the most renowned of the verses written to honor the heroine. Here, Longfellow likened Nightingale to the virgin martyr. He paid homage to the Crimean heroine, the "Lady with the Lamp," as he cast her as the avatar of all that was "noble" and "good" in "heroic womanhood." Yet, even as they elevated Nightingale, Longfellow's verses worked to constrain the heroine. They placed her in an arc of female sacrifice that ministered and nurtured, rather than in a lineage of social reform that challenged and critiqued. Like the light she spread, Longfellow's Nightingale seemed to "pass" and "flit," magically and effortlessly. Her work was not that of mind and muscle, but of sympathy and soul.[64]

Along with poetry, visual culture proved to be especially effective in stabilizing an image of a feminine Nightingale. In the mid-nineteenth century, it had the advantage, along with poetry, of being reproducible and transmissible. In no small measure, an image in the *Illustrated London News* cultivated Nightingale's celebrity in Victoria's time and in our own (Figure 5.2).[65] Here, Nightingale was pictured walking through the wards at Scutari with her legendary Turkish lamp. The image did much to popularize the stern and forbidding Nightingale – a woman whose appearance, as an admirer would later recall, was "not one of beauty but of character – firm English character."[66] It was disseminated far and wide, shaping subsequent representations, such as Jerry Barrett's in *The Mission of Mercy* (1856–1858). This group portrait, which includes a gentle and demure Nightingale, rather than a severe and dominating one, has occupied pride of place in London's National Portrait Gallery

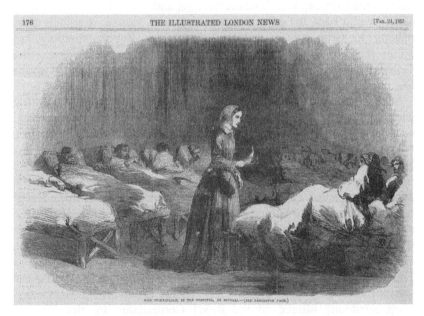

Figure 5.2 Florence Nightingale. Wood engraving. Illustrated London News. February 24, 1855. National Portrait Gallery, London

since 1993. And, well before its hanging there, the painting influenced the iconography of the £10 note that circulated in Britain between 1975 and 1994. Some have lamented its predominance in visual culture and popular consciousness.[67] But these images suggest the staying power of a legend. They remind us, too, of the deep desires for national heroes and the entrenched work of gender norms, in the Victorian era and beyond.

***

The popular understanding, in the wake of the war, was that Florence Nightingale had "saved the British army" even while she ruined her own health.[68] It is now accepted that Nightingale suffered from brucellosis, a bacteria-borne chronic disease that led to her Crimean fever and her subsequent invalidism.[69] Debilitated by the ailment, Nightingale appeared in public only infrequently for the remainder of her life until her death in 1910, well after the close of the Victorian era. In Nightingale's own words, she lived as a "prisoner" in her own home, a victim of "illness and overwork."[70] The public readily accepted Nightingale's self-fashioning around her chronic condition. Yet, the image of Nightingale as an invalid obscures her life's labors in the aftermath of the Crimean War. The overarching understanding of Nightingale as an invalid runs the risk of capturing her as passive; it equally risks making the Crimea the apex of her life's work. Popular memory and public commemoration continue to fuse the two. However, the Crimean campaign did not mark the conclusion of Nightingale's active life, but instead, the very beginning.[71]

Nightingale was, for one, a stern critic of the medical profession during and after the war.[72] She had proven a formidable and often frustrating, adversary for the Royal Army Medical Corps while at Scutari. As a public favorite, she enjoyed distinct advantages. She emerged as the greatest guardian of the soldier and the fiercest foe of cholera. As her star rose, the fortunes of the Royal Army Medical Corps fell.[73] The Royal Army Medical Corps was short on staff, provisions, and goodwill. From top to bottom, its members exhibited incompetence and indifference in the public mind; they failed to keep up with the demands of the war and the exigencies of the age.[74] The troubles of the Royal Army Medical Corps and its doctors did not end with the declaration of peace, however. If Nightingale had challenged the Army's medical leadership during the war, she damned it in the aftermath. Particularly notable was her excoriating testimony offered to the Royal Commission on the Sanitary Condition of the Army in 1858.[75] There, Nightingale lashed out about the filthy halls, drunken orderlies, and medical incapacities of the Army's hospitals, and especially that at Balaklava, which she had visited in 1855. To hear her tell it, all was "dirt and disorder."[76]

Critics have long held that Nightingale's claims were sweepingly distorted, exaggerated, and even libelous. From the Crimean moment to the present, skeptics have maintained that Nightingale and her nurses wrongly claimed credit for countering the cholera.[77] During and after the war, an understanding of Nightingale's unusual, even superhuman effectiveness, and, with it, an acceptance of her staggering, perhaps magical, successes pervaded.[78] But the numerical evidence unsettles a decisive conclusion.[79] Nightingale and her nurses might, in fact, have made matters worse at Scutari. It was not her initiatives, but, instead, improvements in water and sanitation that reversed the death rate, many now argue.[80] Yet, Nightingale's legend has served, in its day and beyond, to overshadow such critiques.

Nightingale employed her legend in the service not simply of critiquing the medical establishment, but also with the purpose of improving patient care. Her work here was enabled, in large part, by a national subscription yielding an award of £50,000.[81] As the war came to a close, enthusiasts across the nation had contributed their guineas to the Nightingale Fund. It was a collection meant to offer long-standing recognition to the patriotic and charitable acts of Nightingale and her nurses. Nightingale delivered on the hopes of the Subscription Fund in founding the Nightingale Training School for Nurses at St. Thomas' Hospital, the first secular training ground for nurses in Great Britain. It made the so-called Nightingale nurse a prototype throughout the English-speaking world. And it provided a template for education across Britain, the empire, and the globe.[82]

But Nightingale's influence did not end there. In her later years, she was an exemplar of liberal-minded reform. Vigorously and forcefully, she engaged in the reworking of the War Office, often sparring with foes – and friends – from her Crimean days. She sought to improve sanitary conditions in India, too. For these causes, she wrote prolifically. Shelves of publications fill library bookcases; thousands of letters fill England's archives. Nightingale was an innovator, additionally, in statistics. A formidable statistician herself, she developed her well-known rose, or coxcomb, graphs to communicate to the medical community and the broader public the extent of deaths by disease in the East.[83] Alongside these pursuits, Nightingale wrote amply about spiritual life and about women's roles. With others of her generation, she kept a distance from the suffrage campaign. Yet she became, in the twentieth century, a foremother, if not an unproblematic one, for first- and second-wave feminism.[84]

These contributions notwithstanding, Nightingale's identity in the public sphere remained that of a "semi-invalid" in her later life.[85] Nightingale scarcely left her bedroom in London's modest South Street after 1896.[86] She was particularly notable as an absent presence when it came to anniversaries and occasions having to do with the Crimean War. With her usual regrets, she routinely expressed her long-standing affection for, and loyalty to, Britain's soldiers. Offering words directly to the veterans, she pointed them toward godliness and temperance.[87] It is fitting to imagine her addressing veterans of the Charge of the Light Brigade, another lot of heroes from the Crimean War, through Edison's phonograph in 1890.[88] In those early years of recorded sound, she must have seemed to the aging veterans something of a spectral presence – a beloved voice from beyond. Though her public appearances grew rarer, Nightingale's reputation expanded. By the turn of the century, Nightingale had become, in the public mind, an exemplar of "Christian charity," the "Queen of Nurses," and the "Soldier's Friend."[89] Several accolades granted late in life recognized this status. Nightingale received the Freedom of the City of London in 1908. Legendarily, she accepted the honor with her typical self-abnegation, asking that the funds routinely spent on a gold casket be routed to charity. In her final year, she attained the Order of Merit, becoming the first woman to hold the status.[90] At her life's end, then, Nightingale's public presence had an inverse relationship to her reputation: the less she went out in public, the more her legacy seemed to grow.

At no time, though, did her absence make the hearts of the nation and the world grow fonder than on the occasion of her passing. In mid-August, 1910, telegraph wires the world over were abuzz with startling news: "Florence Nightingale is dead."[91] The Lady with the Lamp was no more, having expired from heart failure on Saturday, August 13 at her London home.[92] Her death prompted an outpouring of feeling – not just in London, but also across Britain, the empire, and even the English-speaking world. In reaches far and wide, the name of Nightingale had become a "household word."[93] Notices of sorrow, pride, and regret issued from all directions. Tributes upheld Nightingale as a singular figure, rivaling monarchs in stature and enjoying "a halo almost of sanctity."[94]

The encomiums to the deceased reformer issued at the time of Nightingale's death recall the lionization of the Lady with the Lamp at the end of the Crimean War. This time, as they mourned and mythologized the heroine, admirers introduced Nightingale to a new generation of

Britons.[95] As they wrote in the press and preached from the pulpit, those who paid tribute to Nightingale recalled the young heroine of the Crimean War. They told tales of her early days, including her birth to privilege in Italy, her proclivity for care among the poor, and her call to sacrifice in the Crimea. In the process, they solidified the Lady with the Lamp as the paragon of Victorian virtue. She was superhuman in her capacities and godlike in her character. "Myths and saints have been made out of less inspiring material," the *Daily Graphic* claimed.[96] The Nightingale to whom these admirers paid tribute held many qualities worthy of emulation. The embodiment of modesty, the incarnation of Christianity, and the personification of generosity, Nightingale was the epitome of English womanhood. If these qualities had been essential to the construction of the living Nightingale, they were equally, if not more, vital to the characterization of the deceased exemplar.[97]

In an act that was taken as a hallmark of her modesty, Nightingale had protested against the notion of a public funeral. Given her long-standing imprint and her far-reaching influence, however, there were calls among the general public and in military quarters alike for such an occasion.[98] Ultimately, a memorial service at London's St. Paul's Cathedral allowed an audience of 4,000 to remember Nightingale, just a week after she passed away. Hundreds of applications for attendance flooded the War Office. Priority was granted to Crimean veterans and Nightingale nurses, who occupied 2,500 of the seats.[99] Representatives of the Indian Medical Service and Chelsea Pensioners also filled out the audience. The memorial service shaped the legacy of the woman it sought to honor. Not only did the occasion tether Nightingale's life and the Crimean War. It also cemented her ties to Christendom. Those assembled at St. Paul's Cathedral remembered Nightingale by singing the hymn that was the favorite of this Christian crusader: "The Son of God Goes Forth to War."[100] These understandings extended into other memorial occasions honoring Nightingale, including a concurrent service at York Minster, where the Bishop of Beverly bid farewell to an "ideal Christian woman."[101]

There was a sense that Nightingale would have found the village burial that followed the metropolitan ceremony more suited to her tastes. A plain wooden casket draped with a simple white cashmere shawl traveled by train from London's Victoria railway terminus to Romsey's small station. Flanked by soldiers whose regiments had fought in the Crimea long ago, the casket moved on a dreary and gloomy day through quiet village streets with lowered blinds and blackened shutters. It traversed lonely roads and remote corners before making its way to St. Margaret's, East Wellow, a church dating to 1215 (Figure 5.3). It was there that

Hearse Florence Nightingales Funeral

FUNERAL OF
FLORENCE NIGHTINGALE
1910

The Guards following up the hill
Florence Nightingales Funeral
Passing near Snelgroves grave in
The Churchyard. And Captains grave
in the field to left

Figure 5.3 Florence Nightingale's funeral and burial. "Bygone Hampshire" album compiled by Florence H Suckling, 97M81/23/23. Romsey Borough Archive. Hampshire Record Office

Nightingale's parents lay buried and it was there that she had worshipped as a young girl. There, Nightingale was buried, alongside her parents, in a gesture that reminded mourners of her maiden status. The casket arrived to a church overflowing with visitors. The crowds notwithstanding, the contrast between the London memorial, a grand, even global occasion, and the country graveside ceremony, a quiet and intimate affair, was striking. At St. Margaret's, villagers and farmers had gathered to remember a familiar figure and in some cases, a friend.[102] The occasion linked Nightingale, a cosmopolitan leader who was born in Italy and who traveled widely, to a rural people and a rural landscape. It was an association that reached back to her prime, when admirers from across England visited Lea Hurst, and one that persisted after her death, when pilgrims from across the Atlantic traveled to Nightingale's grave.[103]

Recurring as a memory of the day, in newspaper accounts and in oral histories alike, was the abundance of flowers sent both to London and to East Wellow to pay tribute to Nightingale. At St. Margaret's Church, flowers covered the casket, surrounded the grave, and filled the church. They came from locations far and wide, from Germany and from Tanzania, and from people known and unknown. An especially notable contribution was that from Queen Alexandra, who had sent a wreath of lilies, orchids, and white roses in the form of a Cross. The note that it bore expressed the admiration of millions the world over: "In grateful memory to the greatest benefactress of suffering humanity."[104] A humbler tribute that tugged at the heartstrings came from seven-year-old Stella Foster, who included the following note: "To dear Miss Nightingale. Please may my wreath be put with the other flowers? I picked the heather and made it myself."[105] Others, too, paid tribute, including the International Council of Nurses, which was on its way to becoming a custodian of Nightingale's memory, and the North of England Women's Suffrage Society, which sought to lay claim to Nightingale's legacy.

As these floral tributes suggest, a striking range of admirers attached themselves to Nightingale at her life's end. Some may have been motivated by love of country or by the mythology of history. Others might have had professional or political aims. As they joined in the act of mourning Nightingale, they participated in a shared civic and emotional project. Once again, at her death, Nightingale's legacy offered a social bond that connected the polity through tears.[106] The Lady with the Lamp had served as a unifying figure during the Crimean War; she performed a similar function after her death. This was a welcome thing as domestic politics in Britain hurtled toward militancy, among workers and among women, and as the global order lurched toward war. Nurses and veterans, journalists and hagiographers, cosmopolitans and villagers: all participated in marking Florence Nightingale's passing in the summer of 1910. She connected rich and poor and young and old.[107] Her life bridged the nineteenth century and the twentieth, just as it embraced saintliness and science.

At her passing, Nightingale remained linked – fused, even – to the event that had made her into a heroine: the Crimean War. The association filled the pages of the press; it was evident on occasions of pageantry. Time and again, Crimean veterans, or the regiments associated with the Crimea, appeared at occasions meant to celebrate the Lady with the Lamp. There was an understanding, finally, that Nightingale had a special connection to the veterans of the Crimea, as heroes and relics of the nineteenth century. Nowhere is this more evident than in a frequently reprinted vignette of a Mr. Kneller, the Crimean veteran of Romsey, who stood at Nightingale's grave. In the Crimean War, Kneller had fought with the 23rd Regiment of Foot Soldiers. On the occasion of Nightingale's burial, he remembered the young heroine: "Like a spark in the embers of his dwindling mind," there came "the apparition of the lady who came softly along the beds at night carrying in her hand a lantern."[108] The elderly veteran thus became the repository of national memory, while upholding Nightingale as a national heroine.

***

There were many efforts to memorialize Nightingale in the immediate aftermath of her passing and also in the decades beyond. Attesting to her exceptional place in the lore of a Christian nation was a campaign for sanctification in the Anglican Church.[109] This effort to immortalize Nightingale was unsuccessful. More successful were the measures taken to render Nightingale in stone, in the sacred and civic spaces of London and beyond.[110] The most notable campaign involved a statue at the heart of monumental London. Coordinated by the Florence Nightingale Fund, the design came to fruition in the year 1915, when Arthur G. Walker's statue of the Lady with the Lamp was unveiled at Waterloo Place, just across from the Crimea Memorial. His Nightingale tribute constituted a landmark in memorialization – it was the first metropolitan statue of a woman who was not a royal. As it paid homage to Nightingale, it ushered in a great age of female statuary – with tributes to Emmeline Pankhurst and Edith Cavell appearing not long after. Walker's Nightingale was a young woman, appearing "as she might have been seen walking at night through the wards of the hospital at Scutari," that is, carrying a lamp in her right hand and holding up her skirt with her left.[111] If the statue itself sealed the relationship between Nightingale and the Crimea, so too did the decorative plinth that supported it. The plinth featured sights of Nightingale at work. Its four sides showed her tending to convalescent soldiers, walking through a hospital, meeting military officers, and addressing a group of nurses. Thus, in its very design, the statue buttressed Nightingale's connection to the Crimean War.

The archival records charting the making of the statue show well the ways that the everyday intersected with the monumental, and the mundane with the transcendent. Initial enthusiasm notwithstanding, building the statue was slow and erratic work, complicated by domestic budget crises, international tensions, and, eventually, the onset of the Great War. Some of the labors involved pondering routine matters such as gas mains, traffic flows, and street names. Yet, even this last was freighted with significance. The Metropolitan Board of Works was concerned that renaming Waterloo Place as Crimea Place might offend the Russians, tenuous allies in the early days of the Great War. Fundraising too was a preoccupying matter. From the outset, the Nightingale Fund worked methodically and steadfastly to raise funds, printing plaintive appeals in the nation's newspapers and writing personal letters to many. So desperate was the Fund's leadership for contributions that it even considered placing a collection box at the base of the Crimea Memorial, the eventual home of the statue. MPs and mayors made their contributions, but it was, primarily, the "small subscriptions" that had been offered up from "nurses, soldiers, and sailors" that built the statue.[112]

The individual most associated with the effort was the War Office's Sydney Holland. Holland immersed himself in the minutiae of the arrangements and their greater meanings. He came to identify the statue as his life's calling – in his own words, his "one successful bit of work!"[113] His most decisive act was also the most ambitious in logistical and interpretive terms. Holland hatched a plan to move the statue of War Office Secretary Sidney Herbert, Nightingale's sponsor in the East and her partner in reform, to Waterloo Place. It was, he confessed, a "pretty thought."[114] "The beauty of the idea is the propriety of the heroes of the Crimea together," Holland waxed.[115] For Holland, the effort to join the statues was well worth it, for it would rewrite the unfulfilled desires of the past, at least as he understood them. It would change Nightingale's life course and correct history's path, resolving it in a conjugal plot. It would serve to contain the ambitions and eccentricities of a historically problematic woman. "I believe Sidney Herbert wanted to marry her," said Holland of Nightingale, who had famously eschewed marriage vows in her lifetime.[116] In a decisive show of earnest ambition rarely seen in prosaic Office of Works papers, Holland declared of his eventual success at Waterloo Place, where the statues are now coupled, "When I am dead, remember of me only this."[117]

Holland was not alone in anthropomorphizing the statue, and, thereby, attaching his own desires to it. As they made the stone tribute into a living monument, contributors to the daily press similarly enlivened the stone lady. When it announced the statue's completion in 1915, the *Times* found in it the attributes that had come to be associated with Nightingale's character: her "characteristic qualities of strength of will irradiated by an expression of great sweetness and sympathy." Even the opening ceremony itself came, in the press coverage, to reflect Nightingale's nature. This was, in truth, an accident of history rather than the intent of the planners. In the somber and sensitive early years of World War I, an unveiling ceremony – and especially one that might unsettle the alliance with Russia by raising the specter of the Crimea – could strike the wrong key. The statue was thus uncovered without fanfare, with three workmen who worked quietly and unceremoniously removing the tarp on a cold morning in early 1915.[118] It was, in the *Daily Mail*'s estimation, an incident worthy of Nightingale and her modesty. The great lady herself could not have wanted a "simpler ceremony."[119]

The *Daily Mail*'s account of the unveiling recalled its coverage of Nightingale's funeral in more ways than one. If a nod to Nightingale's modesty presented one common ingredient, a reminder of her links to the Crimea, as embodied by its aging veterans, offered another. There were few in attendance for the statue's early morning debut. But among them was one witness – an elderly Crimean veteran – who remembered Nightingale as a young woman. The *Daily Mail* gave the "old gentleman" the last word as it offered up a Victorian memory to its modern readership. "What a grand work she did!" the onetime subaltern exclaimed of the Crimean heroine. Together, the statue and the soldier worked to soothe a weary nation engaged in a vicious war and facing an uncertain future. As he expressed his gratitude, the old soldier bound past and present and produced comfort and consensus. "Thank God for Florence Nightingale," he exclaimed.[120]

The Nightingale statue became a site of pilgrimages and commemorations in years to come (Figure 5.4). It was a destination for the last of the Crimean veterans.[121] It attracted visitors from Britain, the United States, and elsewhere.[122] These visitors participated themselves in the ongoing work of cultivating Florence Nightingale's legacy as they linked it to their own understandings of the past and to their personal hopes for the future. On a misty evening in 1924, Mr. T.W. MacAlpine of Finchley paid tribute at Nightingale's statue. He found himself inspired by an optical illusion that was wrought by the London fog. The moonlit fog produced

LONDON.—Florence Nightingale and Crimean Monument, Waterloo Place.

Figure 5.4 Florence Nightingale Monument, Waterloo Place, Westminster. Postcard. 1910s. Mary Evans Picture Library/Grenville Collins Collection

the appearance of a light burning from the statue's lamp. Moved by this sight, MacAlpine made a suggestion to the Board of Works. Might it install an electric light inside of the stone lamp, so recalling the image of

Nightingale as she had appeared at Scutari? The Office of Works thanked the petitioner, but it could not oblige. MacAlpine may not have succeeded in his quest, but his appeal demonstrates the ways in which the statue provided yet another site for kindling the legends of the Lady with the Lamp.[123]

***

There were those who sought to put Nightingale, literally and metaphorically, on a pedestal after her death – to erect likenesses of her and to spread the myth of the lamp. There were others who aimed to wrest the real Nightingale from legend. Still others sought to dethrone the Victorian idol. Understandings of, and uses of, Florence Nightingale shifted in the twentieth century. Many Britons turned away from their Victorian upbringings. They sought out a new order that was modern in terms of its cultural venues and its gendered mentalities. These realignments occurred against the backdrop of the world wars, which transformed understandings of national history and everyday society. Outgrowths of these conflicts included the professionalization of nursing and the internationalization of humanitarianism. In these contexts, Nightingale became a new sort of heroine. No longer was the Lady with the Lamp the personification of Victorian sentiment: saccharine and sweet; she was instead the exemplar of nineteenth-century modernity: professional and pragmatic.[124]

Writing just after her death, in 1913, Nightingale's first official biographer, Edward Tyas Cook, sought to distinguish the "real Florence Nightingale" from the "legendary."[125] This was no small challenge for Cook. The biographer was well aware that Nightingale lore held great force in its longevity and ubiquity, with its elements of privileged birth and nurturing proclivities, and of sacrificial nature and invalid life. Stories of Nightingale as she nursed a wounded dog and images of the Lady with the Lamp were woven into the national fabric.[126] Yet, the task of pushing against this legend was, Cook believed, a worthy one. In his mind, the real Florence Nightingale was not just different from, but also greater than the legend: more interesting, more accomplished, and even more likeable. Rather than an angel or martyr, Cook argued, Nightingale was an administrator and a reformer. She was not driven by goodness, as many presumed. Instead, she was guided by discernment. Nightingale's power lay not in a soft heart, but rather in a sharp mind. One admirer had quipped, notably, that she had the "clearest brain in man or woman." As he delineated Nightingale's accomplishments, Cook chose, ultimately, to provide a portal onto his protagonist's career, rather than onto her character.[127]

Cook's interpretation had a long afterlife itself. It came to inform the work of Lytton Strachey, who built his 1918 portrait of Nightingale in *Eminent Victorians* atop the biographer's understanding. In a phrasing that was resonant with the campaign to erect the statue in high gear, Cook had claimed, "Florence Nightingale was by no means a plaster saint."[128] Cook may have endeavored to soften stone notions, but Strachey, borrowing from him, sought to shatter a false idol. It was part of his effort to relieve twentieth-century bohemians of their Victorian household gods.[129] Strachey endeavored to dethrone Nightingale, taking her down along with Cardinal Manning, General Gordon, and Thomas Arnold. His Nightingale was not a young dreamer, but a delusional maiden; not a purposeful reformer, but a ruthless matron; not a beloved elder, but a doddering relic. To convey Nightingale's nature in her prime of life, Strachey reached to the animal and spirit worlds. His Nightingale was ruthless and animal-like, alternatively an "eagle" or a "tigress."[130] She was capable of "demonic frenzy."[131] She stirred fear in adversaries and in friends alike, bringing about the death, Strachey argued, of Sidney Herbert. But time, age, and senility would curb these tendencies. The end of Strachey's sketch has Nightingale as a "fat old lady" descending toward an "amiable senility," uttering, upon receipt of the Order of Merit, only the simple words: "too kind, too kind."[132]

With his penchant for spice and his desire for drama, critics noted, Strachey managed to create a popular work. Cook's authoritative text had sought to prize Nightingale's life away from the realm of myth and situate it within a world of truth. It was not, however, broad in its appeal. Strachey's portrait of Nightingale fared differently. *Eminent Victorians* may have been a production of a literary bohemia, but it enjoyed affordable reprinting in the interwar years and well after. Additionally, it became the basis for adaptations to stage, radio, and screen. One notable example is Reginald Berkeley's play, *The Lady with a Lamp*, which debuted at the Garrick Theatre in 1929.[133] Its star, Edith Evans, received plaudits for her performance. Assisted by several make-up changes, Evans depicted Nightingale at several junctures across her long life.[134] The production offered its interwar audience lessons about the "muddle in the Crimea" long ago and the sociability of the Victorian drawing room of bygone days. But its central concern was a love triangle between a childish and churlish Florence Nightingale, a henpecked and ineffective Sidney Herbert, and a petty and heartbroken Elizabeth Herbert. Resolution comes only after Herbert's death, when the two women are left to reckon with one another in what must have been a resonant plot device for a generation that had lost its men in the onslaught of the Great War. The aggrieved Elizabeth serves as a mouthpiece for larger critiques of

Nightingale and her so-called "mad desire for power." But the rivalry between the two women, and the demonic ambition of the protagonist, are tamed in the play's final scene, when an aged Nightingale, "apple-cheeked" and "smiling," is wheeled onto stage. In this closing bedside scene, Nightingale receives an investiture into the Order of Merit and forgiveness from Elizabeth Herbert. Just as Strachey's Nightingale had, Berkeley's matron declares that it is all "too kind."[135]

Such portraits persisted through the interwar and postwar eras, appearing on BBC radio and television, and in a biopic starring Anna Neagle.[136] Among those who criticized these representations for their overreliance on Strachey were two of Florence Nightingale's great nieces, Lady Stephen, born Barbara Shore-Smith, and Mrs. Vaughn Nash, born Rosalind Shore-Smith. Strachey, they alleged, had deviated far from the evidence in constructing his Florence Nightingale – he had a "medieval witch-finder's capacity" for drama and distortion.[137] As a result, those who relied upon Strachey as they adapted Nightingale's life for the stage and the screen missed the mark. They failed to understand Nightingale and her world. Particularly improbable was Berkeley's rivalry between Florence Nightingale and Elizabeth Herbert. Equally out of place was all of the "twentieth-century twaddle about sex."[138] If the nineteenth century had worshipped Nightingale as an "insipid saint," the twentieth century had its own limits in understanding. This was all too evident in the "child-like pleasure" with which it rebelled against the nineteenth-century's exemplars. It was not, Lady Stephen held, that Nightingale did not have her faults. Yet, these faults were distinctly Victorian ones stemming not from being too impetuous or undersexed, but instead from being excessively religious or overworked.[139]

These questions about popular culture point to a challenge faced by Nightingale's twentieth-century interlocutors, admirers and critics alike. There was a tendency, in many quarters, to see Nightingale as transcendent; yet, as her nieces and defenders showed, she was very much a woman of her age, even as she towered over it. Nightingale lived a life of "faith, ardor, and singleness of purpose."[140] This was something with which the feminists of the twentieth-century's first wave, and later, of its second, had to reckon as they considered her legacies.[141] Nightingale had written copiously not only on nursing, sanitation, and spirituality, but also on women's position in society. In *Cassandra*, she assessed the limitations of the gilded cage into which she had been born, as she sought to follow her calling and perform her work. Yet she, like many other women of her generation, including Harriet Martineau and George Eliot, distanced herself from the organized campaign for the suffrage. Ray Strachey addressed Nightingale's vexing position when she reprinted *Cassandra* in her landmark feminist text *The Cause*, published in 1928, the year of the Representation of the People Bill. Although a forerunner to feminism, Nightingale offered "only an incomplete and exhausted sympathy with the organized women's movement."[142]

It proved easier for those in the nursing profession to make Nightingale into a foremother in the interwar era.[143] Nursing had become an increasingly important profession, both nationally and internationally, in the wake of the Great War. The case of Edith Cavell, a nurse executed in Belgium as a spy, was only the best-known instance of nursing heroics in the conflict.[144] It added another martyr, a more starkly literal one, to the pantheon of nurses. More generally, there was an understanding that Nightingale had paved the way for the work of women as nurses during the Great War. The words of Dame Alicia Lloyd Still, the Matron of St. Thomas' Hospital from 1913 to 1937, typify the ideals of those daughters of the Victorian era who sought to burnish Florence Nightingale's memory in a changed world.[145] According to the Matron, it was Nightingale's innovations that had allowed "so very many women" to "restore to health and usefulness" so very many men "who were wounded, gassed, and stricken with grave illnesses" during World War I.[146] Still's language is reminiscent of that used during the Crimean War, when female nurture appeared to be the salvation for male frailty. It was updated here, however, with professional and technological terminology befitting the twentieth century.

There was a pervasive understanding that the nursing profession itself, more than any statue or accolade, was the "true memorial" to Nightingale.[147] The profession was, to use the words of Lucy Ridgely Seymer, "a living monument" that made Nightingale's name known in Britain and across the globe.[148] Aware of their debts to Nightingale, nursing organizations emerged as leading stewards of Nightingale's memory and of her ambitions during the interwar years. One campaign aspired to save Nightingale's residence on South Street and to transform it into a vital memorial for nursing. It was the hope of the National Council of Nurses of Great Britain that the South Street residence might become a hub for nursing education, "the Mecca of the nurse," to use an Orientalizing phrase, notable given Nightingale's own travels to the East.[149] But the funds did not materialize and the plan did not succeed. Some years later, the London County Council decorated the geographical site with one of its signature historical blue plaques.[150] In the 1930s, however, the house languished, its holdings picked over by souvenir hunters.[151]

More successful efforts to remember Nightingale and to refashion her legacy occurred concurrently in other quarters of the changing nursing profession. One organization to embrace Nightingale as its foremother was the International Red Cross. It took its inspiration from the Lady with the Lamp as it sought to manage war through humanitarianism.[152] In the 1930s the organization designated Nightingale's birthday, May 12, as Red Cross Day. Ritual and performance became important elements of this occasion, observed in London and elsewhere. One central feature was the laying of a wreath at the Nightingale statue.[153] Another was the performance of pageants. Typically, these performances offered an arc of improvement from biblical times to the present, with Nightingale's story a critical feature in its unfolding.[154] As these rituals indicate, Nightingale became, in the tense interwar period, a truly international figure.[155] Not just a national icon, she was an "international pioneer" with an "international spirit."[156] She was, to borrow the phrasing of George Newman, a physician and medical officer, the "treasured possession of the human family all over the world."[157]

Yet, even in the midst of these internationalist gestures, Nightingale remained at heart an English heroine and London the hub of her enduring legacy. In the years leading up to World War II, an institution at the heart of London became the preeminent custodian of Nightingale's memory and the primary repository of her possessions. This was St. Thomas' Hospital, where Nightingale had opened her Training School in 1860. Relics connected to Nightingale piled up at the hospital, where plans to build a museum unfolded in the interwar era. Interest in the material artifacts of the Crimea, their preservation, and their salvage was high across this epoch. Not only were the last veterans and nurses dying out; those who held family linkages were entering their latter days. Pictures of Nightingale, letters from her, bracelets of plaited hair, and dried oranges given to soldiers – all arrived at the hospital. With these offerings came claims of connections to Nightingale and to her world on the part of elderly Britons, all relics in their own right. One octogenarian, Mrs. Reiss, reported that she had, as an eight-year-old girl, witnessed the laying of the foundation stone at St. Thomas' Hospital in 1868.[158] There were more material claims to connection as well. Mary Gormand sent in a treasured brooch containing a locket of Nightingale's hair, which had been passed to her by an aunt who had nursed under Nightingale.[159] With its vital capacities, hair was an especially powerful link to the Lady with the Lamp, cherished and treasured across generations. Gormand's gift was not, in fact, the only specimen of its kind to arrive. A Miss Buckeridge offered up a lock of white hair that she herself had salvaged from Nightingale's grave, just one week after the funeral.[160]

These artifacts came to the attention of the public in special exhibitions beginning in the 1930s and extending into the postwar era, as

St. Thomas' Hospital solidified its status as the repository of Nightingale relics.[161] With the Blitz ravaging London and targeting the South Bank of the Thames, the museum's opening was long thwarted. But relics were visible on important anniversaries. There were exhibitions marking the centenary of the Crimean War and the Training School, in 1954 and in 1960. There was another commemorating the sesquicentennial of Nightingale's birth, in 1970. Eventually, the showcased objects formed a collection that opened to the public as the Florence Nightingale Museum in 1989.[162]

The Blitz, for its part, may have slowed the building of a permanent museum, but it inflected the collections, as the fate of one of its treasures lays bare. The object in question was the carriage ridden by Nightingale in the Crimea. It had been offered to the hospital on the part of the Chesterfield Town Council in 1930. Nightingale had opposed the display of the carriage in her own lifetime.[163] Regarded as a sign of her modesty, this act of opposition was of a piece with long-standing understandings of the simple vehicle. During the Crimean War, it had suggested Nightingale's effacing nature. By the twentieth century, it came to connote Britain's resilient spirit. The critical occasion bringing these narratives of the modest Nightingale and the sacrificing nation together was the enemy bombing of London during World War II. Among the many locales damaged in the Blitz's nightly air raids was the hospital. The carriage sustained particular harm. Its desecration gave way to acts of philanthropy and salvage that proved, on the one hand, just how sacred possessions linked to Nightingale had become, and, on the other, just how ingenious voluntarism in the midst of the war could be. Residents of a nation at war sought not only to preserve lives and land; they sought as well to safeguard history and meaning. To this end, two leading lights of the transport industry came to the rescue, as they fused artisanal custom with philanthropic capitalism. Wellan's of Esher, a venerable Surrey firm with a long-standing history of coach building, repaired the old carriage. Granville Bradshaw, a renowned automobile engineer in the modern day, stepped in to fund the endeavor (Figure 5.5).[164]

This was not, however, the only story of regeneration to come out of the damage. Replete with meaning, the carriage proved notably generative of expressions of affection and acts of reuse. In a thrifty and inspired example of salvage, Mr. Sewell, a devoted hobbyist and an ordinary Briton, made meaningful use of a spoke from the bombed vehicle. The artifact had passed to him from a relative working as a government advisor on war damage claims. Inspired by the story of Nightingale, he embarked on a "labor of love": he fashioned the discarded spoke into a lamp. Sewell gifted his craft to St. Thomas' Hospital in 1942.[165] In his rendering of the

Figure 5.5 St. Thomas' Hospital. Return of Florence Nightingale's carriage to the hospital. 1942. LCC Photograph Library. London Metropolitan Archives

object, Sewell fused two elements of Britain's island story – the Lady with the Lamp and the Spirit of the Blitz – into one. A tribute to heroism, sacrifice, and duty across the ages, Sewell's creation testifies, yet again, to the important place occupied by Nightingale in the nation's material culture and in its imagined lore.

***

What sort of place would Florence Nightingale occupy in a postwar Britain, a nation on the cusp of transformation through the rise of the welfare state and the end of empire? Against the winds of change, Nightingale remained a staple of the island story and a heroine of Middle England, as an anecdote from the *Daily Mail* suggests. In 1957, when 400 English schoolboys at the Redruth County Grammar School in Cornwall were asked to list the women they most admired, two names rose to the top. The contenders included movie stars Sabrina, Jane Mansfield, and Bridget Bardot, as well as the more familiar "mother." But the names of Joan of Arc and Florence Nightingale outstripped them all, with Nightingale, the heroine of the Crimean War, topping the list.[166] Nightingale's name may have been a household word. She was not, however, a static icon in the postwar moment. At that time, efforts on behalf of the government and the nursing establishment sought, simultaneously, to celebrate Nightingale and her achievements and to understand the Victorian heroine anew. Nightingale served, from the 1950s onward, as a bridge between the Victorians and the moderns. In the postwar era, the Lady with the Lamp became a beacon of the improving light of science and of the process of professionalization.

Scholars in Victorian Studies may see in these contours of the postwar Nightingale a personification of their own academic project, which also has its roots in the 1950s. At that time, scholars and laypeople alike looked to the Victorian epoch to find a harbinger of their contemporary society. Living a century apart, the mid-Victorians shared with their Cold War contemporaries a commitment to reason, progress, and improvement.[167] This understanding is evident, for instance, in Cecil Woodham-Smith's rendition of Florence Nightingale. Before probing the Charge of the Light Brigade, Woodham-Smith had explored the Lady with the Lamp. She followed in the footsteps of Edward Tyas Cook, writing forty years earlier. Within her widely reviewed biography, Woodham-Smith sought to understand Nightingale as a complex figure who reflected the complexity of her age. In Woodham-Smith's hands, Nightingale emerged as a woman with "contradictory attributes": "both deeply practical and deeply superstitious, both affectionate and steely hard, both rebellious and long-suffering." It was these ingredients that allowed Nightingale to do her work, and it was these tendencies that led her, unfortunately, to be misunderstood.[168] In a clash recalling those of the interwar moment, Woodham-Smith and others found themselves at odds with the producers of a 1951 film, *The Lady with a Lamp*, starring Anna Neagle. When it came to matters of design, the film aspired to great accuracy. Miss Neagle used Nightingale's very lamp, lent to the producers by the United Services Museum.[169] Yet when it came to Nightingale's character, the film was mired in myth. In a film that veered closer to legend than to accuracy, the rendition of Nightingale, the heroine, inspired sympathy and condescension, not fear and admiration.

There were further efforts to recognize, and to salute, a Nightingale who was, at once, a Victorian heroine and a modernizing influence. These antinomies were evident during the Nightingale Centenary, celebrated in 1954. The year witnessed a full calendar of events including exhibitions and tributes not just in London, but in Istanbul, too, designed to commemorate Nightingale's contributions in the Crimea. In many ways, these events were nostalgic, paying tribute to Florence Nightingale's legend, to the Victorian age, and to British global dominance.[170] But they were also forward looking, at least to a degree, as they celebrated the rise of professional nursing and transnational partnership, if in careful and conservative ways.

The centennial commemorations had an uncanny way of repeating the scripts of the Crimean War itself, as the belated, and ultimately unrealized, efforts of the War Office indicate. It was, of course, Sidney Herbert's War Office that had sent Nightingale to the Crimea in the mid-nineteenth century. One hundred years on, its twentieth-century heir aspired to claim its place as the progenitor of modern nursing. Yet, the War Office displayed a lack of foresight once again, as it had in the Crimea. Its efforts came off too slowly to take shape and too late to be realized. The War Office hoped to offer up an exhibit, "100 Years of Army Nursing," at the Time and Life Building in Bond Street, located in London's West End. The show would have enticed viewers with a stunning array of Nightingale relics that was designed to kindle awe for the heroine and hope for the future. This Nightingaliana, as it was called, was to offer a starting point for a larger story about the rise of Army nursing.[171] The heavily and deliberately scripted show was to feature uniforms as they were worn through the ages, and also operating theaters as they had developed across a century. Ideally, the exhibition's arc would invite visitors to tie their own lives to this glorious trajectory of "service and adventure."[172] If one of its goals was to commemorate the life of Florence Nightingale, another was to recruit young women to join the Queen Alexandra Royal Army Nursing Corps (QARANC). So deliberate was the War Office in this aspiration that it planned for the exhibition experience to culminate in conversations with nurses in uniforms offering opportunities for recruitment.[173] These grand designs notwithstanding, the War Office's plans came too late and its efforts fell short. Lacking time, money, and relics, the War Office realized that it could not offer up a suitable exhibition. According to Sidney Rogerson, the Army had been outflanked when it came to centennial celebrations, with dates on the calendar taken and relics of Nightingale's life sent elsewhere.[174]

The nursing establishment had outsmarted the War Office once again. As if to repeat the script of the Crimean War, the former succeeded where the latter had failed. The cornerstone of the success was an October 1954 exhibition held at the Royal College of Surgeons in conjunction with St. Thomas's School of Nursing. The display was the labor of Lucy Ridgely Seymer, a registered nurse, a nursing historian, and a custodian of Nightingale's memory. Seymer's finely wrought and nicely documented exhibition garnered considerable praise as the outcome of grit and devotion. In the months leading up to the exhibit, the indefatigable

Seymer searched widely for relics, approaching individuals and collections for Nightingale treasures to comprise a worthy display commemorating the departure for Scutari one hundred years on. Despite the general willingness, there were those who were hesitant in parting with their treasures. Notably missing was Athena, Nightingale's beloved owl, which had been stuffed and preserved for posterity. Its current owner, Captain H.G. Gorton, had protested the hazards of balancing the stuffed owl on his bicycle for transport. But there was no dearth of objects. A Scutari hospital scarf, a soldier's water bottle, and a walking stick accompanied Nightingale's hair locks, lace collars, and alpaca dress. Visitors could admire a model of Nightingale's famous carriage, too, as well as a draft copy of Longfellow's "Santa Filomena" (Figure 5.6).[175] The one-day affair culminated with a reception that featured as honored guests the Ambassadors to Britain from France and Turkey, as it linked the partnerships of the past to the diplomacy of the future.[176]

Held on November 4, a memorial service at Westminster Abbey capped off the London events in 1954. It gestured to the past as it

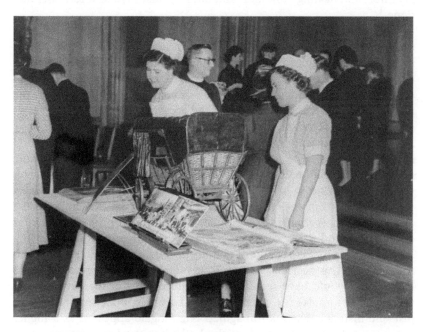

Figure 5.6 Nightingale carriage model at Crimean centenary. Photograph. 1955. HO1/ST/NCPH/A/V/E/016. London Metropolitan Archives. Guy and St. Thomas' NHS Foundation Trust

commemorated the arrival of Nightingale and her troops at Scutari, exactly 100 years before. It looked to the future as it celebrated the vital profession of nursing that had flourished ever since. The November occasion, the second such event in 1954, was preceded by another service, held at St. Paul's Cathedral in May and attended by 3,000 nurses.[177] Once again, legions of QARANC officers and nurses gathered at the Abbey in their regalia, following a wreath-laying ceremony at the Nightingale statue. Not only did the occasion link Nightingale to the Army; it tied her, once again, to Christendom – to the Church of England specifically and to Protestantism more generally. Catholic nurses were, in fact, warned that the occasion would be a Protestant affair. Just as they had at her funeral, those assembled sang Nightingale's favorite hymns, including, of course, "The Son of God Goes Forth to War." They also heard the words of the Dean of Westminster Abbey, who thanked God for Nightingale's "courage and devotion," her "energy and enterprise," and her "deep compassion and abounding charity," all qualities associated with the vocation of Victorian nursing. He shared with the nurses of the twentieth century the hope that they might bring "comfort and healing" to "souls and bodies," just as their forerunner had done.[178]

What might Florence Nightingale have thought of this occasion? This is a question prompted time and again by the archival record itself. Take, for instance, the example of the funeral. Nightingale had expressed a wish for a private burial, and not a public ceremony. However, given the broad desire for a memorial at a time of uncertainty, there was a sense among the planners that she would have allowed the occasion on behalf of the greater good. At the centenary, planners similarly looked to an imaginary Nightingale who watched over the event. Once again, this invocation served their immediate needs. Nightingale functioned not simply as the object of celebration, but equally as its moral compass. This role is evident in an effort to address the question of how many military nurses should travel from their barracks to London for the November 1954 events. Was it worthwhile for military nurses to leave their stations for a week to attend a service lasting a few hours? Lieutenant Colonel J.C. Lambkin, the officer in charge of military hospitals, determined that it was not. He based his decision, moreover, in Nightingale's imagined wisdom: clearly, she would have seen that the requirements of the patients outweighed the impulse for celebration.[179] Lambkin's decision represents just one instance where an imagined Nightingale appeared as a higher conscience. In the coming years, the Lady with the Lamp continued to serve as a superego for the nursing profession as it navigated changing demands in a postwar world.[180]

In more ways than one, the London events of 1954 conjured up a vital Florence Nightingale, who could forcefully remind admirers of the glory of the Victorian past while rightfully steering participants toward the responsibilities of the twentieth century. The same could be said for the even more robust series of events in Istanbul and environs, which served not simply to honor Florence Nightingale, but also to respond to the current moment. On the part of the Turkish state, there was a philatelic tribute in the form of a commemorative stamp issued in 1954, more than fifteen years in advance of Britain, which would do the same in 1970. More generally, the Turkish nursing establishment and the Foreign Office took the lead in concert as they planned a Florence Nightingale Week that melded education and entertainment. The offerings included nursing exhibitions, health fairs, and a film showing across Istanbul. For the Turkish nursing establishment, it was an opportunity to showcase postwar modernity. For the British Foreign Office, it was an occasion for renewing a friendship between the two nations. To this end, there was an array of events – the unveiling of a memorial plaque at Haydarpasha Cemetery, right near Scutari Hospital; a wreath-laying in Taksim Square followed by a ceremonial crossing of the Bosporus; and cocktail parties and tea parties that brought the nations, once allies and later foes, together again. As they honored the legacy of Florence Nightingale, these occasions looked to her life as a bridge between past and present and between East and West. An object of celebration and a tool of diplomacy, Nightingale was a symbol for cooperation in a new age.[181]

The Istanbul events may have been peripheral to the consciousness of most in Great Britain. There were, however, other initiatives on the part of the nursing establishment and the British state ensuring that the Lady with the Lamp retained a place at the heart of national history and national myth over the coming decades. Exhibitions organized by St. Thomas' Hospital in 1960 and 1970 commemorated the centennial of the Training School and the sesquicentennial of Nightingale's birth, tracing the progress from Sairey Gamp to the modern nurse and celebrating the legacy of the Lady with the Lamp.[182] The issue of a stamp, also coinciding with the Nightingale Sesquicentennial, had a broader reach. It debuted in 1970, along with several others that were part of a General Anniversaries Edition. There were stamps marking the 650th Anniversary of the Declaration of Arbroath, the 350th Anniversary of the Sailing of the Mayflower, the 150th Anniversary of the Royal Astronomical Society, and the 75th Anniversary of the International Cooperative Alliance. As a group, these stamps celebrated events upholding the broad liberal values of sovereignty, toleration, and innovation.[183] Additionally, Nightingale appeared on a £10 note five years later, in 1975. She was a trailblazer here as elsewhere, with the currency becoming a space to recognize eminent Victorians, and, eventually, a Georgian: Charles Dickens, Charles Darwin, and Jane Austen each later assumed the place once occupied by Florence Nightingale.[184]

Taken together, the 9d stamp and the £10 note solidified Nightingale's state-sanctioned role as a secular saint and an exemplary Briton. These milestones occurred alongside broader efforts to inculcate the values associated with Nightingale into the popular mind and to write her legacy into Britain's island story. In 1970, for instance, the Post Office released an education pack available to schools across the nation to accompany the Nightingale stamp. It offered hands-on exercises for schoolchildren: they might act out the scene of Nightingale's past where she informed her parents of her wish to nurse, write letters as if they were ladies in Scutari's Hospital ward, or consider the qualities of a nurse as suggested in advertisements in the papers. The materials and the exercises situated Nightingale as a portal onto the Victorian age. Yet, they also understood her as a transcendent subject, who could offer lessons about perseverance, improvement, and innovation. The mother of modern nursing and a reformer of great vision, the Post Office's Nightingale was a "practical genius." She prized pragmatism above ideology, the education pack noted, as it sought to safeguard against a radicalization of the Lady with the Lamp. At the moment of the stamp's issue and in the years following, second-wave feminists reckoned with Nightingale's legacy as they searched for foremothers to their movement. Nightingale had, notably, distanced herself from efforts for the vote. For many in the second wave, however, feminism meant economic, social, and cultural transformations of the sort that Nightingale had advocated; electoral reform was only a start. For the Post Office, however, the lines were clear. Florence Nightingale may have been "a powerful woman in a man's world."[185] She was not, in its assessment, a feminist. In the hands of the Royal Post, Nightingale was a beacon of progress, not a bellwether of revolution.

One final effort to place Nightingale at the center of nursing history and national lore came from the Florence Nightingale Foundation. Its efforts came to fruition in the year 1989, when the Florence Nightingale Museum opened, at long last, in a set of tucked away rooms at St. Thomas' Hospital. It remained open there for more than three decades. In this collection derived from holdings at the hospital and donations from nurses, Nightingale emerged as the progenitor of modern nursing and as a worthy progressive heroine. In taking up this line of interpretation, the Museum tied together the understandings of Nightingale that had come to maturity during the postwar epoch, giving them wider exposition.[186] It was, in the words of the *British Medical Journal*, a tribute to an "extraordinarily varied and productive life," that of a helpmeet, nurse, and reformer.[187] Together, Nightingale's words and her possessions told the story of her industrious career and its many victories. Displays included a medical chest, a family piano, and a childhood book. There were also curiosities, such as cutlery made from bayonets and the shell of Nightingale's own pet tortoise.[188] The object most associated with Nightingale was, of course, the famous Lamp. Much like imaginations of the East from the Victorian period, the object was, itself, a surprise or even a disappointment. "Far from being shiny and Aladdin-style," a reporter for the *Evening Standard* explained, "it is a simple round Turkish camp light topped by a lid and handle."[189] On the whole, the Museum was a great success, even exceeding expectations, despite its unprepossessing location. "Imagine the best museum you know," reported the *Nursing Standard*, "and this is comparable."[190] Heaping on even higher praise, the *Times* determined that the collection gave its visitors a "new feeling for the importance of the nursing profession."[191]

In many ways, the Museum's site, on the grounds of St. Thomas' Hospital, was a fitting one for a collection dedicated to Nightingale, who had pioneered secular nursing education there over a century before. But the consolidation of the holdings raised questions about the place of Nightingale in the nation's history and the role of the Museum in curating it. Was Nightingale the heroine of a profession or the heroine of a nation? If the former, artifacts associated with her memory belonged at the hospital. If the latter, they might reside elsewhere. This was the very logic applied by the Trustees of the National Portrait Gallery when they bought, in a highly publicized sale, two paintings by Jerry Barrett depicting scenes from the Crimean War: "The Queen's Visit to Wounded Soldiers" and "The Mission of Mercy: Florence Nightingale at Scutari." These were purchases enabled by skilled fundraising, aggressive bidding, and institutional savvy. The result of negotiations among funding sources, auction houses, and competing institutions, the 1993 purchase was a "major coup" for the National Portrait Gallery. In advance of the sale, the acquisition of the paintings had been a subject of contention. The Nightingale Museum held that its proper context was the collection devoted to the nursing profession, while the Portrait Gallery maintained that it belonged within a national story. Even after the sale, the Crimean War Research Society hoped for a "high profile loan" to the Florence Nightingale Museum. Yet the rival institution has been stalwart in the position that the works are not the property of the nurses, but rather the property of the nation. Of "paramount importance" to Britain's history, they remain in the National Portrait Gallery as "an inspiration to future generations."[192]

Figure 5.7 Detail from The Mission of Mercy: Florence Nightingale Receiving the Wounded at Scutari, by Jerry Barrett, Oil on Canvas, 1857. Ian Dagnall Computing/Alamy Stock Photo

The Museum may have been thwarted in 1993, but it remained, as it had promised, a dynamic hub of Nightingale's legacy. It reopened with a new design in 2010, to mark the centenary of Nightingale's death.

Hailed as a "huge imaginative success," the new arrangement divided Nightingale's story into three sections chronicling her young life, her Crimean crusade, and her later years. Curators employed a new museology that sought to interpret rather than to describe. They looked to color to perform some of the narrative work, as they took visitors from zone to zone. The collection retained a focus on objects, showcasing Nightingale's iconic Turkish lamp and her haunting owl Athena. A novel feature was its interactive display, enlivened by peepholes to peer through, drawers to open, and videos to watch. The display placed Nightingale in an expansive world, among the classical ruins witnessed in her youth and the sordid hospitals reformed in the Crimea. With an avowed mission to move beyond the myths, the installation conjured a vision of Nightingale, flawed and human, yet impressive and transformative. Hers was a generative life, paving the way for thousands of women to follow in Nightingale's "footsteps," serving in combat from World War II to Afghanistan.[193] As a whole, the collection offered a fulsome tribute to a "pioneering vision." Even in 2010, Nightingale's light continued to burn, "like a beacon in our modern world."[194]

***

During her lifetime, Florence Nightingale was a uniting figure: the Lady with the Lamp and the heroine of the Crimea. After her death, the meanings attached to Nightingale shifted across time, with the image of the Victorian helpmeet giving way to the ideal of the modernizing reformer. Yet, Nightingale retained the status of national heroine all the same, her proverbial lamp continuing to inspire many. As this chapter has shown, the efforts to lionize Nightingale came from state and civil society alike. They occurred on all scales and in many locations, through monumental events and in personal tributes, through metropolitan occasions and in far-flung actions. Taken together, these acts worked, again and again, to uphold Florence Nightingale as the foremost heroine of the Crimean War, and to solidify her role as a leading figure in Britain's island story.

The need for cohesion and consensus at the Crimean moment propelled Nightingale to the forefront of national consciousness, where she remained from the nineteenth century into the twenty-first. Yet, Nightingale faced criticisms from the outset, with her work and her legend finding skeptics in early days. There were those who doubted Nightingale's crusade at its inception, and there were critics in the Royal Army Medical Corps, not to mention among the rival nursing sisterhoods in the East. Army officers regarded her as domineering and supercilious – "an interfering pain in the neck," to use the 1990s parlance of the *Guardian*. Even her nurses found her heavy handed. These sentiments, cautiously voiced in the nineteenth century, found wider expression in the twentieth century, with the discovery of documents and the sale of letters.[195] Broader cultural critiques of Nightingale took shape as well, as the work of Lytton Strachey and his popularizers demonstrated. Across these years, critics additionally unsettled orthodoxies about the very efficacy of Nightingale's labors in the East. While she pioneered modern statistics and modern nursing, she did not, singlehandedly, defeat the cholera. Some of her remedies, such as the use of water from contaminated sources rather than alcohol that threatened insobriety, proved to do more harm than good.[196]

It was in the end, however, the nursing profession itself, along with the National Health Service (NHS), that dealt Nightingale a decisive blow. Nightingale had long stood preeminent as the organizing figure of the nursing profession in the popular mind. She was also an organizing symbol and a recurring touchstone in public discussions of nursing, particularly as administered through the NHS. As in her lifetime, Nightingale was a polyvalent figure, called upon to buttress opposing views and to address changing situations. She was malleable enough to be a proto-feminist heroine, while also serving as a throwback to Victorian duty. Some cast her as a forward-thinking fashionista, while others considered her a duty-bound drudge. Several imagined her as a crusader for the labor rights and salaries of nurses, whereas many invoked her as a critic of the NHS. Time and again, Nightingale's name was pressed into service in the consideration of nursing's best practices. What would Florence Nightingale do, polemicists asked?[197]

Oftentimes, it proved advantageous to invoke Nightingale and her legacy. But this advantage waned sharply as the new millennium approached. By that time, the ideal of the Nightingale nurse had become a straitjacket.[198] In a profession that drew heavily upon the ranks of Black, Asian, and Minority Ethnic Britons, the figure of Nightingale, "white, middle class, wealthy and Protestant," was out of sync. This was a matter that extended beyond the issue of identity. Nightingale's sense of duty and her insistence on deference were "outdated." During its long career that lingered well beyond its prime, Nightingale's system had produced an elite band of "robotic acolytes," critics judged.[199] And her myth, if not her reality, encouraged a stifling subservience to male doctors.[200]

With these criticisms at hand, the NHS cast off the stranglehold of Nightingale in 1999, at the annual meeting of UNISON, the United Kingdom's service union. In Brighton, 460,000 NHS staff and 250,000 nurses took Nightingale off of her pedestal, determining that she was no longer the role model for the profession. Their referendum was, by and large, symbolic. Its immediate result was to press the International Congress of Nurses to switch International Nurses Day from Nightingale's birthday to a day that was more appropriate for a new generation of nurses and more resonant with the current moment. To date, this request remains unfulfilled. There was, however, a more conse- quential, and more long-standing, effect of the vote. It created a breach into which a new nursing heroine might pass. More appealing fore- mothers included the Roman Catholic Joanna Bridgeman or the Quaker Elizabeth Fry. For health visitor Wendy Webster, the decision was of a piece with the dethroning of fleeting gods everywhere. "All over Eastern Europe statues of Lenin are being taken off of their pedestals," she noted as she linked the revolution among the nurses to larger histor- ical stages.[201]

Along with Elizabeth Fry and Joanna Bridgeman, the nurses intro- duced a new foremother at the Brighton convention. This was Mary Seacole, a Jamaican creole healer. Denied a place in Nightingale's band, she had traveled on her own to the Crimea, where she set up a hospital and a hotel. By the year 1999, Britons with an interest in nursing history, gender history, and Black British history had cultivated an interest in Seacole. Her rise to prominence has unsettled simple understandings of Florence Nightingale as the leading lady of the Crimean War. In our own century, the name of Mary Seacole has rapidly become a household word. The milestones have been many: Seacole's selection as the greatest Black Briton in the year 2004, the hanging of her likeness in the National Portrait Gallery in 2005, the introduction of her life's story into the national curriculum in 2007, and the completion of a statue honoring her in 2016. The fruit of the efforts of the Mary Seacole Memorial Statue Appeal, the statue sits on the grounds of St. Thomas' Hospital, looking across the river at the Houses of Parliament and residing meters away from the site of the Nightingale Museum. The statue's unveiling has engendered debates about the propriety of the location, the nature of nursing, and the contours of Britain. Their vitality attests to the formative qualities of the Crimean past and to the long afterlife of a Victorian war.

6   The Foremother

If we need any proof that the Crimea's legacies continue to shape Britain in the present, we need only visit the grounds of St. Thomas' Hospital on the South Bank of the Thames. There, at the institution where Florence Nightingale initiated her pioneering program of nursing education, stands a statue of Mary Seacole, a Caribbean-born healer and a recent inclusion into the pantheon of Victorian worthies. The magisterial tribute, the work of sculptor Martin Jennings, looks out across the river and gazes on the Houses of Parliament. Unveiled in 2016, the sculpture appears as a triumphant notice of Seacole's rise to prominence in the national imaginary. Yet, Seacole's ascent to visibility was anything but inevitable. Seacole's offers to help during the conflict were shunned time and again. She made her way, nonetheless, to the Crimea at the height of the war. While there, she hosted soldiers in her British Hotel and she traversed battlegrounds to comfort them. Although beloved by the troops during the war, she was forgotten soon afterward. In the late twentieth century, Seacole reemerged as a community exemplar in Black, Asian, and Minority Ethnic communities. By the beginning of the twenty-first century, she had ascended to become a national heroine.[1] Like Seacole's travels to the Crimea, the narrative of her rediscovery is a story of success against obstacles and a story of the strength of community. It attests to the generative capacity of a Victorian war in producing cultural inheritances that continue to resonate in Britain today.

Mary Seacole carved a place for herself in history with her 1857 autobiography, the *Wonderful Adventures of Mrs. Seacole in Many Lands.* Through its publication, Seacole simultaneously claimed her place in the Crimea's annals and sought out funds for her well-being. In her appeal, Seacole wrote her way into the narrative of the Crimean War, portraying herself as an adventurer, a healer, and a custodian. She offered up a portrait that had traction not just in the Victorian period, but well beyond, spotlighting her roles as mother, entrepreneur, and friend. Republished in 1984, Seacole's autobiography enabled her rise as a community exemplar in the twentieth century and her ascent as a national heroine in the twenty-first.[2] In her literary legacy, she offered herself up as a foremother to the contemporary Black presence in Great Britain and as a role model for minority populations across the nation. For these audiences, she has provided a set of strategies for making claims to history and belonging in contemporary Britain. Her text also exposes long histories of what we now call institutional or systemic racism. Just as Seacole appealed to her Victorian readers to support her in her hour of need, she offers contemporary Britons a lever for historical redress. Her story urges modern readers to understand and indict the wrongs of the past. It also inspires these very readers to imagine new futures in twenty-first-century Britain.

It was not uncommon, at least in the early days of Seacole's rediscovery, to cast her as the "Black Florence Nightingale," a counterpart to the Crimean War's best-known heroine.[3] But this is a limited characterization, as Seacole's resurgence demonstrates. This characterization has produced dead-end debates about the racial identity of Mary Seacole and countless contentions about the professional ideal of modern nursing. These matters have proven sticking points for those who have been jealous to guard Nightingale's place in the national pantheon of heroines, whatever its scope, and for those who have been anxious to patrol the boundaries of the British nation, whether symbolic or real. A leading light on her own terms, Seacole is more than just a compensatory figure. She exemplified distinct virtues, not of bureaucratic administration, angelic womanhood, and steely isolation, but of brave entrepreneurship, warm care, and robust sociability. Her story offers up its own resources for use in a twenty-first-century Britain. Seacole's afterlife has enabled the imagination of shared ties, the forging of associational life, and the redressing of historical wrongs. As her story shows, the Crimea and its afterlife are at the heart of debates about Britishness and belonging, in the past, present, and future.

***

Had it not been for Seacole's autobiography, she might be an unknown in twenty-first-century Britain. Allusions to Seacole's deeds and sacrifice do survive in the British press and in personal letters. The satirical magazine *Punch* offered an encomium to her in verse.[4] A set of visual sources that span media, to include print, photography, painting, and sculpture contributes to the historical record as well (Figure 6.1). Yet the protagonist's own memoir, The *Wonderful Adventures of Mrs. Seacole in Many Lands,* published in 1857, provides the fullest exposition not just of Seacole's

Figure 6.1 Mary Seacole. Photograph. 1850s. Winchester College. In aid of Mary Seacole Memorial Appeal. Mary Evans Photo Library

deeds, but also of her character. In this autobiography-cum-travelogue, Seacole rendered a vivid and humorous account of her life's story, from her birth in Jamaica at the turn of the nineteenth century to her labors in the Crimea in the mid-Victorian age. Here, Seacole not only recorded her labors as a nurse and as an entrepreneur. She also outlined her virtues as an exemplar of pluck and endurance, and as a provider of warmth and care. In its own time, Seacole's text had an immediate purpose: to garner funds to provide the roving heroine with support in her middle and older age. As she sought out security, Seacole wrote herself into the story of the Crimean War. With her narrative, Seacole claimed her place in the rolls of adventurers and fighters; she foregrounded her distinctive role as a Creole woman caring for British soldiers in the theater of war, all the while. Seacole's text has served ends that its author could not have imagined. It has provided a catalogue of transhistorical virtues of resilience and resourcefulness that have informed Seacole's rehabilitation within

minority communities and health-care circles alike. Ultimately, the autobiography has offered an invitation to belonging, and a critique of exclusions, for a multiethnic Britain.

At the time of her rediscovery in the later twentieth century, Seacole
became known as the Black Florence Nightingale. She had herself
referred to her better-known counterpart, whom many understood as
a rival, as "that Englishwoman whose name shall never die, but sound
like music on the lips of British men until the hour of doom."[5] Seacole
borrowed many elements surrounding the legend of the former when she
sketched her own story. Like Nightingale, Seacole cultivated an interest in
healing at a young age. She nursed a doll, just as her better-known
Crimean counterpart had legendarily done. Like Nightingale, Seacole
was also an avid student of the sciences and crafts of nursing. Seacole
did not have to look far for examples of nursing and medical care. She
learned in her earliest days not from travel abroad, but rather from her
own mother, a boarding housekeeper and a healer in her own right, who
cared for soldiers and invalids in Jamaica. Like Nightingale, Seacole went
to great lengths to obtain knowledge and skill: for instance, she performed
a postmortem exam on a child who had died from cholera. Early life
provided a training ground for fighting cholera, not only in Kingston,
Jamaica, but also in Cruces, Panama, where Seacole became the disease's
"greatest foe," to use her own words.[6] Her Caribbean and Central
American travels gave her experience in treating dysentery and diarrhea
as well. There, as in the Crimea, she addressed these ailments with
a combination of medical know-how and home remedies. It is fair to say
that Seacole surpassed Nightingale's efforts as a wartime nurse. While
Nightingale concerned herself largely with the hospital at Scutari, Seacole
put herself literally "under fire."[7] For this reason, Seacole has served as an
inspiration for wartime nursing in both her deeds and her spirits. As she
told it, the risks to life and limb were more than worth the sacrifice. Whilst
in the Crimea, Seacole was rewarded, time and again, with "grateful
words" and with "smile[s]."[8]

Seacole's renown in her own time, as in ours, did not just hinge on her
healing acumen. It lay equally with her entrepreneurial drive, which
found an outlet in the face of the war's mismanagement.[9] She honed
her entrepreneurialism, like her nursing skills, in her native Jamaica.
According to the autobiography, Mary Seacole came into business hon-
estly, by blood and by upbringing. In her early years, she tried her hand at
merchandizing, bringing pickles and West Indian preserves to England
and selling shell work in New Providence. She pursued the art of a hotelier
in Cruces and developed the craft of a restaurateur in Gorgona. The hard-
scrabble world of the Caribbean, with its thievery and swindling, provided

a good training ground for her later ventures in the Crimea, where she set up the British Hotel, which included a mess table, living quarters, and a store, along with her business partner, Mr. Day. The firm of Seacole and Day was expert in procuring goods amidst the war's scarcity. Together, Seacole and Day supplied their patrons with coveted staples like potatoes, carrots, turnips, and greens, which they brought from Balaklava harbor to the British Hotel. And Seacole herself was a formidable caterer. Dubbed England's "own Vivandière" by *Punch*, she had an array of talents that could impress even the French chef, Alexis Soyer.[10] The war's end brought about the ruin of the firm, leaving Seacole without capital and with a need to write her autobiography, so as to secure resources for the latter part of her life.

Seacole's autobiography was, thus, a campaign for support. When she wrote her own story, she wrote her way into the conscience of the nation. To this end, Seacole outlined her exemplarity. She fashioned herself as a Victorian worthy in her own time, and she became a role model, to use contemporary parlance, in ours. Many aspects of her character antici-pated those qualities lauded by Samuel Smiles in his best seller, *Self Help*, published in 1859, just two years after Seacole released her autobiography.[11] Like Smiles's entrepreneurs and inventors, Seacole was a portrait in perseverance and ingenuity. And like them, she exhibited these qualities from a young age. Losses early on, of her mother and then of her husband, left Seacole alone in the world, to forge her way as best as she could. "I have always turned a bold front to fortune," she explained.[12] Key to her success was her unflappable character. In the face of danger, loss, and disappointment, she never let herself get down. If Seacole was, in part, a portrait in self-reliance resembling the heroes of *Self Help*, she was, equally, a profile in courage recalling the literature of muscular Christianity.[13] Her story was not just an example of rational enterprise. It was equally, if not more, an instance of rollicking adventure. A widowed woman alone in a rough world, she exhibited the wherewithal required for dealing with hucksters, outlaws, and thieves. Human, natural, or animal, nothing was too much for her – the swindlers of the Caribbean, the winds of the Black Sea, or the fleas of the Crimea.

But there were, for Seacole, barriers and challenges that the real-life heroes of Samuel Smiles's didactic prose and the fictional protagonists of muscular Christianity's adventure tales did not face. Some of these had, of course, to do with Seacole's place as a woman and a widow alone in the world. There were, as well, the realities and indignities of color and race. As a Creole born to a free, mixed-race Jamaican woman and a Scotch military man, Seacole's own relationship to these taxonomies was complicated.[14] According to the comic periodical, *Punch*, Seacole had a "berry brown face, with a kind heart's trace."[15] She described herself as a "Yellow Doctress."[16] A woman with "good Scotch blood coursing" through her veins, she was "only a little brown," neither "wholly white" nor "entirely black," either.[17] As later critics have noted, Seacole herself exploited hierarchies of race and color to create sympathies with her English readership and even to underpin the British project of empire. She drew lines between herself and other figures in her midst, such as her "black cook" Francis and the natives of the Americas.[18] But she also fell victim to what we now recognize as institutional racism. This was not, as Seacole told it, the crude American racism of chattel slavery and debasing epithets. But it was responsible, all the same, for her own exclusion from official channels of access to the Crimea. Three times, Seacole was denied in her appeal to aid the soldiers suffering in the East. She was turned away by the War Office, by the Crimean Fund, and by Florence Nightingale herself. She met a chilly reception by Nightingale and her nurses when she passed through Scutari, where she spent the night with welcoming washerwomen and less hospitable rats. These sorts of slights and exclusions required great perseverance and resourcefulness. Seacole put her resolve and ingenuity to work as she labored to reach the battlefront and to fulfill her destiny. "I made up my mind that if the army wanted nurses, they would be glad of me, and with all the ardor of my nature, which ever carried me where my inclination prompted, I decided that I *would* go to the Crimea," she declared.[19] Armed with this strong mindedness and resolve, Seacole became, in her own right and in her own words, a "Crimean *heroine*."[20]

Mary Seacole looked to the words of others to substantiate her own claims to Crimean heroism. The book's preface, written by another Crimean luminary, William Howard Russell, lauded Seacole for her "singleness of heart, true charity, and Christian works."[21] Moreover, the soldiers in her care testified to her labors as a "doctress, nurse and 'mother.'"[22] In the years since its reemergence, a scholarly consensus has emerged around the autobiography wherein readers have understood the persona of "mother" as essential to the author-heroine's literary and public success.[23] In the Crimea, ailing soldiers hailed the Jamaican healer as "Mother Seacole," or, alternatively, as "Aunty Seacole."[24] In her autobiography, Seacole was sure to let her English readership know this designation. It was one that allowed her to blunt the dangers of difference wrought by sex and race and to kindle support, both emotional and financial. It also signaled a particular brand of care that was feminine and nurturing. Ultimately, the persona of mother allowed her to mitigate the threats wrought by sexual and racial difference. By writing herself not as the other, but instead as a mother, Seacole produced the solidarity and sympathy that allowed her to improve her financial situation after the war and to secure her place in history.

Florence Nightingale, herself, was ambivalent at best about this sort of coddling care. It certainly seeped into her legend, but she deemed it a distraction from the bureaucratic and systematic aspects of nursing. Seacole, for her part, was far happier to build upon the understanding of herself as a nurturing presence for the English troops. "Their calling me mother was not altogether without meaning," she declared.[25] As she sought to explain this status and to defend its legitimacy, Seacole pointed to her long-standing dedication to the British Army. Along with other Creoles, she had ministered to the "sick and suffering" English, felled by cholera and tropical disease, in the Caribbean.[26] In the Crimea, she provided the feminine work of care for the sick at the British Hotel and the pastoral work of shepherding the dead across life's threshold. Time and again, she offered up comfort for the ailing and forlorn men. One especially poignant moment had her at the bedside of a dying soldier. With Seacole by his side, he imagined, in his last moments, that he was in a different place, surrounded by his wife and children in his English "village home."[27]

In the Crimea, Seacole offered far more than medicine and steward-ship. Even more importantly, she provided "things suggestive of home and its comforts."[28] At the British Hotel, war weary soldiers could find Irish stew, Welsh rarebit, and rice pudding, as well as cigarettes, tea, and currant jelly, and also sandwiches, pies, and tarts. Seacole served sponge cakes and lemonade that "tasted of home."[29] She did not disappoint at the Yuletide, when she joined in the effort to procure ingredients for Christmas puddings and mince pies. "I wonder if the people of other countries are as fond of carrying with them everywhere their home habits as the English,"[30] the Caribbean-born hotelier mused. "I think not. I think there was something purely and essentially English in the determination of the camp to spend the Christmas-day of 1855 after the good old 'home' fashion,"[31] she declared after the fall of Sebastopol, as the troops anticipated their return to Britain. Finally, Seacole was delighted, at the war's end, to see the attentions of the weary soldiers turn to theatrical productions, cricket matches, and competitive races. With regard to the last, she was struck particularly by the ways in which the race managers "had contrived to imitate the old familiar scenes at home."[32] It may seem surprising that a Caribbean-born woman held such a finely honed sense of the English taste for home. However, the fact that she was in such strong possession of this understanding is of a piece with her own history and that of the empire. It was, additionally, reflective of Seacole's aspirations and her immediate financial goals.

Seacole's ability to produce home for the peripatetic English soldiers had
its origins, of course, in her native Jamaica, where she and her mother had
cared for troops well in advance of the Crimean War. And her ability not
just to cook up a sense or feeling of home during the War, but to stir up its
visceral and affective associations in her writings afterward, was an effective tool in her autobiography.[33] It produced a shared ground between the
Creole healer from Jamaica and her English readership in the
metropole.[34] Ultimately, this commonality led the English to open up
their hearts, and their pockets, in her support, at least for a time.

Yet one of the most poignant aspects of Seacole's predicament had to
do with the nature of home itself. Seacole may have cooked up home for
many, but where did it reside for her? A born traveler and a steady servant,
Seacole herself felt most at home while serving the soldiers of England
and feeding the armies of Europe. Though she welcomed the closing of
the curtain of battle, Seacole was not among those who greeted the
departure from the peninsula with celebration. For the bulk of the adventurers, the opportunity to go back to Britain was a long-awaited return.
They arrived to fanfare, with some embraced in humble homes and others
feted in fancy balls. But it was different for the cosmopolitan Seacole, who
made home everywhere, but was at home nowhere. For Seacole, among
the last to leave the Crimea, the war's end was a melancholy one; it meant
the loss of community and of comfort. "And yet all this going home
seemed strange and somewhat sad," she confessed. "Sometimes I felt
that I could not sympathize with the glad faces and happy hearts of those
who were looking forward to the delights of home." There were, though,
those with whom she felt a true fellowship, those soldiers "by choice and
necessity, as well as by profession," those "lounger[s] with a blank face,
taking no interest in the bustle of departure." They had "no home to go
to" beyond the front.[35] Like roving soldiers, she found comfort in the
fellowship of wartime. For Seacole, the end of the war meant the end of
community, the end of purpose, and the end, perhaps, of home.[36] It was
a painful predicament, one that resonated powerfully with Seacole's
champions in diaspora at the time of her text's rediscovery, some 130
years after the Crimean War.

A particular power of Seacole's narrative is that it offers multiple
opportunities for redemption: for Seacole and for her English contemporaries, and, by extension, for her self-proclaimed heirs. In rhetorical
and personal terms alike, Seacole maneuvered between difference and
similarity, between isolation and camaraderie, and between alienation
and home. Though Seacole's text was remarkably wide ranging, just as
her own adventures had been, the experience of her traveling life was
notably intimate and reassuringly small, at least as she recorded it. She

ministered, in fact, to the fighters of many nations in what she herself called "that one common language of the whole world – smiles."[37] And recurring through her autobiography is the theme of friendship. Seacole's world, as she narrated it, tended to assume the shape of a traveling regiment – convivial, warm, and supportive.[38] Time and again, en route to the Crimea and while there, Seacole stumbled upon old friends and cultivated relationships with new ones. And, though she bade a tearful farewell to the troops in the Crimea, Seacole found comfort, she tells readers, in the streets of London. "Wherever I go I am sure to meet some smiling face," she reports. "In omnibuses, in river steamboats, in places of public amusement, in quiet streets and courts, where taking short cuts I lose my way oft-times, spring up old familiar faces": all reminders of her Crimean campaign. "Where, indeed, do I not find friends," she concludes.[39]

Why did Seacole lean so heavily on friendship as a theme in her life story and as a lesson from her text? The reasons are many. Friendship was, of course, a strange by-product of war. But the appeal to friendship on the Jamaican healer's part was not merely documentary; it performed significant emotional work as well. Portraying war as an exercise in friendship blunted its ravages, taming its horrors and making it appear jolly. In turn, such a maneuver produced comfort and kinship among Seacole's readers, leading them to donate to her cause. Additionally, it provided reassurance for Seacole in the form of a reminder that home could be found in diaspora. Years later, in a similar vein, Seacole's autobiography offered a resource for Black Britons, as they struggled to claim a home, and a history, in the mother country.

But what, for Seacole, was the nature of this friendship? The autobiographer suggested, in her text, that friendship was born not only of mutual affinities, but also of shared debt. A common feeling arose when Seacole encountered comrades from the front in London's streets. Typically, she noted, these fellow travelers looked back on a time characterized not just by shared affection, but also by mutual indebtedness. To this effect, Seacole characterized these occasions of reunion with an old friend as moments when she and a veteran of the war shared in the recollection of the epoch. The war was a time, in Seacole's own words, "when I was of use to him and he to me."[40] Seacole's hope in recalling this debt is clear. It allowed her to make a gentle appeal for support to her benefactors. In broader terms, Seacole's text allowed, eventually, for the expression of a debt writ large. This is the colonial debt carried by Britain with regard to its colonies, and especially its slaveholding colonies in the Caribbean. In years to come, Seacole's text was a reminder, for her latter-day champions, of their rightful place in Britain's history. As they claimed Seacole as a foremother, they claimed their own places in the nation's unfolding and in its present.

***

"I have witnessed her devotion and her courage ... and I trust that England will never forget one who has nursed her sick, who sought out her wounded to aid and succor them and who performed the last offices for some of her illustrious dead."[41] With this encomium, William Howard Russell introduced Mary Seacole to the British reading public in 1857.[42] In his injunction, he offered his support to Seacole, who had returned to England after the war in a state of insecurity. On the heels of the conflict, the differing fates of Mary Seacole and Florence Nightingale appeared in sharp relief. Writing under the pen name of "Da Meritis," one advocate inquired of the disparity in the *Times*: "While the benevolent deeds of Florence Nightingale are being handed down to posterity with blessings and imperishable renown, are the humbler actions of Mrs. Seacole to be entirely forgotten?" "Da Meritis" called attention to the reversal of fortune that had befallen Seacole, "that good old soul whose generous hospitality has warmed up many a gallant spirit on the chilly heights of Balaklava." Having survived the war, Seacole faced a harder trial in the "worst storm of all – the gale of adversity that followed."[43] Other writers joined the chorus, as they lobbied on Mary's behalf in the pages of the press.[44] Still other forms of support came Seacole's way. Soldiers from the Crimea offered her miniature medals.[45] Subscription funds took up monies in her honor. Finally, the Seacole Fund's Grand Military Gala, which played host to no fewer than eleven bands, one thousand performers, and 80,000 visitors at the Royal Surrey Gardens, occurred over four days in the summer of 1857, to be followed by another fete a decade later.[46] Yet, despite this flurry of attention, England did not heed Russell's plea across the *longue durée*. Instead, Mary Seacole lived in relative obscurity, although not in penury, until her 1881 death in London.[47] While later life saw the dimming of Seacole's reputation, her death nearly extinguished her star, leaving her to be forgotten for the better part of a century.

The twentieth-century campaign to resurrect Seacole began not in Britain, but in the heroine's native home: Jamaica led the way in efforts to remember Mary and to enshrine her as a national heroine. There, Seacole was never entirely forgotten.[48] Remembrance efforts accelerated, however, with the Crimean centenary in 1954 and with Jamaican independence in 1962. In the later years of the twentieth century, her name became prominently displayed at locales devoted to Seacole's own crafts of healing and hospitality. In Kingston, the headquarters of the Jamaican Nurses Association is called the Mary Seacole House and a hospital ward bears the heroine's name. In Mona, a residence hall at the University of the West Indies has Seacole's moniker emblazoned on it as well. Seacole's imprint extended beyond the built environment: nursing associations adopted Mary as a foremother and radio shows featured her life story. In Jamaica, Mary Seacole attained a level of national sanction in the 1990s, receiving a posthumous Order of Merit and appearing on a postage stamp, too.[49]

The metropolitan campaign to restore Seacole's name and to refurbish her legacy followed on the inroads made in Jamaica. Between the 1970s and the 1990s, there were many efforts to claim Seacole as a foremother, whether as a trailblazer in the making of the nursing profession or as a forerunner to the Black presence in Britain. Piecemeal and quotidian, this grassroots work transpired across urban Britain, in London especially, but also in cities like Liverpool and Bristol, which were home to sizeable Black, Asian, and Minority Ethnic populations.[50] These efforts occurred in club meetings and in community centers, and in local libraries and in borough offices. Seacole was the concern of ladies' luncheons and fringe theatres, of community centers and youth discos. The campaign for restoration was a labor of love, perseverance, and conviction by the early champions of Mary Seacole. These efforts are chronicled in mimeographed sheets and in local newspapers. Though they occurred in intimate venues and in makeshift spaces, they eventually had significant impact and broad effect. In the end, they delivered on William Howard Russell's plea, made nearly a century and a half before, to remember Mary Seacole and her contributions to the nation.[51]

Concerted efforts to honor Seacole took shape in 1973, with a campaign to restore Mary's grave, located in St. Mary's Catholic Cemetery in Kensal Green, North London. Together, the Lignum Vitae Club, an association of Jamaican women in London, the UK Jamaican Nurses Association, and the Commonwealth Nurses War Memorial Fund took up this effort. Their labors, and Seacole's resting place, are marked by a stone with the following tribute: "Here lies Mary Seacole, 1805–1881, of Kingston, Jamaica: A Notable Nurse Who Cared for the Sick and Wounded in the West Indies, Panama, and on the Battlefields of the Crimea, 1854–1856." Yearly, on the anniversary of Seacole's May 14 death, the graveside provides the site for a wreath-laying ceremony, followed by a luncheon and a lecture. On these occasions, custodians of Mary's memory – including Jamaican women, minority nurses, and Black historians – joined in the yearly occasions led by the Friends of Mary Seacole and later the Mary Seacole Memorial Association.[52]

The campaign to rekindle Seacole's legacy took off in more thorough-going ways in the 1980s. In the midst of the racial discontent of Margaret Thatcher's Britain, Mary Seacole, like Black British history more generally, offered an avenue for redress and a beacon of hope. "Perhaps ... the centenary of her death will see popular interest develop in this extraordinary woman," wrote Ziggi Alexander and Audrey Dewjee, who launched a multipronged effort to bring visibility to Seacole and other Black Britons.[53] Together, they organized a touring exhibit, "Roots in Britain," under the auspices of Brent Library Services in 1980.[54] *Dragon's Teeth,* an antiracist magazine for children, lauded the exhibit for putting to rest the misconception that there was no Black presence in Britain preceding the 1948 arrival of the SS Empire Windrush, which brought over 500 Jamaicans to England after the Second World War.[55] Not only did the exhibit chart the long history of Black people in Britain; it worked simultaneously to lift Seacole out of "obscurity." In the wake of the exhibit, she became "a symbol for Black nurses, civil rights groups, and the women's liberation movement."[56]

Alexander and Dewjee's labor in republishing Seacole's *Adventures* proved even longer lasting in its impact. This was an act that effectively sealed the Jamaican heroine's legacy. The climate was right, with Seacole's autobiography reappearing in the same year that Peter Fryer published *Staying Power,* which brought attention to the long history of Black people in Britain.[57] In 1984, Falling Wall Press, a small publishing house based in Bristol, England, released Seacole's autobiography-cum-travelogue. The text was perfectly matched to Falling Wall's mission of publishing texts of feminist, socialist, and minority interest. By the time of Falling Wall's reprinting, there were "barely half a dozen copies of the original, cheap cardboard-backed" edition to be found.[58] The few copies that existed had languished, inaccessible, with the "leaves unopened" on the shelves of university libraries.[59] Critics acclaimed the book's arrival as part of the blossoming of the Black British book trade. *Dragon's Teeth* noted that, "for Afro–Caribbean and other people of African extraction and indeed, for any reader interested in human experiences, this book is a must."[60] Soon, attention eclipsed this audience, with Seacole gaining currency among scholarly audiences across the Atlantic, as the 1988 release of the text as part of the Schomburg Library of Nineteenth-Century Black Women Writers announced.[61] Over the following years, interest in Seacole and in her text only grew. In 2005, the year of the bicentenary of Seacole's birth, the mainstreaming of her memory achieved another set of landmarks, including the publication of her *Adventures* as a Penguin Classic.

As this chronology indicates, the promulgation of Seacole's text, and of her story, was a gradual process. Moreover, it had its skeptics along the way. From the beginning, there were many who sought to challenge the absorption of Seacole into British history and English culture. A case in point is the *Spectator*'s Roy Kerridge. His trenchant 1984 review, "Black Nightingale," provides a window onto a reception far different from the warm and unequivocal one offered in the Black press and in popular history circles. Like many fellow reviewers, Kerridge hailed Seacole's text at its republication for its literary merit and its human interest: "Wonderful indeed are the true adventures of Mary Seacole, written by herself," he declared. "A brisk, jolly Creole lady of Jamaica, who bustled about the world curing the sick, carrying victuals to soldiers and opening hotels wherever she went, she was justly famous in her day," wrote the critic, who found in the roving figure's narrative delightful echoes of Twain's *Huckleberry Finn* and Dickens's *Martin Chuzzlewit*.[62] Kerridge appreciated Seacole's *Adventures* as a nineteenth-century literary enterprise, but he was less enamored of contemporary efforts to adopt her as a foremother to the Black presence in Britain. For one, the *Spectator*'s reviewer found the desire to claim roots in Britain dating to 1550, and hence to slavery and empire, politically questionable and opportunistic.[63] Instead, he subscribed to a postwar narrative of modernity and choice, wherein colonial subjects came to the mother country by free will and for opportunity. Kerridge's misgivings resided additionally in two further matters. He was skeptical, first, of the claim that Seacole was Black, given her own particular racial negotiations in her day. And he was doubtful, second, of the power of identity as a framework for politics, which he oversimplified as he launched an arch and uncharitable critique:

The revival of Mary Seacole's fame owes something to the urge to "give back history to black children" so that they can "identify" with figures from the English past. Why history, adventure and heroism need to have a color at all is seldom explained. Many white children admire Mohammed Ali and my own boyhood hero was Uncle Remus. James Bond and Superman, who are white, and the Incredible Hulk, who is green, greatly appeal to many coloured children. In order to make Mary Seacole into a complete English Black History in herself, her life has been misrepresented. I have seen a school play, brilliantly acted, in which she invented a miraculous cure for cholera, a fact that was later "suppressed" by white racists. Whatever would good Mother Seacole say if she knew that she had become a heroine of Black Power?[64]

It is worthwhile to examine Kerridge's words against the grain. Admittedly scathing, they provide a glimpse onto a moment in the adoption of Mary Seacole as a community heroine. They reveal, albeit in scorn, the creativity that educators brought to Black children and Black communities as they sought to kindle historical consciousness and to forge a sense of home. And they show, although vituperatively, the central role of Mary Seacole in this project. In his review, Kerridge diagnosed what he uncharitably called "Seacole syndrome," the desire to locate Black roots in Britain in early modern slavery rather than in postwar immigration. For Kerridge, this desire was manifest across London's multiethnic neighborhoods. "It is hard to cross [the London borough of] Brent *without* looking at Mary Seacole, whose clumsy portrait features in every Black Rights Centre in the Harrow Road," Kerridge declared. "Painted in garish colors, it appears on a school playground wall next to a portrait of Chairman Mao."[65]

It is chafing to reckon with the ways that Kerridge used the hyperbole of racial concern and the authority of aesthetic judgment to enable his rant. Yet, his words are valuable as a time capsule of sorts that captures, in a manner that is painfully unsympathetic, the community-based and home-grown nature of efforts to make Seacole into an exemplar. Community centers and school playgrounds were just two of the spaces where Seacole became visible in the later twentieth century. Seacole found a place in many corners of the urban landscape and in the civic practices of Black communities during the later years of the twentieth century. This was, of course, thanks in part to the efforts of Alexander and Dewjee. Yet, there were others as well who played their roles in weaving Mary Seacole into the sociocultural fabric of everyday life as they sought to honor a Crimean heroine and to make a postcolonial home.

Another contemporary leader in this project was Connie Mark, a Jamaican-born nurse who emigrated to London in the postwar era, just as Seacole had done a century before. Beginning in 1983, Mark steered the Friends of Mary Seacole, which assumed a custodial role as it made Mary Seacole's grave the center of its mission. It planned yearly wreath-laying ceremonies, with luncheons and lectures. It labored to safeguard the grave, raising funds for costly maintenance, gilt work, and refurbishment.[66] Mark and her organization extended their mission across London as they sought to consecrate the home where Seacole had lived in Portman Square with one of London's iconic blue plaques. Working alongside the Greater London Council's Ethnic Minorities Unit, they managed to have a plaque installed on International Women's Day in 1985. It was a step toward placing Seacole in a pantheon of heroines, albeit a temporary one. The plaque remained in place for three years, only to be taken down with a building demolition in 1988. Seacole and her partisans were left waiting nearly twenty years, until 2007, for another.[67]

Connie Mark and the Friends of Mary Seacole extended their attentions beyond graves and monuments.[68] The Friends offered potlucks with Caribbean food, discos for youth, and even school plays of the sort derided by Kerridge. In other words, they kindled community and hospitality, just as Mary Seacole had done. They aimed, ostensibly, to sear Mary Seacole into the consciousness of a new generation. Connie Mark's efforts had their roots in her personal history; she hoped that she might redress the omissions of her youth. "I was brought up in Jamaica and never knew anything about [Seacole]," Mark later explained. "She is a good role model for us all." In fact, Seacole proved a role model even in suggesting the mechanisms for her own recognition. In the nineteenth century, Seacole used her business acumen and her public savvy to secure her success. In the twentieth century, Mark and the Friends of Mary Seacole reached to Caribbean businesses and the Black press as they made their appeals. Using methods reminiscent of their foremother, they sought to knit Seacole into the hearts and minds of the community.[69] Ultimately, in her energies and commitment, Connie Mark resembled something of the spirit of Mrs. Seacole. Seacole had, in the nineteenth century, inspired poetry, most notably the tribute in *Punch*. Laboring a century after Seacole's death, Connie Mark, her great advocate, inspired verse too. This memorable couplet at the end of a tribute suggests well the spirit of Seacole and her champion: "Fight on Connie Mark, Lead us out of the dark."[70]

These words point to the sense of urgency associated with efforts not merely to remember Seacole, but equally to redress systemic racial inequities in Margaret Thatcher's Britain. Focused on health care, these efforts were initially incremental and local in their manifestations. In 1980s Liverpool, for instance, the Mary Seacole House sought to advance minority mental health. This day center for a multicultural community offered assistance to those who needed help sorting bills and provided facilities for those who hoped to take showers.[71] In the following decades, Mary Seacole's name came to be associated with minority health, community nursing, and medical training. By hitching Seacole's name to these endeavors, reformers sought, at once, to celebrate the Caribbean heroine and to address inequities in medical access. This goal was historically important, given the role that Black Britons had played in the expansion of the health-care system in the age of the welfare state.[72] In the early 1990s, the NHS remained the largest employer of Black Britons.[73] There was, however, a color bar in the nursing establishment, where white nurses enjoyed the majority of leadership positions and where Black nurses tended to work the lion's share of night shifts. All in all, the profession continued to overlook nursing's "Black face," despite the critical roles played by women of color.[74] Mary Seacole's name offered an avenue to recognize, if not necessarily to redress, these injustices. The Department of Health launched a Mary Seacole Leadership Award complete with cash prize to honor Black, Asian, and Minority Ethnic nurses. In the 1990s and after, several universities opened research centers, education buildings, and special rooms that took Mary Seacole's name: DeMontfort University, the University of Wolverhampton, and the London School of Hygiene and Tropical Medicine. Capping off these efforts, Professor Dame Elizabeth Anionwu, a nurse, an educator, and a pioneer in the treatment of sickle cell anemia, established the Mary Seacole Centre for Nursing Practice at Thames Valley University, now the University of West London.[75]

Beginning in the 1980s, theater provided yet another venue for staging Seacole, herself a master of self-fashioning, as a heroine for a multicultural Britain. Fringe and community theaters featured plays about Seacole, whose lively character and indomitable spirit have proved appealing for audiences large and small. In 1989, for instance, Dual Control Theatre Company put on Michael Bath's play, "Black Legend," at the Oval House Theatre in London.[76] Over the years, Black actresses found in Seacole a source of fascination and a fount for inspiration. One-woman shows about Seacole appeared in venues from the Edinburgh Fringe Festival to London's Rosemary Branch Theatre, and from the National Portrait Gallery to the Florence Nightingale Museum. Nineteen ninety-nine witnessed the three-week run of Sherlina Chamberlain's show, "For Queen and Country," which celebrated the nurse's story of personal overcoming against all obstacles. Particularly inspiring were Seacole's "determination and strength." In Chamberlain's words, "she went anywhere and did everything she wanted to do and more."[77] Along with Chamberlain, Cleo Sylvestre, an English film, television, and stage actress of mixed-race descent, took inspiration from Seacole. Sylvestre's relationship with the heroine began in 1984, when she read the reissued autobiography and discovered an "amazing story." Fascinated by Seacole's resourcefulness, determination, and ingenuity, Sylvestre long harbored the desire to design a one-woman show.[78] She delivered on this dream with "The Marvelous Adventures of Mary Seacole," first performed in 2005. Through her own script, and "with great warmth," Sylvestre brought "to life Mary's humor, flamboyance, dignity, and determination." In the words of the promotional materials, she provided a living tribute to "a woman of immense personal bravery who refused to be categorized as a victim or let prejudice deter her" – in other words, "an inspiring role model for all."[79]

Finally, London's museums played their part to lodge Seacole in the national consciousness. In 1992, for instance, Seacole became the subject of a new partnership between the Florence Nightingale Museum, located on the South Bank of the Thames, and the Black Cultural Archives, housed in Brixton. Leading figures at both institutions – the Florence Nightingale Museum's Alex Attewell and the Black Cultural Archives' Sam Walker – brought their organizations together to share expertise, research, and artifacts. Their collaboration resulted in an exhibit, "The Life and Times of Mary Seacole," which ran simultaneously at both locales. For both institutions, the display vaulted attendance to new levels, as it brought the collections to new constituencies, including Afro-Caribbean teenagers and nurses. The exhibit extended its reach beyond central London, continuing as a traveling show appearing at borough museums, public libraries, and local schools, to name just some locales.[80]

The exhibit opened at the Black Cultural Archives to great fanfare on May 20, 1992. There were Jamaican and British dignitaries in attendance. Isolde O'Neill playing Florence Nightingale and Sherlina Chamberlain dressed as Mary Seacole gave the occasion theatrical flair (Figure 6.2). Sam Walker had worked assiduously – and not without frustration – to

Figure 6.2 Jamaican High Commissioner Ellen Bogle, Sherlina Chamberlain as Mary Seacole, Isolde O'Neill as Florence Nightingale, and Diane Abbot, MP. Press opening. Exhibition on the life of Mary Seacole. 1992. BCA/6/7/4. Copyright Black Cultural Archives

ensure an ample press presence.[81] The *Guardian* gave national notice of the occasion with the headline, "Nursing Pays Debt to Forgotten Heroine," as it brought its readers' attentions to the "Black unknown who rivaled Nightingale in the Crimean War." Journalist David Brindle told that Seacole's name had "slipped from the history books because she was an outsider, did not conform, and was Black."[82] Organs of the local and ethic press followed suit with their own notices of the occasion. "Heroism Acknowledged at Last," proclaimed the *Voice*; "Key Role in Black History" touted the *Hackney Gazette*; "Overdue Celebration Held for Life of Neglected Black Leader" read the *Nursing Times*.[83] The sentiments of those in attendance echoed the headlines, with Connie Mark declaring, "I am really thrilled that this project has come this far. Mary Seacole was a fine Caribbean woman who was blocked out of history because she was Black. She never received half the recognition of Florence Nightingale."[84] Others followed these expressions as they welcomed the march of Mary Seacole from margin to center, applauding her belated arrival "in the public eye."[85] And the directors of the two institutions were, purportedly, both delighted with the final shape of the display.

The exhibit that garnered such publicity and such praise was, in fact, a modest one, made up of four panels of laminated board that featured text and photography telling the story of Mary Seacole. In the exhibit's rendering, Seacole was a heroine not only for her own time, but also for the millennium's end. With its eye to the present, the exhibit began with the context of the 1990–1991 Gulf War and its aftermath. There were images of scorpions and scarves to give a flavor of the desert and its peoples; there were renderings of grenades and amputation saws to give a sense of the challenges of late twentieth-century warfare. The message here was that the nursing heroics of the Victorian past provided a foundational point on a trajectory that extended to Britain's present. Once they had established this understanding, the exhibit's designers transported visitors back to the Crimean War. Subsequent panels made Seacole into a leading figure of the mid-nineteenth century as they informed viewers about Mary's medicinal practices, social world, and London Life. In these object-driven panels, visitors beheld an array of images. Depictions featured rats, stale bread, and a bone-saw, as well as a lancer's helmet and medical tweezers. Taken together, the representations of these objects made tangible the trials and tribulations of the battlefront. As it guided visitors between past and present, the exhibit offered a vision of Seacole as a heroine for the Victorian era and a resourceful role model beyond.[86]

The display attracted attention not only at the Black Cultural Archives, but also at the Florence Nightingale Museum. Yet, its stint on the South

Bank of the Thames sparked critiques as well. The temporary exhibit saluting Mary Seacole appeared meager in relation to a permanent museum celebrating Florence Nightingale.[87] In the face of this disparity, critics longed for a "strong image" of Mary Seacole.[88] A Black nurse who visited the exhibition lamented that the Nightingale Museum "over-powered" the Seacole display. For this troubled visitor, the exhibition revealed a "racial imbalance" at the heart not just of the exhibit, but of the nursing profession itself. To tour the exhibit was to revisit daily slights and long-standing inequities; it was akin to "reliving the last twenty years [in nursing]."[89] Another visitor to express concerns about the exhibit was a teacher from multiracial Peckham, located in south London. From a pedagogical vantage point, she hoped for a more vivid display for her class of ten-year-old students. "Mary Seacole didn't stand out enough against Florence Nightingale," this educator wrote. "You know how you've got the model of Florence Nightingale? You should have one of Mary Seacole. Children like real life-size things. What did Mary Seacole wear? The exhibition did not tell us about that. Also, more ought to be made of the fact that she nursed under gunfire."[90] These critiques do not simply reveal the disappointments generated by the display; they also showcase the hopes that visitors brought to the exhibit. Namely, exhibition-goers held out the wish that the display might rectify the injustices of past wrongs and offer a direction for a better future, much like Mary Seacole herself.

The aspirations that informed these criticisms were not lost on the organizers themselves. They may have fallen short in the minds of some critics, yet they hoped to make Seacole into an exemplar of the Victorian past and a guide for a millennial future. These intentions were developed extensively in the education packet accompanying the exhibition, which included a sound recording narrated by Sherlina Chamberlain. The packet was available for purchase in England's schools, where Mary Seacole was gradually assuming a place in the curriculum. This collection of mimeographed sheets titled "Mary Seacole, The Jamaican Heroine of the Crimean War" placed a premium on interactive and experiential learning. It was filled with activities pegged to primary school skills. Students might engage in drawing activities, playacting, and oral histories as they explored Mary Seacole's story alongside their own.[91]

The *Black Briton* welcomed the work performed by this initiative in bringing what it termed "Afro-centricity" into England's classrooms.[92] Yet it is important to note that the packet framed Seacole not as a rival to Florence Nightingale, but, instead, as a companion. The real and imagined relationship between the Crimean War's two heroines, one long-standing and the other ascendant, was an overarching preoccupation, especially among Nightingale's stewards and partisans. There was a sense, even among those sympathetic to Seacole, of a finite economy of heroines. Would Seacole's rise lead to Nightingale's fall from grace? The Florence Nightingale Museum's Alex Attewell understood well the immovable barriers that had prevented Seacole from accompanying Nightingale to the East during the nineteenth century. And he grasped, too, the institutional racism that thwarted Seacole's rise to prominence in the twentieth. Yet, he worried that Nightingale's reputation might be collateral damage in Seacole's ascent. The curriculum packet assuaged such concerns, as it framed the two women not as rivals, but as compliments.[93]

The result of this effort at balance was the production of an idealized story about the Victorian era suitable for the turn of the millennium. Here, the story of Nightingale and Seacole took shape as an account of shared struggle for these two "greatest women of the nineteenth century" who were, together, a portrait in diversity, one a "white English woman" and the other a "black Jamaican." They may not have been partners, but they were fellow travelers along the improving arc of the nineteenth century and nurturers of its destiny. In the context of the education packet, their collective story was a narrative of feminist labor, of antiracist action, and of shared overcoming. "These two women by their knowledge, skills, humanitarianism, great enterprise and sheer merit transcended the sexist and racist constraints imposed on women and Black people in their time," explained text. Moreover, the effects of their notably feminine "brand of heroism" were truly transformative. Together, they changed the nature of war, where "death usually wins." Instead, in the exhibit's interpretation, Nightingale and Seacole were united in a drive to save lives.[94]

Taken together, the joint exhibition and its auxiliary efforts helped to lay the groundwork for discussions of Mary Seacole in the twenty-first century, when the heroine ascended to a national stage. For instance, the embrace of a shared path for these woman worthies anticipated continued conflicts over the conceptual place of Seacole in the National Curriculum and the literal placement of the healer's statue at St. Thomas' Hospital. These efforts on the part of the Black Cultural Archives and the Florence Nightingale Museum paved the way, too, for other refrains, among them, the continued framing of Seacole's story as one of overcoming. Those who lauded the exhibit and its accompanying efforts returned, again and again, to the sense that Seacole was exemplary for her persistence, especially in relation to the barriers that arose in the face of patriarchy and racism. "Mary Seacole always beat off obstacles," the critic Nigel Pollitt declared.[95] This sort of resourcefulness was something that the heroine bequeathed to her twentieth and twenty-first century heirs. Much like Winston Churchill had been an exemplar of the Blitz spirit of persever- ance, Seacole could, too, be an exemplar of lifelong resourcefulness. Indeed, those who had sought to revive her name had exhibited exactly this trait themselves. If Seacole had overcome obstacles to make it to the Crimea in the nineteenth century, then those who sought to rekindle her memory and to preserve her legacy had done the same in the twentieth. This was the case for the librarians and the publishers, the community health reformers and the fringe actors, and the curators and the educators – all made efforts to bring Seacole from margin to center. Working with a spirit of overcoming and can-do, they had succeeded like their very subject herself. Like Mary Seacole, they worked against the odds. Like the plucky woman and ingenious entrepreneur, they relied upon scant resources and limited opportunities. In the process, they created opportunity and remade history.

***

Together, the work of self-fashioning on the part of the Jamaican nurse during the nineteenth century, along with the efforts at rediscovery and recognition made during the later twentieth century, have had far- reaching results. They have provided the necessary preconditions for the twenty-first-century ascendance of Mary Seacole as a national icon. Over the past twenty years, Seacole has claimed a place as a mainstay of Britain's public culture. She features in its leading museums, in its national curriculum, and in its monumental spaces. Her ascent appears as an arc of triumph: a great success story in the refashioning of England's Victorian past for the utility of Britain's multiracial present. Seacole is a versatile role model: a plucky, entrepreneurial self-starter. Yet, Seacole's has never been a story of uninterrupted ascent. Her twenty- first-century rise has had its share of twists and turns along the way. These moments have functioned as flashpoints for debates. On one level, these debates have concerned the profession of nursing, the politics of inclu- sion, and the nature of race. While contemporary in their concerns, these disputes tapped into long histories regarding the privilege of belonging, the nature of home, and the mantle of heroism that date back to the Crimean War. Across their torsions, Seacole remains, at once, a vector of controversy and a vehicle for inclusion.

The first critical episode in Seacole's twenty-first-century rise to prominence was, as *History Today* noted, a "remarkable story," the result not so much of careful planning as of serendipitous accident.[96] In late 2002, a painting surfaced at a local auction in Warwickshire's

Shipston-on-Stour. In the most material of ways, the painting's story recalled Seacole's own. Encased in an unremarkable contemporary frame, the canvas of note had long served as the backing for another piece of art. A work in oil bearing the date of 1869, this painting had been neglected, forgotten, and nearly lost, just like the nineteenth-century heroine it represented. After an unnamed Oxfordshire family divested itself of the work, the painting found its way from a "posh car boot sale" to a local dealer.[97] Seeking to know more about the canvas, the dealer approached the Order and Medals Research Society. Surely this organization might be able to identify the dusky-complexioned woman who posed heroically with three medals – the Turkish Crimea Medal, the French Legion of Honor, and the Turkish Medjidie – on her chest. When it learned of the painting, the society contacted Helen Rappaport, a historian then at work on a biography of Mary Seacole. Some years later, Rappaport recalled, "as soon as I saw it, I knew it was Mary." Struck by the importance – and the value – of this discovery, Rappaport spent a "long and nail biting" six months negotiating with the dealer and borrowing the funds to purchase the painting, until the portrait was her own.[98]

Newly in possession of her prize, Helen Rappaport approached England's National Portrait Gallery, located in London's Trafalgar Square. Since the nineteenth century, indeed, since the years just after the Crimean War, the Portrait Gallery offered a rendition of national history through its collection of images of worthies, all drawn from life or during their subjects' lifetimes. Might the Seacole portrait take its place among these images of the nation's heroes? Though it was keen to find out, the Gallery was also circumspect, and thus subjected the painting to close scrutiny. The convergence of the appearance of the portrait with Seacole's rise to fame was so serendipitous that the painting might well be a hoax. The Gallery entertained three possibilities: the portrait was rendered from a live sitting, or at least executed during Seacole's lifetime; it was made after her death; or, it was a recent work and a forgery, an opportunistic production got up in response to Seacole's rising reputation. Only the first would qualify it for hanging at Trafalgar Square.[99]

The National Portrait Gallery went through its paces to get an answer, with its curators proceeding through many steps. When they first approached the portrait, curators compared the work to the eight extant renderings of Mary Seacole – among them, a bust by Count Gleichen held in Jamaica, a *carte de visite* made after the Crimean War, and the image in *Punch* of "Our Own Vivandière" (Figure 6.3).[100] When it appeared that the oil painting matched up, the Gallery sought out a forensic analysis performed by Libby Sheldon, a conservator at

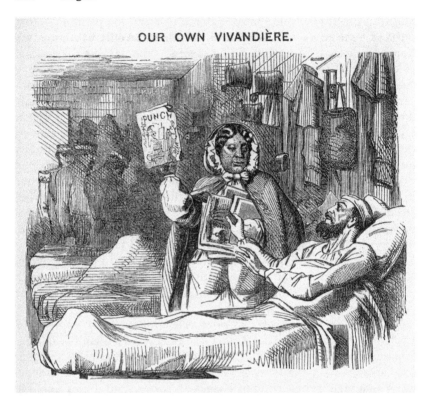

OUR OWN VIVANDIÈRE.

Figure 6.3 "Our Own Vivandière," *Punch*, May 30, 1857. Chronicle/
Alamy Stock Photo

University College London. Aided by stereo microscope and electron
microscope, Sheldon examined the painting. She determined that its
palette – its crimson reds on the Creole scarf, its Prussian blue on the
subject's clothing, and the vermillion gold on the medals – appeared
typical of pigments used in the nineteenth century, and specifically the
1860s and 1870s. The academic style of the portrait, with its lighting
and its pose, was of a piece with the era as well. So, too, was the wooden
panel that supported the work of art, which appeared on a well-used
canvas. As she sought to uncover the painting's story, Sheldon
uncovered no fewer than eight layers of paint. In each instance, the
pigments that she found were available in the nineteenth century. With
her thorough and technical analysis, Sheldon thus put doubts to
rest.[101]

As she worked with the painting, Sheldon uncovered a signature in the form of the initials "ACC." These three letters were the initials of Albert Charles Challen, a little-known London artist. The archival traces of Challen are thin on the ground. Born in Islington in 1847, Challen lived subsequently in Hammersmith, where he listed himself on the 1861 census as an art student and after that in Camberwell, where he counted himself, in 1871, as an artist. His life was cut short by an early death in 1881, when he was only thirty-four years old. Challen's brief life and his little-known work may have been lost to history had it not been for the discovery of the portrait. Its ascent to a national stage was a fine vindication for a young artist who had, in 1869, submitted the painting to be considered for display at the Royal Academy. Only 1,320 of the 4,500 offered up for consideration found their way into the Academy's Exhibition; Challen's was not among them.[102]

Just as the provenance of the painting became clear, Mary Seacole attained even greater fame and luster. In January 2004, Helen Rappaport had written to the National Portrait Gallery with optimism and excitement. It was, she reported, a "dead cert" [sic] that Mary Seacole was to be enshrined as the Greatest Black Briton.[103] Rappaport's intelligence did not disappoint. In February 2004, Seacole attained this title in an online poll. This poll was a form of reparative politics that sought to address the racial myopia of a similar contest in 2003, sponsored by the British Broadcasting Company with the hope of identifying the 100 greatest Britons. As it pointed to the most revered Britons, the 2003 poll had upheld and reinvigorated an island story of ingenuity, royalty, and leadership. Heading the list was Winston Churchill, who was joined in the top ten by Elizabeth I and the recently deceased Diana, Princess of Wales. Charles Darwin and Isambard Kingdom Brunel found their way into the number, as did William Shakespeare and John Lennon. The fact that there were no Black Britons stoked the call for the 2004 vote. This poll vaulted Seacole to greater national renown. She was, more and more, an inspirational figure, a symbol of overcoming against the obstacles of race, gender, and injustice. Helen Rappaport put these matters well a few years later when she claimed of Seacole, "Here was a woman who crossed the classic divides of her time – race, gender, and social class and never let anyone put her down. I love the way she bucked the system and she did it her own way."[104] Seacole may have been "ignored" by history, the *Guardian* noted at the moment of the 2004 vote, yet she was "undeterred" in her own time.[105]

Having long kept the oil painting under wraps, the National Portrait Gallery issued a press release in January 2005. "Lost Portrait of Mary Seacole Discovered," it announced, as it reported the news of what Director Sandy Nairne heralded as a "wonderful" development. In its publicity, the Gallery participated in the project of shaping Seacole as the "famous Black nurse." The Gallery thereby ascribed to Seacole a racial identity that had been up for grabs and a professional identity that would be subject to debate. The Gallery added fuel to the fire of rivalry between Seacole and Nightingale as well. As it promoted its treasure, it noted that Mary Seacole had been "overshadowed" by her nursing contemporary. Unlike Nightingale, Seacole "did not come from a wealthy middle-class background"; nor did she enjoy formal training. Seacole's life was no less inspirational, however.[106] Perhaps, in fact, it was more so. As it reached for a common refrain, the Gallery described Seacole's life as a story of overcoming – of rising above both the limitations for women and the prejudices of race. She was a beacon for ethnic minorities, for health-care professionals, and for women challenging stereotypes; she embodied the spirit of a twenty-first-century nation.

In launching its publicity, the National Portrait Gallery worked to modernize Seacole's story. In planning the installation, the Gallery sought to recast nineteenth-century history. Upon the painting's debut at Trafalgar Square, Helen Rappaport welcomed the placement of the work in what she called its "natural home."[107] Challen's portrait has hung, since 2005, among the nineteenth-century works just by the door-way in Room 23, at the very "heart of the gallery."[108] There, it has enabled the reinterpretation of the nineteenth century, albeit within limits. As if to supplant old history with new, Seacole's portrait replaced works depicting Lord Cardigan and the Coalition Ministry. Today, the portrait remains in Room 23, in a gallery titled "Expansion and Empire." It shares space there with painted and sculptural renderings of the long nineteenth century's household goddesses and heroic mainstays. Among these, we can count Queen Victoria, Florence Nightingale, Robert Baden-Powell, and General Charles Gordon. Such a hang brings Seacole, considered by the Gallery as an avatar of "humanity, compassion, and indomitable spirit," into Britain's island story.[109] This is, on the one hand, a bold act of incorporation and a notable rewriting of the Victorian age. Yet, in the end, it is limited as a gesture of disruption. The hang does little to disturb a narrative of civilization and conquest, but instead incorporates Seacole in its arc. It underscores Seacole's own need to curry favor with power, rather than to disrupt it wholesale.[110]

Since its hanging, the portrait has attracted its skeptics, including a dogged art dealer who visited the Gallery multiple times. Doubtful of the painting's profile, the subject's makeup, and the sitter's medals, this visitor feared it was a hoax.[111] Yet most museumgoers embraced the painting. Almost immediately, the portrait became an object of great interest among community leaders. They wrote to the Gallery seeking out reproductions in the form of posters and postcards. One request came from the Mary Seacole Housing Association, which provided young adults of Afro-Caribbean heritage with vocational training and living skills. Just as its work built on its eponym's commitment to aiding a population in need, so too might its beneficiaries find inspiration in the Jamaican nurse's image.[112] Another solicitation came from Geoff Taylor, the mayor of the exceedingly diverse London borough of Hackney. The London Mayors' Association meeting had brought Taylor to the Gallery. On the heels of his visit, he expressed his delight at the portrait's presence and its prominence. So pleased was Taylor with the painting that he hoped to take home a reproduction. "I popped into the shop to get a postcard of the portrait but found none," he lamented. A postcard would be a true boon, he explained, not just for himself, but also for Hackney. "Many people in this borough and beyond regard Mary Seacole as a role model and heroine," he explained. "We have various institutions named after her and her story is widely known."[113] This hope was realized shortly after the hanging, when the Gallery released a postcard and transmitted images for widespread use.

Mary Seacole's 2005 debut at the National Portrait Gallery vaulted the forgotten heroine to a new level of renown. Not only did the Gallery display Seacole's portrait. It played its role, too, in extending her visibility well beyond Trafalgar Square – into schools and into homes via prints, postcards, and stamps (Figure 6.4). These actions were part of a still larger contemporaneous effort devoted to remembering Mary Seacole and to reproducing her story during the year that marked the bicentenary of her birth. The year 2005 witnessed many tributes to Mary Seacole across venues and across media. The Florence Nightingale Museum put on a year-long exhibition. Channel Four produced an hour-long documentary, "Mary Seacole: The Real Angel of the Crimea."[114] She became a mainstay of the BBC. There were commemorative services across the metropolis, at Westminster Cathedral in Victoria and at St. Martin's Church in Kensal Rise.[115] The publishing industry played its role, too, in mainstreaming Mary Seacole, launching its share of chronicles, including Jane Robinson's biography and a spate of children's books.[116] And the release of a Penguin edition of Mary Seacole's autobiography in 2005 attested further to her prominence. More and more, Seacole's name graced structures in London and elsewhere devoted to health, nursing, and education. By 2005, her name was emblazoned on a Home Office building in the City of Westminster, an inner London borough. There, Seacole assumed her place alongside two other Victorian worthies, Robert Peel and Elizabeth Fry.[117]

Figure 6.4 National Gallery commemorative stamp featuring Mary Seacole Portrait. 2006. Neftali. Alamy Stock Photo

As these examples suggest, Seacole had become, by the first decade of the twenty-first century, a figure worthy of national stewardship, on the one hand, and an exemplar addressing community needs, on the other. It was in the spirit of cultivating both that the Ministry of Education introduced Mary Seacole into the national curriculum in 2007. Seacole had long appeared as a feature of children's education in London and in multiracial communities beyond. The inclusion of Mary Seacole into the elementary curriculum nationalized the possibility of studying the Jamaican heroine, though it did not mandate it. Instead, it left room in curriculum design to address community imperatives and to consider local needs. When they introduced students in years three through six to the nineteenth century, teachers could choose Seacole as a figure of study, alongside such Victorian icons as Isambard Kingdom Brunel and David Livingstone. This circumspect act of curricular inclusion was a timely, if belated act of historical revision alongside the bicentenary of the slave trade's abolition. The year 2007 witnessed commemorative efforts across urban Britain, with the public reckoning, often for the first time, with slavery's legacy in the United Kingdom. Rendering more visibility to the Jamaican-born heroine was a blue plaque, a historical marker honoring Seacole at Soho Square, unveiled in the same year. Through inroads such as these, a host of reflective Britons sought redemption through education and civic action some two hundred years on.[118]

Seacole's incorporation into the National Curriculum answered a call for reflection, but in the following years it became a flashpoint of dissent.[119] In 2013, the *Daily Mail* let loose the plans of Conservative Education Secretary Michael Gove to take Seacole out of the curriculum, at a moment when calls for increasing her prominence were intensifying.[120] Gove operated with a zero-sum understanding of history. His concern was that the inclusion of the likes of Seacole took room away from the standard fare of British greats, among them Winston Churchill and the Kings and Queens of England. Gove's plans opened up a vitriolic discussion that pitted Seacole's defenders against her critics. A twenty-first-century contest, this battle played not only in the newspaper and periodical press, but also in online petitions and opinion sites. Defenders of Seacole's place in the curriculum, including Operation Black Vote, spoke of her efficacy as a role model and her potential for closing the achievement gap.[121] Opponents, such as the *Daily Mail*, the *Spectator*, and Nightingale acolytes, pushed back against this defense.[122] They called into question the framing of Seacole as a nursing forerunner and as a Black woman. In their minds, the first was a mischaracterization of a traditional healer and enterprising hotelier. And as they saw it, the second was a stretch for a woman who was, putatively, three-quarters white. By subjecting Seacole to a color test and by nodding to essentialism, these critics sidestepped the violences of slavery and empire. Their attacks, furthermore, echoed those of Roy Kerridge, launched over two decades before. In their portrayal, the cult of Mary Seacole was the outgrowth of "political correctness run amuck," the product of the "deluded and hysterical liberal-left," and the ferment of "imbecility and absolutism." "It may be good politics, but it is poor history," the *Daily Mail* quipped of the fascination with Mary Seacole. Following on in the *Spectator*, Robert Liddell declared, with archness and condescension, that the case of the Jamaican nurse revealed more about the present than about the past. The phenomenon of Mary Seacole had a lot to say, in his words, "about our present society and how it came to be so brain-damaged." "Let the kids marvel at how a nice woman who wasn't really very Black came to be revered as a Black icon," he continued, as he reinforced the notion of an Anglo-Saxon nation, "because, unsurprisingly, given the make-up of British society prior to the 1950s, they couldn't find anyone else."[123]

Gove's efforts were, ultimately, thwarted, in a campaign that revealed what the *Independent* called "people's power in action."[124] Some applauded this success, while others regarded it as a pyrrhic victory, perhaps not unlike the Crimean War itself: while the retention campaign may have succeeded in its immediate object, it did not offer a larger critique of the whitewashing of history as a legacy.[125] Yet, it was a generative moment, in more ways than one. Perhaps the most remarkable monument to the 2007 contest that remains is a painting by Cameroon-born artist Adjani Okpu-Egbe, shown in an exhibition in Tel Aviv in 2016 and now housed in a private collection in London.[126] With his hallmark style, Okpu-Egbe depicted an abstracted Seacole in a pan-African palette of greens, yellows, and reds. The words "Michael Gove-Hands Off" appear in bold relief on her dress. Okpu-Egbe's Seacole pushes back against the charges that Seacole was neither black nor a nurse. Her skin tone is dark; the packet in her hands reads "Jamaican herbs." Finally, the painting leaves a punctuating message with its title and text: "Politics of Mary Seacole and the Whiteman's Pathetic and Pathological Obsession with the Appropriation of Everything Good" (Figure 6.5).[127]

The battle over the curriculum unfolded just as plans for the most ambitious tribute to Mary Seacole were coming to fruition. This effort involved a statue of Mary Seacole, unveiled on June 30, 2016. The work of sculptor Martin Jennings, the stone tribute sits today on the South Bank of the Thames, looking across the river and facing the Houses of Parliament. It bears the distinction of being the first public sculpture of a named Black woman in Britain. Jennings's work occupies a prominent place on the grounds of St. Thomas' Hospital, where Florence Nightingale had initiated secular nursing training. It is a work on a grand scale, with the statue weighing 1.5 tons and a backing disc coming in at five tons. At three meters in height, and with a 4.5-meter backing, the sculpture takes its place on the horizon, where it can be seen from the nearby Westminster Bridge (Figure 6.6). It is, in short, of monumental enough proportions to counter, at least for the foreseeable future, the tendencies to erase, airbrush, and fade Seacole from history. While ultimately successful, the campaign for the statue – the literal materialization of

Figure 6.5 *The Politics of Mary Seacole*. Painting by Adjani Okpu-Egbe. Mixed media on canvas. Private collection. Photograph by Claudia Rodrigues. Permission of the Artist

the efforts to cement Seacole onto the national landscape – was hard won. It came at a staggering expense, costing upwards of £500,000.[128] Its twists and turns show the renewed promise that Seacole, a Crimean healer, holds today for Black Britons, and for the nation more generally, even as they point to her enduring role as a cultural flashpoint.

The Mary Seacole Memorial Statue Appeal guided the efforts to build the tribute. At its helm were two leading stewards: Lord Clive Soley, a onetime Member of Parliament for Hammersmith and the Chair of the Appeal, and Dame Elizabeth Anionwu, a sickle cell researcher and nursing educator. The hopes and words of each reveal nicely the aspirations of

Figure 6.6 Official unveiling of the Mary Seacole Memorial Statue by Martin Jennings. 2016. Photo by author

those who worked to realize the statue. Soley's investment in Seacole dated back to the 1980s, when he attended a wreath laying at the Jamaican nurse's grave. After hearing laments about Seacole's erasure from history, Soley vowed, one day, to redress these omissions. In pressing for the statue, Soley aspired to address a national debt to the past – a debt not just to Seacole, but to a generation of Afro-Caribbean women who had toiled in Britain's service a century after their foremother had. "Britain was not alone in 1939 and 1940," claimed Soley, as he upended the well-known bluster of Winston Churchill. Among those who had served the nation were scores of "remarkable women" who had traveled from the Caribbean to Britain, leaving their homes at the mother country's "hour of need" to become part of a "vast reservoir of support for the ideas of freedom and democracy" that the web of empire had provided.[129] If Lord Soley sought to recognize past debts, Dame Anionwu hoped to make a deposit on the future. Anionwu had long been a steward of Seacole's memory as a chronicler of her predecessor's history and as a trailblazer in preserving her legacy. She shared with many other supporters of the statue the conviction that Mary Seacole occupied a critical place in a multicultural Britain, and especially in a National Health Service where 79 percent of the workforce was female, and a good part of that from Black, Asian, and Minority Ethnic communities.[130] In this context, Mary Seacole was a role model. She may have lived in the past, but she was a beacon for the future. To use the words of Elizabeth Anionwu, "England may have forgotten Mary, but her rediscovery could not have been more timely. Her life, her views and her legacy have real meaning in modern, diverse Britain. That is why the statue, a lasting memorial and a major London landmark, stands as an inspiration to today's young people."[131]

The challenges and the opportunities alike of redressing the past and speaking to the present were not lost on sculptor Martin Jennings. For Jennings, the opportunity to design the statue was at once an encounter with alterity and an exercise in commonality. As he explained, "I wondered how I could represent meaningfully someone so different from me, who lived in a time so different from our own."[132] But if Seacole, the Black Jamaican nurse, was a figure from a distant past, she was also an exemplar for Jennings's own present. As others had noted, she was a role model who had overcome manifold obstacles with her indomitable spirit. She offered lessons for the present day and for the future. To express this potential, Jennings noted, was the challenge facing public monuments in the twenty-first century. His subject may have lived during the nineteenth century, but Jennings eschewed ossified Victorian sculptural practices as he sought to design a monument for the twenty-first. As he saw it, the current moment valued humanity over heroism; it acknowledged that even the most lauded among us have our "feet of clay."[133] With this in mind, Jennings rejected the protocols of the nineteenth century. "I didn't want to sculpt a mere pastiche of Victorian statuary as it would leave [Mary's] story seeming significant only to the history of the mid-nineteenth century," he explained. "If, however, I could find some way of grounding her against a backdrop of her own time and place, as literally as possible, then paradoxically I might be able to emphasize with more force the relevance of her story today."[134] In the process, Jennings aspired to use the monument not only to interpret the past, but also to transform, in his own words, "the way we see ourselves."[135]

Jennings's plan was this. As a part of his installation, he would construct a backing disc depicting the very ground in the Crimea where Seacole had run her British Hotel. To achieve this goal, Jennings and his team traveled to the Crimea, as the nineteenth century's adventurers had. They made it just in time, visiting the peninsula in the latter part of 2013, only months before the 2014 Russian invasion. While there, Jennings combined old and new technologies, using nineteenth-century maps and digital mapping techniques to locate the ground and to image the Crimean soil. Where the British Hotel had once stood, they found "small shards of broken glass," remnants of the bottle store that had been "calcified by Crimean earth." There were also pieces of shrapnel from other battles fought on the same ground a century later, during World War II. "Some small corners of the earth seem forever destined to be battlefields," declared Jennings.[136] His team took an impression of this continual battleground to create the backing disc, encasing into it a piece of the Crimea's "real history" in the form of a shard of glass.[137] He relied, afterward, on the disc to perform much of the statue's work of providing universal lessons for the present, while honoring Mary Seacole's contributions in the past. Describing the disc, Jennings explained that "history reaches forward from that war long ago towards our own time."[138] The disc served as a reminder, as well, that a "battlefield is metaphorical and each of us has our own." When it came to Mary Seacole and to her legacy, this was a battle for inclusion, waged in her own time and in ours. Seacole and her supporters had often found themselves "stonewalled," to use Jennings's language. In his rendering, he explained, "Mary turns her back on this stone wall. It is now part of her monument, a monument of pain cast in bronze. Undaunted, this battlefield nurse with the overflowing heart hitches up her skirts and marches into history. Treated as if she didn't belong, she has come to belong to us all."[139]

The sense of collective ownership of Seacole's legacy was evident in the project of fundraising for the statue. It was an uphill struggle over a number of years. Large and small donations came from many sectors of society, including business, education, and health care. Unions gave in Mary Seacole's name. There were contributions from the Army regiments whose members Seacole had aided during the Crimean War. Government funding came through in the form of a Treasury grant offered to charities representing, in the words of Treasury Secretary George Osborne, the "'very best of values.'"[140] There were those with public roles, and there were, as well, ordinary citizens who contributed to the effort. The JustGiving site used to bring in funds in the final push provides a record of what Seacole meant to the public during the 2010s. While the means of fundraising was far different, the site recalled the sentiments offered up by the guardians of the Light Brigade at the fin de siècle, not to mention those of the proponents of Nightingale who provided monies for her statue in the shadow of World War I. One donor gave to honor the memory of a great aunt, "a nurse who told me about Mary Seacole back in the 80s." Another gift came from "eleven-year-old Lucy who is currently working on her school Hero Project and chose Mary Seacole." Lucy was determined to give when she discovered that "there was no statue for her hero." And a third contribution came from an "NHS Stalwart," who declared themselves "proud to be a healthcare worker in the company of a great person and humbled by such a role model."[141]

Together, these donations and accompanying sentiments buoyed the process of completion. The ceremonial unveiling of the statue at St. Thomas' Hospital at the end of June 2016 celebrated the resourcefulness and perseverance of Mary Seacole herself and of the very campaign to honor her. Baroness Shreela Flather, one of the Trustees of the Mary Seacole Memorial Statue Appeal, twinned the Victorian heroine and the twenty-first-century appeal in her own tribute. "Not unlike Mary, the Appeal has faced many obstacles, each one a stepping stone to achieving a shared vision," she declared. But in the end, the statue was "a true reflection of Mary's resilience, character, sense of purpose, and adventure."[142] Other supporters similarly hailed Seacole, and, in the process, refashioned her as a heroine for the twenty-first century on the occasion of the unveiling. Leaders from England's Afro-Caribbean community, representatives from Jamaica, and arts consultants praised Seacole for her resilience and her entrepreneurialism. They were joined by voices from the Army, the National Health Service, and St. Thomas' Hospital. Admirers saluted Seacole as a "pioneering Jamaican" and as a "trailblazer." They lauded her "compassion, determination, discipline, character, and courage," and also her "personal warmth." Seacole was, at once, an exemplar of ingenuity and a paragon of humanity.[143] She was "an inspirational role model" and "a courageous and passionate woman who put others before herself."[144] Worked over for a new century, the Victorian heroine seemed to have something to offer to everyone, almost.

Critics of Seacole and the statue remained among Florence Nightingale's most stalwart defenders. The year 2016 marked nearly a century since the unveiling of the tribute to Florence Nightingale, without fanfare and in the shadow of the Great War. A century later, the statue of the English nurse remained at Waterloo Place, which lay across the Thames, just a mile to the north. The Seacole statue's unveiling occurred just one week after the Brexit referendum. At that time, questions of national purpose and national belonging loomed large. In this immediate context, the relationships between Nightingale and Seacole took on a special charge. To be sure, the sense of a rivalry between the two Crimean heroines had grown across the prior decade, as Seacole's star had risen. The new discovery of incendiary correspondence from Nightingale inflamed assessments of the rivalry.[145] While some of this hostility dated back to the Victorian era, still more came from the staging of the current day. Take, for instance, the "Horrible Histories" renderings of Seacole and Nightingale, which delivered an understanding of these two "Vile Victorians," in the language of Children's BBC, to younger generations. These snippets pitted the heroines against each other in a historical competition for attention and in witty repartee.[146] Similar tensions and tonalities informed complaints about the Seacole statue on the part of Nightingale's partisans.[147] If there were to be a statue of Seacole, some critics held, it should not sit at St. Thomas' Hospital, the preserve of Florence Nightingale. Seacole, they claimed, held an oblique relationship to the profession of nursing at best. To intrude her upon the hospital grounds was to disrespect a profession and its founder. Adding insult to injury was the fact that Seacole's statue dwarfed Nightingale's in size.[148]

It is important to note that there were stewards of Nightingale's legacy, and also of St. Thomas' Hospital itself, who took exception to these challenges. Natasha McEnroe, Director of the Florence Nightingale Museum in 2016, was galled by the return, once again, to the notion of a jealous and petty rivalry between the women; the sense that these two leading figures were enmeshed in a cat fight, not only in their lives, but well beyond their deaths, too, was one that was ultimately demeaning and diminishing – for Nightingale, for Seacole, and for all women.[149] Official word from the Hospital sought to put a stop to the mud-slinging. On the occasion of the unveiling, the Hospital's leadership welcomed the statue to St. Thomas's grounds. The Seacole tribute there could do no harm to Nightingale's legacy, for the latter was, after all, "memorialized at the very heart of the hospital." Drawing upon an earlier refrain, Sir Hugh Taylor, then the Chair of the Guy's and St. Thomas's NHS Foundation Trust, noted that both women were "remarkable figures" in their own rights – "Victorian women who, in different ways and for different reasons, are still role models today."[150]

***

The Mary Seacole Memorial Statue Appeal was successful in its efforts to install the Jamaican healer on Britain's landscape of heroes, both literally and metaphorically. With its work on the statue completed, the organization that oversaw its erection turned its attention to the promulgation of Seacole's legacy more broadly. As the Mary Seacole Trust, it seeks, now, to steward Mary's memory for the future, to care for her statue, and to further the contemporary values that have come to be associated with the historical figure. In its own words, the Trust imagines a Britain that is "fairer, more inclusive, and more harmonious." To do so, it encourages a citizenry that is "compassionate, entrepreneurial, and hard working."[151] Its efforts have extended from enrichment in primary schools to training for NHS managers to curatorship of nursing's broader history. In its hands, Seacole is more than a foremother of the Black presence in Britain – more, even, than an inspiration for the nation's youth or the nursing profession. Her legacy exceeds the concrete limits of her statue, however substantial those may be.

Like the other protagonists of the Crimean moment, Mary Seacole has become a staple of the national story. Attributes of her life's experience as expressed in the struggle for diversity and inclusion now inform British public culture. Aspects of Seacole's character such as entrepreneurialism and resourcefulness now inform the nation's shared values. Seacole may have been an outsider – and she may remain so in some quarters. But the dynamics of Mary Seacole's own Crimean afterlife offer a powerful account of promulgation, and assimilation – and perhaps, some might argue, of cooptation by a neoliberal order. Looking back, Mary Seacole's ability to cultivate loyalty among British soldiers and the British public worked, in some regards, to undergird the empire and the structures that enabled it. As recent critics of the institutionalization of diversity have shown, moreover, appeals to inclusion risk bolstering a dominant culture and its interests. Finally, as canny scholars of Seacole have demonstrated, she was not so much anticolonial as she was entrepreneurial.[152]

Still, Seacole's presence in the Crimea and its afterlife unsettles a traditional narrative of the war and its legacies. Those personifications of masculine duty, the Chargers, and that avatar of feminine sacrifice, Florence Nightingale, have served to underwrite insular notions of white Englishness. And although it has long extended its reach beyond a color bar, the Victoria Cross has been a tool of imperial and military hegemony. As an adventurer and a healer in her own time, and as a foremother and a role model in ours, Mary Seacole disrupts these boundaries. Her installation into the pantheon of national heroes and her placement within a constellation of island stories challenge the way we understand Britain's past, present, and future. Her life reminds us that there was no single island story. Great Britain was connected to other islands in histories of empire and to faraway peninsulas in stories of war.[153] Its island story, moreover, is subject to revision, just like the Crimean War itself.

Afterword: Do and Die

It is difficult to know when, and how, to end a book on afterlives. The Crimean War was a bounded affair, taking place in the mid-nineteenth century. Though the war itself was finite, its legacies have endured across centuries, from the nineteenth, through the twentieth, and into the twenty-first. Wartime experiences gave rise to new institutions and new heroes who played central roles in a modernizing nation; they also generated a set of cultural repertoires and shared affects that recurred across time. As they reckoned with family histories and with national pasts, and as they grappled with geopolitical transitions and with social change, ordinary Britons – and the English especially – looked time and again to the Crimean War as a resource. But it was no monolithic touchstone. A complex event, the mid-Victorian war generated the possibilities for a multifaceted afterlife, as the six chapters of this book have shown.

The war sent battling Britons and their companions to the Crimea, located at a periphery of Europe. There and along the way, they negotiated terrains, allies, and enemies that were all unfamiliar. While the engagement in the East opened up new worlds, it also showed the English to be reluctant Europeans, turning away from the continent at the conflict's end. If cultural dynamics were one thing to negotiate, battlefield encounters were another. The British came out on the winning side, of course, but the war was full of blunders, not least the Charge of the Light Brigade, an occasion that has come to exemplify a particularly English capacity to embrace disaster and to turn defeat into glory.

With its triumphs and with its losses, the Crimean War played its part in shaping two forms of military masculinity that have informed British manhood ever since. While the conflict was a harbinger of later military encounters, it was equally a throwback to earlier ones. As such, it featured hand-to-hand combat and feats of bravery that stoked an appetite for gallant tales. Those few who performed signal acts of valor and lived to tell the tales enjoyed a new honor that married democracy and chivalry: the Victoria Cross. The war engendered acts of valor, but it was also more than full of stories of misfortune. As the front line in facing loss, combatants took care of their comrades, combining acts of bravery and acts of compassion; they wrote letters to the home front, performed last rites, and maintained memorials. In the Crimea, heroes of combat were also men of feeling.[1]

The Crimean War is known even more for its heroines, who stepped into the breach wrought by mismanagement and who seized opportunities to care for male combatants. Florence Nightingale, the Lady with the Lamp, captured the national imagination when she traveled with a band of nurses to Scutari to battle the cholera and challenge the Royal Army Medical Corps. Her popularity and her presumed competence provided a feminine rebuke to institutional failings. A heroine of the war effort in her own right, Mary Seacole broke through her share of barriers. She brought comfort to the soldiers as she created home and cultivated friendship on the Crimea's battlefields.

The exemplars of nationhood, masculinity, and femininity offered up by the war have proven salient across centuries. There may be some chance in their recurrence, but this book has revealed patterns as well. Life cycle changes among the generation of Crimean veterans and their descendants brought renewed attention to the war, time after time. So too did later military conflicts and Crimean anniversaries themselves. More generally, moments of transition and crisis on a national scale moved the Crimean conflict to the front of the public mind. The mid-Victorians' war garnered renewed attention on occasions of imperial pressure, decline, and decolonization; it has come to the fore at turning points in the relationship to Europe. The Crimean War, with the questions and challenges that it opened, has attained pressing salience at junctures when the state's capacities to care for its citizens have come into question. Finally, shifts in the gender order and the racial makeup of Britain have called, repeatedly, on the values and the protagonists of the Crimean conflict.

The afterlife of a war does not end with the publication of a book on the subject. In fact, one measure of the success of this book will be if it prompts its readers to look for traces of the Crimea in the years to come, especially in the service of sharpening historical analysis, making social critique, and forging cultural understanding. For now, the year 2020 provides a final opportunity to assess the continuing purchase of the Crimean War. 2020 saw more than its share of challenges across the globe, and certainly in Europe and the Anglosphere. The coronavirus pandemic transformed daily life; racial reckoning has made addressing anti-Black violence ever more urgent. In Britain, 2020 also figured in the history books as the year that Brexit was finally done. To limn this year through the themes of the book is to show, once again, the notable resonance of the Crimea and its legacies at a time of crisis and reckoning.

The war's verses and affects, its ideals and institutions, and its heroes and lessons were all manifest in 2020. One hundred seventy-five years on, the conflict continues to supply an optic for understanding public opinion, a referent for assessing structures of feeling, and a touchstone for expressing ideals to emulate.

Britain began and ended 2020 with Brexit. It left the European Union at the stroke of midnight on January 31. As 2020 drew to a close, Prime Minister Boris Johnson avoided a no-deal Brexit with just days to spare, settling on a trade deal with the EU on December 24. This exit from the European Union closed a chapter in the long, ambivalent history of engagement with the continent. The Crimean War was not the origin of this ambivalence, yet it was an occasion for its expression as a matter of national policy and individual selfhood. Diplomatically speaking, a radical critique of continental entanglement existed from the war's outset, articulated by Richard Cobden and John Bright. Additionally, in the aftermath of the Paris Peace Conference, many Britons looked away from the continent.[2] In more personal terms, the adventurers bound for the Crimea brought with them an ambivalent attitude of semi-detachment that had long characterized the English.[3] They may have looked eagerly to wartime encounters, but they sought to recreate England again and again along the way. The Brexit campaign drew upon similar tropes, often detrimentally, as it advocated a turn away from continental engagement in favor of life at home.[4]

The best-known military maneuver of the Crimean conflict provides a particularly resonant chord for the bathos of Brexit. Journalist Fintan O'Toole has persuasively linked Brexit to the cult of "heroic failure," a notion epitomized by the Charge of the Light Brigade.[5] In the aftermath of the Charge, the lines between disaster and success became irretrievably blurred, thanks in no small part to the verses of Tennyson. The work of the poet laureate lyricized the capacity to transform disaster into victory, and triumph into defeat, lodging this collective mental habit at the heart of the national mind.[6] "There is something genuinely magnificent in this English capacity to embrace disaster," O'Toole observed.[7] He found the apogee of this embrace in the Brexit referendum, wherein Leave voters lost sight of their nation's power and privilege. Instead, they imagined themselves as colonized by Brussels, leaping headlong into the abyss of a chimerical liberation.[8]

Described by one critic as "irrepressibly English," Prime Minister Boris Johnson led the way in getting Brexit done.[9] Not yet Prime Minister in the summer 2019, he declared in a ballyhooed media appearance that he would implement the referendum, "come what may, do or die."[10] The Eton-educated Johnson had been known to misuse Victorian poetry, most notably when he recited Kipling's "Mandalay" in Burma just a few years before.[11] On this subsequent occasion, pundits held that Johnson had misquoted – and misunderstood – Tennyson. It is possible that Johnson was borrowing from Scottish Poet Robert Burns.[12] But cultural brinksmanship and political jockeying pointed more frequently to Tennyson, whose "do and die" encapsulated the tragic duty of the Light Brigade. Critics capitalized on the opportunity to draw parallels between the two ill-fated descents, one into the Valley of Death and the other into the chasm of Brexit. One likened the Brexiteers to the 17th Lancers, perhaps the best-known regiment in the Charge, whose motto was "Death and Glory."[13] And another held that the dash toward Brexit was a charge wrapped in the Victorian debris of the *Boy's Own Paper*, with its "hints of valor."[14] For Leave proponents, it offered the possibility of transforming "the soul-sapping humdrum of everyday economics" into a "wider, more glorious narrative of British derring-do."[15]

The Brexit cause relied not only upon an ideal of heroic failure, but also upon a mythologized past of going it alone. World War II – and particularly the Blitz and Dunkirk – are set pieces in this narrative.[16] Seventy-five years on, the numbers of its veterans have dwindled, and those who remain approach the century mark. Like Crimean combatants in times past, these elderly men have served as exemplars of military valor, modeling bravery, selflessness, and the stiff upper lip. One such figure is Flying Officer John Cruickshank, who was, in 2020, the last surviving Victoria Cross recipient to fight in World War II and the only Cross winner ever to reach 100 years of age. At Cruickshank's centenary, the *Telegraph* extolled a life of adventure in its twilight of repose. On July 17, 1944, Cruickshank, a Scottish airman, had sunk a German U-boat despite being wounded an astounding seventy-two times. Determined to bring his crew to safety, he refused morphine so that he could successfully land his plane after having his wounds dressed.[17] The airman was surprised in the war's aftermath by the granting of the Cross: an award had never crossed his mind while doing his duty. This modest bearing lasted a lifetime for the "quiet, unassuming gentleman with a great sense of humor." On turning 100 in May 2020, Cruickshank declined a cake from the Royal Air Force, not wanting to "make a fuss."[18] The character of this Victoria Cross hero has a timeless quality, but Cruickshank's deeds were imparted in new ways. In prior centuries, the *London Gazette* had announced the feats of Victoria Cross heroes. In 2020, the airman's act of valor became the subject of a tweet: "John Cruickshank served in the @Royal Air Force as a Flying Officer. In 1944 he was wounded 72 times during an attack on a German U-boat, but still managed to sink it."[19]

If valor was one characteristic of the military masculinity forged in the Crimea, another was care. Exemplifying this quality was another World War II veteran who attracted yet broader attention across the year 2020, becoming a national hero. As he approached his 100th birthday in the spring of 2020, Tom Moore, a Yorkshireman whose tour of duty had taken him to India and Sumatra, launched a different campaign. He waged this one much closer to home – in his back garden. Moore and his family hatched a plan to have the elderly veteran walk 100 lengths of his Dorset garden, completing ten lengths per day with the help of his walker. They hoped to garner support for the beleaguered National Health Service, and especially for NHS Charities Together, with funds going to aid essential workers who had fallen ill with COVID-19, then in the first stages of ravaging Great Britain. The efforts went viral, with the campaign raising nearly £39 million.[20] Moore's story struck a chord of common feeling across the year 2020; it brought together a beloved, if fraying narrative, that of Britain's Finest Hour, and a cherished yet imperiled institution, the National Health Service.[21] Captain Tom, as he became known, was an ideal man for the moment. As his daughter explained, "He's a typical Yorkshireman, very stoic, very controlled, and takes everything in his stride. We always knew that he was this incredible gem of a man, but we never had any idea that his story would capture the hearts of a nation."[22] In the face of this meteoric rise, Captain Tom became the subject of a painting, a best-selling autobiography, and even the BBC's end-of-year London light show.[23] He enjoyed another claim to fame as the oldest Briton to have a pop single top the UK charts. Ultimately, Captain Tom achieved knighthood, with the honor personally granted in July 2020 by Queen Elizabeth, who came out of quarantine to recognize the beloved veteran.[24] It was a moment of intimate royal ceremony reminiscent of Queen Victoria, who honored the military across her lifetime as she sought to offer comfort and promote loyalty. Like the heroes of yore, Sir Captain Tom proved similarly to be a symbol of unity, with his story attracting admiration across political and generational divides. His appeal was evident once again at the moment of his death from coronavirus contracted while undergoing treatment for pneumonia in early February 2021, with Britain under yet another lockdown as it confronted a new COVID-19 strain.[25] On that occasion, Conservative Prime Minister Boris Johnson and Labor Party Leader Kier Starmer both referred to Captain Sir Tom Moore as a "beacon of hope."[26]

Like the Crimean War, the coronavirus pandemic engendered a hunger for heroes in the face of trial and mismanagement. On both occasions, medical mismanagement proved to be a common ingredient, especially at the outset. The Royal Army Medical Corps stumbled in addressing cholera in the Crimea; nearly 175 years on, the British government dallied in its initial response to the coronavirus. In keeping with Brexit, the nation chose a path that differed from much of continental Europe's, initially delaying a lockdown in favor of the pursuit of herd immunity in 2020. A U-turn and Boris Johnson's own hospitalization came not long after. As part of the effort to change the course, the National Health Service went to war against the virus, building emergency hospitals. Once again, the name of Florence Nightingale, the angel of the Crimea, came to the fore. Against the specter of the shortage of ICU beds in Italy, military regiments, including the Royal Anglian Regiment and the Royal Gurkha Rifles, labored alongside NHS staff to construct a 4,000-bed facility at London's ExCel Centre. They named the hospital the NHS Nightingale as they set out to battle the virus. London's was only the flagship of the NHS Nightingale wards dedicated to the evisceration of the coronavirus. NHS Nightingales quickly popped up, too, in Manchester, Birmingham, Bristol, and Harrogate, with plans for Exeter and Sunderland scratched before delivery. In the end, it was a case of spectacular overpreparation, at least in the virus's first round of assault, with many of the hospitals closing within weeks of opening.[27]

Nightingale was not simply a name emblazoned on buildings during the first phase of the pandemic. She was also a yardstick for assessing response. This use of Nightingale as a higher conscience hearkens back to the twentieth century. Time and again, those in a changing nursing profession asked themselves, "What would Florence Nightingale do?" The question resurfaced as Britain wrestled with the coronavirus. Proponents observed that Nightingale was the original messenger of the "Wash Your Hands" campaign, which dates back to her 1859 *Notes on Nursing*. She was also an innovator in statistics, so important for tracking and understanding disease and its spread. In May 2020, Carola Hoyos asked how Nightingale would have "tackled COVID-19" in the pages of the *Guardian*. The question allowed Hoyos to imagine Nightingale as a twenty-first-century leader. No longer the "Lady with the Lamp," she would be the "Statistician with the Spreadsheet." In her twenty-first-century incarnation, Nightingale's celebrity would assume a different form, characterized by a formidable Twitter presence of her own making. Perhaps, Hoyos envisioned, in a rebuke to the many male mishandlers of the coronavirus, Nightingale might even be a head of state, effectively battling COVID-19 like Germany's Angela Merkel or New Zealand's Jacinda Ardern.[28]

Nightingale was already to have been in the spotlight in 2020, named by the World Health Organization as the Year of the Nurse and the

Midwife in honor of the 200th anniversary of the icon's birth. There were noted creations in honor of Nightingale's roles across the sacred and the secular, with a new window installed at Romsey Abbey depicting Nightingale's call from God, and a trademarked Barbie in Mattel's Inspiring Women Range. On her birthday, May 12, the Houses of Parliament provided a backdrop for an image, part Nightingale and part contemporary nurse. It was projected in light, along with the words, "Our nation thanks those who care." An array of other events was long in the planning, including a refurbished exhibit at London's Florence Nightingale Museum, a memorial service at St. Paul's Cathedral, and a history walk around Derby. In a cruel twist of fate, the coronavirus lockdown caused delays and cancellations. This confluence was particularly damaging for the Florence Nightingale Museum, which closed its doors indefinitely in early 2021.[29] Run by a private charity, the Museum had planned for a banner year on the occasion of the bicentenary. Its future in peril, the Museum looked to a GoFundMe and a charity auction, where supporters could purchase a Hampshire tour, a signed photograph of Teresa May, a Fortnum and Mason hamper, or a tour of Nightingale's Hampshire. These and other items pitched Nightingale as the apotheosis of a traditional England.[30] At her bicentenary, Nightingale continued to operate in two registers, as a trailblazing statistician and potential head of state, on the one hand, and as a focus for nostalgia and a symbol of rural England, on the other.

Among the items donated to the auction were two provided by Trevor Sterling, the Chair of the Mary Seacole Trust. Sterling offered up two books: a souvenir tribute to the statue at St. Thomas' Hospital and a Penguin edition of Seacole's autobiography. The act was a gesture of solidarity and support from the Trust, which played a part in publicizing the auction. Thanks to the work of the Trust, not to mention to the actions of its predecessors, Seacole occupies a place on the civic and physical landscape of Britain that now rivals Nightingale's. Having fulfilled its initial ambition of erecting the Seacole statue, the Trust now oversees education and diversity initiatives. Seacole's legend continues to inspire artistic production across genres. Jackie Sibblies Drury's play, *Marys Seacole*, debuted in New York in 2019; multicolored billboards paying tribute to the heroine appeared all around London in 2020; and a feature film devoted to the heroine was slated to appear soon after.[31] Like the name of Florence Nightingale, that of Seacole was also pressed into service in the fight against the coronavirus. The first NHS Seacole Centre, devoted to coronavirus recovery, opened its doors in Surrey in May 2020 in a refurbished military hospital. As the NHS noted, its task of "rehabilitative care" resonated with Seacole's own concern for soldiers.[32]

The use of Seacole's name, and her vision, in the provision of health care has its own history. Beginning in the 1980s, communities seeking to address inequities in local health and in health education for Black, Asian, and Minority Ethnic Britons had rallied under Mary Seacole's name. COVID-19 put disparities in health, along with the importance of BAME care workers, into sharp relief.[33] On the occasion of its opening, the NHS noted that the Seacole Centre paid homage in its name to the many BAME workers among its staff.[34] In 2020, across the nation, the labors of these workers, along with their vulnerabilities, were evident throughout the coronavirus pandemic, which claimed the lives of hundreds of NHS workers, many from Black, Asian, and Minority Ethnic populations. In Britain more generally, as in the United States, the virus wrought disproportionate destruction on communities of color, giving rise to assessments of the many health inequalities that stem from long-standing racial injustices.[35]

The inequalities laid bare by the coronavirus stoked the fires of the protests against white supremacy and in favor of Black Lives Matter during the summer 2020. Global in scale, they focused in Britain on the interrogation of past and present. "The U.K is not innocent," claimed protestors, as they doubled down on the legacies of the transatlantic slave trade which had enriched private citizens and built cities. In Britain, the defining moment of the protests came with the toppling into Bristol harbor of the statue of Edward Colston, erected in 1895 to honor the city's favorite son and philanthropist, himself an early slave trader.[36] Colston's was only the first statue to be unseated in a national reckoning with the legacies of slavery and empire. This reckoning has opened up promises to reevaluate existing monuments. It has also prompted calls for new statues, perhaps of Chartist William Cuffay or of footballer Jack Leslie, maybe of Notting Hill Carnival founder Claudia Johnson or of Black Panther Olive Morris.[37]

Will Seacole remain a heroine among new generations of Britons who are interested in dismantling old pieties and old statues? A 2020 auction of a Seacole bust by Count Gleichen suggests the heroine's enduring value. The bust sold for over £101,000, 101 times the initial estimate, to Billy Peterson. Involved in making a feature-length film about Seacole, Peterson planned to deposit the bust in a public collection.[38] Yet, while Seacole's story remains highly compelling, it does not, necessarily, point the way to social revolution. Though heroic, Seacole did herself employ hierarchies of color in her attempt to curry favor with her English readership, even as she rebuked American racism. And, rather than overturning power structures, she ultimately labored in their service, tending to the men of the British armed forces. She is a role model among professionals, a beloved foremother among older generations, and a curricular mainstay for schoolchildren. The Black Lives Matter protests gave the Mary Seacole Trust an occasion to restate its mission and to reup the heroine's legacy. In their wake, Vice-Chair Lisa Rodrigues offered up Seacole as beacon for a Britain righting itself after the Windrush Scandal and reckoning with the realities of structural racism. She publicly renewed the Trust's commitment to the "values of Mary Seacole, a woman of color who never took no for an answer in her quest to help others." "What would Mary do today?" Rodrigues asked. "I think she would listen, speak up when she saw things that were wrong, and encourage people to make their protests passionately and peacefully. And she would never give up in the fight for fairness and equality."[39]

***

When I set out to write about the Crimean War, I aspired to rescue it from its Victorian obscurity. Perhaps it is not so obscure after all. I may have held this belief because I spent many years researching and writing in the long shadow of World War I's centenary. The Crimean War was not forgotten. Instead, its legacies remain strikingly resonant.[40] The mid-Victorian war was a generative one, its mismanagement leading to improvement, its blunder to redemption. Reverberations of the Crimea are to be found between forgetfulness and remembering, and between amnesia and trauma. Its elements are sometimes trivialized, with its remnants a sort of Victorian detritus.[41] Yet, it has had an unexpectedly rich and varied afterlife. The Crimean War gave rise to a set of actors and institutions, and, with these, to a set of affects and experiences. All have held a remarkable persistence in British life. Surprisingly regenerative, they shape popularly held values and contours of belonging. If there is a question about why the Crimean War should matter in a twenty-first century Britain, reckoning with its own past and facing an uncertain future, this is the reason why.

Notes

Introduction: The Reason Why

1. Michael Howard, "Someone Had Blundered," *New Statesman and Nation*, November 14, 1953, pp. 609–10, Liddell Hart Military Archive 15/1/27, Kings College, London.
2. Cecil Woodham-Smith, *The Reason Why: The Story of the Fatal Charge of the Light Brigade* (Constable, 1953).
3. "Book of the Month," *Daily Mail*, November 6, 1953, p. 6, issue 17925, and "Success Still Surprises Her," *Daily Mail*, November 5, 1953, p. 6, issue 17925, *Daily Mail Historical Archive* (hereafter *DMHA*).
4. See, among others, Clive Ponting, *The Crimean War* (Chatto and Windus, 2004), vii.
5. On the evolution of this image, see Mark Bostridge, *Florence Nightingale: The Making of an Icon* (Farrar, Straus, and Giroux, 2008), 251–54.
6. This book is deeply archival in a traditional sense, but it is also enabled by massive digitization projects. For an influential account of the effects of digitization on historical research, see Lara Putnam, "The Transnational and the Text-Searchable: Digitized Sources and the Shadows They Cast," *American Historical Review* 121, no. 2 (April 2016): 377–402.
7. Other important considerations of the Crimea's long legacies include Rachel Bates, "Curating the Crimea: The Cultural Afterlife of a Conflict" (PhD diss., University of Leicester, 2015); A. L. Berridge, "Off the Chart: The Crimean War in British Public Consciousness," *19: Interdisciplinary Studies in the Long Nineteenth Century* 20 (2015); Glenn Fisher, "The Crimea and Indian Mutiny Veterans' Associations of the 1890s" (PhD diss., University of Cardiff, 2020).
8. For one early articulation, see Kellow Chesney, *Crimean War Reader* (Frederick Muller, 1960), 224.
9. This turn of phrase is inspired by Richard Altick's *The English Common Reader* (University of Chicago Press, 1957). For a different account of reading practices in the 1950s, see Christopher Hilliard, "'Is it a Book that You Would Even Wish Your Wife or Servants to Read?': Obscenity Law and the Politics of Reading in Modern England," *American Historical Review* 118, no. 3 (June 2013): 653–78. On writing, see Christopher Hilliard, *To Exercise our Talents: The Democratization of Writing in Britain* (Harvard University Press, 2006). This production of a common readership relied on a process of racial exclusion. See, for an influential and prescient iteration of this

process, Chris Waters, "'Dark Strangers' in Our Midst: Discourses of Race and Nation in Britain, 1947–1963," *Journal of British Studies* 36, no. 2 (1997): 207–38.

10. George Malcolm Thompson, "The Reason Why," *Evening Standard*, November 5, 1953, Liddell Hart Military Archive 15/1/27, Kings College, London. On Victorianism and modern reinventions, see, among others, Miles Taylor and Michael Wolff, *The Victorians since 1901: Histories, Representations, and Revisions* (Manchester University Press, 2004); Simon Joyce, *The Victorians in the Rearview Mirror* (Ohio University Press, 2007). On the postwar moment and its modernity, see especially Becky Conekin, Frank Mort, and Chris Waters, "Introduction," in *Moments of Modernity: Reconstructing Britain, 1945–1964*, edited by Becky Conekin, Frank Mort, and Chris Waters, 1–21 (Rivers Oram Press, 1999).

11. See, especially, Raphael Samuel, *Theatres of Memory: Past and Present in Contemporary Culture* (Verso, 1994), 27.

12. Stephanie Barczewski, *Heroic Failure and the British* (Yale University Press, 2016).

13. Fintan O'Toole, *Heroic Failure: Brexit and the Politics of Pain* (Head of Zeus, 2018), 70, 73.

14. In the British context, see, among others, George Behlmer and Fred Leventhal, eds., *Singular Continuities: Tradition, Nostalgia, and Identity in Modern British Culture* (Stanford University Press, 2000); Owen Hatherley, *The Ministry of Nostalgia* (Verso, 2016); Patrick Wright, *On Living in an Old Country: The National Past in Contemporary Britain* (Verso, 1985).

15. Of this number, 4,500 were killed in action or from wounds resulting from action. Of those remaining, approximately half died of disease and half came out of the War wounded. Michael Clodfelter, *Warfare and Armed Conflicts: A Statistical Encyclopedia of Casualty and Other Figures, 1492–2015*, 4th ed. (McFarland, 2017).

16. The literature here is vast and growing. I am indebted for my understandings to a long, transnational bibliography. Some important and recent works in the context of British wartime, and particularly World War I, include T. G. Ashplant, Graham Dawson, and Michael Roper, eds., *The Politics of War Memory and Commemoration* (Routledge, 2000); Laura Clouting, *A Century of Remembrance* (Imperial War Museum, 2018); Stephen Heathorn, *Haig and Kitchener in Twentieth-Century Britain: Remembrance, Representation, and Appropriation* (Ashgate, 2013); Jessica Meyer, ed., *British Popular Culture and the First World War* (Brill, 2008); Janet S. K. Watson, *Fighting Different Wars: Experience, Memory, and the First World War* (Cambridge University Press, 2004); Ross J. Wilson, *Cultural Heritage of the Great War in Britain* (Ashgate, 2013); Jay Winter, *Sites of Memory, Sites of Mourning: The Great War in European Cultural History* (Cambridge University Press, 1995); Jay Winter, *Remembering War: The Great War between Memory and History in the Twentieth Century* (Yale University Press, 2006); Bart Ziino, ed., *Remembering the First World War* (Routledge, 2015). On the Second World War, see, among others,

Philippa Levine and Susan Grazyel, eds., *Gender, Labour, War, and Empire: Essays on Modern British History* (Palgrave, 1999); Lucy Noakes and Juliette Pattinson, eds., *British Cultural Memory and the Second World War* (Bloomsbury, 2014).

17. For its articulation of the cultural workings of afterlife, I am especially indebted to Jennifer Wenzel's *Bulletproof: Afterlives of Anticolonial Prophecy in South Africa and Beyond* (University of Chicago Press, 2009). I owe a debt as well to Jordanna Bailkin, *The Afterlife of Empire* (University of California Press, 2012); Karen Inouye, *The Long Afterlife of Nikkei Wartime Incarceration* (Stanford University Press, 2016); Kristin Ross, *May '68 and its Afterlives* (University of Chicago Press, 2002). They do not use the term in the title of their text, but Trudi Tate and Kate Kennedy work productively with the notion of afterlife in their consideration of the legacies of the Armistice. See Trudi Tate and Kate Kennedy, eds., *The Silent Morning: Culture and Memory after the Armistice* (Manchester University Press, 2013), especially "Introduction: 'This Grave Day,'" 1–16, particularly p. 13. On a different note, Daniel Loss effectively uses the notion in his consideration of the persistence of religious institutions in a secular age. See Daniel S. Loss, "The Institutional Afterlife of Christian England," *Journal of Modern History* 89 (2017): 282–313.

18. Some have used the term mnemohistory. See, e.g., Marek Tamm, *Afterlife of Events: Perspectives on Mnemohistory* (Palgrave, 2015); Stephen Heathorn, "The Mnemonic Turn in the Cultural Historiography of Britain's Great War," *Historical Journal* 48, no. 4 (December 2005): 1103–24.

19. On history and the everyday, see Laura Carter, "The Quennells and the 'History of Everyday Life' in England, c. 1918–69," *History Workshop Journal* 81 (Spring 2016): 106–34; Billie Melman, *The Culture of History: English Uses of the Past, 1800–1953* (Oxford University Press, 2006).

20. Historians of the twentieth century have recently unpacked the valences of this term to great effect, especially as it coalesced in the post-World War II era. See Clare Langhamer, "'Who the Hell are Ordinary People?': Ordinariness as a Category of Historical Analysis," *Transactions of the Royal Historical Society* 28 (2018): 175–95. For earlier work on ordinary people and nation building, see Robert Colls, *Identity of England* (Oxford University Press, 2002); Simon Featherstone, *Twentieth-Century Popular Culture and the Forming of English Identity* (Edinburgh University Press, 2009).

21. Robert Saunders, "Myths from a Small Island: The Dangers of a Buccaneering View of British History," at www.newstatesman.com/politics/uk/2019/10/myth s-small-island-dangers-buccaneering-view-british-history.

22. On associational life in Britain, see Penelope Ismay, *Trust among Strangers: Friendly Societies in Modern Britain* (Cambridge University Press, 2018); James Vernon, *Distant Strangers: How Britain Became Modern* (University of California Press, 2014).

23. This book takes up an interest in scale among British historians, as it addresses intimate and family life alongside broader social, military, and national developments. Some of the foremost examples placing intimate life

in broader contexts include Deborah Cohen, *Family Secrets: Shame and Privacy in Modern Britain* (Oxford University Press, 2013); Seth Koven, *The Match Girl and the Heiress* (Princeton University Press, 2015); Judith Walkowitz, *Nights Out: Life in Cosmopolitan London* (Yale University Press, 2012).

24. Raphael Samuel and Paul Thompson, eds., *The Myths We Live By* (Routledge, 1990) is helpful on the commingling of private and public myth here. See "Introduction," 1–22, especially p. 15.

25. Leading assessments of everyday engagements with the past include Hazel Carby, *Imperial Intimacies: A Tale of Two Islands* (Verso, 2019); Alison Light, *Common People: In Pursuit of my Ancestors* (University of Chicago Press, 2015); Raphael Samuel, *Theatres of Memory: Past and Present in Contemporary Culture* (Verso, 1994); Raphael Samuel, *Island Stories: Unraveling Britain*, ed. Alison Light with Sally Alexander and Gareth Stedman Jones (Verso, 1994).

26. Paul Ward's *Britishness since 1870* provides helpful frameworks for thinking about the relationships between the institutional and the everyday in making national identity and national life. See Paul Ward, *Britishness since 1870* (Routledge, 2004), especially "Introduction: Being British," 1–13.

27. The same can be said of Victorian war poetry in relation to that of World War I. See Tai-Chun Ho, "Tyrtaeus and the Civilian Poet of the Crimean War," *Journal of Victorian Culture* 22, no. 4 (2017): 503–20 and "The Afterlife of Thomas Campbell and 'The Soldiers Dream' in the Crimean War," *19: Interdisciplinary Studies in the Long Nineteenth Century* 20 (2015). On poetry and the production of war's legacies, see Alisa Miller, "Rupert Brooke and the Growth of Commercial Patriotism in Britain, 1914–1918," *Twentieth-Century British History* 21, no. 2 (June 2010): 141–62.

28. On the twentieth and twenty-first-century histories of Trafalgar Square, see Shanti Sumartojo, *Trafalgar Square and the Narration of Britishness, 1900–2012* (Peter Lang, 2013). On the use and fashioning of Napoleon, see Gavin Daly, "British Soldiers and the Legend of Napoleon," *The Historical Journal* 61, no. 1 (March 2018): 131–53; Stuart Semmel, "British Uses for Napoleon," *MLN* 120, no. 4 (2005): 733–46 and *Napoleon and the British* (Yale University Press, 2004). On the nineteenth-century's limits and specificities of commemoration, see Jennifer L. Allen, "National Commemoration in an Age of Transnationalism," *Journal of Modern History* 91 (March 2019): 109–48.

29. On the Crimea as an effect of empire building, see Kelly O'Neill, *Claiming Crimea: A History of Catherine the Great's Southern Empire* (Yale University Press, 2017). For a recent reinterpretation of the Pax Britannica, see Priya Satia, *Time's Monster: How History Makes History* (Harvard University Press, 2020), chapter 1, especially p. 83.

30. Byron Farwell, *Queen Victoria's Little Wars* (Harper and Row, 1972; Norton reprint 1985) and recently, Stephen M. Miller, ed., *Queen Victoria's Wars: British Military Campaigns, 1857–1902* (Cambridge University Press, 2021). For new interpretations of the nineteenth century as a century of warfare, see Antoinette Burton, *The Trouble with Empire: Challenges to Modern British*

Imperialism (Oxford University Press, 2015); Nasser Mufti, *Civilizing War: Imperial Politics and the Poetics of National Rupture* (Northwestern University Press, 2015). It is noteworthy that this is the work of feminist and postcolonial scholars. While it was not necessarily the explicit aim of that work, earlier scholarship on feminism and prostitution had the effect of foregrounding the militarization of everyday life in the nineteenth century. See Philippa Levine, *Prostitution, Race, and Politics: Policing Venereal Disease in the British Empire* (Routledge, 2003); Judith R. Walkowitz, *Prostitution and Victorian Society: Women, Class, and the State* (Cambridge University Press, 1980). On 1857 and its reverberations, see Jill C. Bender, *The 1857 Uprising and the British Empire* (Cambridge University Press, 2016). On the long shadow of the Sepoy Revolt, see Kim Wagner, *Amritsar 1919: An Empire of Fear and the Making of a Massacre* (Yale University Press, 2019).

31. For a more extensive explanation, see Winfried Baumgart, *The Crimean War, 1853–1856*, 2nd ed. (Bloomsbury, 2020), chapters 1–2.

32. The conflict mobilized over 1.5 million troops and took the lives of nearly 300,000, many of whom died of disease, most notably from cholera. When it came to Great Britain, there were 100,000 troops fighting under the Union Jack, one-fifth of whom lost their lives.

33. On the Napoleonic Wars as total war, if not necessarily imperial war, see David A. Bell, *The First Total War: Napoleonic Europe and the Birth of Warfare as We Know It* (Hougton Mifflin, 2007).

34. Susan R. Grayzel expertly surveys the imperial turn in the historiography of World War I in "Belonging to the Imperial Nation: Rethinking the History of the First World War in Britain and its Empire," *Journal of Modern History* 90, no. 2 (June 2018): 383–405. See, among other titles, Santanu Das, ed., *Race, Empire, and First World War Writing* (Cambridge University Press, 2011); Priya Satia, *Spies in Arabia: The Great War and the Cultural Foundations of Britain's Covert Empire in the Middle East* (Oxford University Press, 2008); Heather Streets-Salter, *World War I in Southeast Asia: Colonialism and Anticolonialism in an Era of Global Conflict* (Cambridge University Press, 2018); Jay Winter, ed., *The Cambridge History of the First World War* (Cambridge University Press, 2014). On the German imperial case, see Michelle Moyd, *Violent Intermediaries: African Soldiers, Conquest, and Everyday Colonialism in German East Africa* (Ohio University Press, 2014). For an up-to-date review of the Italian case, see Roberta Pergher, "An Italian War? War and Nation in the Historiography of the First World War," *Journal of Modern History* 90, no. 4 (December 2018): 863–99.

35. An important new piece of literary criticism addressing the global effects of the War is Nicholas Birns, "Sable Seas: The Crimean War's Global Reach and 1850s Literariness," *Victorian Studies* 63, no. 2 (2021): 169–192.

36. For recent reinterpretations that highlight the role of the Navy, see Peter Duckers, *The Crimean War at Sea: Naval Campaigns against Russia, 1854–6* (Pen & Sword, 2011); Andrew Lambert, *The Crimean War: British Grand Strategy against Russia, 1853–1856* (Ashgate, 2011); Andrew Rath, *The Crimean War in Imperial Context, 1854–1856* (Palgrave Macmillan, 2015); Trudi Tate, *A Short History of the Crimean War* (I. B. Tauris, 2019), chapter 5.

37. There is important recent work on the Russian and Ottoman experiences. For a new account of the Russian experience, see Orlando Figes, *The Crimean War: A History* (Metropolitan, 2011); Mara Kozelsky, *Crimea in War and Transformation* (Oxford University Press, 2019). For the Ottoman experience see Candan Badem, *The Ottoman Crimean War (1853–1856)* (Brill, 2010).
38. There are many outstanding narrative histories of the War. These include Figes, *Crimean War*; Ponting, *Crimean War*; John Sweetman, *The Crimean War* (Osprey, 2001); Trevor Royle, *Crimea: The Great Crimean War* (Little, Brown, 1999); Tate, *Short History of the Crimean War.*
39. On the nineteenth-century army as an institution, see, among others, Byron Farwell, *For Queen and Country: A Social History of the Victorian and Edwardian Army* (Viking, 1981); Edward M. Spiers, *The Army and Society, 1815–1914* (Longman, 1980).
40. Trudi Tate, "Sebastopol: On the Fall of a City," *19: Interdisciplinary Studies in the Long Nineteenth Century* 20 (2015).
41. Particularly excellent on the Army's peninsular campaign, material culture, and cultural legacies is Alastair Massie, ed., *A Most Desperate Undertaking: The British Army in the Crimea, 1856–1856* (National Army Museum, 2003).
42. See, among others, Peter Mandler, *The English National Character: The History of an Idea from Edmund Burke to Tony Blair* (Yale University Press, 2007), 68, and more generally, on the nineteenth century, Chapters 2–4.
43. For an analysis of this notion and the myths surrounding it as it developed under Wellington, see Edward J. Cross, *The British Soldier Under Wellington* (University of Oklahoma Press, 2013), chapter 1.
44. See Stefanie Markovits, *The Crimean War in the British Imagination* (Cambridge University Press, 2009); Holly Furneaux, *Military Men of Feeling: Emotion, Touch, and Masculinity in the Crimean War* (Oxford University Press, 2016). See also Margery Masterson, "Dueling, Conflicting Masculinities, and the Victorian Gentleman," *Journal of British Studies* 56, no. 3 (2017): 605–28. Beyond Britain, see Peter Guardino, *The Dead March: A History of the Mexican-American War* (Cambridge University Press, 2017); Kristin Hoganson, *Fighting for American Manhood: How Gender Politics Provoked the Spanish-American and Philippine-American Wars* (Yale University Press, 2000). On World War I, see Nicoletta Gullace, *"The Blood of our Sons": Men, Women, and the Renegotiation of British Citizenship during the Great War* (Palgrave, 2002); Jessica Meyer, *Men of War: Masculinity and the First World War in Britain* (Palgrave, 2009); Joanna Bourke, *Dismembering the Male: Men's Bodies, Britain, and the Great War* (Reaktion Books, 1996). On World War II, see Sonya Rose, *Which People's War?: National Identity and Citizenship in Britain, 1939–1945* (Oxford University Press, 2003). More generally see Stefan Dudnik, Karen Hagemann, and John Tosh, eds., *Masculinities in Politics and War: Gendering Modern History* (Manchester University Press, 2004). On imperial masculinities, see Heather Streets, *Martial Races: The Military, Race, and Masculinity in British Imperial Culture, 1857–1914* (Manchester University Press, 2004); Kate Imy, *Faithful Fighters: Identity and Power in the British Indian Army* (Stanford University Press, 2019).

45. For a recent and lucid consideration of mismanagement, see Tate, *Short History of the Crimean War*, Introduction, especially pp. 6, 10.
46. The points above have been told, and retold, by many authors. One particularly readable distillation is Ian F. W. Beckett, *The Victorians at War* (Hambledon & London, 2003; Bloomsbury, 2006), chapter 17, "The First Modern War," 161–78. For a recent argument about the Crimean War's mixed modernity, see Tate, *Short History of the Crimean War*, 163. On the war and reform, see Olive Anderson, *A Liberal State at War: English Politics and Economics during the Crimean War* (St. Martin's Press, 1967). On the aftereffects of the war and Army reform, see, e.g., John Sweetman, *War and Administration: The Significance of the Crimean War for the British Army* (Scottish Academic Press, 1984). Hew Strachan makes the point that the process of reforming the Army began before the Crimean War's outbreak in *The Reform of the British Army, 1830–1854* (Manchester University Press, 1984). See also Hew Strachan, *From Waterloo to Balaclava: Tactics, Technology, and the British Army, 1815–1854* (Cambridge University Press, 1985).
47. Mark Bostridge offers one corrective in *Florence Nightingale*.
48. On the Cardwell Reforms, see Edward M. Spiers, *The Late Victorian Army, 1868–1902* (Manchester University Press, 1992), chapter 1; Albert V. Tucker, "Army and Society in England, 1870–1900: A Reassessment of the Cardwell Reforms," *Journal of British Studies* 2, no. 2 (May 1963): 110–41.
49. On care relations and the Crimea, see Furneaux, *Military Men of Feeling*, chapters 3, 4, 6, and Conclusion.
50. See Thomas W. Laqueur, "Bodies, Details, and the Humanitarian Narrative," in *The New Cultural History*, ed. Lynn Hunt (University of California Press, 1989), 176–204; Caroline Shaw, *Britannia's Embrace: Modern Humanitarianism and the Imperial Origins of Refugee Relief* (Oxford University Press, 2015).
51. Literary romanticists have been especially influential in shaping understandings of mediation and war: Mary Favret, *War at a Distance: Romanticism and the Making of Modern Wartime* (Princeton University Press, 2009); Philip Shaw, *Waterloo and the Victorian Imagination* (Palgrave, 2002); Lily Gurton-Wachter, *Watchwords: Romanticism and the Poetics of Attention* (Stanford University Press, 2016). Historians of the epoch have also contributed energetically to this literature: Karen Hagemann, *Revisiting Prussia's Wars against Napoleon: History, Culture, and Memory*, trans. Pamela Selwyn (Cambridge University Press, 2015); Catriona Kennedy, *Narratives of the Revolutionary and Napoleonic Wars: Military and Civilian Experience in Britain and Ireland* (Palgrave Macmillan, 2013), especially Introduction and chapter 1. The proliferation of genres of and expression after World War I is significant for my understanding too. See, among others, Jay Winter, *War Beyond Words: Languages of Remembrance from the Great War to the Present* (Cambridge University Press, 2017).
52. For an assessment of Victorian military history as a history of blunder, see, among others, Denis Judd, *Someone Has Blundered: Calamities of the British*

Army in the Victorian Age (Arthur Barker, 1973). For a more general assessment of blunders in British culture, see Stephanie Barczewski, *Heroic Failure.*

53. On Fenton's contributions to the understandings – and misunderstandings – of the War, see, Duncan Anderson, *Glass Warriors: The Camera at War* (Collins, 2005), 1–26; Sophie Gordon (with Louise Pearson), *Shadows of War: Roger Fenton's Photographs of the Crimea, 1855* (Royal Collection Trust, 2017); Jennifer M. Green, "Stories in an Exhibition: Narrative and Nineteenth-Century Photographic Documentary," *Journal of Narrative Technique* 20, no. 2 (Spring 1990): 147–66; Jennifer Green-Lewis, *Framing the Victorian: Photography and the Culture of Realism* (Cornell, 1996), chapter 4; Helen Groth, "Technological Mediations and the Public Sphere: Roger Fenton's Crimea Exhibition and 'The Charge of the Light Brigade,'" *Victorian Literature and Culture* 30, no. 2 (2002): 553–70. For a recent consideration of military history that makes use of Fenton's work, see David R. Jones, *The Crimean War, Then and Now* (Pen & Sword, 2017); on visual representation beyond photography, see, Ulrich Keller, *The Ultimate Spectacle: A Visual History of the Crimean War* (Routledge, 2013); Sergiusz Michalski, "War Imagery between the Crimean Campaign and 1914," in *War and Art: A Visual History of Modern Conflict,* ed. Joanna Bourke (Reaktion, 2017), 44–79 and Markovits, *Crimean War,* chapter 4 and Afterword; on the French case, see Katie Hornstein, *Picturing War in France, 1792–1856* (Yale University Press, 2017) and Julia Thoma, *The Final Spectacle: Military Painting under the Second Empire, 1851–1867* (Walter de Gruyter, 2019).

54. Gavin Williams, ed., *Hearing the Crimean War: Wartime Sound and the Unmaking of Sense* (Oxford University Press, 2019).

55. Along with Furneaux and Markovits, see John Peck, *War, the Army, and Victorian Literature* (St. Martin's, 1998), chapter 2 and Cynthia Dereli, *A War Culture in Action: A Study of the Literature of the Crimean War Period* (Peter Lang, 2003).

56. Rachel Teukolsky, "Novels, Newspapers, and Global War: New Realisms in the 1850s," *Novel: A Forum on Fiction* 45, no. 1 (2012): 31–55.

57. Jack Fairey, *The Great Powers and Orthodox Christendom: The Crisis over the Eastern Church in the Era of the Crimean War* (Palgrave Macmillan, 2015).

58. Markovits, *Crimean War,* chapter 2; Sarah Ross, "Brave Hermeneutics, The Eastern Question, and Kingsley's *Hypatia,*" *Victorian Studies* 60, no. 3 (Spring 2018): 412–33.

59. On the war and the production of the aggregate, see Elaine Hadley, "Nobody, Somebody, and Everybody," *Victorian Studies* 59, no. 1 (Autumn 2016): 65–86.

60. On these senses and their association with World War I, see Santanu Das, *Touch and Intimacy in First World War Literature* (Cambridge University Press, 2009).

61. The literature on gender and war is now vast. A pioneering volume was Miriam Cooke and Angela Woollacott, eds., *Gendering War Talk* (Princeton University Press, 1993).

62. See, among others, Mary Poovey, *Uneven Developments: The Ideological Work of Gender in Mid-Victorian England* (University of Chicago Press, 1988), chapter 6.

63. Markovits, *Crimean War,* chapter 2. A foundational text here is Donald E. Hall, ed., *Muscular Christianity: Embodying the Victorian Age* (Cambridge University Press, 1994).

64. Furneaux, *Military Men of Feeling.* For a different variety of literary masculinity, see James Eli Adams, *Dandies and Desert Saints: Styles of Victorian Masculinity* (Cornell University Press, 1995).

65. Christopher Herbert, *War of No Pity: The Indian Mutiny and Victorian Trauma* (Princeton University Press, 2008).

66. The words are taken from Rudyard Kipling's "White Man's Burden," which was originally published in the *Times.* See Rudyard Kipling, "The White Man's Burden," *Times,* no. 35744, February 4, 1899, *Times Digital. Archive* (hereafter *TDA*).

67. The now classic text on the island nation is, of course, Linda Colley's *Britons: Forging the Nation, 1707–1837* (Yale University Press, 1992). For historical tensions between formations of English and British identity, see, among others, Krishan Kumar, *The Making of English National Identity* (Cambridge University Press, 2003).

68. On the history of empire as a palimpsest for British national life, see Dane Kennedy, "The Imperial History Wars," *Journal of British Studies* 54 (January 2016): 5–22.

69. On veterans and old age, see Kate McLoughlin, *Veteran Poetics: British Literature in the Age of Mass Warfare* (Cambridge University Press, 2018), Introduction. On war and generation, see, recently, Joel Morley, "Dad 'never said much' but . . Young Men and Great War Veterans in Day-to-Day-Life in Interwar Britain," *Twentieth-Century British History* 29, no. 2 (June 2018): 199–224; Michael Roper, "The Bush, the Suburbs, and the Long Great War," *History Workshop Journal* 86 (Autumn 2019): 90–113. On generational history as an approach, see Abosede George, Clive Glaser, Margaret D. Jacobs, Chitra Joshi, Emily Marker, Alexandra Walsham, Wang Zheng, and Bernd Weisbrod, "Conversation: Each Generation Writes its Own History of Generations," *American Historical Review* 123, no. 5 (2018): 1505–46; R. F. Foster, *Vivid Faces: The Revolutionary Generation in Ireland, 1890–1923* (Allen Lane, 2014).

70. See Paula M. Krebs, *Gender, Race, and the Writing of Empire: Public Discourse and the Boer War* (Cambridge University Press, 1999); Kenneth O. Morgan, "The Boer War and the Media, 1899–1902," *Twentieth-Century British History* 13, no. 1 (January 2002): 1–16.

71. For an assessment of the relevance of World War I in the early days of World War II, see Joel Morley, "The Memory of the Great War and Morale during Britain's Phoney War," *Historical Journal* 63, no. 2 (March 2020): 437–67.

72. On the Korean War as a forgotten war, and on the function of forgetting in postwar societies, see Grace Huxford, "The Korean War Never Happened: Forgetting a Conflict in British Culture and Society," *Twentieth-Century British History* 27, no. 2 (June 2016): 195–219 and also Grace Huxford's *The Korean War in Britain: Citizenship, Selfhood, and Forgetting* (Manchester University Press, 2018).

73. The three-volume collection, *Patriotism: The Making and Unmaking of British National Identity* (Routledge, 1989), edited by Raphael Samuel, had its roots in the moment of the Falklands War. See also Ward, *Britishness since 1870*, 6.
74. On the cultural history of decolonization, see, among others, Wendy Webster, *Englishness and Empire, 1939–1965* (Oxford University Press, 2005); Stuart Ward, *British Culture and the End of Empire* (Manchester University Press, 2001). For a broader, European perspective see Elizabeth Buettner, *Europe after Empire: Decolonization, Society, and Culture* (Cambridge University Press, 2016).
75. Nicole Eustace, Eugenia Lean, Julie Livingston, Jan Plamper, William M. Reddy, and Barbara H. Rosenwein, "Conversation: The Historical Study of Emotions," *American Historical Review* 117, no. 5 (December 2012): 1487–531. Recent notable works in the contexts of modern British history include, but are not limited to, Emma Griffin, "Emotions of Motherhood: Love, Culture, and Poverty in Victorian Britain," *American Historical Review* 123, no. 1 (February 2018): 60–85; Joanna Lewis, *Empire of Sentiment: The Death of Livingstone and the Myth of Victorian Imperialism* (Cambridge University Press, 2018); Claire Langhamer, *The English in Love: The Intimate Story of an Emotional Revolution* (Oxford University Press, 2013); Michael Roper, *The Secret Battle: Emotional Survival in the Great War* (Manchester University Press, 2009).
76. One provocative effort here is Dominic Sandbrook's *The Great British Dream Factory* (Allen Lane, 2015).
77. This question has been at the heart of debate among literary critics, especially. See, notably, "The Manifesto of the V21 Collective," at http://v21collective.org/manifesto-of-the-v21-collective-ten-theses.
78. George Malcolm Thompson, "The Reason Why," *Evening Standard*, November 5, 1953, Liddell Hart Military Archive 15/1/27, Kings College, London.
79. Benjamin Morgan, "Fin du Globe: On Decadent Planets," *Victorian Studies* 58, no. 4 (Summer 2016): 609–35; Chris Otter, Alison Bashford, John L. Brooke, Frederik Albritton Jonsson, and Jason M. Kelly, "Roundtable: The Anthropocene in British History," *Journal of British Studies* 57, no. 3 (July 2018): 568–96.
80. Jacob Rees-Mogg, *The Victorians: Twelve Titans Who Forged Britain* (W. H. Allen, 2019).
81. Ronjaunee Chatterjee, Alicia Mireles Christoff, and Amy R. Wong, "Undisciplining Victorian Studies," *Los Angeles Review of Books*, July 10, 2020, at https://lareviewofbooks.org/article/undisciplining-victorian-studies/. One outgrowth of this call is the new website and project, "Undisciplining the Victorian Classroom," at https://undiscipliningvc.org/index.html.
82. For some classic expositions of these values, see Asa Briggs, *Victorian People: A Reassessment of Persons and Things* (University of Chicago Press, 1955), especially Introduction and chapter 2; Walter Houghton, *The Victorian Frame of Mind, 1830–1870* (Yale University Press, 1957). It is notable that these classics were published around the time of the Crimean War's centenary; this is also when the journal, *Victorian Studies*, commenced publication.

83. For a values-based approach that addresses Englishness in the years leading up to the Crimean War, see Paul Langford, *Englishness Identified: Manners and Character, 1650–1850* (Oxford University Press, 2000). Particularly a wartime necessity, the collective notion of morale took its shape as well under the aegis of nineteenth-century liberalism, too. See Daniel Ussishkin, *Morale: A Modern British History* (Oxford University Press, 2017). On liberalism, the Crimean War, and patriotism, see Jonathan Parry, *The Politics of Patriotism: English Liberalism, National Identity and Europe, 1830–1866* (Cambridge University Press, 2006). A recent assessment of the period that takes a values-based approach is Angus Hawkins, *Victorian Political Culture: "Habits of Heart and Mind"* (Oxford University Press, 2015).

84. Victorian values have long underwritten conservativism and its programs. For a diagnosis of this phenomenon, see Wright, *On Living in an Old Country*, 169–73. For a conservative academic example of the veneration of Victorian virtues, see Gertrude Himmelfarb, *The De-Moralization of Society: From Victorian Virtues to Modern Values* (Knopf, 1995), especially Prologue and chapters 1–2. For popular, right wing usage, see, most recently, Rees-Mogg, *Victorians*. Kim A. Wagner calls this a caricature of Victorian values in his *Observer* review, "Rees-Mogg's Book is 'Sentimental Jingoism and Empire Nostalgia,'" *The Observer*, May 19, 2019, at www.theguardian.com/books/2019/may/19/jacob-rees-mogg-victorians-sentimental-jingoism-and-empire-nostalgia.

85. On the saturation of everyday life with war and violence, see Joanna Bourke, *Deep Violence: Military Violence, War Play, and the Social Life of Weapons* (Counterpoint, 2015).

86. See, among others, Sebouh David Aslanian, Joyce E. Chaplin, Ann McGrath, and Kristin Mann, "Conversation-How Size Matters: The Question of Scale in History," *American Historical Review* 118, no. 5 (December 2013): 1431–72.

87. David Armitage and Jo Guldi, *The History Manifesto* (Cambridge University Press, 2014); Deborah Cohen and Peter Mandler, "*The History Manifesto*: A Response," and David Armitage and Jo Guldi, "*The History Manifesto*: A Reply to Deborah Cohen and Peter Mandler," *American Historical Review* 120, no. 2 (April 2015): 530–42 and 543–54.

88. This work joins with recent scholarship that tracks long chronologies to understand life and representation in British modernity. See, for instance, Cohen, *Family Secrets;* Nadja Durbach, *Many Mouths: The Politics of Food in Britain from the Workhouse to the Welfare State* (Cambridge University Press, 2020); Erika Rappaport, *A Thirst for Empire: How Tea Shaped the Modern World* (Princeton University Press, 2017).

89. For a broader, important discussion of war and masculinity across the nineteenth century, see Michael Brown, Anna Maria Barry, and Joanne Begiato, eds., *Martial Masculinities: Experiencing and Imagining the Military in the Long Nineteenth Century* (Manchester University Press, 2019).

90. On the Imperial War Museum as a repository of war memory itself, see, among others; Jennifer Wellington, *Exhibiting War: The Great War, Museums and Memory in Britain, Canada, and Australia* (Cambridge University Press, 2017).

91. On the stakes of the competing stories of these two figures, and for a nuanced history of the nursing profession more generally that seeks to get beyond myth, see Anne Borsay and Billie Hunter, "Nursing and Midwifery: Historical Approaches," in *Nursing and Midwifery in Britain since 1700* (Palgrave, 2012), 5.
92. On envisioning a multicultural Britain, see, among others, Yasmin Alibhai-Brown, *Imagining the New Britain* (Routledge, 2001) and Bhikhu Parekh et al., *The Future of Multi-Ethnic Britain* (Profile Books, 2000). Two new histories of the making of multicultural Britain across the twentieth century include Jordanna Bailkin, *Unsettled: Refugee Camps and the Making of Multicultural Britain* (Oxford University Press, 2018) and Wendy Webster, *Mixing It: Diversity in World War Two Britain* (Oxford University Press, 2018).
93. Cecil Woodham-Smith, *The Great Hunger: Ireland, 1845–1849* (H. Hamilton, 1962). See also Christine Kinealy, "'The Historian is a Haunted Man': Cecil Woodham-Smith and *The Great Hunger*," *New Hibernia Review* 12, no. 4 (Winter 2008): 134–43.

1   The Adventurers

1. Mary Seacole, *Wonderful Adventures of Mrs. Seacole in Many Lands*, ed. Sarah Salih (1857; Penguin, 2005), 69. For a recent appraisal, see Antoinette Burton, "Writer-Travelers and Fugitives: Insider-Outsiders," in *The Cambridge History of Black and Asian British Writing*, ed. Susheila Nasta and Mark U. Stein (Cambridge University Press, 2020), 40–53.
2. Neil Kent, *Crimea: A History* (C. Hurst, 2016), Introduction, especially p. 2.
3. Kent, *Crimea*, Introduction, especially p. 2.
4. Seacole, *Wonderful Adventures*, 75.
5. Seacole, *Wonderful Adventures*, 11, 75.
6. On military travel in earlier conflicts, see Joseph Clarke and John Horne, "Introduction," in *Militarized Cultural Encounters in the Long Nineteenth Century: Making War, Mapping Europe*, ed. Joseph Clarke and John Horne (Palgrave, 2018), 1–22. In this volume, see also Joseph Clarke, "Encountering the Sacred: British and French Soldiers in the Revolutionary and Napoleonic Mediterranean," 49–74, and Catriona Kennedy, "Military Ways of Seeing: British Soldiers' Sketches from the Egyptian Campaign of 1801," 197–222.
7. See Kent, *Crimea*, chapter 4.
8. Elizabeth Berkeley Craven, *A Journey through the Crimea to Constantinople* (G. G. J. and J. Robinson, 1789), 184.
9. Craven, *Journey through the Crimea*, 191.
10. Mary Holderness, *Journey from Riga to the Crimea, with Some Account of the Manners and Customs of the Colonists of New Russia* (Sherwood, Gilbert, and Piper, 1827), 144, www4.wlv.ac.uk/btw/authors/1075.
11. James Edward Alexander, *Travels to the Seat of War in the East, through Russia and the Crimea in 1829* (H. Coburn and R. Bentley, 1829), 247, 259.
12. On the romantic Crimea, see also Kent, *Crimea*, chapter 5.

13. Anthony Grant, *An Historical Sketch of the Crimea* (Bell and Daldy, 1855), 1. See also The Reverend Thomas Milner, *The Crimea, Its Ancient and Modern History* (Longman, Brown, Green, and Longmans, 1855).
14. Grant, *Historical Sketch*, 1.
15. Grant, *Historical Sketch*, 2.
16. Grant, *Historical Sketch*, 111.
17. Grant, *Historical Sketch*, 4.
18. See, for instance, "The War in the East," *Illustrated London News*, October 8, 1853, p. 297, issue 648 (hereafter *ILN*), *Illustrated London News Historical Archive* (hereafter *ILNHA*).
19. See, for instance, Orlando Figes, *The Crimean War: A History* (Metropolitan, 2011), 304–11.
20. On these sources, see Gavin Daly, "British Soldiers and the Legend of Napoleon," *Historical Journal* 61, no. 1 (March 2018): 131–53.
21. Thomas Wood Correspondence: Letters to his wife Fanny, July 1, 1854, Wood Family Collection, ACC/1302/239, London Metropolitan Archives; Frances Isabella Duberly, *Mrs. Duberly's War: Journal and Letters from the Crimea*, ed. Christine Kelly (Oxford University Press, 2008), 208.
22. "Going to the War," *ILN*, February 18, 1854, p.145, issue 669, *ILNHA*. See also "Ready for the Conflict," *ILN*, March 4, 1854, p. 181, issue 671; "A Chaplain in the Crimea, the Account of Haydon Aldersey Taylor," November 22, 1854, 2005–09–151, National Army Museum, Templer Study Centre, Chelsea, UK (hereafter NAM); Letters and Papers of Col. Hugh Robert Hibbert, Letter to Mary Caroline Henrietta Hibbert, Mainly Relating to Service in the Crimean War, 1854–1855, April 4, 1854, DHB/2, Cheshire Archives and Local Studies, Chester, UK.
23. Somerset J. Gough Calthorpe and George Cadogan, *Cadogan's Crimea* (Athenaeum, 1980), 9–10.
24. See, for example, Letters of William John Rhodes, January 29, 1855, MS 7866, Wellcome Library, London, UK.
25. See, for example, Duberly, *Mrs. Duberly's War*, 3.
26. Major G. G. Clowes, "Letters from Crimea and India," May 4, 1854, NAM 1995–04–21. For the American Civil War, see David Anderson, "Dying of Nostalgia: Homesickness in the Union Army during the Civil War," *Civil War History* 56, no. 3 (September 2010): 247–82.
27. Seacole, *Wonderful Adventures*, 76. See also Clowes Letters, May 12–14, 1854, NAM 1995–04–21; Notes and Draft Account of Sister Sarah Anne Terrot's Experiences, Nursing the Wounded in the War, RAMC 1752/3, Wellcome Library, pp. 5–8.
28. See, for example, Letters from William John Rhodes, February 18, 1855, MS 7866, Wellcome Library.
29. See, for example, Letters from William John Rhodes, March 1, 1855, MS 7866, Wellcome Library.
30. William Howard Russell, *The British Expedition to the Crimea* (Routledge, 1877), 14.

31. Jervoise Smith, "Journal of a Visit to the Crimea, on Behalf of the Commissioners of the Crimean Army Fund," January 22, 1855, Add MSS 22583, West Sussex Record Office, Chichester, UK.

32. The foundational text here is, of course, Edward Said, *Orientalism* (Pantheon Books, 1978). A seminal consideration of travel writing is Mary Louise Pratt, *Imperial Eyes: Travel Writing and Transculturation* (Routledge, 1992). For a more recent discussion of Britain and the Near East, see Michelle Tusan, *Smyrna's Ashes: Humanitarianism, Genocide, and the Birth of the Middle East* (University of California Press, 2012).

33. Duberly, *Mrs. Duberly's War*, 10.

34. Letters of Frederick Cockayne Elton, no. 47, April 2, 1856, NAM 1988–01-3 and "A Chaplain in the Crimea, the Account of Haydon Aldersey Taylor," December 5, 1854, NAM 2005–09–151; Letters from William John Rhodes, December 31, 1855, MS 7866, Wellcome Library; "Sketch in the Streets of Constantinople," *ILN*, January 28, 1854, p. 69, issue 665, *ILNHA*; Duberly, *Mrs. Duberly's War*, 13.

35. Jervoise Smith, "Journal of a Visit to the Crimea, on Behalf of the Commissioners of the Crimean Army Fund," December 30, 1854, Add MSS 22583, West Sussex Record Office. On the place of the *Arabian Nights* in early and mid-Victorian culture, see Melissa Dickson, "Jane Eyre's 'Arabian Tales': Reading and Remembering the *Arabian Nights*," *Journal of Victorian Culture* 18, no. 2 (2013): 198–212.

36. William Montgomery-Cuninghame Letters, August 2, 1854; August 9, 1854, HRO 1509, Hampshire Record Office, Winchester, UK.

37. Letters of George Henry Waller, August 17, 1855, CR 341/324/44, Warwickshire County Record Office, Warwick, UK.

38. Letters and Papers of Col. Hugh Robert Hibbert, Letter to Mary Caroline Henrietta Hibbert, May 9–10, 1854, DHB/4, Cheshire Archives and Local Studies; Seacole, *Wonderful Adventures*, 78.

39. "A Chaplain in the Crimea, the Account of Haydon Aldersey Taylor," December 5, 1854.

40. Duberly, *Mrs. Duberly's War*, 13.

41. Duberly, *Mrs. Duberly's War*, 14

42. Letters and Papers of Col. Hugh Robert Hibbert, Letter to Mary Caroline Henrietta Hibbert, May 9–10, 1854.

43. Letter from Lieutenant Alfred Howell to his Brother, Stephen Howell, Kertche [sic], November 24, 1855, NAM 1972–08–51.

44. Smith, "Journal of a Visit to the Crimea," December 30, 1854.

45. Philip Warner, ed., *Letters Home from the Crimea: A Young Cavalryman's Campaign from Balaklava and Sebastopol to Victory* (Windrush Press, 1999), 203.

46. Smith, "Journal of a Visit to the Crimea," January 22, 1855. Another officer to write extensively and fondly about the baths was Major Robert Poore. See Letters of Major Robert Poore, 8th Hussars, 1854–1858, NAM 1995–04–22, especially January 1, 1856.

47. Typescript Copies of Letters from Fred and Fitz Maxse to their Parents, February 21, 1864, MP4332, West Sussex Record Office.

48. "The Landing in the Crimea," *ILN*, September 23, 1854, p. 269, issue 703, *ILNHA*.

49. Letters and Papers of Col. Hugh Robert Hibbert, Letter to Mary Caroline Henrietta Hibbert, September 9–12, 1854, DHB/10, Cheshire Archives and Local Studies.

50. Alexander, *Travels to the Seat of War*, 261.

51. Letters and Papers of Col. Hugh Robert Hibbert, Letter to Mary Caroline Henrietta Hibbert, September 9–12, 1854.

52. Duberly, *Mrs. Duberly's War*, 174.

53. Charles Henry Scott, *The Baltic, the Black Sea, and the Crimea* (Richard Bentley, 1854), 240.

54. Letters and Papers of Col. Hugh Robert Hibbert, Letter to Mary Caroline Henrietta Hibbert, October 13, 1854, DHB/13, Cheshire Archives and Local Studies.

55. Letters of Major Andrew Campbell Knox Lock, May 16, 1855, WKR.B2. ZA, Kent Record Office, Maidstone, UK.

56. See, for instance, Letters of Lt. Col. Edward Legge, May 22, 1856, f. 18, F/LEG/0836, London Metropolitan Archives; Travel Journal of Frederick Legge, May 23, 1856, F/LEG/0896, London Metropolitan Archives, pp. 18–19.

57. Journal, September 19, 1854, Papers of Alexander Kinglake, GBR/0012/MS Add.7633 5/1, Department of Manuscripts and University Archives, Cambridge University Library, Cambridge, UK.

58. Letters of Frederick Cockayne Elton, especially no. 20, April 22, 1855, NAM 1988-01-3; see also William Montgomery-Cuninghame Letters, April 12, 1856, HRO 1509, Hampshire Record Office.

59. On the power of things to connote sentiment and belonging, see John Plotz, *Portable Property: Victorian Culture on the Move* (Princeton University Press, 2008).

60. Letters and Papers of Col. Hugh Robert Hibbert, Miscellaneous Crimean Items, April 4, 1854, DHB/70, Cheshire Archives and Local Studies.

61. Letters and Papers of Col. Hugh Robert Hibbert, Letter to Mary Caroline Henrietta Hibbert, January 29, 1855, DHB/19, Cheshire Archives and Local Studies.

62. See, e.g., Letters from William John Rhodes, March 1, MS 7866, Wellcome Library.

63. I am influenced here by leading work among literary scholars on Victorian thing culture and material culture. Elaine Freedgood, *The Ideas in Things: Fugitive Meaning in the Victorian Novel* (University of Chicago Press, 2006); Deborah Lutz, *Relics of Death in Victorian Literature and Culture* (Cambridge University Press, 2015); Plotz, *Portable Property*; Talia Schaffer, *Novel Craft: Victorian Domestic Handicraft and Nineteenth-Century Fiction* (Oxford University Press, 2011).

64. On Tatar hospitality, see, e.g., Letters of Lt. Col. Edward Legge, May 24, 1856, f. 32, F/LEG/0836, London Metropolitan Archives.

65. William Howard Russell, *Russell's Dispatches from the Crimea, 1854–1856*, ed. Nicolas Bentley (Hill and Wang, 1967), 272–73; Craven, *Journey*

through the Crimea, 117–18; Scott, *Baltic, the Black Sea, and the Crimea*, 214–15.

66. Scott, *Baltic, the Black Sea, and the Crimea*, 147.
67. A Soldier, *A Knouting for the Czar!* (George R. Wright, 1855), 5. See also William Morris, *The Three Sergeants, or Phases of the Soldier's Life* (Effingham Wilson, 1858), 220–21. Anti-Russian sentiment was evident in poetry as well. See Rev. T. R. I. Laugharne, ed., *A Bundle of Reeds from the Alma & C.* (Whitnash Press, 1854).
68. See, e.g., Russell, *British Expedition to the Crimea*, 84.
69. Surgeon John Netten Radcliffe found the habits of the Turks when it came to timekeeping and tasking especially frustrating: Transcripts of the Crimean War Letters of John Netten Radcliffe, January 12 to March 21, 1856, NAM 2009–08–38, especially March 21, 1856. See also Adam Von Gurowski, *A Year of the War* (D. Appleton, 1855).
70. George Buchanan, *Camp Life as Seen by a Civilian* (James Maclehose, 1871), 157. See also Letters of William Markham, July 12, 1854, RAMC 436/1/2, Wellcome Library; Russell, *British Expedition to the Crimea*, 56.
71. Letters and Papers of Col. Hugh Robert Hibbert, Letter to Mary Caroline Henrietta Hibbert, May 9–10, 1854.
72. Scott, *Baltic, the Black Sea, and the Crimea*, 308.
73. Russell, *Dispatches from the Crimea*, 145.
74. Seacole, *Wonderful Adventures*, 98.
75. Rudyard Kipling, "The White Man's Burden," *McClure's Magazine* 12, no. 4 (February 1899).
76. "A Chaplain in the Crimea, the Account of Haydon Aldersey Taylor," December 18, 1854, NAM 2005–09–151.
77. See, for instance, "The Turks Conveying the Sick to Balaklava," *ILN*, March 17, 1855, p. 260. Portfolio of cuttings from the *Illustrated London News*, Courtesy of Mr. J. E. Crisp, RAMC 27, Wellcome Library.
78. Letters of John Netten Radcliffe, January 12 to March 21, 1856, especially March 21, 1856.
79. On Turkish savagery, see Clowes Letters, July 3, 1854, NAM 1995–04–21; Letter from Studholme-Brownrigg to Spencer Stanhope, June 8, 1855, Spencer Stanhope Collection, SpSr 10/4/1, West Yorkshire Archive Service, Bradford, UK.
80. Letters and Papers of Col. Hugh Robert Hibbert, Letter to Mary Caroline Henrietta Hibbert, May 9–10, 1854.
81. Letters and Papers of Col. Hugh Robert Hibbert, Letter to Mary Caroline Henrietta Hibbert, May 9–10, 1854.
82. See, e.g., Letters from William John Rhodes, July 13, 1855, MS 7866, Wellcome Library.
83. Russell, *Dispatches from the Crimea*, 26.
84. Seacole, *Wonderful Adventures*, 94.
85. Sparling Marcus, "A Zouave: Roger Fenton in Borrowed Zouave Uniform," Fenton Crimean War Photographs, Library of Congress Prints and Photographs Online, at www.loc.gov/pictures/item/2001697657.

86. Letters and Papers of Col. Hugh Robert Hibbert, August 18, 1854, DHB/8, Cheshire Archives and Local Studies; Warner, ed., *Letters Home from the Crimea*, 22.
87. See, e.g., Letters from William John Rhodes, February 8, 1855, MS 7866, Wellcome Library.
88. Letters of Frederick Cockayne Elton, especially no. 12, January 28, 1855, NAM 1988–01–3.
89. Russell, *British Expedition to the Crimea*, 169.
90. Russell, *British Expedition to the Crimea*, 169.
91. Letters of Sergeant General Robert Wyatt Meadows to his Sister, December 10, 1855, NAM 1987–03–24.
92. Letters and Papers of Col. Hugh Robert Hibbert, Letter to Mary Caroline Henrietta Hibbert, July 27, 1855, DHB/31, Cheshire Archives and Local Studies.
93. Surgeon John Netten Radcliffe used the exclamation "Hurrah!" similarly. Letters of John Netten Radcliffe, January 12 to March 21, 1856, especially March 21, 1856.
94. On the military and the making of manhood, see Rebecca Friedman, "Masculinity, the Body, and Coming of Age in the Nineteenth-Century Russian Cadet Corps," *Journal of the History of Childhood and Youth* 5, no. 2 (2012): 219–38; and Jennine Hurl-Eamon, "Youth in the Devil's Service, Manhood in the King's: Reaching Adulthood in the Eighteenth-Century British Army," *Journal of the History of Childhood and Youth* 8, no. 2 (2015): 163–90.
95. Letters of George Henry Waller, February 29, 1856, CR 341/324/94, Warwickshire County Record Office.
96. Letters of George Henry Waller, February 24, 1856, CR 341/324/91, Warwickshire County Record Office.
97. See Papers of Alexander William Kinglake, See GBR/0012/Ms Add.7633, Packets 14–18, Department of Manuscripts and University Archives, Cambridge University Library, Cambridge, UK.
98. On the former, see Stuart Semmel, "Reading the Tangible Past: British Tourism, Collecting, and Memory after Waterloo," *Representations* 69 (2000): 9–37. On the latter, see note 56 above.
99. M. S., "Ten Days in the Crimea," *Macmillan's Magazine* 5 (1862): 301–11, especially p. 305.
100. M. S., "Ten Days in the Crimea," 309.
101. Teresa Grey, *Journal of a Visit to Egypt, Constantinople, the Crimea, Greece, Etc. in the Suite of the Prince and Princess of Wales* (Smith, Elder, 1869).
102. William Howard Russell, *A Diary in the East during the Tour of the Prince and Princess of Wales*, vol. 2 (Routledge, 1869), 568.
103. Grey, *Journal of a Visit*, 154.
104. Grey, *Journal of a Visit*, 172.
105. "The Crimea Revisited," *ILN*, May 22, 1869, p. 511, issue 1539, *ILNHA*.
106. Russell, *Diary in the East*, 523.
107. Grey, *Journal of a Visit*, 173.

108. Grey, *Journal of a Visit*, 194.
109. Russell, *Diary in the East*, 524–25, 538.
110. On war writing and the pastoral, see Kate McLoughlin, *Authoring War: The Literary Representation of War from the Iliad to Iraq* (Cambridge University Press, 2011), chapter 3.
111. Russell, *Diary in the East*, 523.
112. Russell, *Diary in the East*, 542.
113. Russell, *Diary in the East*, 569.
114. "The Crimea Revisited," *ILN*, June 19, 1869, p. 622, issue 1544, *ILNHA*.
115. Russell, *Diary in the East*, 547.
116. See also Kent, *Crimea*, chapter 7, especially p. 115; for an earlier assessment, see William Jesse, *Notes of a Half-Pay in Search of Health* (James Madden, 1841), 117.
117. Grey, *Journal of a Visit*, 191.
118. Russell, *Diary in the East*, 566.
119. "Sir Evelyn Wood on the Crimea," *Times*, August 8, 1895, p. 8, issue 34605, *TDA*.
120. Evelyn Wood, *The Crimea in 1854 and 1894* (Chapman and Hall, 1895); see also Evelyn Wood, "The Crimea in 1854, and 1894," *Fortnightly Review* 56, no. 334 (1894): 469–97.
121. Wood, *Crimea in 1854 and 1894*, 69.
122. Wood, *Crimea in 1854 and 1894*, viii.
123. William James Garnett to Bertha Garnett, October 22, 1903, DDQ/9/4/24 and "Journey Round the Black Sea, 1903," DDQ/9/6/WJG2, Lancashire Archives, Preston, UK.
124. See, also, "A Visit to the Crimea Fifty Years After," n.d., V/4/6/9, Papers of Brigadier General Sir James Edward Edmonds, Liddell Hart Military Archives, Kings College, London, UK.
125. "Journey Round the Black Sea, 1903."
126. "Journey Round the Black Sea, 1903."
127. See Eric G. Zuelow, *A History of Modern Tourism* (Palgrave, 2016).
128. Ménie Muriel Norman, "In the Haunted Crimea," *Contemporary Review* 78 (July 1900): 38–57. Norman is known now by her maiden name, Dowie.
129. "Visit to the Crimea Fifty Years After."
130. Norman, "In the Haunted Crimea," 42.
131. "Visit to the Crimea Fifty Years After."
132. British critics went to pains to portray Russians as allies in the years after 1907's Anglo-Russian Entente and during the Great War. See Michael Hughes, "Searching for the Soul of Russia: British Perceptions of Russia during the First World War," *Twentieth Century British History* 20, no. 2 (2009): 198–226.
133. "Advance of General Wrangel's Army," *Daily Mail*, June 11, 1920, p. 5, issue 7543, *DMHA*.
134. "Help for Russian Refugees," *Times*, March 1, 1921, p. 10, issue 42657, *TDA*. See also Vladimir Poliakoff, "The Darkest Hour," *Times*, November 16, 1920, p. 8, issue 42569, *TDA*.

135. An American Traveler, "4s for a Loaf under Soviet Rule," *Daily Mail*, October 27, 1931, p. 3, issue 11078, *DMHA*.
136. "Bolshevist Atrocities on Moslems," *Times*, December 23, 1919, p. 9, issue 42290, *TDA*; "Cannibalism In The Crimea," *Times*, July 24, 1922, p. 7, issue 43091, *TDA*. On the human costs of war and revolution, and on British responses, see, for instance, Michelle Tusan, "'Crimes against Humanity': Human Rights, the British Empire, and the Origins of the Response to the Armenian Genocide," *American Historical Review* 119, no. 1 (February 2014): 47–77; Tehila Sasson, "From Empire to Humanity: The Russian Famine and the Imperial Origins of International Humanitarianism," *Journal of British Studies* 55 (July 2016): 519–37.
137. See Kent, *Crimea*, chapter 8.
138. "The Crimea," *Times*, April 17, 1944, p. 5, issue 49832, *TDA*.
139. "Main Defence Line of Sevastopol Broken," *Times*, May 9, 1944, p. 4, issue 49851, *TDA*.
140. "Sevastopol Captured," *Times*, May 10, 1944, p. 4, issue 49852, *TDA*.
141. Kent, *Crimea*, 139.
142. Private Papers of Lt. Col. T. J. Cowen, MBE: Diary, Imperial War Museum Archives, London, 17512, 1945, pp. 23–24 (hereafter, IWM).
143. They may also have taken inspiration from intelligence officers working earlier in the century. See Satia, *Spies in Arabia*.
144. Cowen Diary, 1.
145. Cowen Diary, 4.
146. Cowen Diary, 2.
147. Cowen Diary, 22.
148. Private Papers of Miss. G. I. Hutchinson, Documents, 2896, Letter to Her Sister, February 1945, p. 1, IWM.
149. Cowen Diary, 13.
150. Cowen Diary, 9.
151. Cowen Diary, 17–18.
152. Hutchinson Letter, 3.
153. Cowen Diary, 16–17.
154. Hutchinson Letter, 3.
155. Cowen Diary, 13–14. Mary Louise Roberts notes that alcohol was free-flowing among the US troops in France. See *What Soldiers Do: Sex and the American GI in France* (University of Chicago Press, 2014).
156. Cowen Diary, 16–17.
157. Cowen Diary, 16.
158. Cowan Diary, 12.
159. Cowan Diary, 10.
160. Jonathan Steele, "Riding Again into the Valley of Death: Jonathan Steele, on a Rare Visit to a Crimean Battlefield, Retraces the Charge of the Light Brigade," *Guardian*, November 2, 1991, p. 27.
161. Cowen Diary, 20.
162. "Motor-Cycling in South Russia," *Daily Mail Atlantic Edition* [Berengaria, Eastbound], May 8, 1925, p. 19, issue 337, *DMHA*.

163. Simon Tisdall, "Good Health," *Guardian*, July 7, 1979, p. 13, issue 41332.
164. "Yalta: The Gem of the Crimea," Intourist Brochure, K09/1032, IWM.
165. Kent, *Crimea*, chapter 10, especially p. 144.
166. "Drive Your Car to the Crimea," *Daily Mail*, October 31, 1955, p. 2, issue 18518. See also "A Crimean Welcome," *Daily Mail*, April 3, 1956, p. 8, issue 18648; "Sebastopol Open to Tourists," *Daily Mail*, March 30, 1959, p. 7, issue 19574, *DMHA*.
167. "Yalta: The Gem of the Crimea."
168. Vladimir Ankudinov, "Getting to Know Russia," *Guardian*, December 7, 1960, p. 17, issue 35593.
169. Tisdall, "Good Health," 13.
170. Tisdall, "Good Health," 13.
171. "Autumn Sunshine in Russia – Its 70 Degrees Plus!," *Guardian*, June 1, 1988, p. 7.
172. Errol Morris, *Believing is Seeing: Observations on the Myths of Photography* (Penguin, 2011), 21; Trader Horn, "Through the Looking Glass in Old Crimea," *Guardian*, December 11, 1993, p. 11.
173. Guy Walters, "Charge of the Holiday Brigade," *Daily Mail*, October 16, 2004, p. 53, issue 33704, *DMHA*.

2   The Dutiful

1. Barczewski, *Heroic Failure and the British*, chapter 3.
2. Trudi Tate, "On Not Knowing Why: Memorializing the Light Brigade," in *Literature, Science, Psychoanalysis, 1830–1970: Essays in Honour of Gillian Beer*, ed. Helen Small and Trudi Tate (Oxford University Press, 2003), 160–80, especially p. 164.
3. For an account of the actions of the Heavy Brigade, see, for example, "Incidents of the Battle of the 25th," *John Bull and Britannia*, November 18, 1854, p. 725, issue 1771, *British Library Newspapers Part I: 1800–1900* (hereafter *BLN Part 1*).
4. See, for instance, Alexander William Kinglake, *Invasion of the Crimea*, Students' edition: abridged by G. S. Clarke, Sr. (Blackwood, 1899).
5. For one rendition of the event, see "The Charge of the Light Brigade," *Review of Reviews* 5, no. 29 (May 1892): 491, *British Periodicals, ProQuest* (hereafter *BPPQ*).
6. See, for instance, "A Vindication of Major-General the Earl of Lucan from Lord Raglan's Reflections about His Conduct in the Action at Balaklava," *Athenaeum*, July 14, 1855, p. 812, issue 1446; "Truths and Untruths about the Balaklava Charge," *Examiner*, June 28, 1856, p. 402, issue 2526; "Lord Cardigan's Chesnut [Sic] Horse," *London Review of Politics, Society, Literature, Art and Science* 6, no. 154 (June 13, 1863): 626; Archibald Forbes, "The Battle of Balaclava," *Contemporary Review* 59 (January/ March 1891): 428–40; Russell V. Steele, "The Light Brigade," *Saturday Review of Politics, Literature, Science, and Art* 156, no. 4073 (November 18, 1933): 520–21, all in *BPPQ*; George Charles Bingham, *Speech of Major General the Earl of Lucan, Delivered in the House of Lords* (Thomas

Hatchard, 1855); A Cavalry Officer, *The British Cavalry at Balaklava* (Charles Evans, 1855); Crimean Commission and the Chelsea Board, *Correspondence between Major-Gen the Earl of Lucan, KCB, and Gen Bacon, in Reference to the Pamphlet Entitled The English Cavalry at Balaclava* (G. J. Palmer, 1855); George Charles Bingham, *Reply of Major Gen the Earl of Lucan, KCB, Chelsea Inquiry* (Thomas Hatchard, 1856); George Ryan, *Was Lord Cardigan a Hero at Balaklava?* (James Wield, 1855).

7. On the news and the sense of anticipation in the press at this moment more generally, see "Before Sebastopol," *The Lady's Newspaper*, October 28, 1854, p. 259, issue 409, *BLN Part 1*.

8. Leader Comment, *Morning Chronicle*, November 2, 1854, p. 4, issue 27412, *BLN Part 1*; "Latest Intelligence," *Times*, November 4, 1854, p. 6, issue 21890 and Leader Comment, *Times*, November 6, 1854, p. 6, issue 21891, *TDA*.

9. Leader Comment, *Times*, November 13, 1854, p. 6, issue 21897 and Leader Comment, *Times*, November 6, 1854, p. 6, issue 21891, *TDA*. Captain Soame Gamber Jenyns of the 13th Hussars warned his family that, while they might "read many accounts of that disastrous day," that of the *Times'* special correspondent was "the only true account" that was going around. Typewritten transcription of a series of letters sent from the Crimea by Capt. Soame Gamber Jenyns, 13th Hussars, May 8, 1854 to January 27, 1856, NAM 2011–03–09.

10. "Latest Intelligence," *Times*, November 4, 1854, p. 6, issue 21890, *TDA*.

11. Leader Comment, *Times*, November 13, 1854, p. 6, issue 21897, *TDA*.

12. On the work of Russell in the Crimea, see Stefanie Markovits, "Rushing into Print: 'Participatory Journalism' in the Crimean War," *Victorian Studies* 50, no. 4 (Summer 2008): 559–86 and Markovits, *Crimean War*, chapter 1; Teukolsky, "Novels, Newspapers, and Global War" and more recently her *Picture World: Image, Aesthetics, and Victorian New Media* (Oxford University Press, 2020), chapter 2. More generally, see Kate McLoughlin, "War in Print Journalism" and John R. Reed, "The Victorians and War," in *The Cambridge Companion to War Writing*, ed. Kate McLoughlin (Cambridge University Press, 2009), 47–59 and 135–47.

13. Our Special Correspondent, "The Operations of the Siege," *Times*, November 14, 1854, p. 8, issue 21898, *TDA*. Russell's article was reprinted in many places. See, for instance, "Grand Cavalry Attack near Balaklava," *The Lady's Newspaper*, November 18, 1854, p. 305, issue 412, *BLN Part 1*.

14. See, for instance, typescript transcript of letter written by Australian Steamer, Sir William Gordon, Bart, 17th Lancers, to his mother, October 30, 1854, NAM 1983–10–132.

15. Manuscript transcript of two letters written to his father by Capt. Godfrey Charles Morgan, 17th Lancers, dated Balaklava October 27 and 31, 1854, describing the Charge of the Light Brigade; associated with the Battle of Balaklava, Crimean War (1854–1856), NAM 1979–03–2; bound duplicated typescript transcript of twenty-seven letters written by or relating to Maj. G. G. Clowes, 8th Hussars, of the period May 1854 to November 1859; associated with the Crimean War (1854–1856) and the

Indian Mutiny (1857–1859), NAM 1995–04–21; and typescript transcript of a letter written by Lt. Hedworth Hylton Jolliffe, October 28, 1854, NAM 1979–07–148.

16. Papers of Troop Sgt. Thomas Williamson, 11th Hussars, 1836–1870; associated with the Crimean War, includes: correspondence, music and a press cutting from *The Times*, NAM 1992–05–25.

17. Capt. Godfrey Charles Morgan letters, October 27 and 31, 1854; Lt. Hedworth Hylton Jolliffe letter, October 28, 1854; press cutting from the *Australian Sunday Times* of February 2, 1997 reprinting a letter first published in the *Western Illustrated Times* in 1876 giving Pte. Henry Naylor of the 13th Light Dragoons' account of the Charge of the Light Brigade, NAM 1997–05–7; and typescript copies of four letters written by Capt. Thomas Everard Hutton, 4th Light Dragoons after the Battle of Balaklava, October 1854; associated with the Crimean War (1854–1856), NAM 1967–07–16.

18. Lt. Hedworth Hylton Jolliffe letter, October 28, 1854; Sir William Gordon, Bart, letter, October 30, 1854; Capt. Soame Gamber Jenyns letters, May 8, 1854 to January 27, 1856.

19. "The Light Cavalry Charge on the 25th of October," *John Bull and Britannia*, November 18, 1854, p.734, issue 1771, *BLN Part 1*.

20. Capt. Soame Gamber Jenyns letters, May 8, 1854 to January 27, 1856.

21. Maj. G.G. Clowes letters, May 1854 to November 1859; Sir William Gordon, Bart, letter, October 30, 1854; Lt. Hedworth Hylton Jolliffe letter, October 28, 1854; photocopy of a contemporary manuscript transcript of a letter written by Lt. H. E. Handley, 2nd Dragoons, to his mother, dated Balaclava October 27, 1854, where he describes the battle of Balaklava in which he was wounded in the side, NAM 1981–10–69; two manuscript letters from William Archer Amherst, October 23 and 28, 1854; with letters from Frederick Paulet, John Wyatt, and H. M. Addington to Amherst's father, Lord Holmesdale, following the wounding of his son, NAM 1973–05–75.

22. Transcription of the Diary of Bandmaster Frederick Oliver, 20th Regiment of Foot, August 15 to October 30, 1854, especially October 24, 1854, NAM 2003–03–634.

23. Sir William Gordon, Bart, letter, October 30, 1854 and Lt. Hedworth Hylton Jolliffe letter, October 28, 1854.

24. Typescript copy of a letter written by "Robert," A Soldier in the 2nd Dragoons, Describing the Battle of Balaklava, dated "opposite Sevastopol," November 13, 1854, NAM 1972–10–68.

25. O'Toole, *Heroic Failure*, 73.

26. Two typescript copies of letters written by Lt. Henry B. Roberts, Royal Marine Artillery, 1854, to his family from No. 4 Battery, Balaklava, Crimea, NAM 1967–02–36.

27. "The Charge of the Light Cavalry Brigade," *ILN*, November 18, 1854, p. 502, issue 713, *ILNHA*.

28. "The Heroes of Balaklava," *John Bull and Britannia*, November 18, 1854, p. 726, issue 1771, *BLN Part 1*.

29. "The Heroes of Balaklava," *John Bull and Britannia*, November 18, 1854, p. 726, issue 1771, *BLN Part 1*.
30. Sir William Gordon, Bart, letter, October 30, 1854.
31. Capt. Soame Gamber Jenyns letters, May 8, 1854 to January 27, 1856.
32. Charge of the 21st, "Russian Officer's Memories of Balaclava," by an Old Resident in Russia, *Daily Telegraph*, September 7, 1898, p. 4, NAM 1972–03–36.
33. "The Heroes of Balaklava," *John Bull and Britannia*, November 18, 1854, p. 726, issue 1771, *BLN Part 1*; and Maj. G. G. Clowes letters, May 1854 to November 1859. See also Barczewski, *Heroic Failure and the British*; O'Toole, *Heroic Failure*.
34. Letter of Trooper Edward John Firkins, 13th Regiment of (Light) Dragoons, 1854. Manuscript, dated December 27, 1854, Camp before Sebastopol; associated with the Charge of the Light Brigade, Battle of Balaklava, Crimean War (1854–1856), NAM 1986–02–75; Capt. Thomas Everard Hutton, Letters after the Battle of Balaklava, October 1854.
35. Typescript transcript of the Letter Diary of Lt. (later Lt. Col.) Peake Newman, 47th Regiment of Foot, While Serving in the Crimea, August to November 1855, NAM 1996–07–70; Sir William Gordon, Bart, letter, October 30, 1854.
36. William Archer Amherst letters, October 23 and 28, 1854.
37. William Archer Amherst letters, October 23 and 28, 1854; Lt. Henry B. Roberts letters, 1854.
38. Capt. Soame Gamber Jenyns letters, May 8, 1854 to January 27, 1856; five letters written from the Crimea by N. Kingscote, Scots Guards, all addressed "My Dear Mapleton," especially November 13, 1854, NAM 1972–05–28–4; Trooper Edward John Firkins letter, December 27, 1854; Sir William Gordon, Bart, letter, October 30, 1854; and photostat copy of printed pamphlet, *Short Sketch of the 17th Lancers and Life of Sergt-Major J I Nunnerley, late of the Lancashire Hussars* (W. A. Guest, 1892), NAM 1971–08–3.
39. Capt. Soame Gamber Jenyns letters, May 8, 1854 to January 27, 1856.
40. Capt. Thomas Everard Hutton letters after the Battle of Balaklava, October 1854; Sir William Gordon, Bart, letter, October 30, 1854; Lt. Hedworth Hylton Jolliffe letter, October 28, 1854; William Archer Amherst letters, October 23 and 28, 1854; newspaper cutting, apparently from the *Cork Constitution* (Cork, Ireland), March 6, 1912, reproducing a statement by Lord Cardigan relating to the Charge of the Light Brigade, originally published in the *Army and Navy Gazette*, NAM 1990–06–400; Pte. Henry Naylor of the 13th Light Dragoons' account of the Charge of the Light Brigade; *Short Sketch of the 17th Lancers and Life of Sergt-Major J I Nunnerley*.
41. Brothers-in-law Lucan and Cardigan engaged in a vitriolic public contest as each defended himself and his reputation. See, for instance, *Speech of Major General the Earl of Lucan, Delivered in the House of Lords* on Monday, March 19, 1855; Crimean War Correspondence of Alexander William

Kinglake, MS. Add. 9554/3/1–3 (1863), Department of Manuscripts and University Archives, Cambridge University Library, Cambridge, UK.

42. See Markovits, *Crimean War*, chapter 3. See also Stefanie Markovits, "Giving Voice to the Crimean War: Tennyson's 'Charge' and Maud's Battle Song," *Victorian Poetry* 47, no. 3 (2009): 481–503.

43. "Charge of the Light Brigade," *Examiner*, December 9, 1854, p. 780, *BLN Part 1*. On the publication, see also Natalie M. Houston, "Reading the Victorian Souvenir: Sonnets and Photographs of the Crimean War," *Yale Journal of Criticism* 14, no. 2 (Fall 2001): 353–83.

44. For examples, see, among countless others, Richard Maxse Papers, Scrapbook 178, West Sussex Record Office, Chichester, UK; William Bance, *The Battle of Balaclava, or A Ballad* (Published by the Author, 1855); ΠΔ [sic], *Duty; Or, the Heroes of the Charge in the Valley of Balaklava* (Joseph Masters, 1854).

45. Tate, "On Not Knowing Why," 175.

46. Tate, "On Not Knowing Why," 173.

47. See Daniel Hack, "Wild Charges: The Afro-Haitian Charge of the Light Brigade," *Victorian Studies* 54, no. 2 (Winter 2012): 199–225; and Daniel Hack, *Reaping Something New: African-American Transformations of Victorian Literature* (Princeton University Press, 2016), chapter 2.

48. See, for instance, "The Charge of the Light Brigade," *Musical Times and Singing Class Circular* 31, no. 563 (January 1890): 40; "The Charge of the Light Brigade," *Musical Times and Singing Class Circular* 15, no. 359 (January 1873): 725, *BLN Part 1*.

49. "The Charge of the Six Hundred: A Personal Narrative of the Battle of Balaclava, as Told by a Survivor, at His Home in Battersea, and Set Down by Robert Shackleton," 1907, NAM 1988–08–61. See also Private James Lamb, "The Charge of the Light Brigade," *Strand Magazine* 2 (July 2, 1891): 348, *BPPQ*.

50. *The British Cavalry at Balaklava, Remarks in Reply to Lt. Gen the Earl of Lucan's Speech in the House of Lords, Published with an Appendix, by a Cavalry Officer*, p. 5. On the writing of this history, see Crimean War Correspondence of Alexander William Kinglake, MS. Add. 9554/3/1–3, Department of Manuscripts and University Archives, Cambridge University Library, Cambridge, UK.

51. Copies of Reviews from Various Newspapers of the Royal Academy Exhibition which included Elizabeth Thompson's *The Roll Call*, May 2 to June 2, 1874, NAM 1992–10–35; Matthew Lalumia, "Lady Elizabeth Thompson Butler in the 1870s," *Women's Art Journal* 4, no. 1 (Spring-Summer 1983): 9–14, especially p. 10.

52. See, for example, "The Balaklava Banquet," *Standard*, October 9, 1875, p. 6, issue 14976; "The Balaklava Banquet," *Morning Post*, October 26, 1875, p. 6, issue 3223826, *BLN Part 1*. See also *Fete in Commemoration of the Balaklava Charge, Programme* (R. K. Burt, Fleet Street, 1875), NAM 1964–11–55–2.

53. See mounted illustrated menu from the Balaklava Commemoration Banquet held at Alexandra Palace, October 25, 1875, NAM 1992–08–356.

54. "Balaclava Dinner," *Daily Mail*, October 26, 1910, p. 5, issue 4539, *DMHA*; "The Balaclava Anniversary Festival," *ILN*, October 1875, p. 438, issue 1890, *ILNHA*.
55. Two pamphlets: "Rules of the Balaklava Commemoration Society 1877, Including a List of the Then Survivors of the Charge of the Light Brigade"; "Programme of the Golden Commemoration of the Indian Mutiny Veterans at the Royal Albert Hall," December 23, 1907, NAM 1998–06–107.
56. Thomas Dixon, *Weeping Britannia: Portrait of a Nation in Tears* (Oxford University Press, 2015), 185, 8. On associationalism, see also Vernon, *Distant Strangers*. On the sentimental soldier, see Furneaux, *Military Men of Feeling*.
57. Two pamphlets: "Rules of the Balaklava Commemoration Society 1877" and "Programme of the Golden Commemoration."
58. Despite efforts to address these challenges, these deaths persisted into the twentieth century. See, for instance, "Officer's Pitiful End," *Daily Mail*, January 18, 1902, p. 3, issue 1794; and "Crimean Veteran's Death," *Daily Mail*, July 27, 1903, p. 3, issue 2269, *DMHA*. See also Peter Bailey, "Kipling's Bully Pulpit: Patriotism, Performance, and Publicity in the Victorian Music Hall," *Kipling Journal* 85, no. 41 (April 2011): 28–41.
59. Rudyard Kipling, "The Last of the Light Brigade," *St. James's Gazette*, April 28, 1890, p. 3, *BLN Part 1*. See also Rudyard Kipling, *Rudyard Kipling's Verse: Inclusive Edition, 1885–1918* (Doubleday, 1922), 328–30.
60. See, for example, "Last Light Brigade Officer Dies; Kipling Poem Discovered," *New York Times*, November 2, 1913, p. 8, at www .nytimes.com/1913/11/02/archives/last-light-brigade-officer-dies-kipling-poem-discovered-anniversary.html.
61. "Light Brigade Relief Fund," *Lloyd's Weekly Newspaper*, May 15, 1892, p. 9, issue 2582, *BLN Part 1*.
62. "The Light Brigade Relief Fund," *Morning Post*, May 20, 1890, p. 5, issue 36794, *BLN Part 1*.
63. "Who Will Help the Remnant of the Light Brigade?," *Lloyd's Weekly Newspaper*, June 1, 1890, p. 9, issue 2480; "Who Will Help the Remnant of the Light Brigade?," *Lloyd's Weekly Newspaper*, June 8, 1890, p. 9, issue 2481, *BLN Part 1*.
64. "News of the Day," *Birmingham Daily Post*, June 24, 1890, p. 4, issue 9984; "Shipping and Mail News," *Birmingham Daily Post*, July 10, 1890, p. 8, issue 9998, *BLN Part 1*.
65. See, for instance, Alfred Charles Jonas, *An Unassuming Crimean Veteran: Major Read, Thornton Heath, Reprinted from the Croydon Guardian* (London, Guardian Offices,1907); John J. Sullivan, *Our Veterans: Heroes of the Crimea and the Mutiny* (Sherratt and Hughes, 1908); W. T. Jervis-Waldy, *From Eight to Eighty: The Life of a Crimean and Indian Mutiny Veteran* (Harrison and Sons, 1914).
    Examples of local press coverage include "Sheffield Veterans' Gathering," *Sheffield and Rotherham Independent*, January 15, 1900, p. 7, issue 14096; "Darlington Veteran's Dinner," *Northern Echo*, February 20, 1900, p. 4, issue

9347; "Army Veterans' Picnic," *Huddersfield Daily Chronicle*, July 30, 1900, p. 3, issue 10297; "An Interview with a Crimean Veteran," *Devon and Exeter Daily Gazette*, January 10, 1905, p. 10, issue 18140; "Veterans' Last Roll Call," *Manchester Courier and Lancashire General Advertiser*, December 24, 1907, p. 6, issue 15953; "Veterans' Bazaar," *Manchester Courier and Lancashire General Advertiser*, May 22 1908, p. 5, issue 16081; "Dundee Veteran's Adventure," *Evening Telegraph and Post*, May 5, 1919, p. 3, *BLN Part 1*.

66. "Light Brigade Relief Fund," *Morning Post*, August 1, 1890, p. 2, issue 36857; and "Naval and Military," *Daily News*, August 1, 1890, p. 6, issue 13829, *BLN Part 1*.

67. "Light Brigade Relief Fund," *Newcastle Weekly Courant*, April 11, 1891, p. 2, issue 11282, *BLN Part 1*.

68. Leader Comment, *Morning Post*, April 6, 1891, p. 5, issue 37069, *BLN Part 1*. On efforts to increase payments from the fund, see Light Brigade Relief Fund: Attorney-General versus Commissioners of the Patriotic Fund, TS 18/322, The National Archives, Kew, UK (hereafter TNA).

69. "The Light Brigade Relief Fund," *Morning Post*, April 6, 1891, p. 3, issue 37069, *BLN Part 1*.

70. "The Light Brigade Relief Fund," *Standard*, March 4, 1891, p. 2, issue 20797, *BLN Part 1*.

71. "The Balaclava Relief Fund," *Standard*, March 7, 1891, p. 3, issue 20800, *BLN Part 1*.

72. "The Light Brigade Relief Fund," *Lloyd's Weekly Newspaper*, May 15, 1892, p. 9, issue 2582, *BLN Part 1*.

73. "Our Neglected Heroes," *Dundee Courier and Argus*, August 26, 1893, p. 3, issue 12527, *BLN Part 1*.

74. "The Balaklava Banquet," *Saturday Review of Politics, Literature, Science, and Art* 40, no. 1044 (October 30, 1875): 545–46, *BPPQ*.

75. "The Balaklava Subscription," *Saturday Review of Politics, Literature, Science, and Art* 69, no. 1808 (June 21, 1890): 760, *BPPQ*.

76. "Topics of the Week: Our Starving Heroes," *Graphic*, May 24, 1890, p. 578, issue 1069, *BLN Part 1*.

77. Cavendish L. Fitzroy, "The Light Brigade Relief Fund," *Morning Post*, May 22, 1890, p. 5, issue 36796, *BLN Part 1*.

78. W. C. Galton, "The Light Brigade Relief Fund," *Morning Post*, May 26, 1890, p. 3, issue 36799, *BLN Part 1*.

79. On resentment of the Cavalry, see, for instance, Crimean War Letters, 1854–1856, being mainly family letters written home by Assistant Surgeon Edward Mason Wrench, with associated correspondence: collected, collated, and transcribed by Edward Gillam Wrench, 1954, Wre C 4b. nos. 336–337, University of Nottingham Special Collections, Nottingham, UK.

80. "Reminiscences of Balaklava," *ILN*, November 3, 1894, p. 556, issue 2898, *ILNHA*.

81. T. H. Roberts, "When Shall Their Glory Fade?" *Daily Mail*, October 13, 1909, p. 4, issue 4215 and "Far and Near," *Daily Mail*, September 22, 1915, p. 3, issue 6075, *DMHA*.

82. T.H. Roberts, "When Shall Their Glory Fade?" *Daily Mail*, October 13, 1909, p. 4, issue 4215; T. H. Roberts, "Balaclava Survivors Fund," *Daily Mail*, May 15, 1905, p. 4, issue 2833 and T. H. Roberts, "Balaclava Survivors Fund," *Daily Mail*, July 2, 1906, n.p., issue 3187, *DMHA*. See also Title Royal, Crimea and Indian Mutiny Veterans' Association, TNA HO 144/775/124030.

83. Two especially active associations were in Nottingham and Bristol. On the Crimea and Indian Mutiny Veterans' Association of Nottingham and Nottinghamshire, see Files M1373-M1418, Nottinghamshire Archives, Nottingham, UK.

84. "The Last of the 600," *Daily Mail*, October 26, 1907, p. 5, issue 3600, *DMHA*.

85. "Balaclava Dinner," *Daily Mail*, October 25, 1913, p. 3, issue 5477, *DMHA*.

86. "Balaclava Dinner," *Daily Mail*, October 25, 1913, p. 3, issue 5477, *DMHA*.

87. Lara Kriegel, "Living Links to History, or, Victorian Veterans in the Twentieth- Century World," *Victorian Studies* 58, no. 2 (Winter 2016): 298–301.

88. On the War, more generally, as a relic of the past, see, for instance, Major Arthur Griffiths, "The Army in the Victorian Era," *ILN*, May 14, 1911, p. 55, special issue, *ILNHA*.

89. See "Trying to Enlist at 83," *Derby Daily Telegraph*, January 3, 1916, p. 4, issue 11331, *BLN Part 1*. For a similar article on a Crimean Veteran and the Second Anglo-Boer War, see "A Sheffield Crimean Veteran. Lives Again His Experiences," *Sheffield Daily Telegraph*, January 14, 1904, p. 3, issue 15135, *BLN Part 1*.

90. See, for instance, *Yearbook of the Crimea and Indian Mutiny Veterans' Association*, 1896; *Handbook of the Crimea and Indian Mutiny Veterans' Association*, 1892–1912, 40386, Bristol Archives, Bristol, UK. See also Glenn Fisher's recent PhD dissertation, "The Crimea and Indian Mutiny Veterans' Associations of the 1890s."

91. See Photograph, 2014, *Bristol Crimea and Indian Mutiny Veterans' Association*, 1907–1914, 28049.a 29, Bristol Archives, Bristol, UK. On changing notions of manhood in wartime and after, see Michael Roper, "Between Manliness and Masculinity: The 'War Generation' and the Psychology of Fear in Britain, 1914–1950," *Journal of British Studies* 44 (April 2005): 343–62.

92. The classic work here is, of course, Paul Fussell's *Great War and Modern Memory* (Oxford University Press, 1975).

93. Wilfred Owen, "Dulce et Decorum Est," October 1917–March 1918, *First World War Digital Poetry Archive*.

94. www.poetryfoundation.org/poems/57409/epitaphs-of-the-war.

95. John Meredith, *Omdurman Diaries 1898* (Pen and Sword, 1990).

96. Stephen Badsey, *Doctrine and Reform in the British Cavalry, 1880–1918* (Ashgate, 2008).

97. Brian Tilley, *Tynedale in the Great War* (Pen and Sword, 2015), chapter 1.

98. W. T. Massey and General Allenby, "Turks Sabered at Their Guns," *Daily Mail*, November 13, 1917, p. 3, issue 6743, *DMHA*; and Jane Kelly, "At the Cry of 'Charge!,'" *Daily Mail*, December 28, 1996, pp. 34–35, issue 31274, *DMHA*.

99. John Winton, "The Modern Cavalry," *ILN*, July 30, 1983, p. 3, issue 7020, *ILNHA* and Our Special Correspondent, and Exchange, "Rebels Fine Town," *Daily Mail*, July 4, 1936, p. 11, issue 12541, *DMHA*. On the Cavalry in World War I, see also Badsey, *Doctrine and Reform*.

100. For an excellent collective biography of those who participated in the Charge, see Roy Dutton, *Forgotten Heroes: The Charge of the Light Brigade* (InfoDial, 2007).

101. On Balaklava Ned, see http://news.bbc.co.uk/local/northeastwales/hi/peo ple_and_places/history/newsid_8170000/8170593.stm. For interest in other long-lived veterans, see, for instance, "Burial of Scotland's Oldest Veteran," *Aberdeen Daily Journal*, May 26, 1915, p. 6, issue 18841; and "A Crimean Veteran Still Working at 80," *Essex County Chronicle*, June 3, 1910, p. 6, issue 7602, *BLN Part 1*.

102. John Winton, "The Modern Cavalry," *ILN*, July 30, 1983, p. 3, issue 7020, *ILNHA* and Our Special Correspondent, and Exchange, "Rebels Fine Town." See also Badsey, *Doctrine and Reform*.

103. Tate, "On Not Knowing Why," 160.

104. Virginia Woolf, *To the Lighthouse* (Harcourt, 1927). On modernism and First World War writing, see Trudi Tate, *Modernism, History and the First World War* (Manchester University Press, 1998); Das, *Touch and Intimacy in First World War Literature*.

105. John Squire, "The Riddle of the Immortal Charge," *ILN*, November 28, 1953, p. 866, issue 5980, *ILNHA*.

106. Woodham-Smith, *The Reason Why*; "Success Still Surprises Her," *Daily Mail*, November 5, 1953, p. 6, issue 17925, *DMHA*.

107. "Book of the Month," *Daily Mail*, November 6, 1953, p. 6, issue 17925, *DMHA*.

108. "Royal Occasions, a Political Landmark, and Home Items of Particular Interest," *ILN*, December 4, 1954, p. 998, issue 6033, *ILNHA*.

109. Joseph Minogue, "Last Battle for Hero of Light Brigade," *Guardian*, December 28, 1967, p. 2, issue 37779, *Guardian and Observer Digital Archive*. For another manifestation of local interest, see Alfred H. Robinson Scrapbook, volume 3, Clipping from *Beccles and Bungay Journal*, June 6, 1969, 44D91/3, Bradford, West Yorkshire Archive Service.

110. Typescript pamphlet, "Nunnerley and Co at Balaclava, The Story of a Shropshire Hero," written by A. Allwood, 1854, NAM 1968–03–21.

111. Eleven press cuttings, April 1964, relating to the sale at Sotheby's on April 20 of the bugle of W. Brittain, 17th Lancers who reputedly sounded the charge of the Light Brigade at Balaklava, NAM 1976–07–28.

112. Eleven press cuttings, NAM 1976–07–28.

113. Eleven press cuttings, NAM 1976–07–28.

114. Letters, press cuttings, programs, 1854; relating to the Bugle of Tpt. Maj. Joy, 17th Lancers, said to have been used at the Charge of the Light Brigade; with printed pamphlet, "The World's Most Famous Bugle" published in Newcastle, 1906 (c), NAM 1972–03–36.

115. Letters, press cuttings, programs, 1854, relating to the Bugle of Tpt. Maj. Joy, 17th Lancers. On this episode, see Lara Kriegel, "Who Blew the Balaklava Bugle?: The Charge of the Light Brigade and the Afterlife of the Crimean War," *19: Interdisciplinary Studies in the Long Nineteenth Century* 20 (2015).

116. Ian Wright, "The Heavyweight Brigade," *Guardian*, April 13, 1968, p. 7, issue 37870, *Guardian and Observer Digital Archive*.

117. John Gale, "Charge of the Light Brigade? More Like Commanding an Army than Making a Film," *Observer*, March 3, 1968, p. 7, issue 9216, *Guardian and Observer Digital Archive*.

118. See Press Pack for the 1968 Film, "The Charge of the Light Brigade," NAM 2007–02–10.

119. This film is mostly known today for the cruel treatment of horses which led to new US standards for animals in the industry.

120. See Press Pack for the 1968 Film. On Richardson's efforts at historical fidelity, see Correspondence between Sir Basil Liddle Hart and Tony Richardson, July 1966, LH13/65: Films, Liddell Hart Centre for Military Archives, Kings College, London, UK.

121. Alison Adburgham, "The Charge of the Rag Brigade," *Guardian*, March 21, 1968, p. 9, issue 37851, *Guardian and Observer Digital Archive*.

122. I employ this term in an appreciative, if challenging nod to "The Manifesto of the V21 Collective."

123. See Press Pack for the 1968 Film.

124. Michael Billington, "Futuristic Thriller," *ILN*, May 4, 1968, p. 28, issue 6718, *ILNHA*.

125. See Press Pack for the 1968 Film.

126. See, for e.g., John Russell Taylor, "The Charge and the Film," *Times*, April 13, 1968, p. 21, issue 57225, *TDA*.

127. Billington, "Futuristic Thriller"; Wright, "Heavyweight Brigade."

128. "Charge of the Light Brigade Restaurant," September 25, 1965, p. 6, issue 37081, *Guardian and Observer Digital Archive*.

129. O'Toole, *Heroic Failure*, 77.

130. See "The Charge of the Light Brigade," *Judy, or the London Serio-Comic Journal* 30 (January 4, 1882): 10, *BPPQ*.

131. www.nottinghampost.com/trumpeter-brittain-s-bugle-hole-cossack/story-19901513-detail/story.html.

132. www.mirror.co.uk/tv/tv-news/charge-light-brigade-bugle-star-2339839.

133. "Bugle Which Sent 673 Cavalrymen into the 'Valley of Death' in the Charge of the Light Brigade Turns Up on Antiques Roadshow," *Daily Mail*, October 4, 2013, at www.dailymail.co.uk/news/article-2443739/Bugle-sounded-orders-Charge-Light-Brigade-673-cavalrymen-headed-Valley-Death-turns-Antiques-Road-Show.html.

3   The Brave

1. "From the London Gazette," *Daily News*, February 6, 1856, p. 3, issue 3033, *BLN Part 1*.
2. "The New Order of Valour," *Reynolds's Newspaper*, February 10, 1856, p. 6, issue 287, *BLN Part 1*. See also Melvin Charles Smith, *Awarded for Valour: A History of the Victoria Cross and the Evolution of Heroism* (Palgrave, 2008), 43.
3. "Review of Holders of the Victoria Cross in Hyde Park, 26 June, 1956, The Queen's Speech," NAM 1971–12–37.
4. These stipulations were reproduced widely. For the original warrant, see Original Royal Warrant, signed by Her Majesty Queen Victoria, January 29, 1856, 98/1, The National Archives, War Office Records, Kew, UK (hereafter TNA WO).
5. "The Victoria Cross," *Saturday Review of Politics, Literature, Science, and Art* 1, no. 15 (February 9, 1856): 272–73, especially p. 272, *BPPQ*.
6. See, for e.g., O'Byrne, Robert W. *The Victoria Cross: An Official Chronicle of the Deeds of Personal Valour* (O'Byrne Bros., 1865), vii.
7. "Distribution of the Victoria Cross," *Reynolds's Newspaper*, June 28, 1857, p. 5, issue 359, *BLN Part 1*.
8. The annuity was initially £10. It was raised to £50 at the turn of the century, to £100 in 1959 and to £10,000 in 2015. On this last innovation, see Patrick Wintour, "George Osborne to Raise Victoria Cross and George Cross Payments to £10,000," *Guardian*, July 7, 2015, at www.theguardian.com /uk-news/2015/jul/07/george-osborne-to-raise-victoria-cross-and-george-cross-payments-to-10000; Farwell, *Queen Victoria's Little Wars*.
9. Eric Hobsbawm, "Introduction: Inventing Traditions," in *The Invention of Tradition*, ed. Eric Hobsbawm and Terence Ranger (Cambridge University Press, 1983), 2.
10. Beckett, *Victorians at War*, 167.
11. Scott Hughes Myerly, *British Military Spectacle: From the Napoleonic Wars through the Crimea* (Harvard University Press, 1996), 75. See also Introduction and chapters 1–2.
12. Alexis Troubetzkoy, *A Brief History of the Crimean War* (Robinson, 2006), 37.
13. Farwell, *Queen Victoria's Little Wars*, 69.
14. Heather Streets, *Martial Races: The Military, Race and Masculinity in British Imperial Culture, 1857–1914* (Manchester University Press, 2010), 19–22; Myerly, *British Military Spectacle*, 3, 5; Beckett, *Victorians at War*, 176.
15. See, for e.g., Max Hastings, *The Oxford Book of Military Anecdotes* (Oxford University Press, 1985), 223.
16. Streets, *Martial Races*, 19–22.
17. Beckett, *Victorians at War*, 177; Leader Comment, *Morning Chronicle*, June 26, 1857, p. 4, issue 28240, *BLN Part 1*.
18. Troubetzkoy, *Brief History of the Crimean War*, 21.

19. Beckett, *Victorians at War*, 171; Anderson, *Liberal State at War*, 4–5; "The New Order of Valour," *Reynolds's Newspaper*, February 10, 1856, p. 6, issue 287, *BLN Part 1*.

20. Streets, *Martial Races*, 11, 21; Anderson, *Liberal State at War*, 27.

21. Markovits, *Crimean War*, Introduction and chapters 1–2. See also Bradley Deane, "Imperial Boyhood: Piracy and the Play Ethic," *Victorian Studies* 53, no. 4 (Summer 2011): 689–714. On military and imperial masculinity as backward-looking, see John Tosh, "Masculinities in an Industrializing Society: Britain, 1800–1914," *Journal of British Studies* 44, no. 2 (April 2005): 330–42; for preceding notions of chivalry, see Michèle Cohen, "'Manners' Make the Man: Politeness, Chivalry, and the Construction of Masculinity, 1750–1830," *Journal of British Studies* 44 (April 2005): 312–29. See also Bertrand Wyatt Brown's classic study, *Honor and Violence in the Old South* (Oxford University Press, 1986). On World War I and chivalry, see Stefan Goebel, *The Great War and Medieval Memory: War, Remembrance, and Medievalism in Britain and Germany, 1914–1940* (Cambridge University Press, 2007).

22. Smith, *Awarded for Valour*, 26.

23. There was, of course, the Order of the Bath, but it was restricted to officers only, and even this honor precluded lieutenants and captains. See Smith, *Awarded for Valour*, 29, 35, and chapter 2 more generally.

24. Original Warrant found in Correspondence and Papers Concerning the Victoria Cross, 1856–1977, TNA WO 98/1.

25. "The New 'Order of Valour,'" *Lloyd's Weekly Newspaper*, February 10, 1856, p. 3, issue 690, *BLN Part 1*. See also "The New Order of Valour," *Reynolds's Newspaper*, February 10, 1856, p. 6, issue 287, *BLN Part 1*.

26. "The Victoria Cross," *Saturday Review of Politics, Literature, Science, and Art* 1, no. 15 (February 9, 1856): 272–73, especially p. 272, *BPPQ*.

27. "Reward of Valour," *Morning Chronicle*, February 26, 1857, p. 4, issue 28137, *BLN Part 1*. See also "The Victoria Cross," *Leader and Saturday Analyst* 8, no. 362 (February 28, 1857): 206, *BPPQ*.

28. "Spirit of the Press (from *Lloyd's*)," *Caledonian Mercury*, February 28, 1857, p. 6, issue 21037, *BLN Part 1*.

29. "Military Honours," *Saturday Review of Politics, Literature, Science, and Art* 4, no. 108 (November 21, 1857): 461–62, *BPPQ*.

30. See "The Victoria Cross," *Leader and Saturday Analyst* 8, no. 362 (February 28, 1857): 206, *BPPQ*.

31. "Reward of Valour," *Morning Chronicle*, February 26, 1857, p. 4, issue 28137, *BLN Part 1*. See also "The Victoria Cross," *Saturday Review of Politics, Literature, Science, and Art* 1, no. 15 (February 9, 1856): 272–73, especially p. 272, *BPPQ*.

32. "Distribution of the Victoria Cross for Valour," *Liverpool Mercury*, June 29, 1857 (as excerpted from the *Times* of June 27, 1857), p. 6, issue 3001, *BLN Part 1*.

33. "Reward of Valour," *Morning Chronicle*, February 26, 1857, p. 4, issue 28137, *BLN Part 1*.

34. "Summary: From *The Globe,*" *Liverpool Mercury,* February 27, 1857, p. 8, issue 2949, *BLN Part 1.*
35. See, for e.g., Lecture Notes on the Victoria Cross, c. 1945, WKR/BZ/Z6, Kent Archives and Local History Library, Maidstone, UK (hereafter Kent Archives).
36. On the Lucas cross, see Victoria Cross Details of Charles D. Lucas, June 21, 1854, TNA WO 98/3/4.
37. See Victoria Cross: Details of Charles Henry Lumley, 1856–1864, TNA WO 98/3/76; on the Lumley Cross, see also WKR/B2/Z9, Kent Archives.
38. Victoria Cross Details of Private John Alexander, TNA WO 98/3/75.
39. "The Victoria Cross," *Leader and Saturday Analyst* 8, no. 362 (February 28, 1857): 206, *BPPQ.*
40. See, for e.g., Lecture Notes on the Victoria Cross, c. 1945, WKR/BZ/Z6, Kent Archives.
41. Richard Vinen, "The Victoria Cross," *History Today* 56, no. 12 (2006): 50–57.
42. "The Victoria Cross," *Bristol Mercury,* July 4, 1857, Supplement p. 4, issue 3511, *BLN Part 1.*
43. "The Distribution of the Victoria Cross," *John Bull and Britannia,* July 4, 1857, p. 424, issue 1908, *BLN Part 1.*
44. Lord William Lennox, *The Victoria Cross: The Rewarded and their Services* (John Mitchell, 1857).
45. See, for e.g., Extract of Letter from Col. Lacy Yea to General Weatherall, June 15, 1855, CR341/324/31 and Letter from A. Greig to Sir Thomas Wathen Waller, July 3, 1855, CR341/324/36, Waller Family Papers: George Henry Waller, Warwickshire County Record Office, Warwick, UK.
46. See, for e.g., Letter from C. Yorke to Sir Thomas Wathen Waller, December 19, 1856, CR0341/309g, Waller Family Papers. The War Office made note of Waller's gallantry, but it did not award him the Cross – perhaps because Colonel Yea, who might have greased the wheels, had passed away in June of 1855.
47. "Application of Mr. Henry Evelyn Wood, Lieutenant of the 17th Lancers, for the Victoria Cross," TNA WO 32/7307.
48. See Correspondence between Military Secretary, Adjutant General, and Corporal Courtney, April–May 1858, TNA WO 98/2.
49. "Claim by T. Morley, 17th Lancers, for Victoria Cross and Pension," TNA WO 32/7483.
50. Victoria Cross: Awards to be Retrospective from Commencement of Crimean War, Application by Mother of Captain Jary, 12th Lancers, February 1856, TNA WO 32/7299.
51. Victoria Cross: Posthumous Awards Not Admissible, Application by Father of Lieutenant Godfrey, Rifle Brigade, 1856, TNA WO 32/7300.
52. "The New Order of Valour," *Reynolds's Newspaper,* February 10, 1856, p. 6, issue 287, *BLN Part 1.* See, for e.g., "A New Order of Merit," *Reynolds's Newspaper,* February 10, 1856, p. 9, issue 287; and "London Correspondence," *Leeds Mercury,* February 12, 1856, p. 2, issue 6441, *BLN Part 1.*

53. Peter Burroughs, "An Unreformed Army? 1815–1868," in *The Oxford History of the British Army*, ed. David G. Chandler and Ian Beckett (Oxford University Press, 1994), 169, 171.
54. Smith, *Awarded for Valour*, chapter 3, especially p. 50. See also Soldier, "The Victoria Cross," *Times*, October 24, 1901, p. 10, issue 36594, *TDA*.
55. "Military Honours," *Saturday Review of Politics, Literature, Science, and Art* 4, no. 108 (November 21, 1857): 461–62, *BPPQ*.
56. Vinen, "Victoria Cross." On the use of the lash for crimes like drunkenness/sleeping on watch in the Crimea see "Legree in the Army," *Stirling Observer*, January 17, 1856; "The Cat before Sebastopol," *Lloyd's Illustrated Newspaper*, March 4, 1855; "Cat-O'-Nine-Tailing in the Crimea," *Reynolds's Newspaper*, January 27, 1856, *BLN Part 1*.
57. "The New Order of Merit," *Reynolds's Newspaper*, February 10, 1856, *BLN Part 1*.
58. "Savage and Ferocious Treatment of the English Soldier," *Reynolds's Newspaper*, January 6, 1856, *BLN Part 1*.
59. See, for instance, Lennox, *Victoria Cross*, 3.
60. Smith, *Awarded for Valour*, 15.
61. For coverage of the occasion, see "Distribution of the Victoria Cross in Hyde Park by Her Majesty," *ILN*, July 4, 1857, p. 22, issue 867; "The Distribution of the Victoria Cross," *ILN*, July 11, 1857, p. 42, issue 868, *ILNHA*. "Military Honours," *Saturday Review of Politics, Literature, Science, and Art* 4, no. 108 (November 21, 1857): 461–62, *BPPQ*. See also A. L. Haydon, *The Book of the V.C.* (Melrose, 1906), 1–2.
62. Diary of Frederick W. Chesson, August 1854 to October 1855, entry of October 10, 1854, GB 133 REAS/11/2, Rylands Library, University of Manchester, UK.
63. Diary of Frederick W. Chesson, June 1856 to July 1857, entry of June 26, 1857, GB 133 REAS/11/4, Rylands Library, University of Manchester, UK.
64. "The Victoria Cross," *Saturday Review of Politics, Literature, Science, and Art* 1, no. 15 (February 9, 1856): 272–73, especially p. 272, *BPPQ*.
65. Colonial troops became eligible for the award in 1867.
66. See, for e.g., Regenia Gagnier, "'From Fag to Monitor; Or, Fighting to the Front': Art and Power in Public School Memoirs," *Browning Institute Studies* 16 (1988): 15–38. On the enduring appeal of this sort of literature, see Deane, "Imperial Boyhood"; Lara Kriegel, "The Strange Career of Fair Play, or, Warfare and Gamesmanship in the Time of Victoria," in *The Oxford Handbook of Victorian Literary Culture*, ed. Juliet John (Oxford University Press, 2016), 268–83.
67. Victoria Cross Details of Henry Evelyn Wood, Lieutenant, 17th Lancers, TNA WO 98/3/204.
68. "The Jubilee of a Famous Deed of the Mutiny: How Lord Roberts Won the Victoria Cross," *ILN*, January 11, 1908, pp. 2–3, issue 3566, *ILNHA*.
69. Brian Best, *The Victoria Crosses that Saved an Empire: The Story of the VCs of the Indian Mutiny* (Pen and Sword, 2016).
70. On trauma and 1857, see, especially, Herbert, *War of No Pity*.

71. On this Gallery, see Joany Hirchberger, "Democratising Glory? The Victoria Cross Paintings of Louis Desanges," *Oxford Art Journal* 7, no. 2 (1984): 42–51.

72. Victoria Cross Details of Robert James Lindsay, TNA WO 98/3/46.

73. "How the Victoria Cross was Won," *All the Year Round*, May 28, 1859, pp. 50–55, issue 15, *BPPQ*.

74. "The Victoria Cross Gallery," *Athenaeum*, April 7, 1860, p. 480, issue 1693, *BPPQ*. See also "Stories of Soldiers," *Saturday Review of Politics, Literature, Science and Art* 24, no. 617 (August 24, 1867): 262, *BPPQ*.

75. On the opening of the gallery see "Victoria Cross Gallery," *ILN*, June 2, 1860, p. 537, issue 1033–34; and "The Victoria Cross Gallery," *ILN*, July 13, 1861, p. 41, issue 1098, *ILNHA*. On the Wantage Gallery, see Irene Hancock, "The Victoria Cross Gallery and the 'Deeds of Valour,'" Vale and Downland Museum: Local History Series. Reproduced from *The Blowing Stone* (1992–1993).

76. Samuel O. Beeton, *Our Soldiers and the Victoria Cross* (Ward, Lock, and Tyler, 1867). For similar, subsequent publications, see also William Wallingford Knollys, *The Victoria Cross in the Crimea* (Dean and Son, 1876) and J. E. Muddock, *For Valour: The Victoria Cross* (Hutchinson, 1895). For a fictionalized example, see Louisa Thompson, *Winning the Victoria Cross, or the Story of Rex* (Estes and Laurait, 1895).

77. "Our Soldiers and the Victoria Cross," *Examiner*, November 2, 1867, p. 694, issue 3118, *BPPQ*.

78. Beeton, *Our Soldiers and the Victoria Cross*, v.

79. Samuel Smiles, *Self-Help, with Illustrations of Character and Conduct* (John Murray, 1859).

80. "Our Soldiers and the Victoria Cross," *Athenaeum*, 1867, pp. 110–11, especially 110, issue 2074, *BPPQ*.

81. See, for e.g., "'Lucknow' Kavanagh and the Victoria Cross," *Boy's Own Magazine* [Date Unknown], p. 413, issue 11, *BLN Part 1*.

82. Thomas Henry Kavanagh, *How I Won the Victoria Cross* (Ward and Lock, 1860).

83. For this formulation, I am indebted to the work of Stefanie Markovits. See "Rushing into Print," 559–86.

84. "Lucknow Kavanagh," *Chambers's Journal of Popular Literature, Science, and Arts* 14, no. 355 (October 20, 1860): 251–54, especially p. 251, *BPPQ*.

85. "The Victoria Cross," *Saturday Review of Politics, Literature, Science, and Art* 6, no. 145 (August 7, 1858): 129–30, *BPPQ*.

86. Vinen, "Victoria Cross"; "The New Order of Merit," *Morning Chronicle*, February 6, 1856, p. 5, issue 27805, *BLN Part 1*.

87. James Maguire, Late Sergeant 1st Bengal Fusiliers, Removed from Register of Holders of Cross, 1862–1863, TNA WO 32/7359; see also, for e.g., Edward St. John Daniel, Late Lieutenant, Royal Navy, Removed from Register of Holders of Cross, TNA WO 32/7358; Frederick Corbett, Private, Removed from Register of Holders of Cross, TNA WO 32/7485.

88. See Smith, *Awarded for Valour*, 108.

89. See, for e.g., "Presentation of the Victoria Cross on Southsea Common," *ILN*, October 7, 1865, p. 333, issue 1337; and "The Queen at Netley Hospital," *ILN*, May 21, 1898, p. 727, issue 3803, *ILNHA*.

90. See "Saving the Guns at Colenso," National Army Museum Online Collection, at https://collection.nam.ac.uk/detail.php?acc=1970-10-9-1.

91. "The Queen is Not Always Able to Pin on to the Breast of Her Heroes the Victoria Cross 'For Valour', the Pathetic Fact Being That in Many Cases They Have Not Lived to Receive the Coveted Recognition," *ILN*, April 7, 1900, n.p., issue 3181, *ILNHA*.

92. On the Crimean career and death of Archibald Clevland, see Letters and Papers of Archibald Clevland, 1833–1881, D2455/F4/3/3/5, Gloucestershire Archives, Gloucester, UK. See also Thomas Morley, "The Cross of Valor," *Times*, April 24, 1857, p. 10, issue 22663, *TDA*.

93. "Application of J. Morley," TNA WO 32/7483.

94. "A Nottingham Crimean Veteran: Hero of the Balaclava Charge," *Nottingham Daily Guardian*, August 18, 1906, Nottingham and Nottinghamshire Crimea and Indian Mutiny Veterans' Association, M1373–M1418, Nottinghamshire Archives, Nottingham, UK. On the persistence of chivalry in the Edwardian era, see Lucy Delap, "'Thus Does Man Prove his Fitness to Be the Master of Things': Shipwrecks, Chivalry, and Masculinities in Nineteenth- and Twentieth-Century Britain," *Cultural and Social History* 3, no. 1 (2006): 45–74; for an understanding of monarchical politics and traditional institutions as central to provincial consensus, see Frank Mort, "Safe for Democracy: Constitutional Politics, Popular Spectacle, and the British Monarchy 1910–1914," *Journal of British Studies* 58, no. 1 (2019): 109–41.

95. "New Warrant: Superceding All Previous Regulations, 22 May 1920," as printed in Smith, *Awarded for Valour*, 216–18.

96. Sardar Asghar Ali, *Our Heroes of the Great War: A Record of the VCs Won by the Indian Army during the Great War* (Times Press, 1922).

97. See Ronan McGreevy, "The Life and Troubled Times of an Authentic Irish War Hero," *Irish Times Online*, January 30, 2015.

98. George Bernard Shaw, *O'Flaherty, VC*, 1915; Studio City: Players Press, 2001. For an earlier satire and critique, see Lt. Gen. H. J. Stannus, *Curiosities of the Victoria Cross* (Ridgway, 1882).

99. Rudyard Kipling, "Winning the Victoria Cross," in *Land and Sea Tales for Scouts and Guides* (Doubleday, Page, 1923), 3. For another assessment of childhood and war's legacies in the interwar era, see Susannah Wright, "War and Peace: Armistice Observance in British Schools in 1937," *Journal of the History of Childhood and Youth* 13, no. 3 (2020): 426–45.

100. Kipling, "Winning the Victoria Cross," 20–22.

101. Ruth Sheppard, *Extraordinary Heroes: Amazing Stories of Victoria Cross and George Cross Recipients* (Osprey, 2010), 92–93.

102. Frances Smyth, Introduction to *The Only Enemy: An Autobiography*, by Brig. Sir John Smyth (Hutchinson, 1959), 11–13.

103. Smyth, *Only Enemy*, 118.

104. Smyth, *Only Enemy*, 330.

105. *VC Dinner at the Gallery of the House of Lords* (1929), IWM. See also Papers Associated with Victoria Cross Dinner, NAM 1970–09–12 and Invitation Card and Programme to Victoria Cross Dinner, NAM 2001–02–16.
106. Theatre Program with VC Autographs, 1929, Documents.10268, IWM. On the play and its legacies, see Emily Curtis Walters, "Between Entertainment and Elegy: The Unexpected Success of R. C. Sherriff's *Journey's End* (1928)," *Journal of British Studies* 55, no. 2 (2016): 344–73.
107. Smyth, *Only Enemy*, 333.
108. Smyth, *Only Enemy*, 333–34.
109. Victoria Cross Details of James Hewitson, TNA WO 98/8/48.
110. On World War I veterans and disability, see Julie Anderson, *War, Disability, and Rehabilitation in Britain: "Soul of a Nation"* (Manchester University Press, 2011); Jeffrey S. Reznick, *Healing the Nation: Soldiers and the Culture of Caregiving in Britain during the Great War* (Manchester University Press, 2011); Jeffrey S. Reznick, *John Galsworthy and Disabled Soldiers of the Great War* (Manchester University Press, 2009).
111. Correspondence of James Hewitson, Victoria Cross: Provision and General Correspondence, 1948–1970, TNA WO 32/21740.
112. See, for instance, "Full Text of Churchill's Tribute to King George VI," *Sydney Morning Herald*, February 9, 1952, p. 2, *Trove: National Library of Australia*.
113. Sheppard, *Extraordinary Heroes*, 14–15. See also "VCs Decorated," *Times*, December 12, 1945, p. 7, issue 50323, *TDA*. On the culture of the World War II Air Force, see Martin Francis, *The Flyer: British Culture and the Royal Air Force, 1939–1945* (Oxford University Press, 2008).
114. "Another VC for the Gurkhas," *Times*, February 23, 1945, p. 4, issue 50075; "Posthumous VC for Punjabi," *Times*, May 9, 1945, p. 7, issue 50138; "VC for Maori Subaltern," *Times*, June 5, 1943, p. 4, issue 49564, *TDA*.
115. See, for e.g., "Five VCs," *Times*, November 3, 1945, p. 2, issue 49986; Harold Cooper, "A Fijian VC," *Times*, January 19, 1945, p. 5, issue 50045; Our Military Reporter, "Centenary Celebrations of the Victoria Cross," *Times*, June 4, 1856, p. 6, issue 53548, *TDA*.
116. See, for instance, Victoria Cross: Disposal of the Award to the Lt. Hon. C. Furness, June 1946, TNA WO 32/21615.
117. Letter from Maud Sylvester, April 29, 1953, "Coronation Procession: Arrangements for Holders of Victoria Cross or their Widows to be Allocated Seats," 1953, TNA WO 32/16214.
118. "The Victoria Cross Centenary Luncheon," NAM 1965–10–183/17–18; "Papers of the Victoria and George Cross Association," NAM 1986–02–33.
119. On the Centenary and its events, see Our Military Reporter, "A Hundred Years of Heroism: Victoria Cross Exhibition," *Times*, June 15, 1956, p. 12, issue 53558, *TDA*. See also Catalogue of Victoria Cross Centenary Exhibition, TNA AIR 20/9847; Victoria Cross: Service of Thanksgiving at Westminster Abbey, TNA AIR 20/10679; Correspondence Relating to Crimean Relics, Particularly the Victoria Cross Awarded to Sergeant John

Coleman of the 97th, Papers of the Queen's Own Royal West Kent Regiment, WKR/B2/Z13, Kent Archives.

120. See for e.g., Victoria Cross Centenary Celebrations, TNA WO 32/15921; Victoria Cross Centenary Celebrations: Public Relations, Publicity, and Arrangements, TNA WO 32/16920.

121. For the rhetoric of the moment, see "The Opening of the VC Exhibition: Sir Anthony Eden's Tribute," *Times*, June 15, 1956, p. 4, issue 53559; and "For Valour: The Victoria Cross from the Crimea to the Present," *Times*, January 14, 1956, p. 7, issue 53428, *TDA*.

122. On event arrangements, see Celebration of Centenary of the Introduction of the Victoria Cross, Dominions Office and Commonwealth Relations Office, TNA DO 35/6557.

123. On the Lucas cross see, Victoria Cross Details of Charles D. Lucas, June 21, 1854, TNA WO 98/3/4.

124. "Review of Holders of the Victoria Cross in Hyde Park, 26 June, 1956, The Queen's Speech," NAM 1971–12–37.

125. "Review of Holders of the Victoria Cross in Hyde Park."

126. This formulation is taken from Dean Acheson's West Point Speech of December 1962. Douglas Brinkley, "Dean Acheson and the 'Special Relationship': The West Point Speech of December 1962," *Historical Journal* 33, no. 3 (1990): 599–608.

127. Smyth, *Only Enemy*, 306.

128. Smyth, *Only Enemy*, 443.

129. For a late example, see "The Bravest of the Brave Meet under the Big Guns," Press Cutting, *Daily Mail*, May 20, 1981, NAM 1986–02–33.

130. On nostalgia, wartime, and empire in the making of a right-wing mindset, see Camilla Schofield, *Enoch Powell and the Making of Postcolonial Britain* (Cambridge University Press, 2013).

131. See, for example, "The Victoria Cross," *Times*, June 6, 1956, p. 11, issue 53550, *TDA*. See also Authenticity and Disposal of Cross Awarded to Private O'Hea, TNA WO 32/14413.

132. See, for example, Victoria Cross: Provision and General Correspondence, 1948–1970, TNA WO 32/21740.

133. Correspondence Relating to the Victoria and George Cross Association, 1966–1967, Documents.6710, IWM.

134. Album of Signatures of Victoria Cross Winners, 1955–1957, Documents.23385, IWM.

135. Letters of Peter Sharpe to Sir John Smyth, Victoria and George Cross Association, March 27, 1976 and April 4, 1976, NAM 1986–02–33. On letters as archives for accessing ordinary Englishness and its raced meanings, see Amy Whipple, "Revisiting the 'Rivers of Blood' Controversy: Letters to Enoch Powell," *Journal of British Studies* 48, no. 3 (2009): 717–35.

136. Album of Signatures of Victoria Cross Winners, 1955–1957, Documents.23385, IWM.

137. On the nationalism of the Falklands contest, see Ezekiel Mercau, "War of the British Worlds: The Anglo-Argentines and the Falklands," *Journal of British Studies* 55, no. 1 (2016): 146–68.

138. Paul Pickering, "For Even Greater Valour," *Times*, July 8, 1982, p. 10, issue 61280, *TDA*.
139. These were two of the fifteen awarded since World War II.
140. See Victoria Cross: Recommendation for Award for Herbert Jones, Lieutenant Colonel, Parachute Division, 1982, TNA WO 373/188/170; Victoria Cross: Recommendation for Award for Ian McKay, Sergeant, TNA WO 373/188/171.
141. John Cooksey, *Falklands Hero: Ian McKay, The Last VC of the Twentieth Century* (Pen and Sword, 2012); Sheppard, *Extraordinary Heroes*, 97.
142. "Pride of VC's Widow," *Times*, October 11, 1982, p. 1, issue 61359, *TDA*.
143. Harvey Elliott, Defence Correspondent, "For Valour," *Daily Mail*, October 9, 1982, p. 1+, issue 26845; and Lynda Lee-Potter, "I Look Back on my Marriage to H with Nostalgia. He's Still in My Heart and Mind Every Day," *Daily Mail*, March 7, 2002, p. 52, issue 32888, *DMHA*.
144. "This is for H, says Falklands Widow," *Daily Mail*, June 17, 1995, pp. 6–7, issue 30796, *DMHA*.
145. Ian Key, "Fighter Hero's Widow Puts VC Up for Sale," *Daily Mail*, February 9, 1983, p. 3, issue 26947, *DMHA*.
146. A. G. Bolton, Mrs. Ann R. Jones, and Mrs. J. Lee. "Widowed by War," *Daily Mail*, February 14, 1983, p. 21, issue 26951, *DMHA*.
147. "VC fetches £110, 000," *Times*, April 28, 1983, p. 3, issue 61518, *TDA*.
148. June Southworth, "Victims of the VC," *Daily Mail*, March 4, 1983, pp. 20–21, issue 26967, *DMHA*.
149. Michael Horsnell and Ronald Kershaw, "Battle of Britain VC Sale to Highlight Plight of War Widows," *Times*, February 9, 1983, p. 3, issue 61452, *TDA*.
150. "Hypocrisy, Says VC's Son," *Daily Mail*, April 29, 1983, p. 3, *DMHA*.
151. "War Hero's Widow Being Helped," *Times*, April 29, 1983, p. 4, issue 61519, *TDA*.
152. David Williams and Richard Alleyne, "An Anniversary Wedding for the Son of Hero H," *Daily Mail*, June 21, 1997, p. 21, issue 31423; and Denis Cassidy, "Smile that Says: If Only Your Father Could See You Now, Son," *Daily Mail*, April 16, 1991, p. 13, issue 29493, *DMHA*.
153. David Norris, "Surrender," *Daily Mail*, May 31, 1982, p. 1, issue 26733, *DMHA*.
154. John Wilsey, "Hero or Hothead?" *Daily Mail*, March 2, 2002, pp. 48–49, issue 32884, *DMHA*.
155. Edward Verity, "What is the Truth about Colonel H?" *Daily Mail*, July 11, 1996, pp. 24–25, issue 31129, *DMHA*.
156. On the Gallery see, Nigel Steel, Principal Historian, "An Introduction to the Lord Ashcroft Gallery: *Extraordinary Heroes*," The Lord Ashcroft Gallery Press Information, at www.lordashcroftmedals.com/about/lord-ashcroft-gallery. For information on an earlier exhibition held at the Imperial War Museum, see Invitation to Museum Opening, 1970, NAM 1993–02–509.
157. Sheppard, *Extraordinary Heroes*, 106–07.

158. Letter from F. W. A. D. Drummond to Major General R. E. Barnsley, March 18, 1955, Director General Army Medical Services Victoria Cross Fund, Purchase of Awards and Medals, 1955–1958, TNA WO 32/17827.
159. See Michael Ashcroft, Foreword to Sheppard, *Extraordinary Heroes*, 4. See also Michael Ashcroft, *Victoria Cross Heroes* (Headline Review, 2006), especially chapter 1.
160. Neil Tweedie, "Imperial War Museum: Gallery of War Heroes," *Telegraph*, November 6, 2010, at www.telegraph.co.uk/history/britain-at-war/811422 7/Imperial-War-Museum-gallery-of-war-heroes.html.
161. Steel, "An Introduction to the Lord Ashcroft Gallery, at www.iwm.org.uk /sites/default/files/public-document/The_Lord_Ashcroft_Gallery.pdf.
162. Steel, "Introduction to the Lord Ashcroft Gallery"
163. Zarena Aslami, "Victorian Afghanistan, the The Iron Amir, and the Poetics of Marginal Sovereignty," *Victorian Studies* 62, no. 1 (Autumn 2019): 35–60; Antoinette Burton, ed., *The First Anglo-Afghan Wars: A Reader* (Duke University Press, 2014).
164. Nigel Steel, "Introduction" to Sheppard, *Extraordinary Heroes*, 5.
165. Sheppard, *Extraordinary Heroes*, 98–99 and 109.
166. Johnson Beharry, *Barefoot Soldier: A Story of Extreme Valour* (Little, Brown, 2006).
167. Dating back to the Crimean War, the suicide rate for VC winners is far higher than that in the military and the general population, too. For one discussion of the risks that have accompanied the Cross, see John Winton, "The High Price of Valour," *ILN*, September 29, 1989, p. 51, issue 6974, *ILNHA*.
168. "Victoria Cross Recipient Johnson Beharry 'Humiliated' by Trump 'Muslim Ban'" at www.independent.co.uk/news/uk/home-news/donald-trump-muslim-ban-johnson-beharry-victoria-cross-humiliated-a7563451.html.
169. Jaymi McCann, "'Why My Boy Became a Soldier:' Mother of Victoria Cross Hero Reveals her Pride of Para Son," *Express*, March 1, 2015 at www.express.co.uk/news/uk/561103/Rosie-Leakey-Victoria-Cross-war-hero-pride-Para-son-Joshua.
170. For an example of new work on the topic, see Talia Schaffer, "Victorian Feminist Criticism: Recovery Work and the Care Community," *Victorian Literature and Culture* 47, no. 1 (Spring 2019): 63–91.

4   The Custodians

1. Luc Capdevila and Danièle Voldman, *War Dead: Western Societies and the Casualties of War*, trans. Richard Veasey (Edinburgh University Press, 2006). A recent exception is Lucy Noakes's *Dying for the Nation: Death, Grief, and Bereavement in Second World War Britain* (Manchester University Press, 2020).
2. It was not until World War I that the majority of soldiers died on the battlefield, rather than from such extenuating causes as hunger, climate, and disease.
3. Michael Clodfelter, *Warfare and Armed Conflicts: A Statistical Encyclopedia of Casualty and Other Figures, 1492–2015*, 4th ed. (McFarland, 2017), 180.

See also http://necrometrics.com/wars19c.htm, which gives 21,000 as the figure.

4. George Dodd, *Pictorial History of the Russian War, 1854-5-6* (W. and R. Chambers, 1856), 196.

5. Drew Gilpin Faust, *This Republic of Suffering: Death and the American Civil War* (Vintage, 2009).

6. Photocopy of Contemporary Copy of a Letter from Sergeant R. Yeasbley, 67th Regiment of Foot, to his Parents, September 22, 1854, describing the Battle of the Alma, NAM 1995–06–38.

7. Furneaux, *Military Men of Feeling*; for an American counterpart, see Frances M. Clarke, *War Stories: Suffering and Sacrifice in the Civil War North* (University of Chicago Press, 2011).

8. On Dickens and Death more generally, see Claire Wood, *Dickens and the Business of Death* (Cambridge University Press, 2015); on the material culture of death, see Lutz, *Relics of Death in Victorian Literature and Culture.*

9. On nineteenth-century cemeteries, see, David Charles Sloane, *The Last Great Necessity: Cemeteries in American History* (Johns Hopkins University Press, 1991); Peter Thorsheim, "The Corpse in the Garden: Burial, Health, and the Environment in Nineteenth-Century London," *Environmental History* 16 (2011): 38–68.

10. The religious nature of the war in lived experience and in cultural production do not receive the attention they should in recent scholarship; Sarah Ross successfully brings these matters to the fore in "Brave Hermeneutics."

11. See, for example, Pat Jalland, *Death in the Victorian Family* (Oxford University Press, 1996), 25 and ff.

12. On letters and emotion in a later conflict, see Kate Hunter, "More than an Archive of War: Intimacy and Manliness in the Letters of a Great War Soldier," *Gender and History* 25, no. 2 (August 2013): 339–54.

13. See, for example, manuscript Letter written by Private Edward Garnett of the 13th Prince Albert's Light Infantry from Sebastopol, February 1, 1856, to his sister Eliza, NAM 2005–10–54; Two manuscript letters from William Archer Amherst, October 23 and 28, 1854, with letters from Frederick Paulet, John Wyatt, and H. M. Addington to Amherst's Father, Lord Holmesdale, following the wounding of his son, NAM 1973–05–75; Crimean War Letters and Papers of Major George Harry Smith Willis, 77th East Middlesex Regiment, NAM 2004–10–168; Manuscript Letter written on the Back of a Printed Russian Form from S/Sgt. J. Brown to his Parents, September 13, 1855, telling of the Fall of Sebastopol, NAM 1973–04–27; Letter, September 20, 1854, associated with Lt. George Clay, 19th (The 1st Yorkshire North Riding) Regiment of Foot, relating to the Battle of the Alma, Crimean War, NAM 1989–08–18; Transcript of a Letter from Sergeant Joseph Pickford, First Battalion Rifle Brigade, dated "Camp before Sebastopol," April 9, 1855, to his Father Mr. J. D. Clarke of Great Coram Street, Russell Square, London, NAM 1992–04–111; Manuscript Letter, with Typescript Transcript, written by Thomas Harrison, unknown regiment, from Constantinople, describing his experiences during the Crimean War, NAM 2001–06–92; Copy of letter written from George

Allen, 44th Regiment, to his Parents from Sebastopol, October 1854, NAM 1998–06–142; Typed Transcript of Six Letters from Lt. Nichol Graeme, 90th Regt of Foot, Written to a Family Friend from the Crimea, February 1855, especially p. 7, NAM 2009–06–10.

14. The effort to manage these statistics at the time of the Great War was a herculean one. See, for instance, the War Office's *Statistics of the Military Effort of the British Empire During the Great War* (HMSO, 1922), 237.

15. Letter written by Lt. Alfred Howell, Dated Kertche [sic], Crimea, Land Transport Corps, at Turkish Contingent, to his brother Stephen Howell, November 24, 1855, NAM 1972–08–51.

16. Sergeant R. Yeasbley letter, September 22, 1854.

17. Two manuscript letters, to "My dear Cousin" from Alexander Hood, a private or NCO of the 42nd (Royal Highland) Regiment of Foot, dated "Heights of Balaclava" January 15 and February 24, 1855, NAM 1978–05–47.

18. Transcripts of the Crimean War letters of John Netten Radcliffe, January 12, 1855 to March 21, 1856, written to family members whilst serving as a surgeon attached to Omar Pasha's headquarters with the Turkish Army (1854–1855), NAM 2009–08–38; Bound duplicated typescript transcript of twenty-seven letters written by or relating to Maj. G. G. Clowes, 8th Hussars, May 1854 to November 1859, NAM 1995–04–21; Alexander Hood letters, January 15 and February 24, 1855; George Allen letter, October 1854; Crimean War Letters and Papers of Major George Harry Smith Willis.

19. Sergeant R. Yeasbley letter, September 22, 1854; Extracts from Diaries of Commissary General A. W. Downes, compiled at the express desire of his widow, Alice Mary Downes, January 28, 1855, NAM 1998–02–198. For treatment of this subject, see also William Howard Russell, *The British Expedition to the Crimea* (Routledge, 1877), 70, 126, 256–57, 483, 491.

20. The burials of Army privates were often far less personal than the rites provided for officers. See, for instance, Extracts from Diaries of Commissary General A. W. Downes, January 28, 1855.

21. Lt. Alfred Howell letter, November 24, 1855.

22. On the treatment of Russian dead by the Turks, see two typescript copies of letters written by Lt. Henry B. Roberts, Royal Marine Artillery, 1854, especially October 27, 1854, to his family from No. 4 Battery, Balaklava, Crimea, NAM 1967–02–36. See also Letter from Cornet James Gunter, 1st King's Dragoon Guards, in the Crimea, to his brother, on the aftermath of the Battle of the Tchernaya, August 27, 1855, NAM 1999–03–40.

23. Letter, with typescript transcript, from George Ratcliff (1836–1879), Land Transport Corps, Crimea, May 6, 1856, possibly to his parents (?), letter written on the day peace was proclaimed, writes about celebrations, and of death from fever of Joe Saddler, possibly Cpl. Joseph Sadlier (?), NAM 2000–12–577; and Six manuscript letters written to his mother by Lt. H. J. Alderson, 10th Bn Royal Artillery, August 1854–March 1855, NAM 1980–11–54.

24. Collection of letters relating to Pte. Joseph Reid, Rifle Brigade, eighteen letters from Pte. Joseph Reid to his family, Reid served in Canada, 1849–

1852, and in the Crimea where he died in January 1855; One letter from his namesake, John Reid, informing his family of his death; copy of the letter from John Reid; twenty transcripts of the letters from Joseph Reid and John Reid, NAM 1999–03–130.

25. George Ratcliff letter, May 6, 1856. The burials of Army privates were often far less personal than the rites provided for officers. See also Extracts from Diaries of Commissary General A. W. Downes, January 28, 1855; Correspondence of Florence Nightingale and Arthur Hugh Clough, March 12, 1859, MS 7204, Wellcome Library, London, UK.

26. For examples of privates' letters, see also letter written by Private John Rose, 50th Regt, to his Parents, dated Varna, August 28, 1854, NAM 2000–02–94; Letter from David Lobley to his sister, April 25, 1856, written at a camp before Sevastopol, NAM 2002–07–174; Edward Garnett letter, February 1, 1856.

27. On deaths at the Battle of Inkerman, see *The Night after the Battle of Inkerman: Lord Raglan's Delayed Dispatches, Sunday, November 5, 1854* (Thomas Hatchard, 1854), 5–7.

28. Letter from Godfrey Morgan to Margaret Caroline Clevland, mother of Archibald Clevland, November 12, 1854, Letters and Papers of Archibald Clevland, D455/F4/3/3/5, Gloucestershire Archives, Gloucester, UK.

29. For an Army Doctor's moving account of deaths in battle, see Letter, September 10, 1855, from Assistant Surgeon T. Egerton Hale, to his Parents, RAMC/270: Box 28, Wellcome Library.

30. Letters flowed into Scutari Hospital as well in great volume, so much so that the Postmaster General had to implement a special system for delivering them. Posters issued by the Postmaster General relating to the sending of Letters to the Troops in the Crimean War, NAM 1998–05–4–1.

31. Photocopy and typed transcript of a letter from Florence Nightingale to Mrs. Sarah Ann Spofforth, on the death of her son Edward Nixon Spofforth at Scutari; also a transcript of a letter from Spofforth to his brother Robert, after running away from home to join the Army in the ranks, NAM 2009–03–2; Photocopy of a Manuscript Letter dated January 21, 1856 written by Arthur Helling, regiment unknown, from a Ward at Scutari Hospital, NAM 2005–07–732.

32. There were many books and pamphlets published for individual and collective use. See, for instance, R. W. Browne, *Tracts for Soldiers: Selected by the Reverend R. W. Browne* (SPCK, 1854); Reverend E. P. Hannam, *The Hospital's Manual or Soldier's Guide in the Hour of Sickness, to Which is Prefixed a Short Service for the Use of Military Hospitals* (SPCK, 1854); R. W. Browne, *The Soldier's Funeral* (SPCK, 1856); A Clergyman of the English Church, *A Tribute to the Slain in the Crimea, or, Solemn Prayers for those who Cannot Pray for Themselves* (Joseph Masters, 1855); *Proclamation of a Day of Solemn Fast, Humiliation, and Prayer: 28 February 1855* (F. and W. Thomson, 1855); Soldiers' Friend and Army Scripture Readers' Society, *Report on Mr. Mathieson's Labours at the East* (The Society, Printed at Cambridge Printing Press, 1855). On these practices more generally, see Philip Williamson, "State Prayers,

Fasts and Thanksgivings: Public Worship in Britain, 1830–1897," *Past and Present* 200, no. 1 (August 2008): 121–74.

33. Simon Goldhill, "A Mother's Joy at Her Child's Death: Conversion, Cognitive Dissonance, and Grief," *Victorian Studies* 59, no. 4 (2017): 636–57.

34. Manuscript transcript of three letters, dated October 1854, relating to the death of Lt. Henry George Teesdale, Royal Engineers, of fever and dysentery, caught after being wounded at the Alma; also included is a leaf from Teesdale's grave, NAM 1977–04–17.

35. Four manuscript letters associated with Pte. G. Burdis, 47th Regt, 1854–1855, NAM 1963–11–151.

36. Faust, *Republic of Suffering*; see also Samantha Matthews, *Poetical Remains: Poets' Graves, Bodies, and Books in the Nineteenth Century* (Oxford University Press, 2004).

37. See Clodfelter, *Warfare and Armed Conflicts*, 180.

38. The toll has long been counted as 620,000, but recent research has given the total of 750,000. See Guy Gugliotta, "New Estimate Raises Civil War Death Toll," *New York Times*, April 2, 2012, at www.nytimes.com/2012/0 4/03/science/civil-war-toll-up-by-20-percent-in-new-estimate.html.

39. James Gibson, *Memoirs of the Brave: A Brief Account of the Battles of the Alma, Balaklava, and Inkerman, with Biographies of the Killed and a list of the Wounded* (Effingham Wilson, 1855); John Colborne and Frederic Brine, *Memorials of the Brave, or Resting Places of our Fallen Heroes in the Crimea and at Scutari* (Ackermann, 1858); John Colborne and Frederic Brine, *Graves and Epitaphs of our Fallen Heroes in the Crimea and Scutari* (L'Enfant and Hodgkins, 1865).

40. See "A Soldier's Death and Burial," *Daily News*, November 20, 1854, p. 3, issue 2653; "A Soldier's Death and Burial," *Newcastle Guardian and Tyne Mercury*, November 25, 1854, p. 3, issue 459; "Miscellaneous," *Newcastle Courant*, November 24, 1854, issue 9390; "Births, Deaths, Marriages, and Obituaries," *Paisley Herald*, November 25, 1854, p. 3; "A Soldier's Death and Burial," *Leicester Chronicle*, November 25, 1854, issue 2296; "Incidents in the Siege of Sebastopol," *Chester Chronicle and Cheshire and North Wales General Advertiser*, November 25, 1854, p. 2, issue 150; "Her Majesty's Approbation of the Army," *Norfolk Chronicle and Norwich Gazette*, November 25, 1854, p. 4, issue 4387; "Siege of Sebastopol," *Leicestershire Mercury and General Advertiser*, November 25, 1854, p. 1, issue 959, *BLN Part 1*.

41. On Wellington's funeral, see Cornelia D. J. Pearsall, "Burying the Duke: Victorian Mourning and the Funeral of the Duke of Wellington," *Victorian Literature and Culture* 27, no. 2 (1999): 365–93; Peter W. Sinnema, *The Wake of Wellington: Englishness in 1852* (Ohio University Press, 2006). On the dead as exemplars in the years leading up to the death of Wellington, see David McAllister, *Imagining the Dead in British Literature and Culture, 1790–1848* (Palgrave Macmillan, 2018).

42. Christopher Hibbert, *The Destruction of Lord Raglan: A Tragedy of the Crimean War, 1854–1855* (Little, Brown, 1961), 296. See also

Edward Woollcombe, *Funeral Sermon to the Late Lord Raglan, Preached in the Chapel Royal, Whitehall, the Seventh Sunday after Trinity, July 22, 1855* (Bell and Daldy, 1857); An Englishman and a Civilian, *Lord Raglan, a Would-be Sacrifice to a Ribald Press* (James Ridgway, 1855).

43. Two manuscript memorandums written by Col. C. A. Windham after the battle of Inkerman, November 6, 1854; one announces the arrangements for the burial of officers of the 4th Division killed in the battle, the other announces arrangements for the funeral of Lt. Gen. Sir George Cathcart, NAM 1972–08–13.

44. Many officers' bodies were moved to the site and buried there in individual, dedicated graves. See Letter from William Fielding to his Father, Camp before Sebastopol, February 25, 1856, CR2017/W2, Warwickshire County Record Office, Warwick, UK.

45. "The Officers' Cemetery, Cathcart-Hill," *ILN*, June 16, 1855, p. 611, issue 748, *ILNHA*.

46. Col. C.A. Windham manuscript memorandums, November 6, 1854.

47. Our Special Correspondent, "Our Graves in the Crimea," *Times*, July 26, 1856, p. 9, issue 22430, *TDA*. See also William Howard Russell, *Russell's Dispatches from the Crimea, 1854–1856*, ed. Nicolas Bentley (Hill and Wang, 1967), 498; "Monumental Remains of the Crimean War," *ILN*, August 23, 1856, p. 199, issue 817, *ILNHA*.

48. Pierre Nora, "Between Memory and History: *Les Lieux de Mémoire*," *Representations* 26 (Spring 1989): 7–24, especially p. 7. Also helpful here are Elizabethada A. Wright, "Reading the Cemetery, Lieu de Mémoire par Excellance," *Rhetoric Society Quarterly* 33, no. 2 (Spring 2003): 27–44; Elizabethada A. Wright "Rhetorical Spaces in Memorial Places: The Cemetery as a Rhetorical Memory Place/Space," *Rhetorical Society Quarterly* 35, no. 4 (Fall 2005): 51–81.

49. "Cathcart's Hill," *Morning Post*, July 10, 1856, p. 3, issue 25747, *BLN Part 1*.

50. Prayers and other rituals at home also provided ways to remember the dead. See, for instance, A Clergyman of the English Church, *Tribute to the Slain in the Crimea*.

51. Cathcart's Hill, December 16, 1854, Watercolor by William Simpson, NAM 1992–01–115. For one example of a reproduction, see The Graves in the Fort on Cathcart's Hill, Tinted Lithograph by C. Haghe after William Simpson, NAM 1972–11–78. For other views, see Carlo Bossoli. *The Beautiful Scenery and Chief Places of Interest throughout the Crimea* (Day, 1856).

52. Colborne and Brine, *Graves and Epitaphs of our Fallen Heroes*.

53. Fenton's photographs of Cathcart's Hill can be found in boxes 15 and 24, Roger Fenton Photography Collection: Series I, Crimean War, Harry Ransom Humanities Research Center, University of Texas. For other examples of photographs, see James Robertson, Photograph: Camp of the 2nd, 4th, and Light Divisions from Cathcart's Hill, NAM 1970–4–55–1; Photograph 77th Regiment Cemetery, Crimea, by James Robertson, 1856,

Crimean War Scrapbook of Major (later Colonel) George Henry Smith Willis, 77 Foot, NAM 1994–01–1–417–24.

54. These words originally appeared in the *Times*: Our Special Correspondent, "The British Expedition," *Times*, October 8, 1855, p. 7, issue 22179, *TDA*. Some of the examples of reprinting include the following, "The Graves on Cathcart's Hill," *Sheffield Daily Telegraph*, October 9, 1855, p. 4, issue 105; "Cathcart's Hill and Cemetery," *Reynolds's Newspaper*, October 14, 1855, p. 10, issue 270; "The Cemetery of Cathcart's Hill," *Newcastle Journal*, October 20, 1855, p. 7, issue 1229; and "The Tombs on Cathcart's Hill," *Royal Cornwall Gazette, Falmouth Packet, and General Advertiser*, October 19, 1855, p. 7, issue 2730, *BLN Part 1*.

55. See, among others, David Blight, *Beyond the Battlefield: Race, Memory, and the American Civil War* (University of Massachusetts Press, 2002); David Wharton Lloyd, *Battlefield Tourism: Pilgrimage and the Commemoration of the Great War in Britain, Australia, and Canada, 1919–1939* (Berg, 1998); Stephen Miles, *The Western Front: Landscape, Tourism, and Heritage* (Pen and Sword, 2016); Nicholas J. Saunders, "Crucifix, Calvary and Cross: Materiality and Spirituality in Great War Landscapes," *World Archaeology* 35, no. 1 (2003): 7–21.

56. See, for instance, General the Marquis of Hereford, *Rough Notes of a Tour in the Crimea in 1880* (William Clowes, 1881), CR114A/649/1–3, Warwickshire County Record Office.

57. On Army wives as subjects of history, see Paul Huddle, "Victims or Survivors: Army Wives in Ireland during the Crimean War, 1854–56," *Women's History Review* 26, no. 4 (August 2017): 541–54.

58. James Fergusson, "The Graves at Sebastopol," *Times*, June 24, 1858, p. 7, issue 23028, *TDA*.

59. James P. Hammet and John E. Gowen, "Graves in the Crimea," *Times*, June 14, 1860, p. 9, issue 23646; and Montague Gore, "The Crimean Graves," *Times*, June 2, 1860, p. 12, issue 23636, *TDA*.

60. A Crimean, "To the Editor of the Times," *Times*, October 22, 1862, p. 7, issue 24383, *TDA*; and "Colonel Gowen and the English Graveyard on Cathcart-Hill, Sebastopol," *ILN*, August 10, 1861, p. 133, issue 1102, *ILNHA*.

61. John E. Gowen, "The Crimean Graves," *Times*, May 11, 1869, p. 12, issue 26434, *TDA*.

62. See, for instance, "The Crimea Revisited," *ILN*, May 22, 1869, p. 511, issue 1539, *ILNHA*.

63. Russell, *Diary in the East*, 540.

64. See, for instance, "The Crimea Revisited," *ILN*, June 5, 1869, p. 514, issue 1542, *ILNHA*.

65. G. Arbuthnot, "The Graves in the Crimea," *Times*, May 4, 1869, p. 5, issue 26428, *TDA*.

66. Russell, *Diary in the East*, 540–41.

67. T. Brocklebank and J. H. Law, "Soldiers' Graves in the Crimea," *Times*, November 30, 1869, p. 4, issue 26608, *TDA*.

68. Teresa Grey, *Journal of a Visit to Egypt, Constantinople, the Crimea, Greece, Etc. in the Suite of the Prince and Princess of Wales* (Smith, Elder, 1869), 187–88.

69. "The Crimea Revisited," *ILN*, June 5, 1869, p. 514, issue 1542, *ILNHA*. Contrast was a tool for identifying British failure and negligence in many areas of the war effort and aftermath. See, for instance, Surgeon General T. Longmore, *The Sanitary Contrasts of the British and French Armies during the Crimean War* (Charles Griffin, 1883).

70. Russell, *Diary in the East*, 540–41.

71. H. Daniell, Colonel, late Coldstream Guards, "The Crimean Cemeteries," *Times*, June 25, 1873, p. 11, issue 27725, *TDA*.

72. "A National Scandal," *Reynolds's Newspaper*, May 16, 1869, p. 5, issue 979, *BLN Part 1*; "The Crimea Revisited," *ILN*, June 5, 1869, p. 574, issue 1542, *ILNHA*.

73. "The British Graveyards in the Crimea," *Sheffield Daily Telegraph*, October 12, 1872, p. 3, issue 5413; "Multiple News Items," *Standard*, October 14, 1872, p. 5, issue 15041; "Naval and Military," *Bath Chronicle*, October 17, 1872, p. 6, issue 5947, *BLN Part 1*.

74. J. Adye and C. Gordon, *Report on the Crimean Cemeteries* (HMSO, 1873).

75. British Cemeteries in the Crimea, vol. 3, 1870–1880, The National Archives, Kew, UK, Foreign Office (hereafter, TNA FO). See TNA FO 65/1510, August 18, 1872 and January 10, 1873.

76. Soldier, "The British Graves in the Crimea," *Times*, August 6, 1873, p. 5, issue 27761, *TDA*.

77. "The Cemeteries in the Crimea – The Condition," *Times*, October 28, 1874, p. 11, issue 28145, *TDA*.

78. TNA FO 65/1510, November 12, 1877 and October 23, 1880.

79. "The Crimean Graves," *Times*, March 8, 1875, p. 11, issue 28257, *TDA*. See also TNA FO 65/1510, October 23, 1875, January 24, 1877, April 13, 1877, and July 23, 1877.

80. British Cemeteries in the Crimea, vol. 4, 1881–1895, TNA FO 65/1511, f. 6–12, February 1881; TNA FO 65/1511, f. 27–29, May 11, 1881.

81. G. E. Stanley, "British Cemeteries in the Crimea," *Times*, June 8, 1881, p. 6, issue 30215, *TDA*.

82. TNA FO 65/1510, December 8, 1880.

83. S. G. H. and E. L. F., "The British Cemetery in the Crimea," *Times*, May 5, 1881, p. 10, issue 30186; and Tourist, "The British Graves in the Crimea," *Times*, August 19, 1873, p. 3, issue 27772, *TDA*.

84. TNA FO 65/1511, f. 17–18, May 1, 1881.

85. TNA FO 65/1511, ff. 39–55, June 10, 1882, August 18, 1882, August 31, 1882, September 10, 1882, and October 24, 1882; TNA FO 65/1510, November 16, 1880.

86. These visitors included Lady Estcourt, the widow of the dead Estcourt, and Emily Cathcart, daughter of the fallen General. See Crimean Cemetery, 1883–1884, CR114A/715/8, Warwickshire County Record Office.

87. Walter B. Paton, "The British Graves in the Crimea," *Times*, March 9, 1883, p. 12, issue 30763, *TDA*.

88. W. J. Codrington, "The British Graves in the Crimea," *Times*, May 5, 1883, p. 10, issue 30812, *TDA*.

89. TNA FO 65/1511, f. 84–87, May 23, 1884.

90. TNA FO 65/1511, f. 134, December 22, 1890.

91. TNA FO 65/1511, f. 150–155, May 21, 1894; f. 156–159, April 12, 1894.

92. TNA FO 65/1511, f. 162, June 3, 1891; f. 164–165, August 17, 1892; f. 166–167, n.d.

93. TNA FO 65/1511, f. 156–159, April 12, 1894.

94. See TNA FO 65/1511, f. 198–200, November 30, 1894; f. 201–202, October 3, 1894; f. 205, February 13, 1895; f. 207, February 14, 1895; f. 210, January 9, 1895; f. 213, February 22, 1895; f. 217, March 19, 1895; f. 218, March 23, 1895.

95. On later twentieth-century efforts regarding the cemetery at Therapia, see Disposal of Therapia Crimean War Graves Cemetery, Istanbul, and Reversion to Nature of Cemetery, Foreign Office, Central Department, and Commonwealth Office, Southern European Department, Foreign and Commonwealth Office Files, National Archives, TNA FCO 9/1472.

96. See TNA WO 43/1032, Crimean War Cemeteries on the Shores of the Bosporus. Arrangements for their Permanent Care and Conservation; Proposal to Appoint a Resident Gardener at Scutari, 1856–57.

97. "The Great Cemetery at Scutari," *ILN*, January 27, 1855, p. 80, issue 725; and T. C., "Holiday Rambles," *ILN*, October 2, 1886, p. 363, issue 2476, *ILNHA*.

98. "The Great Cemetery at Scutari," *ILN*, January 27, 1855, p. 80.

99. These were at Kululu, Therapia, Smyrna, Sinope, Abydos, and Renkioi.

100. On the remuneration of Sergeant Lyne, see Scutari and Karadeniz Bogazi, Bosporus: Expenditure on Upkeep of Cemeteries, 1879–1883, Treasury Board Papers and In-Letters, National Archives, Treasury TNA T1/16314.

101. See Memorials and Graves, War Memorials: Design, Transportation, and Erection by Baron Marochetti of Memorial at Scutari, Crimea, to British Army and Navy Personnel who Fell in the War with Russia, 1855–1859, TNA WO 32/5999.

102. See TNA WO 32/5999, October 21, 1857.

103. See TNA WO 32/5999, March 24, 1858 and May 4, 1858.

104. See TNA WO 32/5999, May 24, 1858.

105. See TNA WO 32/5999, September 2 and 14, 1858.

106. See TNA WO 32/5999, May 10, May 22, and May 26, 1858.

107. See TNA WO 32/5999, May 10, 1858.

108. See TNA WO 32/5999, June 17, 1858.

109. On the Church, see Ministry of Defense Papers, 1970–77, relating to Casualties, Cemeteries, Memorials and Historical Memorials, in particular the Maintenance of those in the Crimea and the Crimea Memorial Church, NAM 2001–05–598; Photocopies of Items Relating to the Crimea Memorial Church, Istanbul, NAM 1975–12–130.

110. Cemetery at Scutari, 1913: TNA FO 195/2450/81; Burial Grounds: Maintenance of British Cemetery at Scutari, 1909–1926, Treasury: Supply Department, TNA T161/239/19; Transfer of Graves of Naval,

Military, and Air Force Personnel from Erdek to Haidar Pasha Cemetery, Turkey, Records of the Navy Board and Board of Admiralty, 1927–1931, TNA ADM1/8727/140.

111. "The Crimean Dead," *Times*, September 8, 1923, p. 7, issue 43441, *TDA*.
112. "Hero's Lonely Burial," *Daily Mail*, September 19, 1905, p. 3, issue 2942, *DMHA*.
113. See Minute Book: Nottingham and Nottinghamshire Crimea and Indian Mutiny Veterans' Association, 1936–37, M1373 and Typescript History of the Nottingham and Nottinghamshire Crimea and Indian Mutiny Veterans' Association, M1405, Nottinghamshire Archives, Nottingham, UK.
114. See, among other histories, G. Kingsley Ward and Major Edwin Gibson, *Courage Remembered* (HMSO, 1995); Heather J. Kichner, *Cemetery Plots from Victoria to Verdun: Literary Representations of Epitaph and Burial from the 19th Century through the Great War* (Peter Lang, 2012).
115. Rudyard Kipling, *Graves of the Fallen* (HMSO, 1919).
116. www.cwgc.org/.
117. The Commission's principles can be found at www.cwgc.org/who-we-are/. See also Alex King, "The Archive of the Commonwealth Graves Commission," *History Workshop Journal* 47, no. 47 (Spring 1999): 253–59.
118. Your Correspondent in the Near East, "British Graves in Turkey," *Times*, September 11, 1922, p. 6, issue 43133, *TDA*.
119. "The Crimean Dead," *Times*, September 8, 1923, p. 7, issue 43441, *TDA*.
120. Anglo-French Cemetery at New Phaleron: With Plans, 1948–49, TNA FO 286/1393, especially December 30, 1949.
121. Anglo-French Crimean Cemetery at Athens, 1954, TNA FO 369/5036, especially April 12, 1954.
122. Maintenance of British and French Crimean Cemetery: Greece, 1959, TNA FO 369/5438.
123. Athens held the first Olympic Games in 1896. The city bid again as contender in 1944 and 1996, but did not succeed until 2008.
124. TNA FO 369/5036, April 5, 1954.
125. TNA FO 369/5036, April 5, 1954.
126. Disposal of Spare Land adjoining the Anglo-French Cemetery at New Phaleron, Maintenance of British Cemeteries in Greece, 1957, TNA FO 396/5350.
127. See Anglo-French Crimean War Cemetery, Athens, 1967, TNA FCO 47/65, especially October 16 and 23, 1967.
128. "Please Support a British Memorial in the Crimea," by Swordswoman (Louise Berridge), October 23, 2013, Victorian Wars Forum, at www.victorianwars.com/viewtopic.php?t=8700.
129. War Graves in Murmansk and Crimea, 1964, TNA FO 181/1178, especially October 7 and October 24, 1964.
130. Seven Photographic Views of the British Cemetery, Sebastopol, Taken in 1987, includes Cathcart's Hill Cemetery Compound covered with Cooperative Gardens, NAM 1990-01-50.
131. See, for example, the muddle the Duke of Edinburgh stepped into in October 2004, regarding the 150th anniversary of the Charge of the Light

Brigade at www.thetimes.co.uk/article/duke-steps-into-monumental-row-in-crimea-c5g2h8tc6hd.

132. See A. L. Berridge, "The Shame and the Glory," *The History Girls* (blog), September 20, 2013, at http://the-history-girls.blogspot.com/2013/09/the-shame-and-glory-by-l-berridge.html.

133. See Berridge, "The Shame and the Glory."

134. These words appeared on the now-defunct website of the Crimea Memorial Appeal, formerly at crimeaappeal.com.

135. See Berridge, "The Shame and the Glory."

136. Capdevila and Voldman, *War Dead*, x.

137. Rachel Anchor, "A Sore Sight: Britain's Crumbling Crimean Memorials and the Campaign to Restore Them," *Victorian Studies Centre* (blog), University of Leicester, January 11, 2014, at https://victorianstudiescentre.wordpress.com/2014/01/11/a-sore-sight-britains-crumbling-crimean-memorials-and-the-campaign-to-restore-them/.

138. www.independent.co.uk/news/people/silvio-berlusconi-visits-war-memorial-in-crimea-with-vladimir-putin-10499892.html.

139. Joshua Provan, Josh and Historyland, Reply to "Please Support a British Memorial in the Crimea," by Swordswoman (Louise Berridge), February 1, 2016, Victorian Wars Forum.

140. https://victoriansociety.org.uk/news/sheffields-missing-crimean-war-monument.

141. www.bbc.com/news/uk-england-hampshire-27346321.

5   The Heroine

1. See, among others, Lucy Ridgely Seymer, *Florence Nightingale* (Faber & Faber, 1950), 137.

2. See, for instance, "Florence Nightingale," *Daily Graphic*, August 15, 1910, p. 6, 38M49/F9/105, Hampshire Record Office, Winchester, UK.

3. See, for instance, "Florence Nightingale," *Daily Graphic*, August 15, 1910, p. 6.

4. "Recordings by Ms. Vaughan Nash," *Oral History*, 97M72/F725/14–15, Hampshire Record Office.

5. Amy Steedman, *The Story of Florence Nightingale* (T. C. and E. C. Jack, c. 1915), 10.

6. Marion Holmes, *Florence Nightingale: A Cameo Sketch* (Women's Freedom League, 1910), p. 4, *Gale Group Nineteenth-Century Collections Online*. See also Bostridge, *Florence Nightingale*, chapter 3.

7. Carol Helmstadter and Judith Godden, *Nursing before Nightingale, 1815–1899* (Ashgate, 2011), 109.

8. Ellen Creathorne Clayton, *Notable Women: Florence Nightingale, the Soldier's Friend* (Dean and Son, 1860?), 9; Annie Matheson, *Florence Nightingale: A Biography* (Thomas Nelson, 1913), 18.

9. For an account of their correspondence, see Sue M. Goldie, ed., *Florence Nightingale: Letters from the Crimea* (Mandolin, 1997), chapter 1.

10. For the letter, see Goldie, *Florence Nightingale*, 23–25.

11. Clayton, *Notable Women*, 9.
12. Flora Masson, *Florence Nightingale, O.M., By One Who Knew Her* (The Scientific Press, 1910), p. 9, HO1/ST/NC12/5, St. Thomas's Hospital Archive: Nightingale Collection, London Metropolitan Archives (hereafter, Nightingale Collection, LMA); Helmstadter and Godden, *Nursing before Nightingale*, 89; see also Poovey, *Uneven Developments*, chapter 6.
13. This recurring phrase is attributed to Alexander Kinglake. See Royle, *Crimea*, 245.
14. Notes and Draft Account of Sarah Anne Terrot's Experiences Nursing the Wounded in the Crimean War, p. 4, RAMC 1752/3, Wellcome Library, London, UK.
15. Letter to the Editor from "One Who Has Known Miss Nightingale," *Times*, October 25, 1854, p. 7, issue 21881, *TDA*.
16. Edward Tyas Cook, *The Life of Florence Nightingale*, 2 vols. (Macmillan, 1913).
17. See, for example, Cecil Woodham-Smith, *Florence Nightingale: 1820–1910* (Constable, 1950), 17.
18. Anne Summers, "The Mysterious Demise of Sarah Gamp: The Domiciliary Nurse and Her Detractors, C. 1830–1860," *Victorian Studies* 32, no. 3 (1989): 365–86.
19. Letter to the Editor from "One Who Has Known Miss Nightingale," *Times*, no. 21881, (October 25, 1854): 7, *TDA*.
20. "Nurses for the East," *ILN*, November 4, 1854, pp. 446–47, issue 710, *ILNHA*. On Nightingale and Joan of Arc, see also, *The British Red Cross Review*; *Red Cross Day: May 12*, British Red Cross Society, March 1933 Cuttings, Journals, and Pamphlets on Florence Nightingale, GC/236/b/1/5: Box 2, 1913–1933, Wellcome Library.
21. Matheson, *Florence Nightingale*.
22. *The Nightingale Fund: Report of Proceedings at a Public Meeting held in London on November 29, 1855*, HO1/ST/NC18/2/2, Nightingale Collection, LMA. On Nightingale's Christian mission, see also *Derby Telegraph and Weekly County Advertiser*, February 9, 1856, Press Cuttings, HO1/ST/NC14, Nightingale Collection, LMA.
23. "Nurses for the East," *ILN*, November 4, 1854, pp. 446–47, issue 710, *ILNHA*. See also Portfolio of Cuttings, RAMC 27, Wellcome Library.
24. "The Barrack Hospital at Scutari," *ILN*, December 16, 1854, issue 717–18, *ILNHA*.
25. Bostridge, *Florence Nightingale*, 52–53; Notes and Draft Account of Sarah Anne Terrot's Experiences Nursing the Wounded in the Crimean War, 16–17.
26. "Miss Nightingale," *ILN*, February 24, 1855, p. 175, issue 729, *ILNHA*. See also Portfolio of Cuttings, RAMC 27, Wellcome Library.
27. "The Sick and Wounded at Scutari," *Hampshire Advertiser and Salisbury Guardian*, November 25, 1854, p. 3, *Nineteenth Century British Library Newspapers: Part II* (hereafter, *BLN Part 2*); and "The Wounded and the Nurses at Scutaria [sic]," *Hampshire Advertiser and Salisbury Guardian*, December 2, 1854, p. 2, *BLN Part 1*.

28. Notes and Draft Account of Sarah Anne Terrot's Experiences Nursing the Wounded in the Crimean War, 16.
29. Clayton, *Notable Women*, 15.
30. *Statements exhibiting the Voluntary Contributions received by Miss Nightingale for the use of British War Hospitals in the East, 1854, 1855, 1856* (Harrison, 1856), HO1/ST/NC18/002/1, Nightingale Collection, LMA.
31. "Lint," *Derby Mercury*, November 29, 1854, p. 5, *BLN Part 2*; Our Own Correspondent, "The Sick and Wounded Fund," *Times*, November 30, 1854, p. 8, issue 21912, *TDA*.
32. Bostridge, *Florence Nightingale*, 87.
33. See, for example, Notes and Draft Account of Sarah Anne Terrot's Experiences Nursing the Wounded in the Crimean War, 36.
34. Charles Ray, ed., *The Romance of the Nation: The Story of the Crimean War* (Amalgamated Press, 1934–1935); Cuttings, Journals, and Pamphlets on Florence Nightingale, GC/236/b/1/5, Box 2, 1913–1933, Wellcome Library.
35. Florence Nightingale, *Notes on Nursing: What It Is and What It Is Not* (Appleton, 1860).
36. See Bostridge, *Florence Nightingale*, 199.
37. JBB Estcourt, *Diary Written in Crimea, Europe, and England*, D1571/F588, Gloucestershire Archives, Gloucester, UK.
38. See, for example, Papers of Sir John Hall, Principal Medical Officer in the Crimea, April 23, 1856, RAMC 397/F/CO7/39; November 21, 1855, RAMC 397/F/CO22/6; March 9, 1858, RAMC 397/F/CO23/3, Wellcome Library; Angella Johnson, "Letters from Crimean War Major to Mother and Father in England shed an Unflattering Light on the Saintly Lady of the Lamp," *Guardian*, March 7, 1996, p. 6, *BPPQ*.
39. Edith Allbright, "Florence Nightingale Memories," *Daily Mail*, February 14, 1934, p. 10, *DMHA*.
40. See, for example, "The Return of Miss Nightingale to this Country," *Times*, August 15, 1856, p. 6, issue 22447, *TDA*; Anonymous, *Heroines Worthy of the Red Cross* (Dean and Son, 1883).
41. "Miss Nightingale's Carriage at the Seat of War," *ILN*, August 30, 1856, p. 208, issue 818, *ILNHA*.
42. Typescript extracts of letters from General Grey to Mrs. Grey, September 1856, H01/ST/NC/05/003/016, Nightingale Collection, LMA.
43. "The Queen's Present to Miss Nightingale," *ILN*, January 19, 1856, issue 780, *ILNHA*.
44. Letters: Florence Nightingale's Return from the Crimea, Wellcome Library, MS 9063, 1856, especially 9063/8, August 18, 1856, Letter from Mrs. Hamilton Gray.
45. "Miss Nightingale," *Manchester Guardian*, August 30, 1856, p. 5, *Guardian Historical Archive*.
46. Bostridge, *Florence Nightingale*, 261.
47. Bostridge, *Florence Nightingale*, xxi.
48. Peter Quennell, "Florence Nightingale," *Daily Mail*, September 16, 1950, p. 2, *DMHA*.

49. Julianne Smith, "'A Noble Type of Good Heroic Womanhood': The Popular Rhetoric of Florence Nightingale's Enshrinement," *Nineteenth-Century Prose* 26, no. 1 (1999): 59+; Bostridge, *Florence Nightingale*, 254.

50. James Croston, *A Pilgrimage to the Home of Florence Nightingale* (Whittaker, 1862), 31–32.

51. Llewellynn Jewitt, *A Stroll to Lea Hurst, Derbyshire, the Home of Florence Nightingale* (Kent, Paternoster Row, 1855), 20, 12.

52. Jewitt, *Stroll to Lea Hurst*, 7.

53. Jewitt, *Stroll to Lea Hurst*, 8; on the later sale of the home see *Nursing Mirror*, May 25, 1946, HO1/ST/NC13/3/4a, Nightingale Collection, LMA.

54. Clayton, *Notable Women*, 12.

55. Furneaux, *Military Men of Feeling*, chapter 6.

56. A Correspondent, "The Nightingale Fund," *ILN*, March 24, 1856, Portfolio of Cuttings, RAMC 27, Wellcome Library.

57. Frederick Milnes Edge, *A Woman's Example and a Nation's Work: A Tribute to Florence Nightingale* (William Ridgway, 1864), H01/ST/NC12/002, Nightingale Collection, LMA.

58. Susan R. Grayzel, *Women's Identities at War: Gender, Motherhood, and Politics in Britain during the First World War* (University of North Carolina Press, 1999); Susan R. Grazyel and Tammy Proctor, eds., *Gender and the Great War* (Oxford University Press, 2017); Gullace, *"The Blood of Our Sons"*; Virginia Nicholson, *Singled Out: How Two Million British Women Survived without Men after the First World War* (Oxford University Press, 2008); Watson, *Fighting Different Wars*; Angela Woollacott, *On Her Their Lives Depend: Munitions Workers and the Great War* (University of California Press, 1994).

59. Bostridge, *Florence Nightingale*, 25.

60. Bostridge, *Florence Nightingale*, 160.

61. "Miss Nightingale," *Observer*, April 30, 1855, p. 8, *BPPQ*.

62. Ray, *Romance of the Nation*.

63. A recent and illuminating study of Nightingale's life and legacies through the prism of home is Paul Crawford, Anna Greenwood, Richard Bates, and Jonathan Memmel, *Florence Nightingale at Home* (Palgrave Macmillan, 2020).

64. Henry Wadsworth Longfellow, "Santa Filomena: A Poem," *The Atlantic* (November 1857), *Atlantic Magazine Archive*.

65. On nineteenth-century celebrity, see Sharon Marcus, *The Drama of Celebrity* (Princeton University Press, 2019).

66. "Recordings by Ms. Vaughan Nash," *Oral History*, 97M72/F725/14–15, Hampshire Record Office.

67. Judith Moore, *A Zeal for Responsibility: The Struggle for Nursing in Victorian England* (University of Georgia Press, 1998).

68. "Death of Miss Florence Nightingale," *Manchester Guardian*, August 15, 1910, *BPPQ*.

69. D. A. B. Young, "Florence Nightingale's Fever," *British Medical Journal* 311, no. 7021 (1995): 1697–700.

70. Manuscript Copy of Letter from Florence Nightingale Declining Invitation to Attend Balaklava Banquet, October 25, 1875, HO1/ST/NC/05/008, Nightingale Collection, LMA.

71. Cook, *Life of Florence Nightingale*, vol. II (1862–1910), xxvi.

72. On the medical community and heroic masculinity, see Michael Brown, "'Like a Devoted Army': Medicine, Heroic Masculinity, and the Military Paradigm in Victorian Britain," *Journal of British Studies* 49 (July 2010): 529–622.

73. For one example, see Papers of Sir John Hall, RAMC 397/PB1-2, July 28, 1854, Wellcome Library.

74. See, for e.g., Goldie, *Florence Nightingale*, 5–8.

75. Newspaper Clippings, "Defence of the Medical Department: Alleged Neglect of the Wounded at Scutari," RAMC 1139/L105, Wellcome Library; Papers of Sir John Hall, March 9, 1858, RAMC 397/FCO/23/3, Wellcome Library.

76. Papers of Sir John Hall, March 31, 1858, RAMC397/FCO/23/7, Wellcome Library. See also Papers of Sir John Hall, March 14–15, 1858, RAMC 397/FCO/23/27; March 1, 1858, RAMC 397/FCO/23/29; April 23, 1858, RAMC 397/FCO/23/30, Wellcome Library. For a later assessment, see Zachary Cope, "Miss Florence Nightingale and the Doctors," *Proceedings of the Royal Society of Medicine* 49, no. 11 (1956): 907–14, as found in HO1/ST/NC12/21, Nightingale Collection, LMA. Christopher Hibbert, "The Condition of the British Army in the Crimea," *The Victorian Web* at www.victorianweb.org.

77. For an appraisal of this line of argument and a challenge to it, see Christopher J. Gill, and Gillian C. Gill. "Nightingale in Scutari: Her Legacy Reexamined," *Clinical Infectious Diseases* 40, no. 12 (2005): 1799–805.

78. "The Wounded and the Nurses at Scutaria (sic)," *Hampshire Advertiser and Salisbury Guardian*, December 2, 1854, p. 2, *BLN Part 2*.

79. For a challenge to this new orthodoxy see Lynn McDonald, "Florence Nightingale, Statistics and the Crimean War," *Journal of the Royal Statistical Society, Series A* 177, no. 3 (2014): 569–86.

80. Maev Kennedy, "Angel of Mercy or Power-Crazed Meddler?: Unseen Letters Challenge View of Pioneer Nurse," *Guardian*, September 3, 2007, at www.theguardian.com/uk/2007/sep/03/health.healthandwellbeing.

81. *The Nightingale Fund: Report of Proceedings*, H01/ST/NC18/002/2, Nightingale Collection, LMA; "Recognising the Work of Miss Florence Nightingale," *The Sphere*, February 29, 1908, p. 180, RAMC 115–116, Wellcome Library.

82. For an early history, see, Sarah A. Southall Tooley, *The History of Nursing in the British Empire* (S. H. Bousfield, 1906).

83. See Gill and Gill, "Nightingale in Scutari."

84. Elaine Showalter, "Florence Nightingale's Feminist Complaint: Women, Religion, and 'Suggestions for Thought,'" *Signs* 6, no. 3 (Spring 1981): 395–412.

85. Poster and First-Day Postcard, Florence Nightingale Stamps, 1970, H01/ST/NC/21/002/005, Nightingale Collection, LMA.
86. For one memory of South Street, see Miss Joanna F. Bonham-Carter, Oral History, 97M72/F725/14–15, Hampshire Record Office.
87. Manuscript Copy of Letter from Florence Nightingale Declining Invitation to Attend Balaklava Banquet, October 25, 1875.
88. Florence Nightingale, "In Aid of the Light Brigade Relief Fund," August 2, 1890, British Library Sound and Moving Image Collection.
89. W. B. Northrop, "A Woman the World Raved About Forty Years Ago," *Daily Mail*, May 7, 1900, p. 12, *DMHA*.
90. Presentation of the Order of Merit, November 29, 1907, HO1/ST/NC9/2, Nightingale Collection, LMA; Presentation of the Freedom of the City of London, March 16, 1908, HO1/ST/NC9/3, Nightingale Collection, LMA.
91. Masson, *Florence Nightingale*, 3.
92. "Florence Nightingale," *Daily Mail*, August 15, 1910, p. 4, *DMHA*.
93. See, for instance, Maude E. Seymour Abbott, *Florence Nightingale* (McGill, 1916), 3.
94. Mary Frances Billington, "Biography of Florence Nightingale," *Daily Telegraph*, August 15, 1910, as printed in [Anonymous], *In Memoriam: To the Late Florence Nightingale* (Neves and Biscoe, 1910), H01/ST/NC10/002, Nightingale Collection, LMA.
95. A. L. Pringle, "Some Recollections of Florence Nightingale," Manuscript, August 23, 1911, HO1/ST/NC12/004/2, Nightingale Collection, LMA.
96. "Florence Nightingale," *Daily Graphic*, August 15, 1910, p. 6; see also "The Lady with the Lamp: Death of Miss Florence Nightingale," *Daily Graphic*, August 15, 1910, 38M49/F9/105, Hampshire Record Office.
97. "The Late Miss Nightingale," *Times*, August 23, 1910, p. 9, issue 39358, *TDA*; "Death of Miss Florence Nightingale," *Manchester Guardian*, August 15, 1910, p. 7, *BPPQ*; "Florence Nightingale," *Times*, August 15, 1910, p. 9, issue 39351, *TDA*; A. L., "Florence Nightingale: Her Aims and Ideals for the Nursing Profession" (1917), Typescript, HO1/ST/NC12/8, Nightingale Collection, LMA.
98. "Miss Nightingale Dies, Aged Ninety," *New York Times*, August 15, 1910, *BPPQ*.
99. "Crimean Veterans and Nurses at St. Paul's," *Daily Mail*, August 18, 1910, *DMHA*.
100. See Memorial Services for the Late Miss Florence Nightingale, August 20, 1910, H01/ST/NC10/3, Nightingale Collection, LMA.
101. "Florence Nightingale," *Observer*, August 21, 1910, p. 7, *BPPQ*.
102. For instance, Mrs. F. Harding Remembers Florence Nightingale's Funeral, AV6/R94/51, Hampshire Record Office.
103. Visit of American Army Nurses and American Red Cross to Grave in East Wellow Churchyard: Program, HO1/ST/NC10/9, Nightingale Collection, LMA; "Florence Nightingale," *Times*, August 16, 1930, p. 13, issue 45593, *TDA*. On the Church more generally see Pamphlet: St. Margaret's Wellow, HO1/ST/NC13/2, Nightingale Collection, LMA.

104. "Miss Nightingale Dies, Aged Ninety," *New York Times*, August 15, 1910, *BPPQ*.

105. "Funeral of Miss Nightingale," *Daily Graphic*, August 22, 1919, pp. 7–10, especially p. 10, 38M49/F9/105, Hampshire Record Office.

106. Dixon, *Weeping Britannia*, 8.

107. "Florence Nightingale," *Observer*, August 21, 1910, p. 7, *BPPQ*; "Death of Miss Nightingale," *Times*, August 15, 1910, p. 8, issue 39351, *TDA*; George Newman, *A Lady with a Lamp: The Case for Red Cross Day* (British Red Cross Society, 1933), HO1/ST/NC12/11, Nightingale Collection, LMA; Masson, *Florence Nightingale*.

108. "Florence Nightingale," *Observer*, August 21, 1910, p. 7, *BPPQ*. See also "A Rustic Burial," *Daily Mail*, August 22, 1910, p. 3, *DMHA*.

109. Edge, *Woman's Example and a Nation's Work*.

110. "Florence Nightingale," *Daily Mail*, February 25, 1915, p. 3, *DMHA*; see also *Minutes of the Florence Nightingale Fund*, HO1/ST/NC/10/001, Nightingale Collection, LMA.

111. Press Cutting, *Times*, January 12, 1915, Work 20/103, Office of Works: Statue of Florence Nightingale, The National Archives, Kew, UK (hereafter, TNA Work).

112. See, for e.g., TNA Work 20/103, Correspondence of Lionel Earle, January 14, 1915; February 5, 1915; February 6, 1915.

113. TNA Work 20/67, Office of Works: Statue of Florence Nightingale, Sydney Holland to Lionel Earle, November 9, 1912.

114. Sydney Holland to Lionel Earle, November 9, 1912.

115. TNA Work 20/67, Office of Works: Statue of Florence Nightingale, Sydney Holland to Lionel Earle, November 26, 1912.

116. Sydney Holland to Lionel Earle, November 9, 1912.

117. TNA Work 20/67, Statue of Florence Nightingale, Sydney Holland to Lionel Earle, November 16, 1912.

118. "The Lady with the Lamp," *Times*, February 24, 1915, p. 11, issue 40786, *TDA*.

119. "Florence Nightingale," *Daily Mail*, February 25, 1915, p. 3, *DMHA*.

120. "Florence Nightingale," *Daily Mail*, February 25, 1915, p. 3.

121. "The Lady of the Lamp," *Times*, May 12, 1931, p. 18, issue 45820, *TDA*; and "Red Cross Day," *Daily Mail*, May 12, 1931, *DMHA*.

122. TNA Work 20/103, Office of Works: Statue of Florence Nightingale, February 19, 1923. See also "Wreath for Miss Nightingale's Statue," *The Nightingale Fellowship Journal*, January 1930, Cuttings, Journals, and Pamphlets on Florence Nightingale, GC/236/b/1/5: Box 2, 1913–1933, Wellcome Library.

123. TNA Work 20/103, Office of Works: Statue of Florence Nightingale, Letter from T. W. MacAlpine, December 12, 1924; Letter from Board of Works, December 16, 1924.

124. See, for instance, Irene Cooper Williams, *Florence Nightingale: A Biography* (George Allen & Unwin, 1931), 12, 245.

125. Cook, *Life of Florence Nightingale*, vol. I (1820–1861), xxiiv.

126. See, for e.g., Steedman, *Story of Florence Nightingale*, 10–11. On anecdotes of childhood promise, see Alison Booth, "A Bestiary of Florence Nightingales: Strachey and Collective Biographies of Women," *Victorian Studies* 61, no. 1 (Autumn 2018): 93–99.
127. Cook, *Life of Florence Nightingale*, vol. I (1820–1861), xxx.
128. Cook, *Life of Florence Nightingale*, vol. II (1862–1910), 424.
129. See, for instance, Simon Joyce, "On or About 1901: The Bloomsbury Group Looks Back at the Victorians," *Victorian Studies* 46, no. 4 (Summer 2004): 631–54. For a recent reconsideration of Stracey's Nightingale, see James Southern, "A Lady 'in Proper Proportions'? Feminism, Lytton Strachey, and Florence Nightingale's Reputation, 1918–39," *Twentieth Century British History* 28, no. 1 (March 2017): 1–28.
130. Lytton Strachey, *Eminent Victorians* (1918; reprint Oxford World's Classics, 2003), 101, 122.
131. Strachey, *Eminent Victorians*, 117.
132. Strachey, *Eminent Victorians*, 141–42.
133. Reginald Berkeley, *The Lady with a Lamp* (1929; reprint Longmans, Green, 1948). See also Garrick Theatre Programme, HO1/ST/NC/11/1, Nightingale Collection, LMA.
134. "Picture Gallery," *Daily Mail*, February 6, 1929, p. 9, *DMHA*.
135. "Picture Gallery," *Daily Mail*, February 6, 1929, p. 9, *DMHA*.
136. Typescript, "They Made History: Florence Nightingale," BBC Television, MS 8588, Wellcome Library, London.
137. See Letters from Rosalind Nash to Victor Bonham Carter, November 13, 1949 and November 23, 1949, 97M72/F725, Hampshire Record Office. For another critique see Edith Gittings Reid, *Florence Nightingale: A Drama* (Macmillan, 1922), 9.
138. Rosalind Nash, "Florence Nightingale: Vicissitudes of a Reputation, by One Who Knew Her," *Manchester Guardian*, May 6, 1929, p. 6, *Guardian Historical Archive*. See also Rosalind Nash, *A Sketch of the Life of Florence Nightingale* (SPCK, 1937).
139. See "The Real Florence Nightingale," *The Woman's Leader and the Common Cause*, February 15, 1929, pp. 11–12, Press Cuttings, 94M72/600, Hampshire Record Office and in Cuttings, Journals, and Pamphlets on Florence Nightingale, GC/236/b/1/5: Box 2, 1913–1933, Wellcome Library.
140. Williams, *Florence Nightingale*, 251.
141. For a new analysis of nineteenth-century feminists' reckonings with Queen Victoria herself, see Arianne Chernock, *The Right to Rule and the Rights of Women: Queen Victoria and the Women's Movement* (Cambridge University Press, 2019).
142. Ray Strachey, *The Cause: A Short History of the Women's Movement in Great Britain* (G. Bell & Sons, 1929) as cited in Showalter, "Florence Nightingale's Feminist Complaint"; see also Williams, *Florence Nightingale* and D. Lammond, *Great Lives: Florence Nightingale* (Duckworth, 1935), 143.
143. Williams, *Florence Nightingale*, 245.
144. See, for instance, A. A. Hoehling, *Edith Cavell* (Cassell, 1958).

145. On Still, see Lucy Seymer, *Dame Alicia Lloyd Still, A Memoir* (Smith and Ebbs, 1953).
146. Correspondence regarding the Nation's Fund for Nurses, Alicia Lloyd Still, April 27, 1920, HO1/ST/NC10/007, Nightingale Collection, LMA.
147. Seymer, *Florence Nightingale.*
148. Seymer, *Florence Nightingale.*
149. Appeal to Buy 10 South Street, especially Letter of April 9, 1930, Ethel Fenwick to Alicia Lloyd Still, HO1/ST/NTS/A16/6, Nightingale Collection, LMA.
150. Cecil Woodham-Smith, "Florence Nightingale," *Times*, April 12, 1954, p. 9, issue 52904; and W. G. Fiske, "Florence Nightingale," *Times*, May 26, 1954, p. 7, issue 52941, *TDA.*
151. Appeal to Buy 10 South Street, especially Letter of November 26, 1930, Alicia Lloyd Still to Ethel Fenwick, HO1/ST/NTS/A16/6, Nightingale Collection, LMA.
152. John Hutchinson, *Champions of Charity: War and the Rise of the Red Cross* (Westview Press, 1996).
153. See, for e.g., Newman, *Lady with a Lamp*; and *British Red Cross Review.*
154. History of Nursing Pageant Programme, Scala Theatre, 1937, HO1/ST/NC/11/002, Nightingale Collection, LMA.
155. On American uses of Nightingale, see Julia Irwin, *Making the World Safe: A Nation's Humanitarian Awakening* (Oxford University Press, 2013).
156. *Appeal by the National Florence Nightingale Memorial Committee of Great Britain for the Florence Nightingale International Foundation*, p. 4, Cuttings, Journals, and Pamphlets on Florence Nightingale, GC/236/b/1/5: Box 2, 1913–1933, Wellcome Library. See also Florence Nightingale International Foundation, HO1/ST/NC10/8, Nightingale Collection, LMA.
157. *The Commemoration of Florence Nightingale: An Oration Delivered by Sir George Newman*, 1938, H01/ST/NTS/Y/79/12, Nightingale Collection, LMA.
158. Papers Relating to the Nightingale Collection, Especially Letter from Mrs. Reiss, H01/ST/NTS/A16/017, Nightingale Collection, LMA.
159. Letter from Mary Gormand, May 21, 1940, HO1/ST/NC22/002, Nightingale Collection, LMA.
160. Lock of Hair with Newspaper Cutting, August 20, 1910, H01/ST/NC/22/003, Nightingale Collection, LMA.
161. See, for instance, "Crimean Exhibition," *Times*, December 20, 1935, p. 11, issue 47252, *TDA*; Typescript Catalogue: Exhibition of Papers Relating to Florence Nightingale, July 1937, H01/ST/NTS/A/16/027, Nightingale Collection, LMA.
162. "Florence Nightingale: Lady with the Paper Lamp," *Daily Telegraph*, January 27, 1989; advance notice; "Eminent Victorian," *Nursing Standard*, February 11, 1989, 20, no. 3, pp. 36–38; "Lady of the Lamp," *Evening Standard*, March 10, 1989. Cuttings found in Museum Opening File, Florence Nightingale Museum, London.
163. Maev Kennedy, "Nightingale's Crimean Carriage Goes on Show," *Guardian*, March 10, 2005 at www.theguardian.com/uk/2005/mar/11/arts.artsnews1.

164. On the Carriage, its damage, and its repair, see Carriage and Other Possessions, Nightingale Collection Prints and Photographs, HO1/ST/NC/PH/B/III/D/003-HO1/ST/NC/PH/B/D/027, Nightingale Collection, LMA.
165. Letters from Mr. W. Mumford and Mr. M. W. Sewell (1942–43), H01/St/NCPH/B/III/D/040, Nightingale Collection, LMA.
166. Frank Duesbury, "Boys Put Sabrina Above Mother," *Daily Mail*, September 24, 1957, p. 7, *DMHA*.
167. The journal *Victorian Studies* first appeared in 1957. For reflections on its relationship to Cold War modernity, see Matthew Rowlinson, "Theory of Victorian Studies: Anachronism and Self-Reflexivity," *Victorian Studies* 47, no. 2 (2005): 241–52; James Vernon, "Historians and the Victorian Studies Question: Response," *Victorian Studies* 47, no. 2 (2005): 272–78, especially 272–75; and Andrew H. Miller, "Response: Responsibility to the Present," *Victorian Studies* 59, no. 1 (2016): 122–26; Miles Taylor, "The Beginnings of Modern British Social History?," *History Workshop Journal* 43, no. 1 (Spring 1997): 155–76.
168. Quennell, "Florence Nightingale." See also Woodham-Smith, *Florence Nightingale: 1820–1910*.
169. "Lady with a lamp—and it's the real one," *Daily Mail*, March 21, 1951, p. 3, *DMHA*.
170. Doris Fincher, "Memory," *Daily Mail*, August 7, 1951, p. 2, *DMHA*; Letter from Elizabeth Copley to Matron, St. Thomas's Hospital, H01/ST/NC/08/013, Nightingale Collection, LMA.
171. Letter from Major General R. E. Barnsley, December 2, 1953, Florence Nightingale Centenary Committee, TNA WO 32/15498.
172. 100 Years of Army Nursing: Notes on the staging of the QARANC Exhibition to open on November 4, 1954, p. 2, TNA WO32/15498.
173. For nearly contemporary concerns about nursing recruitment more generally, see James Barclay, *Why No Nurses: The Nursing Recruitment Problem, Its History, Terms and Solution* (Faber and Faber, 1947). On the empire as an opportunity for recruitment, see Catherine Babikian, "'Partnership Not Prejudice': British Nurses, Colonial Students, and the National Health Service, 1948–1962," *Journal of British Studies* 60, no. 1 (2021): 140–68.
174. Letter from War Office to Lallie Lee Lowis, January 22, 1954, TNA WO 32/15498.
175. See Lucy Seymer Correspondence: Florence Nightingale Centenary Exhibition, HO1/ST/NTS/Y/12/001, 1954, Nightingale Collection, LMA. Seymer was a guiding force behind the 1937 exhibition as well. See H01/St/NTS/Y7/3a, 1937, Nightingale Collection, LMA.
176. See Catalogue of the Centenary Exhibition, Royal Surgeon's Hall, HO1/ST/NTS/Y/12/002, 1954, Nightingale Collection, LMA.
177. "Florence Nightingale Centenary," *Times*, May 13, 1954, p. 8, issue 52930, *TDA*.
178. "Order of Service," as filed on July 26, 1954, TNA WO 32/15498; and Our Own Correspondent, "Honour to Florence Nightingale," *Times*, November 5, 1954, p. 3, issue 53081, *TDA*.
179. J. C. Lambkin to War Office, September 30, 1954, TNA WO 32/15498.

180. Hodder-Williams, John Ernest. *Is That Lamp Going Out?* (Hodder and Stoughton, 1910).

181. See Imperial War Graves Cemeteries: Commemoration of Arrival of Florence Nightingale, 1954, TNA FO 371/112953.

182. On the 1960 exhibition in particular, see the files in HO1/ST/NTS/Y/13 and *Nursing Mirror* Copy of Nightingale Centenary Supplement Illustrated, HO1/ST/NCPH/C/VI/B/075, both in Nightingale Collection, LMA, as well as the 1960 Centenary Exhibition File, Florence Nightingale Museum Archives, Lambeth, London.

183. See First Day Covers, Florence Nightingale Stamp, HO1/ST/NC/21–2, 1970, and Poster with examples of First Day Cover, HO1/ST/NC/21/002/005, both in Nightingale Collection, LMA.

184. Tom Tickell, "Women of Note," *Guardian*, February 19, 1975, p. 15, *BPPQ*.

185. See First Day Covers, Florence Nightingale Stamp, and Poster with examples of First Day Cover.

186. See Cuttings: "Eminent Victorian," *Nursing Standard* 20, no. 3 (February 11, 1989): 36–38; "Nightingale Museum New Tourist Attraction," *Nursing Times*, February 1, 1989, 85, no. 5, np; "Where Florence Nightingale's Inspiration Will Shine On," *Sunday Telegraph*, January 29, 1989; Press Cutting, *British Medical Journal*, February 11, 1989, np, all in Museum Opening File: Florence Nightingale Museum.

187. Press Cutting, *British Medical Journal*, February 11, 1989.

188. "Florence Nightingale: Lady with the Paper Lamp," *Daily Telegraph*, January 27, 1989; "Why Florence Nightingale's Inspiration will Shine On." *Sunday Telegraph*, January 29, 1989, np.

189. "Lady of the Lamp," *Evening Standard*, March 10, 1989.

190. "Eminent Victorian," *Nursing Standard* 20, no. 3 (February 11, 1989): 36–38.

191. Simon Tait, "Nursing an Historic Lamp," *Times*, February 4, 1989, p. 31, issue 63309, *TDA*.

192. On the portrait, see Registered Packet 6202, *The Mission of Mercy: Florence Nightingale Receiving the Wounded at Scutari* by Jerry Barrett (1856), NPG 46/63/2, especially January 6, March 19, and June 8, 1993, National Portrait Gallery Archive, London.

193. Melissa van der Klugt, "Who was the Lady with the Lamp?," *Times*, May 11, 2010, p. 4, issue 69944, *TDA*.

194. van der Klugt, "Who was the Lady with the Lamp?" and Rachel Campbell-Johnston, "The Lady of the Lamp Shines Even Brighter," *Times*, May 3, 2010, p. 43, issue 69937, *TDA*.

195. Johnson, "Letters from Crimean War Major to Mother and Father in England shed an Unflattering Light on the Saintly Lady of the Lamp." See also Allbright, "Florence Nightingale Memories."

196. See, for example, Bostridge, *Florence Nightingale*, 249.

197. The *Daily Mail's* archive across the years provides one avenue for tracking these changes. See, for example, Margaret Lane, "Are Young Nurses Overworked?," January 13, 1934, p. 9; Rafael Sabatini, "Florence

Nightingale," January 29, 1934, p. 18; Miss J. A. A. et al., "Letters," April 27, 1962, p. 12; Celia Haddon, "Florence Nightingale Also Wore Drawers," October 18, 1965, p. 9; Hugh McLeave, "Nurses Seek Pay for Overtime," January 21, 1966, p. 10; Miss Phillis Williamson and Janet Fisher, "Nurses Rule," May 24, 1982, p. 22; John Illman, Medical Correspondent, "Florence Nightingale's NHS Problem," October 25, 1983, p. 3; Myles Harris, "How the NHS Destroyed the Nursing Profession," January 11, 1988, p. 7, *DMHA*.

198. McLeave, "Nurses Seek Pay for Overtime."
199. David Brindle, "Nurses Snuff Nightingale Image," *Guardian*, April 26, 1999, at www.theguardian.com/uk/1999/apr/27/davidbrindle; Jane Kelly, "Feminist, Rebel, and the Ideal Role Model," *Daily Mail*, April 2, 1999, pp. 24–25, *DMHA*.
200. Emily Wilson, Medical Reporter, "Nurses Abandon Florence," *Daily Mail*, April 29, 1999, *DMHA*.
201. See "Health Nurses Ditch Florence Nightingale Image," April 27, 1999, at http://news.bbc.co.uk/2/hi/health/329381.stm.

6   The Foremother

1. For another account of Seacole's rediscovery and reuses, see Samantha Pinto, "'The Right Woman in the Right Place': Mary Seacole and Corrective Histories of Empire," *ARIEL: A Review of International English Literature* 50, nos. 2–3 (2019): 1–31.
2. Mary Seacole, *Wonderful Adventures of Mrs. Seacole in Many Lands*, ed. Ziggi Alexander and Audrey Dewjee, 2nd ed. (Falling Wall Press, February 1984).
3. See, "Pass Notes: No. 1386: Mary Seacole," *Guardian*, April 29, 1999, p. A3. See for instance, Elizabeth Anionwu, *A Short History of Mary Seacole: A Resource for Nurses and Students* (Royal College of Nursing, 2005), 29; Seacole/1, Mary Seacole Collection: Educational Publications, Black Cultural Archives, Brixton, London (hereafter, BCA). A play, *Black Nightingale*, was originally performed in the year 1989.
4. [Tom Taylor], "A Stir for Seacole," *Punch*, December 6, 1856, p. 221, *Punch Historical Archive, 1841–1992*.
5. Mary Seacole, *Wonderful Adventures of Mrs. Seacole in Many Lands* (James Blackwood, Paternoster Row, 1857), 82.
6. Seacole, *Wonderful Adventures*, 37.
7. Seacole, *Wonderful Adventures*, 134.
8. Seacole, *Wonderful Adventures*, 136.
9. See, for instance, Jessica Damian, "A Novel Speculation: Mary Seacole's Ambitious Adventures in the New Granada Gold Mining Company," *Journal of West Indian Literature* 16, no. 1 (2007): 15–36.
10. "Our Own Vivandière," *Punch*, May 30, 1857, p. 221, *Punch Historical Archive, 1841–1992*.
11. Samuel Smiles, *Self Help, with Illustrations of Character and Conduct* (John Murray, 1859).

12. Seacole, *Wonderful Adventures*, 15.
13. On Seacole and Muscular Christianity, see Jessica Howell, "Mrs. Seacole Prescribes Hybridity: Constitutional and Maternal Rhetoric in *Wonderful Adventures of Mrs. Seacole in Many Lands*," *Victorian Literature and Culture* 38, no. 1 (2010): 107–25.
14. See Ron Ramdin, *Mary Seacole* (Haus, 2005), 3, 6. For a reading of Seacole as an expressly Creole text, see Rhonda Frederick, "Creole Performance in *Wonderful Adventures of Mrs. Seacole in Many Lands*," *Gender & History* 15, no. 3 (November 2003): 487–506.
15. [Taylor], "A Stir for Seacole," 221.
16. Seacole, *Wonderful Adventures*, 29.
17. Seacole, *Wonderful Adventures*, 11, 13, 49. On Seacole's own negotiation and construction of race, see Evelyn J. Hawthorne, "Self-Writing, Literary Traditions, and Post-Emancipation Identity: The Case of Mary Seacole," *Biography* 23, no. 2 (2000): 309–31. On race, embodiment, and feeling, see Alisha R. Walters, "'The Tears I Could Not Repress, Rolling Down My Brown Cheeks': Mary Seacole, Feeling, and the Imperial Body," *Nineteenth-Century Gender Studies* 16 no. 1 (2020), at http://ncgsjournal.com/issue161/issue161.html.
18. Seacole, *Wonderful Adventures*, 103. See also, for e.g., p. 38.
19. Seacole, *Wonderful Adventures*, 71.
20. Seacole, *Wonderful Adventures*, 71. On this production, see Loraine Mercer, "I Shall Make No Excuse: The Narrative Odyssey of Mary Seacole," *Journal of Narrative Theory* 35, no. 1 (2005): 1–24, especially p. 2.
21. Seacole, *Wonderful Adventures*, 5.
22. Seacole, *Wonderful Adventures*, 110.
23. See, among others cited in this chapter, Nicole Fluhr, "'Their Calling Me 'Mother' Was Not, I Think, Altogether Unmeaning': Mary Seacole's Maternal Personae," *Victorian Literature and Culture* 34, no. 1 (March 2006): 95–113; Mercer, "I Shall Make No Excuse," 12.
24. Seacole, *Wonderful Adventures*, 90.
25. Seacole, *Wonderful Adventures*, 112.
26. Seacole, *Wonderful Adventures*, 59.
27. Seacole, *Wonderful Adventures*, 160.
28. Seacole, *Wonderful Adventures*, 121. On Seacole and the production of the domestic, see Alison Fletcher, "'Mother Seacole': Victorian Domesticity on the Battlefields of the Crimean War," *Minerva: Journal of Women and War* 1, no. 2 (September 2007): 7–21.
29. Seacole, *Wonderful Adventures*, 91.
30. Seacole, *Wonderful Adventures*, 157.
31. Seacole, *Wonderful Adventures*, 159.
32. Seacole, *Wonderful Adventures*, 157.
33. On Seacole and affect, see Walters, "The Tears I Could Not Repress."
34. On Seacole's use of humor to navigate Englishness, see Angelia Poon, "Comic Acts of (Be)longing: Performing Englishness in *Wonderful Adventures of Mrs. Seacole in Many Lands*," *Victorian Literature and Culture* 35, no. 1 (March 2007): 501–16. On Seacole's use of imitation and

mimicry, see Amy Robinson, "Authority and the Public Display of Identity: *Wonderful Adventures of Mrs. Seacole in Many Lands*," *Feminist Studies* 20, no. 3 (Autumn 1994): 537–57. On Seacole's radical negotiations of community, see Sandra Gunning, "Traveling with Her Mother's Tastes: The Negotiation of Gender, Race, and Location in 'Wonderful Adventures of Mrs. Seacole in Many Lands,'" *Signs* 26, no. 4 (2001): 949–81.

35. Seacole, *Wonderful Adventures*, 164.

36. On the estrangement of the veteran, see Kate McLoughlin, *Veteran Poetics: British Literature in the Age of Mass Warfare* (Cambridge University Press, 2018), Chapter 2.

37. Seacole, *Wonderful Adventures*, 143.

38. For a dramatic portrayal of the regiment as a caretaking unit, see T. W. Robertson, *Ours* (1866), as anthologized in T. W. Robertson, *Six Plays*, with an introduction by Michael R. Booth (Amber Lane Press, 1980), 57–118.

39. Seacole, *Wonderful Adventures*, 170.

40. Seacole, *Wonderful Adventures*, 170. On Seacole as a veteran herself, see Aeron Hunt, "Ordinary Claims: War, Work, Service, and the Victorian Veteran," *Victorian Studies* 61, no. 3 (Spring 2019): 395–418.

41. Seacole, *Wonderful Adventures*, 5.

42. Jane Robinson, *Mary Seacole: The Most Famous Black Woman of the Victorian Age* (Carroll and Graff, 2004), 174.

43. D. A. Meritis, "Mrs. Seacole A Bankrupt," *Times*, November 24, 1856, p. 8, issue 22533, *TDA*.

44. Rokeby, "Mrs. Seacole," *Times*, November 29, 1856, p. 12, issue 22534 *TDA*.

45. Ramdin, *Mary Seacole*, 114–15 and Robinson, *Mary Seacole*, 121.

46. Robinson, *Mary Seacole*, 175; Ramdin, *Mary Seacole*, 113–17.

47. She died in May 1881 and left a sizeable estate worth over £2,600. "Obituary," *Times*, May 21, 1881, p. 7, issue 30200, *TDA*.

48. "Jamaica Portraits and Jamaica History," *Times*, April 22, 1905, p. 8, issue 37688, *TDA*.

49. Deborah Gabriel, "Great Jamaicans: Mary Seacole, 1805–1881," *Jamaican Magazine* (2004), at http://jamaicans.com/maryseac/; Anionwu, *Short History of Mary Seacole*, 30; see also Ramdin, *Mary Seacole*, 125. For stamp examples, see Seacole/10, Mary Seacole Collection: Mary Seacole Stamps, BCA.

50. On the intellectual and cultural politics of the moment more generally, see Rob Waters, *Thinking Black: Britain, 1964–1985* (University of California Press, 2019). On an earlier milieu, see Marc Matera, *Black London: The Imperial Metropolis and Decolonization in the Twentieth Century* (University of California Press, 2015). On the claiming of citizenship, see Kennetta Hammond Perry, *London is the Place for Me: Black Britons, Citizenship, and the Politics of Race* (Oxford University Press, 2016).

51. Anionwu, *Short History of Mary Seacole*, 30–43; see also Seacole/7, Mary Seacole Collection: Teaching Materials, BCA.

52. Elizabeth Anionwu, "Mary Seacole: Her Life," in *A Statue for Mary: The Seacole Legacy*, ed. Jean Gray (Mary Seacole Memorial Statue Appeal,

2016), 13; Seacole/9: Mary Seacole Collection: The Friends of Mary Seacole, BCA.

53. See lithographed typescript leaflet, "Mary Seacole: Jamaican National Heroine and Nurse in the Crimean War (1805? – May 14, 1881)," Published 1981, Brent Library Service, NAM 1981–06–22. See also Ziggi Alexander and Audrey Dewjee, "Mary Seacole," *History Today* 31 (September 1981), Press/13, BCA.

54. Anionwu, *Short History of Mary Seacole*, 33; Seacole/7: Mary Seacole Collection: Teaching Materials, BCA.

55. Press Cutting: Dorothy Kuya, "Roots in Britain," *Dragon's Teeth: Bulletin of the National Committee on Racism in Children's Books* 2, no. 4 (December 1980), Seacole/7, file 2: Mary Seacole Collection, Teaching Materials, BCA. There is now an ample history addressing the longevity of the African presence in Europe. A recent book to receive wide attention is Olivette Otele's *African Europeans: An Untold Story* (Hurst, 2020).

56. Helen J. Seaton, "Another Florence Nightingale? The Rediscovery of Mary Seacole," at www.victorianweb.org/history/crimea/seacole.html.

57. Peter Fryer, *Staying Power: The History of Black People in Britain* (Pluto Press, 1984); Trevor Philipps, "Welcome Relief in the Battle against Racism," *Times*, May 12, 1984, p. 15, issue 61829, *TDA*.

58. Robinson, *Mary Seacole*, 174.

59. From a Correspondent, "Mrs. Seacole," *Times*, December 24 1954, p. 8, issue 53123, *TDA*.

60. Press Cutting: *Dragon's Teeth* 18 (Summer 1984), 14–15, Seacole/7 file 2: Mary Seacole Collection, Educational Materials, BCA.

61. Mary Seacole, *Wonderful Adventures of Mrs. Seacole in Many Lands*, ed. William L. Andrews (Oxford University Press, 1988). On the interpretive effects of republication, see Sandra Pouchet Paquet, "The Enigma of Arrival: The Wonderful Adventures of Mrs. Seacole in Many Lands," *African-American Review* 50, no. 4 (2017): 864–76.

62. Roy Kerridge, "Black Nightingale," *The Spectator*, March 24, 1984, pp. 25–26, especially p. 25, Seacole/9: Mary Seacole Collection, The Friends of Mary Seacole, BCA.

63. For a recent challenge, see Hakim Adi, ed., *Black British History: New Perspectives from Roman Times to the Present Day* (Zed Books, 2019).

64. Kerridge, "Black Nightingale," 25–26, especially p. 26.

65. Kerridge, "Black Nightingale," 25.

66. See Seacole/9, Mary Seacole Collection: Friends of Mary Seacole Papers, BCA.

67. See Seacole/9, Mary Seacole Collection: Friends of Mary Seacole Papers, BCA; Anionwu, *Short History of Mary Seacole*, 36.

68. See BCA 6/7/8, Mary Seacole Exhibition Press Cuttings: "Heroism is Acknowledged at Last," *The Voice*, May 26, 1992, BCA.

69. Seacole/9: Friends of Mary Seacole Papers, BCA.

70. Poem by John Rafferty, Friends of Mary Seacole Papers, Seacole/9, BCA.

71. See Seacole/7, Mary Seacole Collection, Teaching Materials, BCA.

72. See, among others, Jordanna Bailkin, *The Afterlife of Empire* (University of California Press, 2012).
73. On the negotiation of race inside the NHS and beyond, see Roberta Bivins, "Picturing Race in the British National Health Service, 1948–1988," *Twentieth Century British History* 28, no. 1 (March 2017): 83–109.
74. Press Cutting: Paul Crawford, "The Other Lady with the Lamp," *Nursing Times*, March 11, 1992, pp. 56–58, especially p. 57, Seacole/7: file 2, Mary Seacole Collection, Teaching Materials, BCA. For an assessment of immigration discourses around Commonwealth nurses, see Anna Caceres, "Windrush Migrants and 'Our NHS Heroes,'" June 25, 2020, at www .historyworkshop.org.uk/windrush-migrants-and-our-nhs-heroes/.
75. See Anionwu, *Short History of Mary Seacole*. For Anionwu's fascinating life history, see Elizabeth Anionwu. *Mixed Blessings of a Cambridge Union* (Elizan, 2016).
76. See "Black Nightingale" *Playbill*, Seacole/7: file 2, Mary Seacole Collection, Teaching Materials, BCA.
77. Press Cutting: "Tale of an Angel of Mercy," *The Voice*, October 29, 1991, p. 21, Ephemera/391, BCA.
78. Conversation with Cleo Sylvestre, De Beauvoir Square, London, May 5, 2017.
79. Ephemera/36/60, BCA.
80. The file BCA 6/7/3, BCA provides ample documentation of the exhibit.
81. Yet, there were still slights and oversights at this seemingly victorious occasion. There were plenty of newspapers that failed to note the Black Cultural Archives' role in enabling the exhibition, despite its being held on the organization's very premises. For Sam Walker, this was an all too familiar pattern, wherein the black press did not pay heed to black organizations. This all left him "extremely angry," in his own words, frustrated that the BCA was "once again sidelined by the people who should support us." BCA 6/7/3, especially letter of May 14, 1992 from Sam Walker to Brixton's *Weekly Journal*, BCA.
82. David Brindle, "Nursing Pays Debt to Forgotten Heroine," *Guardian*, May 20, 1992, Seacole/7: file 2, Mary Seacole Collection, Teaching Materials, BCA.
83. "Heroism is Acknowledged at Last," *The Voice*, May 26, 1992, BCA; "Key Role in Black History," *Hackney Gazette*, May 29, 1992; "Overdue Celebration Held for Life of Neglected Black Leader," *Nursing Times*, May 27, 1992, BCA 6/7/8, Mary Seacole Exhibition Press Cuttings, BCA.
84. "Heroism is Acknowledged at Last," *The Voice*, May 26, 1992, BCA.
85. "Key Role in Black History," *Hackney Gazette*, May 29, 1992.
86. Nigel Pollitt, "Forgotten Heroine," *Times Educational Supplement,* June 26, 1992, p. 33, Seacole/7: file 2, Mary Seacole Collection, Teaching Materials, BCA.
87. "Mary Seacole Exhibition Evaluation Report to the London Boroughs Grants Committee," December 1992, BCA 6/7/3, BCA.
88. "Mary Seacole Exhibition Evaluation Report to the London Boroughs Grants Committee," December 1992, BCA 6/7/3, BCA.

89. Response on June 26, 1992, Mary Seacole Exhibition Evaluation Report, BCA 6/7/3, BCA.
90. Response on June 29, 1992, Mary Seacole Exhibition Evaluation Report, BCA 6/7/3, BCA.
91. "Teacher's Pack: Mary Seacole, the Jamaican Heroine of the Crimean War," BCA 6/7/3; "Mary Seacole Exhibition: Curriculum Study Notes," BCA 6/7/3, folder 2, BCA. For its innovations, it received plaudits from the *Times Educational Supplement*. Ambitions and hopes for the enterprise may have been national, but the allure was, in truth, regional, with over 50 percent of the 250 packets sold going to schools in the Greater London area.
92. Press Cuttings: *Black Briton*, Friday, November 1, 1991, p. 4, Ephemera/391, BCA.
93. Letter from Alex Attewell to Sherlina Chamberlain, August 8, 1991 and "Mary Seacole Exhibition: Curriculum Study Notes," BCA 6/7/3, folder 2, BCA.
94. "Mary Seacole Exhibition: Curriculum Study Notes," BCA 6/7/3, folder 2, BCA.
95. Pollitt, "Forgotten Heroine," 33.
96. Press Release: *History Today,* February 2005, Mary Jane Seacole Portrait File, NPG39/69/49: Registered Packet 5856, Heinz Archive and Library, National Portrait Gallery, London (hereafter, NPG).
97. Report/F1741, November 2003, Seacole Portrait File, NPG39/69/49.
98. Press Cutting: *Oxford Times,* February 18, 2010, NPG39/69/49.
99. Report/F1741, November 2003, Seacole Portrait File, NPG39/69/49.
100. Curatorial Notes, Seacole Portrait File, NPG39/69/49.
101. Report/F1741, November 2003, Seacole Portrait File, NPG39/69/49.
102. Report/F1741, November 2003, Seacole Portrait File, NPG39/69/49.
103. Email from Helen Rappaport to Peter Funnell, January 22, 2004, Seacole Portrait File, NPG39/69/49.
104. Press Cutting: *Oxford Times*, February 18, 2010, NPG39/69/49.
105. Matthew Taylor, "Nurse is Greatest Black Briton," *Guardian*, February 10, 2004, at www.theguardian.com/uk/2004/feb/10/britishiden tity.artsandhumanities.
106. "Lost Portrait of Mary Seacole Discovered," National Portrait Gallery Press Release, January 11, 2005, NPG39/69/49.
107. "Lost Portrait of Mary Seacole Discovered," National Portrait Gallery Press Release, January 11, 2005, NPG39/69/49. Rappaport remained the painting's owner until 2008, when the Gallery purchased the work for £130,000 with the help of visitor gifts and the Heritage Lottery Fund. Letter from Helen Rappaport to Peter Funnell, July 28, 2008, NPG39/69/49.
108. Email from Sandy Nairne to Peter Funnell, September 10, 2004, NPG39/69/49.
109. Press Cutting: *Oxford Times,* February 18, 2010, NPG39/69/49.
110. Pinto, "'Right Woman in the Right Place.'"
111. Letter from Robert Miller to Peter Funnell, April 7, 2015, NPG 39/69/49.
112. Letter to Sandy Nairne from David Bye, Mary Seacole Housing Association, March 2, 2005, NPG39/69/49.

113. Letter to Sandy Nairne from Geoff Taylor, Speaker of Hackney Council, February 16, 2005, NPG39/69/49.
114. Flyer, Seacole/5: Ephemera, Mary Seacole Collection, BCA.
115. Flyer, Seacole/7: Teaching Materials, Mary Seacole Collection, BCA; Flyer, Ephemera/36/62, BCA.
116. See Emma Lynch, *The Life of Mary Seacole* (Heinemann/Harcourt, 2005). Titles published earlier include Harriet Castor, *Mary Seacole* (Franklin Watts, 1999); Trish Cooke and Anni Axworthy, *Hoorah for Mary Seacole* (Franklin Watts, 2008); Brian Williams, *The Life and World of Mary Seacole* (Heinemann, 2003); published just after this date were Paul Harrison, *Who was Mary Seacole?* (Wayland, 2007); Sarah Ridley, *Mary Seacole and the Crimean War* (Franklin Watts, 2009). On the explosion of this, and related, literatures, see Karen Sands O'Connor, "My (Black) Britain: The West Indies and Britain in Twenty-First Century Nonfiction Picture Books," *Bookbird: A Journal of International Children's Literature* 50, no. 3 (July 2012): 1–11.
117. Anionwu, *Short History of Mary Seacole*, 40.
118. Tim Taylor, "The Mary Seacole Debate: A Teacher's View of the Primary Curriculum," *Guardian*, January 10, 2013, at www.theguardian.com/teacher-network/teacher-blog/2013/jan/10/mary-seacole-primary-curriculum-teachers-gove. On anniversaries, see Katie Donington, Ryan Hanley, and Jessica Moody, eds., *Britain's History and Memory of Transatlantic Slavery: Local Nuances of a National "Sin"* (Liverpool University Press, 2016); David T. Gleeson and Simon Lewis, eds., *Ambiguous Anniversary: The Bicentennial of the International Slave Trade Bans* (University of South Carolina Press, 2012).
119. Greg Jenner, "Michael Gove is Wrong: Mary Seacole Belongs on the School Curriculum," *Huffington Post* (UK), January 6, 2013, at www.huffingtonpost.co.uk/greg-jenner/dropping-mary-seacole-from-schools-curriculum-would-be-a-mistake_b_2415735.html.
120. See, for e.g., Peter Hitchens, "How 'Multiculture' Fanatics Took Mary Seacole Hostage," *Daily Mail*, January 5, 2013, at www.dailymail.co.uk/debate/article-2257668/PETER-HITCHENS-How-multiculture-fanatics-took-Mary-Seacole-hostage.html. See also Hugh Muir, "Why is Gove Trashing Mary Seacole?," *Guardian*, January 6, 2013, at www.theguardian.com/education/2013/jan/06/gove-mary-seacole-black-florence-nightingale. For a recent assessment and retrospective, see Caroline Bressey, "Radical History Then and Now," *History Workshop Journal* 83 (Spring 2017): 217–22.
121. Petition by Operation Black Vote, "Michael Gove, Secretary of State for Education: Keep Mary Seacole on the National Curriculum," at www.change.org/p/michael-gove-secretary-of-state-for-education-keep-mary-seacole-on-the-national-curriculum.
122. Lynn Macdonald, *Mary Seacole: The Making of the Myth* (Iguana Books, 2014).
123. Guy Walters, "The Black Florence Nightingale and the Making of a PC Myth: One Historian Explains How Mary Seacole's Story Never Stood Up," *Daily Mail*, December 30, 2012, at www.dailymail.co.uk/news/article-2255095/The-black-Florence-Nightingale-making-PC-myth-One-historian-explains-Mary-Seacoles-story-stood-up.html; and Rod Liddle,

"How Did Mary Seacole Come to Be Revered as a Black Icon?," *Spectator*, January 2013, at www.spectator.co.uk/2013/01/how-did-mary-seacole-come-to-be-revered-as-a-black-icon/.

124. Kevin Rawlinson, "Another Gove-U Turn: Mary Seacole Will Remain on the Curriculum," *Independent*, February 7, 2013, at www.independent.co.uk/news/uk/politics/another-gove-u-turn-mary-seacole-will-remain-on-the-curriculum-8485472.html.

125. Dan Lyndon-Cohen, "A Response to the Proposed National Curriculum in History," *History Workshop Online*, February 24, 2013, at www.historyworkshop.org.uk/nationalcurriculum/.

126. Email from Adjani Okpu-Egbe, June 12, 2020.

127. See adjaniogpuegbe.com/painting.

128. See, especially, "Community Fundraising" and "The Making of the Sculpture," in Gray, *Statue for Mary*, 73 and 77.

129. Clive Soley, "From a North West London Cemetery to the Southbank," in Gray, *Statue for Mary*, 11.

130. Lisa Rodrigues, "What Mary Seacole Means to Me," in Gray, *Statue for Mary*, 29–30, especially p. 29.

131. Anionwu, "Mary Seacole: Her Life," 13–15, especially p. 13.

132. Martin Jennings, "Against a Battlefield," in Gray, *Statue for Mary*, 17–19, especially p. 17.

133. Jennings, "Against a Battlefield," 18.

134. Jennings, "Against a Battlefield," 17.

135. Jennings, "Against a Battlefield," 19.

136. Jennings, "Against a Battlefield," 18.

137. Soley, "From a North West London Cemetery to the Southbank," 11.

138. Jennings, "Against a Battlefield," 18.

139. Jennings, "Against a Battlefield," 19.

140. Letter from George Osborne to Clive Soley, 11 June 2016, as printed in Gray, *Statue for Mary*, 119.

141. "Mary Seacole Trust," *JustGiving*, at www.justgiving.com/maryseacole memorial.

142. Roxanne St. Clair, "Five-Year Mission," in Gray, *Statue for Mary*, 39.

143. Shreela Flather, "Personal Warmth," in Gray, *Statue for Mary*, 37.

144. Deidre Mills, "A Pioneering Jamaican," and Marsha John-Greenwood, "What it Means to be Great," in Gray, *Statue for Mary*, 33–34 and 45.

145. Helen Rappaport, "The Invitation that Never Came: Mary Seacole after the Crimea," *History Today* 55, no. 2 (February 2005): 9–15. See also Seacole Portrait File, NPG39/69/49.

146. This is evident in the CBBC Horrible Histories Series for Children. See, for instance, "Horrible Histories: Mary Seacole Lyrics," *YouTube* video, 2 minutes, 25 seconds, at www.youtube.com/watch?v=KNkwY7laMlA; "Mary Seacole vs. Florence Nightingale," *YouTube* video, 3 minutes, 22 seconds, at www.youtube.com/watch?v=nc0cht6YfI8. Samantha Pinto also discusses Seacole's appearance in the Horrible Histories. Pinto, "'Right Woman in the Right Place.'"

147. Patrick Vernon, "Rubbishing Mary Seacole is Another Move to Hide the Contributions of Black People," *Guardian*, June 21, 2016, at www .theguardian.com/commentisfree/2016/jun/21/rubbishing-mary-seacole-hide-black-contributions-britain.

148. Simon Usborne, "Mary Seacole v Florence Nightingale: Who Should Have the Taller Statue?," *Guardian,* June 20, 2016, at www.theguardian.com/arta nddesign/shortcuts/2016/jun/20/mary-seacole-florence-nightingale-statue-st -thomas-hospital-row.

149. Kashmira Gander, "Mary Seacole Statue: Why Florence Nightingale Fans are Angry the Crimean War Nurse is Being Commemorated," *Independent*, June 24, 2016, at www.independent.co.uk/arts-entertainment/florence-vs-mary-the-big-nurse-off-a7100676.html.

150. Hugh Taylor, "Mary and Florence," in Gray, *Statue for Mary,* 22.

151. Mary Seacole Trust, "The Mary Seacole Trust," About Us, at www .maryseacoletrust.org.uk/about/.

152. For a critique of institutionalization, see Sarah Ahmed, *On Being Included: Racism and Diversity in Institutional Life* (Duke University Press, 2012); Pinto, "'Right Woman in the Right Place.'"

153. An important recent consideration of the island histories of Britain and Jamaica is Hazel Carby's *Imperial Intimacies: A Tale of Two Islands* (Verso, 2019).

Afterword: Do and Die

1. Furneaux, *Military Men of Feeling*, Introduction.

2. Baumgart, *The Crimean War, 1853–1856*, 227.

3. Stuart Sweeney, *The Europe Illusion: Britain, France, Germany and the Long History of European Integration* (Reaktion, 2019), 78, 335.

4. David Reynolds, *Island Stories: An Unconventional History of Britain* (Basic Books, 2020), Chapter 2.

5. O'Toole, *Heroic Failure*, 1, 7. See also Stephanie Barczewski, *Heroic Failure and the British* (Yale University Press, 2016).

6. O'Toole, *Heroic Failure*, 21, 38, 66. See also Reynolds, *Island Stories*, Chapter 1.

7. O'Toole, *Heroic Failure*, 70.

8. Stuart Ward and Astrid Rasch, "Introduction: Greater Britain, Global Britain," in *Embers of Empire in Brexit Britain*, ed. Ward and Rasch (Bloomsbury, 2019), 3–4; see also Satia, *Time's Monster: How History Makes History*, 275.

9. Guy Verhofstadt, "Boris Johnson's Threat of a No-Deal Brexit Will Not Break EU Unity," *Guardian*, July 31, 2019, at www.theguardian.com/com mentisfree/2019/jul/31/boris-johnson-eu-no-deal-brexit-uk-government-backstop.

10. Tom McTague, "Why the British Take Glory in Defeat," *The Atlantic*, June 27, 2019, at www.theatlantic.com/international/archive/2019/06/what-boris-johnsons-do-or-die-slip-really-means/592717/.

11. Ian Jack, "Boris Johnson Was Unwise to Quote Kipling. But He Wasn't Praising Empire," *Guardian*, October 7, 2017, at www.theguardian.com/commentisfree/2017/oct/07/boris-johnson-kipling-myanmar-mandalay-colonialism.

12. McTague, "Why the British Take Glory in Defeat."

13. John Kiddell, "Boris has Surely Adopted the 17th Lancers' Motto," Letter, *Financial Times*, August 20, 2019, at www.ft.com/content/9b0bf5d4-c402-11e9-a8e9-296ca66511c9.

14. Verhofstadt, "Boris Johnson's Threat of a No-Deal Brexit Will Not Break EU Unity."

15. Julian Cole, "The Vital Misquote in Boris de Pfeffel's Charge of the Shite Brigade," *Voice of the North*, June 30, 2019, at www.voiceofthenorth.net/the-vital-misquote-in-boris-de-pfeffels-charge-of-the-shite-brigade/.

16. See, among others, Reynolds, *Island Stories*, 48, 83–85.

17. Imperial War Museum, "Flying Officer John Alexander Cruickshank V.C.," at www.iwm.org.uk/history/john-alexander-cruickshank-vc.

18. Danielle Sheridan, "Last Surviving World War Two Holder of Victoria Cross Wants "Quiet' Day to Mark 100th Birthday," *Telegraph*, at www.telegraph.co.uk/news/2020/05/20/last-surviving-world-war-two-holder-victoria-cross-wants-quiet/amp/.

19. Ben Philip, "Britain's Last Surviving World War Two Victoria Cross Hero Turns 100," at www.bbc.com/news/uk-scotland-north-east-orkney-shetland-52704526.

20. "Captain Tom Moore Raises £15m for NHS as He Completes Garden Walk," *Guardian*, April 16, 2020, at www.theguardian.com/world/2020/apr/16/coronavirus-capt-tom-moore-raises-12m-nhs-completes-garden-walk.

21. On the postwar moment, in particular, see Owen Hatherley, *The Ministry of Nostalgia* (Verso, 2016).

22. Mark Landler, "The 100-Year-Old Who Raised $40 Million for UK Health Workers," *New York Times*, May 15, 2020, at www.nytimes.com/2020/05/15/world/europe/captain-tom-moore.html.

23. "London's 2021 Fireworks. Happy New Year Live! BBC," *YouTube* video, 10 minutes, 1 second, January 1, 2021, at www.youtube.com/watch?v=MpJIg_3DnLk&ab_channel=BBC.

24. "Captain Tom Moore Knighted by the Queen During Outdoor Ceremony at Windsor Castle," *YouTube* video, 3 minutes, 51 seconds, July 17, 2020, at www.youtube.com/watch?v=xBIMV5NebrI; Tobias Harper, *From Servants of the Empire to Everyday Heroes: the British Honours System in the Twentieth Century* (Oxford, 2020).

25. Stephen. Bates, "Captain Sir Tom Moore Obituary," *Guardian*, February 4, 2021, at www.theguardian.com/society/2021/feb/02/capt-sir-tom-moore-obituary

26. Caroline Davies and Yohannes Lowe, "Captain Sir Tom Moore Dies at 100 After Testing Positive for Covid," *Guardian*, February 2, 2020, at www.theguardian.com/uk-news/2021/feb/02/captain-sir-tom-moore-dies-at-100-after-testing-positive-for-covid

27. "Coronavirus: How NHS Nightingale Was Built in Just Nine Days," at www.bbc.com/news/health-52125059; Denis Campbell and Rowena Mason,

"London NHS Nightingale Hospital Will Shut Next Week," *Guardian*, May 4, 2020, at www.theguardian.com/world/2020/may/04/london-nhs-nightingale-hospital-placed-on-standby; https://www.england.nhs.uk/2020/04/nhs-steps-up-coronavirus-fight-with-two-more-nightingale-hospitals/.

28. Carola Hoyos, "How Would Florence Nightingale Have Tackled Covid-19," at www.theguardian.com/society/2020/may/05/how-would-florence-nightingale-tackled-covid-19-200-year-anniversary; https://www.florence-nightingale.co.uk/covid-19/.

29. Robert Dex, "Florence Nightingale Nursing Museum Closes For 'Foreseeable Future' as Visitor Numbers Collapse," *Evening Standard*, January 6, 2021, at www.standard.co.uk/news/uk/florence-nightingale-nursing-museum-closes-b674878.html; Geraldine Kendall Adams, "Florence Nightingale Museum Closes Indefinitely to Safeguard its Future," *Museums Journal*, January 8, 2021, at www.museumsassociation.org/museums-journal/news/2021/01/florence-nightingale-museum-closes-indefinitely-to-safeguard-its-future/.

30. https://hansonsauctioneers.co.uk/blog/2020/06/can-boris-johnson-barbie-and-charles-hanson-save-florence-nightingale-museum; https://www.florence-nightingale.co.uk/product/florence-nightingale-barbie-inspiring-women-doll/; https://hansonslive.hansonsauctioneers.co.uk/m/view-auctions/catalog/id/71?page=2.

31. Jackie Sibblies Drury, *Marys Seacole* (Dramatists Play Service, 2019); https://newyorktheater.me/2019/02/25/marys-seacole-review-a-creole-florence-nightingale/; https://www.theatermania.com/off-broadway/reviews/marys-seacole-and-black-female-caretakers_87924.html.

32. "First Seacole Centre Opens Doors as NHS Expands COVID Rehab Services," May 29, 2020, at www.england.nhs.uk/2020/05/first-seacole-centre-opens-doors-as-nhs-expands-covid-rehab-services/; www.england.nhs.uk/2020/05/first-seacole-centre-opens-doors-as-nhs-expands-covid-rehab-services/.

33. Haroon Siddique, "Key Findings from Public Health: England's Report on COVID-19 Deaths," *Guardian*, June 2, 2020, at www.theguardian.com/world/2020/jun/02/key-findings-from-public-health-englands-report-on-covid-19-deaths.

34. Jackie Sibblies Drury's *Marys Seacole* had literally put these workers, and female caregivers especially, on center stage, as it considered the roles of Black health workers across generations.

35. www.bbc.com/news/health-52242856; Haroon Siddique "Historical Racism May Be Behind England's Higher BAME COVID-19 Rate," *Guardian*, June 16, 2020, at www.theguardian.com/world/2020/jun/16/historical-racism-may-be-behind-englands-higher-bame-covid-19-rate.

36. Anna Russell, "How Statues in Britain Began to Fall," *New Yorker,* June 22, 2020, at www.newyorker.com/news/letter-from-the-uk/how-statues-in-britain-began-to-fall

37. www.bbc.com/news/53014592; Gurminder K. Bhambra, "A Statue Was Toppled: Can We Finally Talk about the British Empire?" *New York Times,* June 6, 2012, at www.nytimes.com/2020/06/12/opinion/edward-colston-statue-racism.html?action=click&module=Well&pgtype=Homepage&section=Opinion.

38. "Crimean War Heroine Mary Seacole Statue Sells for £101,000, at www
    .bbc.com/news/uk-england-gloucestershire-53593981; "Film Producer Buys
    Seacole Bust for 101 Times the Estimate," at www.antiquestradegazette.com
    /print-edition/2020/august/2454/news/film-producer-buys-seacole-bust-for-1
    01-times-the-estimate/.
39. www.maryseacoletrust.org.uk/statement-from-vice-chair-lisa-rodrigues-cbe
    -on-black-lives-matter/.
40. "London's 2021 Fireworks. Happy New Year Live! BBC."
41. Bill Schwartz, "Forgetfulness: England's Discontinuous Histories," in
    Embers of Empire in Brexit Britain, ed. Ward and Rasch, 51–52.

Bibliography

Archives

Black Cultural Archives, Brixton, London, UK
Bristol Archives, Bristol, UK
The British Library, London, UK
Cheshire Archives and Local Studies, Chester, UK
Department of Manuscripts, Cambridge University Library, Cambridge, UK
Florence Nightingale Museum Archives, London, UK
Gloucestershire Archives, Gloucester, UK
Hampshire Record Office, Winchester, UK
Harry Ransom Humanities Research Center, University of Texas, Austin, Texas, USA
Heinz Archive and Library, National Portrait Gallery, London, UK
Imperial War Museum Archives, London, UK
The John Rylands Library, University of Manchester, Manchester, UK
Kent Archives and Local History Library, Maidstone, UK
Lancashire Archives, Preston, UK
Liddell Hart Centre for Military Archives, King's College, London, UK
London Metropolitan Archives, Farringdon, London, UK
Manuscripts and Special Collections, University of Nottingham Library, Nottingham, UK
The National Archives, Kew, UK
National Army Museum, Templer Study Centre, Chelsea, London, UK
Nottinghamshire Archives, Nottingham, UK
Royal College of Nursing Library and Heritage Centre, Marylebone, London, UK
Warwickshire County Record Office, Warwick, UK
Wellcome Library, Archives and Manuscripts, London, UK
West Sussex Record Office, Chichester, UK
West Yorkshire Archive Service, Bradford, UK

Periodicals

All the Year Round
Athenaeum

Atlantic
Bath Chronicle
Birmingham Daily Post
Boy's Own Magazine
Bristol Mercury
The British Red Cross Review
Caledonian Mercury
Chambers's Journal of Popular Literature, Science and Arts
Chester Chronicle and Cheshire and North Wales General Advertiser
Contemporary Review
Daily Graphic
Daily Mail
Daily Mail Atlantic Edition
Daily News
Daily Telegraph
Derby Daily Telegraph
Derby Mercury
Devon and Exeter Daily Gazette
Dundee Courier and Argus
Essex County Chronicle
Evening Standard
Evening Telegraph and Post
Examiner
Express
Financial Times
Graphic
Guardian
Hampshire Advertiser and Salisbury Guardian
Huddersfield Daily Chronicle
Huffington Post
Illustrated London News
Independent
Irish Times
John Bull and Britannia
Judy, or the London Serio-Comic Journal
The Lady's Newspaper
Leader and Saturday Analyst
Leeds Mercury
Leicester Chronicle
Leicestershire Mercury and General Advertiser
Liverpool Mercury
Lloyd's Illustrated Newspaper
Lloyd's Weekly Newspaper
London Review of Politics, Society, Literature, Art and Science
Macmillan's Magazine
Manchester Courier and Lancashire General Advertiser
Manchester Guardian

Mirror
Morning Chronicle
Morning Post
Musical Times and Singing Class Circular
New Yorker
New York Times
Newcastle Guardian and Tyne Mercury
Newcastle Journal
Newcastle Weekly Courant
Norfolk Chronicle and Norwich Gazette
Northern Echo
Nottingham Daily Guardian
Nottingham Post
Nursing Standard
Observer
Paisley Herald
Punch
Review of Reviews
Reynolds's Newspaper
Royal Cornwall Gazette, Falmouth Packet, and General Advertiser
Saturday Review of Politics, Literature, Science, and Art
Sheffield Daily Telegraph
Sheffield and Rotherham Independent
Spectator
Sunday Telegraph
St. James's Gazette
Standard
Stirling Observer
Strand Magazine
Sydney Morning Herald
Voice of the North
The Woman's Leader and the Common Cause

Primary and Secondary Sources

P.D. *Duty; or, the Heroes of the Charge in the Valley of Balaklava.* Joseph Masters, 1854.
Abbott, Maude E. Seymour. *Florence Nightingale.* McGill, 1916.
Adams, James Eli. *Dandies and Desert Saints: Styles of Victorian Masculinity.* Cornell University Press, 1995.
Adi, Hakim, ed. *Black British History: New Perspectives from Roman Times to the Present Day.* Zed Books, 2019.
Adye, J. and C. Gordon. *Report on the Crimean Cemeteries.* HMSO, 1873.
Ahmed, Sarah. *On Being Included: Racism and Diversity in Institutional Life.* Duke University Press, 2012.
Alexander, James Edward. *Travels to the Seat of War in the East, through Russia and the Crimea in 1829.* H. Coburn and R. Bentley, 1829.

Ali, Sardar Asghar. *Our Heroes of the Great War: A Record of the VCs Won by the Indian Army*. Times Press, 1922.

Alibhai-Brown, Yasmin. *Imagining the New Britain*. Routledge, 2001.

Allen, Jennifer L. "National Commemoration in an Age of Transnationalism." *Journal of Modern History* 91 (March 2019): 109–48.

Altick, Richard. *The English Common Reader*. University of Chicago Press, 1957.

Anderson, David. "Dying of Nostalgia: Homesickness in the Union Army during the Civil War." *Civil War History* 56, no. 3 (September 2010): 247–82.

Anderson, Duncan. *Glass Warriors: The Camera at War*. Collins, 2005.

Anderson, Julie. *War, Disability, and Rehabilitation in Britain: "Soul of a Nation."* Manchester University Press, 2011.

Anderson, Olive. *A Liberal State at War: English Politics and Economics during the Crimean War*. St. Martin's Press, 1967.

Anionwu, Elizabeth. *Mixed Blessings of a Cambridge Union*. Elizan, 2016.

Anionwu, Elizabeth. *A Short History of Mary Seacole: A Resource for Nurses and Students*. Royal College of Nursing, 2005.

Anonymous. *Heroines Worthy of the Red Cross*. Dean and Son, 1883.

Anonymous. *In Memoriam: To the Late Florence Nightingale*. Neves and Biscoe, 1910.

Armitage, David and Jo Guldi. *The History Manifesto*. Cambridge University Press, 2014.

Armitage, David and Jo Guldi. "*The History Manifesto:* A Reply to Deborah Cohen and Peter Mandler." *American Historical Review* 120, no. 2 (April 2015): 543–54.

Ashcroft, Michael. Foreword to *Extraordinary Heroes: Amazing Stories of Victoria Cross and George Cross Recipients*, by Ruth Sheppard, 4. Osprey, 2010.

Ashcroft, Michael. *Victoria Cross Heroes*. Headline Review, 2006.

Ashplant, T. G., Graham Dawson, and Michael Roper, eds. *The Politics of War Memory and Commemoration*. Routledge, 2000.

Aslami, Zarena. "Victorian Afghanistan, the Iron Amir, and the Poetics of Marginal Sovereignty." *Victorian Studies* 62, no. 1 (Autumn 2019): 35–60.

Aslanian, Sebouh David, Joyce E. Chaplin, Ann McGrath, and Kristin Mann. "Conversation-How Size Matters: The Question of Scale in History." *American Historical Review* 118, no. 5 (December 2013): 1431–72.

Babikian, Catherine. "'Partnership Not Prejudice': British Nurses, Colonial Students, and the National Health Service, 1948–1962." *Journal of British Studies* 60, no. 1 (2021): 140–68.

Badem, Candan. *The Ottoman Crimean War (1853–1856)*. Brill, 2010.

Badsey, Stephen. *Doctrine and Reform in the British Cavalry, 1880–1918*. Ashgate, 2008.

Bailey, Peter. "Kipling's Bully Pulpit: Patriotism, Performance, and Publicity in the Victorian Music Hall." *Kipling Journal* 85, no. 41 (April 2011): 28–41.

Bailkin, Jordanna. *The Afterlife of Empire*. University of California Press, 2012.

Bailkin, Jordanna. *Unsettled: Refugee Camps and the Making of Multicultural Britain*. Oxford University Press, 2018.

Bance, William. *The Battle of Balaclava, or a Ballad*. Published by the Author, 1855.

Barclay, James. *Why No Nurses: The Nursing Recruitment Problem, Its History, Terms and Solution.* Faber and Faber, 1947.

Barczewski, Stephanie. *Heroic Failure and the British.* Yale University Press, 2016.

Bates, Rachel. "Curating the Crimea: The Cultural Afterlife of a Conflict." PhD diss., University of Leicester, 2015.

Baumgart, Winfried. *The Crimean War, 1853–1856.* 2nd ed. Bloomsbury, 2020.

Beckett, Ian F. W. *The Victorians at War.* Hambledon and London, 2003. Reprint, Bloomsbury, 2006.

Beeton, Samuel O. *Our Soldiers and the Victoria Cross.* Ward, Lock, and Tyler, 1867.

Beharry, Johnson. *Barefoot Soldier: A Story of Extreme Valour.* Little, Brown, 2006.

Behlmer, George and Fred Leventhal, eds. *Singular Continuities: Tradition, Nostalgia, and Identity in Modern British Culture.* Stanford University Press, 2000.

Bell, David A. *The First Total War: Napoleonic Europe and the Birth of Warfare as We Know It.* Hougton Mifflin, 2007.

Bender, Jill C. *The 1857 Uprising and the British Empire.* Cambridge University Press, 2016.

Berkeley, Reginald. *The Lady with a Lamp.* 1929. Reprint, Longmans, Green, 1948.

Berridge, A. L. "Off the Chart: The Crimean War in British Public Consciousness." *19: Interdisciplinary Studies in the Long Nineteenth Century* 20 (2015).

Berridge, A. L. "The Shame and the Glory." *The History Girls* (blog). September 20, 2013.

Best, Brian. *The Victoria Crosses that Saved an Empire: The Story of the VCs of the Indian Mutiny.* Pen and Sword, 2016.

Bingham, George Charles (Earl of Lucan). *Reply of Major Gen the Earl of Lucan, KCB, Chelsea Inquiry, Mon, April 28th, 1856.* Thomas Hatchard, 1856.

Bingham, George Charles (Earl of Lucan). *Speech of Major General the Earl of Lucan, Delivered in the House of Lords on Monday, March 19, 1855, on His Recall from His Command in the Crimea.* Thomas Hatchard, 1855.

Birns, Nicholas. "Sable Seas: The Crimean War's Global Reach and 1850s Literariness." *Victorian Studies* 63, no. 2 (Winter 2021): 169–192.

Bivins, Roberta. "Picturing Race in the British National Health Service, 1948–1988." *Twentieth Century British History* 28, no. 1 (March 2017): 83–109.

Blight, David. *Beyond the Battlefield: Race, Memory, and the American Civil War.* University of Massachusetts Press, 2002.

Booth, Alison. "A Bestiary of Florence Nightingales: Strachey and Collective Biographies of Women." *Victorian Studies* 61, no. 1 (Autumn 2018): 93–99.

Borsay, Anne and Billie Hunter, eds. *Nursing and Midwifery in Britain since 1700.* Basingstoke, 2012.

Bossoli, Carlo. *The Beautiful Scenery and Chief Places of Interest throughout the Crimea, from Paintings by Carlo Bossoli.* Day, 1856.

Bostridge, Mark. *Florence Nightingale: The Making of an Icon.* Macmillan, 2008.

Bourke, Joanna. *Deep Violence: Military Violence, War Play, and the Social Life of Weapons.* Counterpoint, 2015.

Bourke, Joanna. *Dismembering the Male: Men's Bodies, Britain, and the Great War.* Reaktion Books, 1996.

Bressey, Caroline. "Radical History Then and Now." *History Workshop Journal* 83 (Spring 2017): 217–22.

Briggs, Asa. *Victorian People: A Reassessment of Persons and Things.* University of Chicago Press, 1955.

Brinkley, Douglas. "Dean Acheson and the 'Special Relationship': The West Point Speech of December 1962." *Historical Journal* 33, no. 3 (1990): 599–608.

Brown, Bertrand Wyatt. *Honor and Violence in the Old South.* Oxford University Press, 1986.

Brown, Michael. "'Like a Devoted Army': Medicine, Heroic Masculinity, and the Military Paradigm in Victorian Britain." *Journal of British Studies* 49 (July 2010): 529–622.

Browne, R. W. *The Soldier's Funeral.* SPCK, 1856.

Browne, R. W. *Tracts for Soldiers: Selected by the Reverend R.W. Browne.* SPCK, 1854.

Buchanan, George. *Camp Life as Seen by a Civilian.* James Maclehose, 1871.

Buettner, Elizabeth. *Europe after Empire: Decolonization, Society, and Culture.* Cambridge University Press, 2016.

Burroughs, Peter. "An Unreformed Army? 1815–1868." In *The Oxford History of the British Army*, edited by David G. Chandler and Ian Beckett, 160–88. Oxford University Press, 1994.

Burton, Antoinette, ed., *The First Anglo-Afghan Wars: A Reader* (Duke University Press, 2014).

Burton, Antoinette. *The Trouble with Empire: Challenges to Modern British Imperialism.* Oxford University Press, 2015.

Burton, Antoinette. "Writer-Travelers and Fugitives: Insider-Outsiders." In *The Cambridge History of Black and Asian British Writing*, edited by Susheila Nasta and Mark U. Stein, 40–53. Cambridge University Press, 2020.

Caceres, Anna. "Windrush Migrants and 'Our NHS Heroes.'" *History Workshop Online.* June 25, 2020.

Calthorpe, Somerset J. Gough and George Cadogan. *Cadogan's Crimea.* Athenaeum, 1980.

Capdevila, Luc and Danièle Voldman. *War Dead: Western Societies and the Casualties of War.* Translated by Richard Veasey. Edinburgh University Press, 2006.

Carby, Hazel. *Imperial Intimacies: A Tale of Two Islands.* Verso, 2019.

Carter, Laura. "The Quennells and the 'History of Everyday Life' in England, c. 1918–69." *History Workshop Journal* 81 (Spring 2016): 106–34.

Castor, Harriet. *Mary Seacole.* Franklin Watts, 1999.

Cavalry Officer. *The British Cavalry at Balaklava, Remarks in Reply to Lt. Gen the Earl of Lucan's Speech in the House of Lords.* Charles Evans, 1855.

Chatterjee, Ronjaunee, Alicia Mireles Christoff, and Amy R Wong, "Undisciplining Victorian Studies." *Los Angeles Review of Books.* July 10, 2020.

Chernock, Arianne. *The Right to Rule and the Rights of Women: Queen Victoria and the Women's Movement.* Cambridge University Press, 2019.

Chesney, Kellow. *Crimean War Reader*. Frederick Muller, 1960.

Clarke, Frances M. *War Stories: Suffering and Sacrifice in the Civil War North*. University of Chicago Press, 2011.

Clarke, Joseph. "Encountering the Sacred: British and French Soldiers in the Revolutionary and Napoleonic Mediterranean." In *Militarized Cultural Encounters in the Long Nineteenth Century: Making War, Mapping Europe*, edited by Joseph Clarke and John Horne, 49–74. Palgrave, 2018.

Clarke, Joseph and John Horne. "Introduction." In *Militarized Cultural Encounters in the Long Nineteenth Century: Making War, Mapping Europe*, edited by Joseph Clarke and John Horne, 1–22. Palgrave, 2018.

Clayton, Ellen Creathorne. *Notable Women: Florence Nightingale, the Soldier's Friend*. Dean and Son, 1860.

A Clergyman of the English Church. *A Tribute to the Slain in the Crimea, or, Solemn Prayers for Those Who Cannot Pray for Themselves*. Joseph Masters, 1855.

Clodfelter, Michael. *Warfare and Armed Conflicts: A Statistical Encyclopedia of Casualty and Other Figures, 1492–2015*. 4th ed. McFarland, 2017.

Clouting, Laura. *A Century of Remembrance*. Imperial War Museum, 2018.

Cohen, Deborah. *Family Secrets: Shame and Privacy in Modern Britain*. Oxford University Press, 2013.

Cohen, Deborah and Peter Mandler, "*The History Manifesto*: A Response." *American Historical Review* 120, no. 2 (April 2015): 530–42.

Cohen, Michèle. "'Manners' Make the Man: Politeness, Chivalry, and the Construction of Masculinity, 1750–1830." *Journal of British Studies* 44 (April 2005): 312–29.

Colborne, John and Frederic Brine. *Graves and Epitaphs of our Fallen Heroes in the Crimea and Scutari*. L'Enfant and Hodgkins, 1865.

Colborne, John and Frederic Brine. *Memorials of the Brave, or Resting Places of our Fallen Heroes in the Crimea and at Scutari*. Ackermann, 1858.

Colley, Linda. *Britons: Forging the Nation, 1707–1837*. Yale University Press, 1992.

Colls, Robert. *Identity of England*. Oxford University Press, 2002.

Conekin, Becky, Frank Mort, and Chris Waters. Introduction to *Moments of Modernity: Reconstructing Britain, 1945–1964*, 1–21. Rivers Oram Press, 1999.

Cook, Edward Tyas. *The Life of Florence Nightingale*. 2 vols. Macmillan, 1913.

Cooke, Miriam and Angela Woollacott, eds. *Gendering War Talk*. Princeton University Press, 1993.

Cooke, Trish and Anni Axworthy. *Hoorah for Mary Seacole*. Franklin Watts, 2008.

Cooksey, John. *Falklands Hero: Ian McKay, the Last VC of the Twentieth Century*. Pen and Sword, 2012.

Craven, Elizabeth Berkeley. *A Journey through the Crimea to Constantinople*. G. G. J. and J. Robinson, 1789.

Crawford, Paul, Anna Greenwood, Richard Bates, and Jonathan Memmel. *Florence Nightingale at Home*. Palgrave Macmillan, 2020.

Crimean Commission and the Chelsea Board. *Correspondence between Major-Gen the Earl of Lucan, KCB, and Gen Bacon, in Reference to the Pamphlet Entitled the English Cavalry at Balaclava*. GJ Palmer, 1855.

Croston, James. *A Pilgrimage to the Home of Florence Nightingale*. Whittaker, 1862.

Daly, Gavin. "British Soldiers and the Legend of Napoleon." *Historical Journal* 61, no. 1 (March 2018): 131–53.

Damian, Jessica. "A Novel Speculation: Mary Seacole's Ambitious Adventures in the New Granada Gold Mining Company." *Journal of West Indian Literature* 16, no. 1 (2007): 15–36.

Das, Santanu. *Touch and Intimacy in First World War Literature*. Cambridge University Press, 2009.

Das, Santanu, ed. *Race, Empire, and First World War Writing*. Cambridge University Press, 2011.

Deane, Bradley. "Imperial Boyhood: Piracy and the Play Ethic." *Victorian Studies* 53, no. 4 (Summer 2011): 689–714.

Delap, Lucy. "'Thus Does Man Prove His Fitness to Be the Master of Things': Shipwrecks, Chivalry, and Masculinities in Nineteenth- and Twentieth-Century Britain." *Cultural and Social History* 3, no. 1 (2006): 45–74.

Dereli, Cynthia. *A War Culture in Action: A Study of the Literature of the Crimean War Period*. Peter Lang, 2003.

Dickson, Melissa. "Jane Eyre's 'Arabian Tales': Reading and Remembering the *Arabian Nights*." *Journal of Victorian Culture* 18, no. 2 (2013): 198–212.

Dixon, Thomas. *Weeping Britannia: Portrait of a Nation in Tears*. Oxford University Press, 2015.

Dodd, George. *Pictorial History of the Russian War, 1854–56*. W. and R. Chambers, 1856.

Donington, Katie, Ryan Hanley, and Jessica Moody, eds. *Britain's History and Memory of Transatlantic Slavery: Local Nuances of a National "Sin."* Liverpool University Press, 2016.

Duberly, Frances Isabella. *Mrs. Duberly's War: Journal and Letters from the Crimea*. Edited by Christine Kelly. Oxford University Press, 2008.

Duckers, Peter. *The Crimean War at Sea: Naval Campaigns against Russia, 1854–6*. Pen and Sword, 2011.

Dudnik, Stefan, Karen Hagemann, and John Tosh, eds. *Masculinities in Politics and War: Gendering Modern History*. Manchester University Press, 2004.

Durbach, Nadja. *Many Mouths: The Politics of Food in Britain from the Workhouse to the Welfare State*. Cambridge University Press, 2020.

Dutton, Roy. *Forgotten Heroes: The Charge of the Light Brigade*. InfoDial, 2007.

Drury, Jackie Sibblies. *Marys Seacole* (Dramatists Play Service, 2019).

Edge, Frederick Milnes. *A Woman's Example and a Nation's Work: A Tribute to Florence Nightingale*. William Ridgway, 1864.

Englishman and a Civilian. *Lord Raglan, a Would-be Sacrifice to a Ribald Press*. James Ridgway, 1855.

Eustace, Nicole, Eugenia Lean, Julie Livingston, Jan Plamper, William M. Reddy, and Barbara H. Rosenwein. "Conversation: The Historical Study of Emotions." *American Historical Review* 117, no. 5 (December 2012): 1487–531.

Fairey, Jack. *The Great Powers and Orthodox Christendom: The Crisis over the Eastern Church in the Era of the Crimean War*. Palgrave Macmillan, 2015.

Farwell, Byron. *For Queen and Country: A Social History of the Victorian and Edwardian Army*. Viking, 1981.

Farwell, Byron. *Queen Victoria's Little Wars*. Harper and Row, 1972. Reprint, Norton, 1985.

Faust, Drew Gilpin. *This Republic of Suffering: Death and the American Civil War*. Vintage, 2009.

Favret, Mary. *War at a Distance: Romanticism and the Making of Modern Wartime*. Princeton University Press, 2009.

Featherstone, Simon. *Twentieth-Century Popular Culture and the Forming of English Identity*. Edinburgh University Press, 2009.

Figes, Orlando. *The Crimean War: A History*. Metropolitan, 2011.

Fisher, Glenn. "The Crimean and Indian Mutiny. Veterans' Associations of the 1890s." PhD diss., University of Cardiff, 2020.

Fletcher, Alison. "'Mother Seacole': Victorian Domesticity on the Battlefields of the Crimean War." *Minerva: Journal of Women and War* 1, no. 2 (September 2007): 7–21.

Fluhr, Nicole. "'Their Calling Me 'Mother' Was Not, I Think, Altogether Unmeaning': Mary Seacole's Maternal Personae." *Victorian Literature and Culture* 34, no. 1 (March 2006): 95–113.

Foster, R. F. *Vivid Faces: The Revolutionary Generation in Ireland, 1890–1923*. Allen Lane, 2014.

Francis, Martin. *The Flyer: British Culture and the Royal Air Force, 1939–1945*. Oxford University Press, 2008.

Frederick, Rhonda. "Creole Performance in *Wonderful Adventures of Mrs. Seacole in Many Lands*." *Gender & History* 15, no. 3 (November 2003): 487–506.

Freedgood, Elaine. *The Ideas in Things: Fugitive Meaning in the Victorian Novel*. University of Chicago Press, 2006.

Friedman, Rebecca. "Masculinity, the Body, and Coming of Age in the Nineteenth-Century Russian Cadet Corps." *Journal of the History of Childhood and Youth* 5, no. 2 (2012): 219–38.

Furneaux, Holly. *Military Men of Feeling: Emotion, Touch, and Masculinity in the Crimean War*. Oxford University Press, 2016.

Fussell, Paul. *The Great War and Modern Memory*. Oxford University Press, 1975.

Gagnier, Regenia. "'From Fag to Monitor; Or, Fighting to the Front': Art and Power in Public School Memoirs." *Browning Institute Studies* 16 (1988): 15–38.

George, Abosede, Clive Glaser, Margaret D. Jacobs, Chitra Joshi, Emily Marker, Alexandra Walsham, Wang Zheng, and Bernd Weisbrod. "Conversation: Each Generation Writes Its Own History of Generations." *American Historical Review* 123, no. 5 (2018): 1505–46.

Gibson, James. *Memoirs of the Brave: A Brief Account of the Battles of the Alma, Balaklava, and Inkerman, with Biographies of the Killed and a List of the Wounded*. Effingham Wilson, 1855.

Gill, Christopher J. and Gillian C. Gill. "Nightingale in Scutari: Her Legacy Reexamined." *Clinical Infectious Diseases* 40, no. 12 (2005): 1799–805.

Gleeson, David T. and Simon Lewis, eds. *Ambiguous Anniversary: The Bicentennial of the International Slave Trade Bans*. University of South Carolina Press, 2012.

Goebel, Stefan. *The Great War and Medieval Memory: War, Remembrance, and Medievalism in Britain and Germany, 1914–1940.* Cambridge University Press, 2007.

Goldhill, Simon. "A Mother's Joy at Her Child's Death: Conversion, Cognitive Dissonance, and Grief." *Victorian Studies* 59, no. 4 (2017): 636–57.

Goldie, Sue M., ed. *Florence Nightingale: Letters from the Crimea.* Mandolin, 1997.

Gordon, Sophie and Louise Pearson. *Shadows of War: Roger Fenton's Photographs of the Crimea, 1855.* Royal Collection Trust, 2017.

Grant, Anthony. *An Historical Sketch of the Crimea.* Bell and Daldy, 1855.

Gray, Jean, ed. *A Statue for Mary: The Seacole Legacy.* Mary Seacole Memorial Statue Appeal, 2016.

Grayzel, Susan R. "Belonging to the Imperial Nation: Rethinking the History of the First World War in Britain and its Empire." *Journal of Modern History* 90, no. 2 (June 2018): 383–405.

Grayzel, Susan R. *Women's Identities at War: Gender, Motherhood, and Politics in Britain during the First World War.* University of North Carolina Press, 1999.

Grayzel, Susan R. and Tammy Proctor, eds. *Gender and the Great War.* Oxford University Press, 2017.

Green, Jennifer M. "Stories in an Exhibition: Narrative and Nineteenth-Century Photographic Documentary." *Journal of Narrative Technique* 20, no. 2 (Spring 1990): 147–66.

Green-Lewis, Jennifer. *Framing the Victorian: Photography and the Culture of Realism.* Cornell University Press, 1996.

Grey, Teresa. *Journal of a Visit to Egypt, Constantinople, the Crimea, Greece, Etc. in the Suite of the Prince and Princess of Wales.* Smith, Elder, 1869.

Griffin, Emma. "Emotions of Motherhood: Love, Culture, and Poverty in Victorian Britain." *American Historical Review* 123, no. 1 (February 2018): 60–85.

Groth, Helen. "Technological Mediations and the Public Sphere: Roger Fenton's Crimea Exhibition and 'The Charge of the Light Brigade.'" *Victorian Literature and Culture* 30, no. 2 (2002): 553–70.

Guardino, Peter. *The Dead March: A History of the Mexican-American War.* Cambridge University Press, 2017.

Gullace, Nicoletta. *"The Blood of Our Sons": Men, Women, and the Renegotiation of British Citizenship during the Great War.* Palgrave, 2002.

Gunning, Sandra. "Traveling with Her Mother's Tastes: The Negotiation of Gender, Race, and Location in 'Wonderful Adventures of Mrs. Seacole in Many Lands.'" *Signs* 26, no. 4 (2001): 949–81.

Gurton-Wachter, Lily. *Watchwords: Romanticism and the Poetics of Attention.* Stanford University Press, 2016.

Hack, Daniel. *Reaping Something New: African-American Transformations of Victorian Literature.* Princeton University Press, 2016.

Hack, Daniel. "Wild Charges: The Afro-Haitian Charge of the Light Brigade." *Victorian Studies* 54, no. 2 (Winter 2012): 199–225.

Hadley, Elaine. "Nobody, Somebody, and Everybody." *Victorian Studies* 59, no. 1 (Autumn 2016): 65–86.

Hagemann, Karen. *Revisiting Prussia's Wars against Napoleon: History, Culture, and Memory.* Translated by Pamela Selwyn. Cambridge University Press, 2015.

Hall, Donald E., ed. *Muscular Christianity: Embodying the Victorian Age.* Cambridge University Press, 1994.

Hannam, Reverend E. P. *The Hospital's Manual or Soldier's Guide in the Hour of Sickness, to which is Prefixed a Short Service for the Use of Military Hospitals.* SPCK, 1854.

Harper, Tobias. *From Servants of the Empire to Everyday Heroes: the British Honours System in the Twentieth Century* (Oxford, 2020).

Harrison, Paul. *Who was Mary Seacole?* Wayland, 2007.

Hastings, Max. *The Oxford Book of Military Anecdotes.* Oxford University Press, 1985.

Hatherley, Owen. *The Ministry of Nostalgia.* Verso, 2016.

Hawkins, Angus. *Victorian Political Culture: "Habits of Heart and Mind."* Oxford University Press, 2015.

Hawthorne, Evelyn J. "Self-Writing, Literary Traditions, and Post-Emancipation Identity: The Case of Mary Seacole." *Biography* 23, no. 2 (2000): 309–31.

Haydon, A. L. *The Book of the V.C.* Melrose, 1906.

Heathorn, Stephen. *Haig and Kitchener in Twentieth-Century Britain: Remembrance, Representation, and Appropriation.* Ashgate, 2013.

Heathorn, Stephen. "The Mnemonic Turn in the Cultural Historiography of Britain's Great War." *Historical Journal* 48, no. 4 (December 2005): 1103–24.

Helmstadter, Carol and Judith Godden. *Nursing before Nightingale, 1815–1899.* Ashgate, 2011.

Herbert, Christopher. *War of No Pity: The Indian Mutiny and Victorian Trauma.* Princeton University Press, 2008.

Hibbert, Christopher. "The Condition of the British Army in the Crimea." *The Victorian,* 2002, *Web.* www.victorianweb.org.

Hibbert, Christopher. *The Destruction of Lord Raglan: A Tragedy of the Crimean War, 1854–55.* Little, Brown, 1961.

Hilliard, Christopher. "'Is it a Book that You Would Even Wish Your Wife or Servants to Read?': Obscenity Law and the Politics of Reading in Modern England." *American Historical Review* 118, no. 3 (June 2013): 653–78.

Hilliard, Christopher. *To Exercise Our Talents: The Democratization of Writing in Britain.* Harvard University Press, 2006.

Himmelfarb, Gertrude. *The De-Moralization of Society: From Victorian Virtues to Modern Values.* Knopf, 1995.

Hirchberger, Joany. "Democratising Glory? The Victoria Cross Paintings of Louis Desanges." *Oxford Art Journal* 7, no. 2 (1984): 42–51.

Ho, Tai-Chun. "The Afterlife of Thomas Campbell and 'The Soldiers Dream' in the Crimean War." *19: Interdisciplinary Studies in the Long Nineteenth Century* 20 (2015).

Ho, Tai-Chun. "Tyrtaeus and the Civilian Poet of the Crimean War." *Journal of Victorian Culture* 22, no. 4 (2017): 503–20.

Hobsbawm, Eric. "Introduction: Inventing Traditions." In *The Invention of Tradition,* edited by Eric Hobsbawm and Terence Ranger, 1–14. Cambridge University Press, 1983.

Hodder-Williams, John Ernest. *Is That Lamp Going Out?* Hodder and Stoughton, 1910.

Hoehling, A. A. *Edith Cavell.* Cassell, 1958.

Hoganson, Kristin. *Fighting for American Manhood: How Gender Politics Provoked the Spanish-American and Philippine-American Wars.* Yale University Press, 2000.

Holderness, Mary. *Journey from Riga to the Crimea, with Some Account of the Manners and Customs of the Colonists of New Russia.* Sherwood, Gilbert and Piper, 1827.

Holmes, Marion. "Florence Nightingale: A Cameo Sketch." *Gale Group Nineteenth-Century Collections Online.* Women's Freedom League, 1910.

Hornstein, Katie. *Picturing War in France, 1792–1856.* Yale University Press, 2017.

Houghton, Walter. *The Victorian Frame of Mind, 1830–1870.* Yale University Press, 1957.

Houston, Natalie M. "Reading the Victorian Souvenir: Sonnets and Photographs of the Crimean War." *Yale Journal of Criticism* 14, no. 2 (Fall 2001): 353–83.

Howell, Jessica. "Mrs. Seacole Prescribes Hybridity: Constitutional and Maternal Rhetoric in *Wonderful Adventures of Mrs. Seacole in Many Lands.*" *Victorian Literature and Culture* 38, no. 1 (2010): 107–25.

Huddle, Paul. "Victims or Survivors: Army Wives in Ireland during the Crimean War, 1854–56." *Women's History Review* 26, no. 4 (August 2017): 541–54.

Hughes, Michael. "Searching for the Soul of Russia: British Perceptions of Russia during the First World War." *Twentieth Century British History* 20, no. 2 (2009): 198–226.

Hunt, Aeron. "Ordinary Claims: War, Work, Service, and the Victorian Veteran." *Victorian Studies* 61, no. 3 (Spring 2019): 395–418.

Hunter, Kate. "More than an Archive of War: Intimacy and Manliness in the Letters of a Great War Soldier to the Woman He Loved, 1915–1919." *Gender and History* 25, no. 2 (August 2013): 339–54.

Hurl-Eamon, Jennine. "Youth in the Devil's Service, Manhood in the King's: Reaching Adulthood in the Eighteenth-Century British Army." *Journal of the History of Childhood and Youth* 8, no. 2 (2015): 163–90.

Hutchinson, John. *Champions of Charity: War and the Rise of the Red Cross.* Westview Press, 1996.

Huxford, Grace. *The Korean War in Britain: Citizenship, Selfhood, and Forgetting.* Manchester University Press, 2018.

Huxford, Grace. "The Korean War Never Happened: Forgetting a Conflict in British Culture and Society." *Twentieth Century British History* 27, no. 2 (June 2016): 195–219.

Imy, Kate. *Faithful Fighters: Identity and Power in the British Indian Army.* Stanford University Press, 2019.

Inouye, Karen. *The Long Afterlife of Nikkei Wartime Incarceration.* Stanford University Press, 2016.

Irwin, Julia. *Making the World Safe: A Nation's Humanitarian Awakening.* Oxford University Press, 2013.

Ismay, Penelope. *Trust Among Strangers: Friendly Societies in Modern Britain.* Cambridge University Press, 2018.

Jalland, Pat. *Death in the Victorian Family.* Oxford University Press, 1996.

Jervis-Waldy, W. T. *From Eight to Eighty: The Life of a Crimean and Indian Mutiny Veteran.* Harrison, 1914.

Jesse, William. *Notes of a Half-Pay in Search of Health*. James Madden, 1841.

Jewitt, Llewellynn. *A Stroll to Lea Hurst, Derbyshire, the Home of Florence Nightingale*. Kent, Paternoster Row, 1855.

Jonas, Alfred Charles. *An Unassuming Crimean Veteran: Major Read, Thornton Heath*. Reprinted from the *Croydon Guardian*. 1907.

Jones, David R. *The Crimean War, Then and Now*. Pen and Sword, 2017.

Joyce, Simon. "On or About 1901: The Bloomsbury Group Looks Back at the Victorians." *Victorian Studies* 46, no. 4 (Summer 2004): 631–54.

Joyce, Simon. *The Victorians in the Rearview Mirror*. Ohio University Press, 2007.

Judd, Denis. *Someone Has Blundered: Calamities of the British Army in the Victorian Age*. Arthur Barker, 1973.

Kavanagh, Thomas Henry. *How I Won the Victoria Cross*. Ward and Lock, 1860.

Keller, Ulrich. *The Ultimate Spectacle: A Visual History of the Crimean War*. Routledge, 2013.

Kennedy, Catriona. "Military Ways of Seeing: British Soldiers' Sketches from the Egyptian Campaign of 1801." In *Militarized Cultural Encounters in the Long Nineteenth Century: Making War, Mapping Europe*, edited by Joseph Clarke and John Horne, 197–222. Palgrave, 2018.

Kennedy, Catriona. *Narratives of the Revolutionary and Napoleonic Wars: Military and Civilian Experience in Britain and Ireland*. Palgrave Macmillan, 2013.

Kennedy, Dane. "The Imperial History Wars." *Journal of British Studies* 54 (January 2016): 5–22.

Kent, Neil. *Crimea: A History*. C. Hurst, 2016.

Kichner, Heather J. *Cemetery Plots from Victoria to Verdun: Literary Representations of Epitaph and Burial from the 19th Century through the Great War*. Peter Lang, 2012.

Kinealy, Christine. "'The Historian is a Haunted Man': Cecil Woodham-Smith and *The Great Hunger*." *New Hibernia Review* 12, no. 4 (Winter 2008): 134–43.

King, Alex. "The Archive of the Commonwealth Graves Commission." *History Workshop Journal* 47 (Spring 1999): 253–59.

Kinglake, Alexander William. *Invasion of the Crimea*. Students' ed. Abridged by G. S. Clarke, Sr. Blackwood, 1899.

Kipling, Rudyard. *Graves of the Fallen*. HMSO, 1919.

Kipling, Rudyard. "The Last of the Light Brigade." *St. James's Gazette*. April 28, 1890.

Kipling, Rudyard. *Rudyard Kipling's Verse: Inclusive Edition, 1885–1918*. Doubleday, 1922.

Kipling, Rudyard. "The White Man's Burden." *McClure's Magazine*. February 1899.

Kipling, Rudyard. "Winning the Victoria Cross." In *Land and Sea Tales for Scouts and Guides*, 1–22. Doubleday, Page, 1923.

Knollys, William Wallingford. *The Victoria Cross in the Crimea*. Dean and Son, 1876.

Koven, Seth. *The Match Girl and the Heiress*. Princeton University Press, 2015.

Kozelsky, Mara. *Crimea in War and Transformation*. Oxford University Press, 2019.

Krebs, Paula M. *Gender, Race, and the Writing of Empire: Public Discourse and the Boer War.* Cambridge University Press, 1999.

Kriegel, Lara. "Living Links to History, or, Victorian Veterans in the Twentieth-Century World." *Victorian Studies* 58, no. 2 (Winter 2016): 298–301.

Kriegel, Lara. "The Strange Career of Fair Play, or, Warfare and Gamesmanship in the Time of Victoria." In *The Oxford Handbook of Victorian Literary Culture,* edited by Juliet John, 268–83. Oxford University Press, 2016.

Kriegel, Lara. "Who Blew the Balaklava Bugle?: The Charge of the Light Brigade and the Afterlife of the Crimean War." *19: Interdisciplinary Studies in the Long Nineteenth Century* 20 (2015).

Kumar, Krishan. *The Making of English National Identity.* Cambridge University Press, 2003.

Lalumia, Matthew. "Lady Elizabeth Thompson Butler in the 1870s." *Women's Art Journal* 4, no. 1 (Spring-Summer 1983): 9–14.

Lambert, Andrew. *The Crimean War: British Grand Strategy against Russia, 1853–1856.* Ashgate, 2011.

Lammond, D. *Great Lives: Florence Nightingale.* Duckworth, 1935.

Langford, Paul. *Englishness Identified: Manners and Character, 1650–1850.* Oxford University Press, 2000.

Langhamer, Claire. *The English in Love: The Intimate Story of an Emotional Revolution.* Oxford University Press, 2013.

Langhamer, Clare. "'Who the Hell are Ordinary People?': Ordinariness as a Category of Historical Analysis." *Transactions of the Royal Historical Society* 28 (2018): 175–95.

Laqueur, Thomas W. "Bodies, Details, and the Humanitarian Narrative." In *The New Cultural History,* edited by Lynn Hunt, 176–204. University of California Press, 1989.

Laugharne, Rev. T. R. I., ed. *A Bundle of Reeds from the Alma & C.* Whitnash Press, 1854.

Lennox, Lord William. *The Victoria Cross: The Rewarded and their Services.* John Mitchell, 1857.

Levine, Philippa. *Prostitution, Race, and Politics: Policing Venereal Disease in the British Empire.* Routledge, 2003.

Levine, Philippa and Susan Grazyel, eds. *Gender, Labour, War, and Empire: Essays on Modern British History.* Palgrave, 1999.

Lewis, Joanna. *Empire of Sentiment: The Death of Livingstone and the Myth of Victorian Imperialism.* Cambridge University Press, 2018.

Light, Alison. *Common People: In Pursuit of My Ancestors.* University of Chicago Press, 2015.

Lloyd, David Wharton. *Battlefield Tourism: Pilgrimage and the Commemoration of the Great War in Britain, Australia, and Canada, 1919–1939.* Berg, 1998.

Longfellow, Henry Wadsworth. "Santa Filomena: A Poem." *The Atlantic.* November 1857.

Longmore, T. *The Sanitary Contrasts of the British and French Armies during the Crimean War.* Charles Griffin, 1883.

Loss, Daniel S. "The Institutional Afterlife of Christian England." *Journal of Modern History* 89 (2017): 282–313.

Lutz, Deborah. *Relics of Death in Victorian Literature and Culture*. Cambridge University Press, 2015.

Lynch, Emma. *The Life of Mary Seacole*. Heinemann/Harcourt, 2005.

Macdonald, Lynn. *Mary Seacole: The Making of the Myth*. Iguana Books, 2014.

Mandler, Peter. *The English National Character: The History of an Idea from Edmund Burke to Tony Blair*. Yale University Press, 2007.

Markovits, Stefanie. *The Crimean War in the British Imagination*. Cambridge University Press, 2009.

Markovits, Stefanie. "Giving Voice to the Crimean War: Tennyson's 'Charge' and Maud's Battle Song." *Victorian Poetry* 47, no. 3 (2009): 481–503.

Markovits, Stefanie. "Rushing into Print: 'Participatory Journalism' in the Crimean War." *Victorian Studies* 50, no. 4 (Summer 2008): 559–86.

Massie, Alastair, ed. *A Most Desperate Undertaking: The British Army in the Crimea, 1856–1856*. National Army Museum, 2003.

Masson, Flora. *Florence Nightingale, O.M., By One Who Knew Her*. The Scientific Press, 1910.

Masterson, Margery. "Dueling, Conflicting Masculinities, and the Victorian Gentleman." *Journal of British Studies* 56, no. 3 (2017): 605–28.

Matera, Marc. *Black London: The Imperial Metropolis and Decolonization in the Twentieth Century*. University of California Press, 2015.

Matheson, Annie. *Florence Nightingale: A Biography*. Thomas Nelson, 1913.

Matthews, Samantha. *Poetical Remains: Poets' Graves, Bodies, and Books in the Nineteenth Century*. Oxford University Press, 2004.

McAllister, David. *Imagining the Dead in British Literature and Culture, 1790–1848*. Palgrave Macmillan, 2018.

McDonald, Lynn. "Florence Nightingale, Statistics and the Crimean War." *Journal of the Royal Statistical Society, Series A (Statistics in Society)* 177, no. 3 (2014): 569–86.

McLoughlin, Kate. *Authoring War: The Literary Representation of War from the Iliad to Iraq*. Cambridge University Press, 2011.

McLoughlin, Kate. *Veteran Poetics: British Literature in the Age of Mass Warfare*. Cambridge University Press, 2018.

McLoughlin, Kate. "War in Print Journalism." In *The Cambridge Companion to War Writing*, edited by Kate McLoughlin, 47–59. Cambridge University Press, 2009.

Melman, Billie. *The Culture of History: English Uses of the Past, 1800–1953*. Oxford University Press, 2006.

Mercau, Ezekiel. "War of the British Worlds: The Anglo-Argentines and the Falklands." *Journal of British Studies* 55, no. 1 (2016): 146–68.

Mercer, Loraine. "I Shall Make No Excuse: The Narrative Odyssey of Mary Seacole." *Journal of Narrative Theory* 35, no. 1 (2005): 1–24.

Meredith, John. *Omdurman Diaries 1898*. Pen and Sword, 1990.

Meyer, Jessica. *Men of War: Masculinity and the First World War in Britain*. Palgrave, 2009.

Meyer, Jessica, ed. *British Popular Culture and the First World War*. Brill, 2008.

Michalski, Sergiusz. "War Imagery between the Crimean Campaign and 1914." In *War and Art*, edited by Joanna Bourke, 44–79. Reaktion, 2017.

Miles, Stephen. *The Western Front: Landscape, Tourism, and Heritage*. Pen and Sword, 2016.

Miller, Alisa. "Rupert Brooke and the Growth of Commercial Patriotism in Britain, 1914–1918." *Twentieth Century British History* 21, no. 2 (June 2010): 141–62.

Miller, Stephen, ed. *Queen Victoria's Wars: British Military Campaigns, 1857–1902*. Cambridge University Press, 2021.

Milner, Rev. Thomas. *The Crimea, Its Ancient and Modern History*. Longman, Brown, Green, and Longmans, 1855.

Moore, Judith. *A Zeal for Responsibility: The Struggle for Nursing in Victorian England*. University of Georgia Press, 1998.

Morgan, Benjamin. "Fin du Globe: On Decadent Planets." *Victorian Studies* 58, no. 4 (Summer 2016): 609–35.

Morgan, Kenneth O. "The Boer War and the Media, 1899–1902." *Twentieth Century British History* 13, no. 1 (January 2002): 1–16.

Morley, Joel. "Dad 'Never Said Much' But… Young Men and Great War Veterans in Day-to-Day-Life in Interwar Britain." *Twentieth Century British History* 29, no. 2 (June 2018): 199–224.

Morley, Joel. "The Memory of the Great War and Morale during Britain's Phoney War." *Historical Journal* 63, no. 2 (March 2020): 437–67.

Morris, Errol. *Believing is Seeing: Observations on the Myths of Photography*. Penguin, 2011.

Morris, William. *The Three Sergeants, or Phases of the Soldier's Life*. Effingham Wilson, 1858.

Mort, Frank. "Safe for Democracy: Constitutional Politics, Popular Spectacle, and the British Monarchy 1910–1914." *Journal of British Studies* 58, no. 1 (2019): 109–41.

Moyd, Michelle. *Violent Intermediaries: African Soldiers, Conquest, and Everyday Colonialism in German East Africa*. Ohio University Press, 2014.

Muddock, J. E. *For Valour: The Victoria Cross*. Hutchinson, 1895.

Mufti, Nasser. *Civilizing War: Imperial Politics and the Poetics of National Rupture*. Northwestern University Press, 2015.

Myerly, Scott Hughes. *British Military Spectacle: From the Napoleonic Wars through the Crimea*. Harvard University Press, 1996.

Nash, Rosalind. *A Sketch of the Life of Florence Nightingale*. SPCK, 1937.

Newman, George. *A Lady with a Lamp: The Case for Red Cross Day*. British Red Cross Society, 1933.

Nicholson, Virginia. *Singled Out: How Two Million British Women Survived without Men after the First World War*. Oxford University Press, 2008.

Nightingale, Florence. *Notes on Nursing: What It Is and What It Is Not*. Appleton, 1860.

Noakes, Lucy. *Dying for the Nation: Death, Grief, and Bereavement in Second World War Britain*. Manchester University Press, 2020.

Noakes, Lucy and Juliette Pattinson, eds. *British Cultural Memory and the Second World War*. Bloomsbury, 2014.

Nora, Pierre. "Between Memory and History: *Les Lieux de Mémoire.*" *Representations* 26 (Spring 1989): 7–24.

O'Byrne, Robert W. *The Victoria Cross: An Official Chronicle of the Deeds of Personal Valour.* O'Byrne Bros., 1865.

O'Connor, Karen Sands. "My (Black) Britain: The West Indies and Britain in Twenty-First Century Nonfiction Picture Books." *Bookbird: A Journal of International Children's Literature* 50, no. 3 (July 2012): 1–11.

O'Neill, Kelly. *Claiming Crimea: A History of Catherine the Great's Southern Empire.* Yale University Press, 2017.

O'Toole, Fintan. *Heroic Failure: Brexit and the Politics of Pain.* Head of Zeus, 2018.

Okpu-Egbe, Adjani. *Politics of Mary Seacole and the Whiteman's Pathetic and Pathological Obsession with the Appropriation of Everything Good.* Painting. Exhibited 2016, Tel Aviv. Private collection. adjaniokpuegbe.com/painting.

Otter, Chris, Alison Bashford, John L. Brooke, Frederik Albritton Jonsson, and Jason M. Kelly. "Roundtable: The Anthropocene in British History." *Journal of British Studies* 57, no. 3 (July 2018): 568–96.

Owen, Wilfred. "Dulce et Decorum Est." *First World War Digital Poetry Archive.* October 1917–March 1918.

Paquet, Sandra Pouchet. "The Enigma of Arrival: *The Wonderful Adventures of Mrs. Seacole in Many Lands.*" *African-American Review* 50, no. 4 (2017): 864–76.

Parekh, Bhikhu, Kate Gavron, Tariq Modood, Robin Richardson, Yasmin Alibhai-Brown, Muhammad Anwar, Colin Bailey, et al. *The Future of Multiethnic Britain.* Profile Books, 2000.

Parry, Jonathan. *The Politics of Patriotism: English Liberalism, National Identity and Europe, 1830–1866.* Cambridge University Press, 2006.

Pearsall, Cornelia D. J. "Burying the Duke: Victorian Mourning and the Funeral of the Duke of Wellington." *Victorian Literature and Culture* 27, no. 2 (1999): 365–93.

Peck, John. *War, the Army, and Victorian Literature.* St. Martin's, 1998.

Pergher, Roberta. "An Italian War? War and Nation in the Historiography of the First World War." *Journal of Modern History* 90, no. 4 (December 2018): 863–99.

Perry, Kennetta Hammond. *London is the Place for Me: Black Britons, Citizenship, and the Politics of Race.* Oxford University Press, 2016.

Pinto, Samantha. "'The Right Woman in the Right Place': Mary Seacole and Corrective Histories of Empire." *ARIEL: A Review of International English Literature* 50, nos. 2–3 (2019): 1–31.

Plotz, John. *Portable Property: Victorian Culture on the Move.* Princeton University Press, 2008.

Ponting, Clive. *The Crimean War.* Chatto and Windus, 2004.

Poon, Angelia. "Comic Acts of (Be)longing: Performing Englishness in *Wonderful Adventures of Mrs. Seacole in Many Lands.*" *Victorian Literature and Culture* 35, no. 1 (March 2007): 501–16.

Poovey, Mary. *Uneven Developments: The Ideological Work of Gender in Mid-Victorian England.* University of Chicago Press, 1988.

Pratt, Mary Louise. *Imperial Eyes: Travel Writing and Transculturation*. Routledge, 1992.

Proclamation of a Day of Solemn Fast, Humiliation, and Prayer: 28 February 1855. F. and W. Thomson, 1855.

Putnam, Lara. "The Transnational and the Text-Searchable: Digitized Sources and the Shadows They Cast." *American Historical Review* 121, no. 2 (April 2016): 377–402.

Ramdin, Ron. *Mary Seacole*. Haus, 2005.

Rappaport, Erika. *A Thirst for Empire: How Tea Shaped the Modern World*. Princeton University Press, 2017.

Rappaport, Helen. "The Invitation that Never Came: Mary Seacole after the Crimea." *History Today* 55, no. 2 (February 2005): 9–15.

Rath, Andrew. *The Crimean War in Imperial Context, 1854–1856*. Palgrave Macmillan, 2015.

Reed, John R. "The Victorians and War." In *The Cambridge Companion to War Writing*, edited by Kate McLoughlin, 135–47. Cambridge University Press, 2009.

Rees-Mogg, Jacob. *The Victorians: Twelve Titans Who Forged Britain*. WH Allen, 2019.

Reid, Edith Gittings. *Florence Nightingale: A Drama*. Macmillan, 1922.

Reynolds, David. *Island Stories: An Unconventional History of Britain*. Basic Books, 2020.

Reznick, Jeffrey S. *Healing the Nation: Soldiers and the Culture of Caregiving in Britain during the Great War*. Manchester University Press, 2011.

Reznick, Jeffrey S. *John Galsworthy and Disabled Soldiers of the Great War*. Manchester University Press, 2009.

Ridley, Sarah. *Mary Seacole and the Crimean War*. Franklin Watts, 2009.

Roberts, Mary Louise. *What Soldiers Do: Sex and the American GI in France*. University of Chicago Press, 2014.

Robertson, T. W. *Ours* (1866). In T. W. Robertson, *Six Plays*, with an introduction by Michael R. Booth, 57–118. Amber Lane Press, 1980.

Robinson, Amy. "Authority and the Public Display of Identity: *Wonderful Adventures of Mrs. Seacole in Many Lands*." *Feminist Studies* 20, no. 3 (Autumn 1994): 537–57.

Robinson, Helen. "Remembering War in the Midst of Conflict: First World War Commemorations in the Northern Irish Troubles." *Twentieth Century British History* 21, no. 1 (January 2010): 80–101.

Robinson, Jane. *Mary Seacole: The Most Famous Black Woman of the Victorian Age*. Carroll and Graff, 2004.

Roper, Michael. "Between Manliness and Masculinity: The 'War Generation' and the Psychology of Fear in Britain, 1914–1950." *Journal of British Studies* 44 (April 2005): 343–62.

Roper, Michael. "The Bush, the Suburbs, and the Long Great War." *History Workshop Journal* 86 (Autumn 2019): 90–113.

Roper, Michael. *The Secret Battle: Emotional Survival in the Great War*. Manchester University Press, 2009.

Rose, Sonya. *Which People's War?: National Identity and Citizenship in Britain, 1939–1945*. Oxford University Press, 2003.

Ross, Kristin. *May '68 and Its Afterlives*. University of Chicago Press, 2002.

Ross, Sarah. "Brave Hermeneutics, the Eastern Question, and Kingsley's *Hypatia*." *Victorian Studies* 60, no. 3 (Spring 2018): 412–33.

Royle, Trevor. *Crimea: The Great Crimean War*. Little, Brown, 1999.

Russell, William Howard. *The British Expedition to the Crimea*. Routledge, 1877.

Russell, William Howard. *A Diary in the East during the Tour of the Prince and Princess of Wales*. Vol. 2. Routledge, 1869.

Russell, William Howard. *Russell's Dispatches from the Crimea, 1854–1856*. Edited by Nicolas Bentley, 1855. Hill and Wang, 1967.

Ryan, George. *Was Lord Cardigan a Hero at Balaklava? Verbatim from the Guinea Editions of the lives of Our Heroes of the Crimea, with Startling Additions*. James Wield, 1855.

Said, Edward. *Orientalism*. Pantheon Books, 1978.

Samuel, Raphael. *Island Stories: Unraveling Britain*. Edited by Alison Light with Sally Alexander, and Gareth Stedman Jones. Verso, 1994.

Samuel, Raphael. *Theatres of Memory: Past and Present in Contemporary Culture*. Verso, 1994.

Samuel, Raphael, ed. *Patriotism: The Making and Unmaking of British National Identity*. Routledge, 1989.

Samuel, Raphael and Paul Thompson, eds. *The Myths We Live By*. Routledge, 1990.

Sandbrook, Dominic. *The Great British Dream Factory*. Allen Lane, 2015.

Sasson, Tehila. "From Empire to Humanity: The Russian Famine and the Imperial Origins of International Humanitarianism." *Journal of British Studies* 55 (July 2016): 519–37.

Satia, Priya. *Spies in Arabia: The Great War and the Cultural Foundations of Britain's Covert Empire in the Middle East*. Oxford University Press, 2008.

Satia, Priya. *Time's Monster: How History Makes History*. Harvard University Press, 2020.

Saunders, Nicholas J. "Crucifix, Calvary and Cross: Materiality and Spirituality in Great War Landscapes." *World Archaeology* 35, no. 1 (2003): 7–21.

Schaffer, Talia. *Novel Craft: Victorian Domestic Handicraft and Nineteenth-Century Fiction*. Oxford University Press, 2011.

Schaffer, Talia. "Victorian Feminist Criticism: Recovery Work and the Care Community." *Victorian Literature and Culture* 47, no. 1 (Spring 2019): 63–91.

Schofield, Camilla. *Enoch Powell and the Making of Postcolonial Britain*. Cambridge University Press, 2013.

Schwartz, Bill. "Forgetfulness: England's Discontinuous Histories." In *Embers of Empire in Brexit Britain*, edited by Stuart Ward and Astrid Rasch, 49–58. Bloomsbury Academic, 2019.

Scott, Charles Henry. *The Baltic, the Black Sea, and the Crimea*. Richard Bentley, 1854.

Seacole, Mary. *Wonderful Adventures of Mrs. Seacole in Many Lands*. James Blackwood, Paternoster Row, 1857.

Seacole, Mary. *Wonderful Adventures of Mrs. Seacole in Many Lands.* Edited by Sarah Salih. Penguin, 2005.

Seacole, Mary. *Wonderful Adventures of Mrs. Seacole in Many Lands.* Edited by William L. Andrews. Schomburg Library of Black Women Writers. Oxford University Press, 1988.

Seacole, Mary. *Wonderful Adventures of Mrs. Seacole in Many Lands.* 2nd ed. Edited by Ziggi Alexander and Audrey Dewjee. Falling Wall Press, 1984.

Semmell, Stuart. "British Uses for Napoleon." *Modern Language Notes* 120, no. 4 (2005): 733–46.

Semmell, Stuart. *Napoleon and the British.* Yale University Press, 2004.

Semmell, Stuart. "Reading the Tangible Past: British Tourism, Collecting, and Memory after Waterloo." *Representations* 69 (2000): 9–37.

Seymer, Lucy. *Dame Alicia Lloyd Still, a Memoir.* Smith and Ebbs, 1953.

Seymer, Lucy Ridgely. *Florence Nightingale.* Faber & Faber, 1950.

Shaw, Caroline. *Britannia's Embrace: Modern Humanitarianism and the Imperial Origins of Refugee Relief.* Oxford University Press, 2015.

Shaw, George Bernard. *O'Flaherty, V.C.,* 1915. Players Press, 2001.

Shaw, Philip. *Waterloo and the Victorian Imagination.* Palgrave, 2002.

Sheppard, Ruth. *Extraordinary Heroes: Amazing Stories of Victoria Cross and George Cross Recipients.* Osprey, 2010.

Showalter, Elaine. "Florence Nightingale's Feminist Complaint: Women, Religion, and 'Suggestions for Thought.'" *Signs: Journal of Women in Culture and Society* 6, no. 3 (Spring 1981): 395–412.

Sinnema, Peter W. *The Wake of Wellington: Englishness in 1852.* Ohio University Press, 2006.

Sloane, David Charles. *The Last Great Necessity: Cemeteries in American History.* Johns Hopkins University Press, 1991.

Smiles, Samuel. *Self-Help, with Illustrations of Character and Conduct.* John Murray, 1859.

Smith, Julianne. "'A Noble Type of Good Heroic Womanhood': The Popular Rhetoric of Florence Nightingale's Enshrinement." *Nineteenth-Century Prose* 26, no. 1 (1999): 59+.

Smith, Melvin Charles. *Awarded for Valour: A History of the Victoria Cross and the Evolution of Heroism.* Palgrave, 2008.

Smyth, Frances. *Introduction to the Only Enemy: An Autobiography by Brig. Sir John Smyth,* 11–13. Hutchinson, 1959.

A Soldier. *A Knouting for the Czar!* George R. Wright, 1855.

Soldiers' Friend and Army Scripture Readers' Society. *Report on Mr. Mathieson's Labours at the East.* The Society, Printed at Cambridge Printing Press, 1855.

Southern, James. "A Lady 'in Proper Proportions'? Feminism, Lytton Strachey, and Florence Nightingale's Reputation, 1918–39." *Twentieth Century British History* 28, no. 1 (March 2017): 1–28.

Spiers, Edward M. *The Army and Society, 1815–1914.* Longman, 1980.

Spiers, Edward M. *The Late Victorian Army, 1868–1902.* Manchester University Press, 1992.

Stannus, Lt. Gen. H. J. *Curiosities of the Victoria Cross.* Ridgway, 1882.

Statements Exhibiting the Voluntary Contributions Received by Miss Nightingale for the Use of British War Hospitals in the East, 1854, 1855, 1856. Harrison, 1856.

Steedman, Amy. *The Story of Florence Nightingale.* T. C. and E. C. Jack, c. 1915.

Strachan, Hew. *From Waterloo to Balaclava: Tactics, Technology, and the British Army, 1815–1854.* Cambridge University Press, 1985.

Strachan, Hew. *The Reform of the British Army, 1830–1854.* Manchester University Press, 1984.

Strachey, Lytton. *Eminent Victorians.* 1918. Reprint, Oxford World's Classics, 2003.

Strachey, Ray. *The Cause: A Short History of the Women's Movement in Great Britain* (1929). Cited in Elaine Showalter, "Florence Nightingale's Feminist Complaint: Women, Religion, and 'Suggestions for Thought.'" *Signs: Journal of Women in Culture and Society* 6, no. 3 (Spring 1981): 395–412.

Streets, Heather. *Martial Races: The Military, Race, and Masculinity in British Imperial Culture, 1857–1914.* Manchester University Press, 2004.

Streets-Salter, Heather. *World War I in Southeast Asia: Colonialism and Anticolonialism in an Era of Global Conflict.* Cambridge University Press, 2018.

Sullivan, John J. *Our Veterans: Heroes of the Crimea and the Mutiny.* Sherratt and Hughes, 1908.

Sumartojo, Shanti. *Trafalgar Square and the Narration of Britishness, 1900–2012.* Peter Lang, 2013.

Summers, Anne. "The Mysterious Demise of Sarah Gamp: The Domiciliary Nurse and Her Detractors, C. 1830–1860." *Victorian Studies* 32, no. 3 (1989): 365–86.

Sweeney, Stuart. *The Europe Illusion: Britain, France, Germany and the Long History of European Integration.* Reaktion, 2019.

Sweetman, John. *The Crimean War.* Osprey, 2001.

Sweetman, John. *War and Administration: The Significance of the Crimean War for the British Army.* Scottish Academic Press, 1984.

Sylvestre, Cleo. Conversation with the Author. De Beauvoir Square, London. May 5, 2017.

Tamm, Marek. *Afterlife of Events: Perspectives on Mnemohistory.* Palgrave, 2015.

Tate, Trudi. "On Not Knowing Why: Memorializing the Light Brigade." In *Literature, Science, Psychoanalysis, 1830–1970: Essays in Honour of Gillian Beer,* edited by Helen Small and Trudi Tate, 160–80. Oxford University Press, 2003.

Tate, Trudi. "Sebastopol: On the Fall of a City." *19: Interdisciplinary Nineteenth Century* 20 (2015).

Tate, Trudi. *A Short History of the Crimean War.* I. B. Tauris, 2019.

Tate, Trudi and Kate Kennedy, eds. *The Silent Morning: Culture and Memory after the Armistice.* Manchester University Press, 2013.

Taylor, Hugh. "Mary and Florence." In *A Statue for Mary: The Seacole Legacy,* edited by Jean Gray, 22. Mary Seacole Memorial Statue Appeal, 2016.

Taylor, Miles. "The Beginnings of Modern British Social History?" *History Workshop Journal* 43, no. 1 (Spring 1997): 155–76.

Taylor, Miles and Michael Wolff. *The Victorians since 1901: Histories, Representations, and Revisions.* Manchester University Press, 2004.

Teukolsky, Rachel. "Novels, Newspapers, and Global War: New Realisms in the 1850s." *Novel: A Forum on Fiction* 45, no. 1 (2012): 31–55.

Thoma, Julia. *The Final Spectacle: Military Painting under the Second Empire, 1851–1867*. Walter de Gruyter, 2019.

Thompson, Louisa. *Winning the Victoria Cross, or the Story of Rex*. Estes and Laurait, 1895.

Thorsheim, Peter. "The Corpse in the Garden: Burial, Health, and the Environment in Nineteenth-Century London." *Environmental History* 16 (2011): 38–68.

Tilley, Brian. *Tynedale in the Great War*. Pen and Sword, 2015.

Tooley, Sarah A. Southall. *The History of Nursing in the British Empire*. S. H. Bousfield, 1906.

Tosh, John. "Masculinities in an Industrializing Society: Britain, 1800–1914." *Journal of British Studies* 44, no. 2 (April 2005): 330–42.

Troubetzkoy, Alexis. *A Brief History of the Crimean War*. Robinson, 2006.

Tucker, Albert V. "Army and Society in England, 1870–1900: A Reassessment of the Cardwell Reforms." *Journal of British Studies* 2, no. 2 (May 1963): 110–41.

Tusan, Michelle. "'Crimes against Humanity': Human Rights, the British Empire, and the Origins of the Response to the Armenian Genocide. *American Historical Review* 119, no. 1 (February 2014): 47–77.

Tusan, Michelle. *Smyrna's Ashes: Humanitarianism, Genocide, and the Birth of the Middle East*. University of California Press, 2012.

Ussishkin, Daniel. *Morale: A Modern British History*. Oxford University Press, 2017.

V21 Collective. "The Manifesto of the V21 Collective." 2015, *Web:* http://v21col lective.org/manifesto-of-the-v21-collective-ten-theses/

Vernon, James. *Distant Strangers: How Britain Became Modern*. University of California Press, 2014.

Vinen, Richard. "The Victoria Cross." *History Today* 56, no. 12 (2006): 50–57.

Von Gurowski, Adam. *A Year of the War*. D. Appleton, 1855.

Wagner, Kim. *Amritsar 1919: An Empire of Fear and the Making of a Massacre*. Yale University Press, 2019.

Walkowitz, Judith. *Nights Out: Life in Cosmopolitan London*. Yale University Press, 2012.

Walkowitz, Judith R. *Prostitution and Victorian Society: Women, Class, and the State*. Cambridge University Press, 1980.

Walters, Alisha R. "'The Tears I Could Not Repress, Rolling Down My Brown Cheeks': Mary Seacole, Feeling, and the Imperial Body." *Nineteenth-Century Gender Studies* 16, no. 1 (2020).

Walters, Emily Curtis. "Between Entertainment and Elegy: The Unexpected Success of R. C. Sherriff's *Journey's End* (1928)." *Journal of British Studies* 55, no. 2 (2016): 344–73.

War Office. *Statistics of the Military Effort of the British Empire during the Great War*. HMSO, 1922.

Ward, G. Kingsley and Major Edwin Gibson. *Courage Remembered*. HMSO, 1995.

Ward, Paul. *Britishness since 1870*. Routledge, 2004.

Ward, Stuart. *British Culture and the End of Empire*. Manchester University Press, 2001.

Ward, Stuart and Astrid Rasch. "Introduction: Greater Britain, Global Britain." In *Embers of Empire in Brexit Britain*, edited by Stuart Ward and Astrid Rasch, 3–4. Bloomsbury, 2019.

Warner, Philip, ed. *Letters Home from the Crimea: A Young Cavalryman's Campaign from Balaklava and Sebastopol to Victory*. Windrush Press, 1999.

Waters, Chris. "'Dark Strangers' in Our Midst: Discourses of Race and Nation in Britain, 1947–1963." *Journal of British Studies* 36, no. 2 (1997): 207–38.

Waters, Rob. *Thinking Black: Britain, 1964–1985*. University of California Press, 2019.

Watson, Janet S. K. *Fighting Different Wars: Experience, Memory, and the First World War*. Cambridge University Press, 2004.

Webster, Wendy. *Englishness and Empire, 1939–1965*. Oxford University Press, 2005.

Webster, Wendy. *Mixing It: Diversity in World War Two Britain*. Oxford University Press, 2018.

Wellington, Jennifer. *Exhibiting War: The Great War, Museums and Memory in Britain, Canada, and Australia*. Cambridge University Press, 2017.

Wenzel, Jennifer. *Bulletproof: Afterlives of Anticolonial Prophecy in South Africa and Beyond*. University of Chicago Press, 2009.

Whipple, Amy. "Revisiting the 'Rivers of Blood' Controversy: Letters to Enoch Powell." *Journal of British Studies* 48, no. 3 (2009): 717–35.

Williams, Brian. *The Life and World of Mary Seacole*. Heinemann, 2003.

Williams, Gavin, ed. *Hearing the Crimean War: Wartime Sound and the Unmaking of Sense*. Oxford University Press, 2019.

Williams, Irene Cooper. *Florence Nightingale: A Biography*. George Allen & Unwin, 1931.

Williamson, Philip. "State Prayers, Fasts and Thanksgivings: Public Worship in Britain 1830–1897." *Past and Present* 200, no. 1 (August 2008): 121–74.

Wilson, Ross J. *Cultural Heritage of the Great War in Britain*. Ashgate, 2013.

Winter, Jay. *Remembering War: The Great War between Memory and History in the Twentieth Century*. Yale University Press, 2006.

Winter, Jay. *Sites of Memory, Sites of Mourning: The Great War in European Cultural History*. Cambridge University Press, 1995.

Winter, Jay. *War Beyond Words: Languages of Remembrance from the Great War to the Present*. Cambridge University Press, 2017.

Winter, Jay, ed. *The Cambridge History of the First World War*. Cambridge University Press, 2014.

Wood, Claire. *Dickens and the Business of Death*. Cambridge University Press, 2015.

Wood, Evelyn. "The Crimea in 1854, and 1894." *Fortnightly Review* 56, no. 334 (1894): 469–97.

Wood, Evelyn. *The Crimea in 1854 and 1894*. Chapman and Hall, 1895.

Woodham-Smith, Cecil. *Florence Nightingale: 1820–1910*. Constable, 1950.

Woodham-Smith, Cecil. *The Great Hunger: Ireland, 1845–1849*. H. Hamilton, 1962.

Woodham-Smith, Cecil. *The Reason Why: The Story of the Fatal Charge of the Light Brigade*. Constable, 1953.

Woolacott, Angela. *On Her their Lives Depend: Munitions Workers and the Great War*. University of California Press, 1994.

Woolf, Virginia. *To the Lighthouse*. Harcourt, 1927.

Woollcombe, Edward. *Funeral Sermon to the Late Lord Raglan, Preached in the Chapel Royal, Whitehall, the Seventh Sunday after Trinity, July 22, 1855*. Bell and Daldy, 1857.

Wright, Elizabethada A. "Reading the Cemetery, Lieu de Mémoire par Excellance." *Rhetoric Society Quarterly* 33, no. 2 (Spring 2003): 27–44.

Wright, Elizabethada A. "Rhetorical Spaces in Memorial Places: The Cemetery as a Rhetorical Memory Place/Space." *Rhetorical Society Quarterly* 35, no. 4 (Fall 2005): 51–81.

Wright, Patrick. *On Living in an Old Country: The National Past in Contemporary Britain*. Verso, 1985.

Wright, Susannah. "War and Peace: Armistice Observance in British Schools in 1937." *Journal of the History of Childhood and Youth* 13, no. 3 (2020): 426–45.

Young, D. A. B. "Florence Nightingale's Fever." *BMJ: British Medical Journal* 311, no. 7021 (1995): 1697–700.

Ziino, Bart, ed. *Remembering the First World War*. Routledge, 2015.

Zuelow, Eric G. *A History of Modern Tourism*. Palgrave, 2016.

Index

For EU product safety concerns, contact us at Calle de José Abascal, 56–1°,
28003 Madrid, Spain or eugpsr@cambridge.org.

www.ingramcontent.com/pod-product-compliance
Ingram Content Group UK Ltd.
Pitfield, Milton Keynes, MK11 3LW, UK
UKHW020401140625
459647UK00020B/2594